BEHAVIOR MANAGEMENT

SYSTEMS, CLASSROOMS, AND INDIVIDUALS

BEHAVIOR MANAGEMENT

SYSTEMS, CLASSROOMS, AND INDIVIDUALS

Jennifer D. Walker, PhD
Colleen Barry, PhD, BCBA-D

PLURAL PUBLISHING INC.

5521 Ruffin Road
San Diego, CA 92123

e-mail: information@pluralpublishing.com
Web site: https://www.pluralpublishing.com

Typeset in 11/15 Stone Serif by Flanagan's Publishing Services, Inc.
Printed in the United States of America by by McNaughton & Gunn, Inc.

Library of Congress Cataloging-in-Publication Data:

Names: Walker, Jennifer D. (Special education teacher), author. | Barry, Colleen (Special education teacher), author.
Title: Behavior management : systems, classrooms, and individuals / Jennifer D. Walker, PhD, Colleen Barry, PhD, BCBA-D.
Description: San Diego, CA : Plural Publishing, Inc., 2022. | Includes bibliographical references and index.
Identifiers: LCCN 2020027013 | ISBN 9781635502244 (paperback) | ISBN 9781635502374 (ebook)
Subjects: LCSH: Behavior modification—Textbooks.
Classification: LCC LB1060.2 .W35 2022 | DDC 370.15/28—dc23
LC record available at https://lccn.loc.gov/2020027013

Contents

Preface xiii

Acknowledgments xv

Reviewers xvii

PART I. FOUNDATIONS OF CLASSROOM MANAGEMENT

Chapter 1. Introduction to Behavior Management 3

Learning Objectives 3

Key Terms 3

Prominent Theorists of Behavior Management 5

    B. F. Skinner 5

    William Glasser 6

    Thomas Gordon 7

    Lee and Marlene Canter 9

    Rudolf Dreikurs 10

    Jacob Kounin 11

    Curwin and Mendler 12

Identifying and Locating Evidence-Based Practices 13

Legal Considerations for Behavior and Consequences 15

    Restraint and Seclusion 18

Landmark Legislation, Policies, and Processes 18

    Manifestation Determination Review (MDR) 18

Conclusion 20

Chapter Summary 20

Chapter 2. Understanding Student Needs 25

Learning Objectives 25

Key Terms 25

Developmental Characteristics 26

    Influence of Cultural, Social, and Environmental Factors 30

Students with Disabilities 37

    Attention Deficit Hyperactivity Disorder 39

    Executive Function Deficits 42

    Emotional and Behavioral Disorders (EBD) 45

Specific Learning Disabilities (SLD) 47

Autism Spectrum Disorders (ASD) 48

Intellectual Disability 53

Conclusion.. 54

Chapter Summary 54

Chapter 3. Basics of Behavior 57

Learning Objectives 57

Key Terms 57

Applied Behavior Analysis 58

Operant Conditioning 58

Selecting and Using Reinforcers.. 61

Schedules of Reinforcement 64

Fixed Ratio (FR) 66

Variable Ratio (VR).. 66

Fixed Interval (FI) 66

Variable Interval (VI).. 67

Positive and Negative Reinforcement 67

Positive Reinforcement 68

Negative Reinforcement 69

Extinction 70

Punishment 71

Conclusion.. 74

Chapter Summary 75

PART II. CLASSROOM MANAGEMENT COMMUNITIES

Chapter 4. School-Wide Systems... 81

Learning Objectives 81

Key Terms 81

Multitiered Systems of Supports 82

Response to Intervention... 82

Positive Behavioral Intervention and Supports (PBIS) 83

PBIS Tiers of Intervention 95

Tier 1.. 95

Tier 2.. 96

Tier 3.. 97

School Safety Plans 98

Conclusion.. 99

Chapter Summary 99

Chapter 5. Classroom Management Collaboration 103
and Communication

Learning Objectives 103
Key Terms 103
Working with Parents 104
  Communicating about Behavior 107
Working with Other Professionals 111
  Paraprofessionals 113
  Coteaching Settings 113
Working with Administration 115
Conclusion 118
Chapter Summary 118

Chapter 6. Setting Up Physical Learning Environments 121

Learning Objectives 121
Key Terms 121
Physical Classroom Setup 122
  Horseshoe 122
  Rows 123
  Clusters or Groups 124
  Pairs 125
  Individual Desks 126
  Tables 127
  Individual Considerations 128
Considerations for Movement and Safety 129
Learning Zones 129
Additional Considerations 131
Classroom Climate 132
Conclusion 135
Chapter Summary 135

Chapter 7. Setting Up the Classroom: Procedures, ... 137
Expectations, Rules, and Prompt Hierarchies 137

Learning Objectives 137
Key Terms 137
Establishing Procedures 138
Establishing Expectations 145
Establishing Rules 147
Hierarchy of Prompts 150
Conclusion 151
Chapter Summary 152

Chapter 8. Engagement, Instruction, and Motivation 155
Learning Objectives 155
Key Terms 155
Motivation 156
Intrinsic Versus Extrinsic Motivation 156
SMART Goals 159
Group Contingencies 161
Dependent Group Contingency 163
Independent Group Contingency 164
Interdependent Group Contingency 165
Considerations 167
Choose Relevant Reinforcers 167
Prerequisite Skills and Attainable Criterion 167
Potential Risks with Group Contingencies 168
Conclusion 169
Chapter Summary 169

PART III. MEETING INDIVIDUAL NEEDS

Chapter 9. Establishing Relationships with Students 175
Learning Objectives 175
Key Terms 175
Best Practices for Positive Relationships 176
Names 176
Sarcasm 178
Power Struggles 178
"Saving Face" 180
Conflict Cycle 181
Behavior-Specific Praise 181
Relationships Between Students 183
Recognizing Diversity and Cultural Differences 186
Relationship-Building Activities 188
Conclusion 192
Chapter Summary 192

Chapter 10. Behavioral Data Collection 195
Learning Objectives 195
Key Terms 195
Identifying and Defining Target Behaviors 197
Methods of Behavioral Data Collection 200

Frequency Counts 202
Duration Recording 203
Time Sampling 203
Momentary Time Sampling 206
Latency 207
Magnitude (Force) 208
Topography 208
Permanent Products 209
Setting Data Collection Timelines 210
Data Collection Tools 213
Considerations for Data Collection 213
Conclusion 216
Chapter Summary 216

Chapter 11. Graphing and Data Analysis 221
Learning Objectives 221
Key Terms 221
Applied Behavior Analysis 222
Single-Subject Design 223
A-B Design 227
Reversal Designs 228
Multiple Baseline Design 230
Visual Displays of Data and Visual Analysis 232
Graphing 233
Visual Analysis 240
Conclusion 243
Chapter Summary 244

Chapter 12. Functional Behavioral Assessment 247
Learning Objectives 247
Key Terms 247
Functional Behavioral Assessment 248
Components of FBA 250
Indirect Assessment Strategies 251
Direct Assessment Strategies 256
Functional Analysis 262
Functions of Behavior 265
Attention 266
Escape 266
Access 267
Automatic 268

Conclusion 268
Chapter Summary 269

Chapter 13. Behavioral Intervention Plans 273
Learning Objectives 273
Key Terms 273
Replacement Behaviors 274
Constructing a Behavioral Intervention Plan 275
    Considerations for Selecting Replacement Behaviors 278
Behavioral Intervention Plans 280
    Setting Event Strategies 280
    Antecedent Event Strategies 282
    Behavioral Teaching Strategies 284
    Consequence Strategies 288
    Extinction 289
    Reinforcement 289
    Redirection 291
    Safety Plans 291
Team Process 292
Conclusion 293
Chapter Summary 293

Chapter 14. Teaching New Skills 297
Learning Objectives 297
Key Terms 297
Behavior Contracts 298
    Definition of Task 298
    Definition of Reward 299
    Task Record 299
Guidelines and Considerations 300
Token Economies 302
    Target Behaviors 302
    Tokens 303
    Backup Reinforcers 303
    Considerations for Token Economies 303
Social Skills 308
    Social Skills Instruction 308
Character Education and Social-Emotional Curriculum 314
    Modeling 315
    Democratic Classrooms 316
    Service Learning 316

Self-Monitoring 317
   Step 1. Define the Target Behavior 317
   Step 2. Choose a Monitoring System 318
   Step 3. Set a Self-Monitoring Schedule 319
   Step 4. Choose a Self-Monitoring Prompt 320
   Step 5. Teach, Practice, and Reinforce 320
   Considerations 321
Conclusion 321
Chapter Summary 322

PART IV.

Chapter 15. Reflective Practices 327
Learning Objectives 327
Key Terms 327
Teacher Self-Reflection 328
   Identify 329
   Gather Data 329
   Questions 331
   Analyze Data 331
   Implement Change 333
Using a UDL Framework 334
Planning for the First Year of Teaching 337
Planning for the 20th Year of Teaching 340
Teacher Stress and Burnout 341
Conclusion 342
Chapter Summary 342

Glossary 345
References 357
Index 367

Preface

In our roles as special education teachers, behavior specialists, behavior analysts, early intervention specialists, and teacher educators, we've had the opportunity to work with a range of students, teachers, administrators, and families. Over the course of 42 years of combined experience in these roles, we've learned that children and teens are simultaneously complex and predictable. Through our experiences and educational backgrounds, we developed this textbook to serve as a pragmatic resource for those embarking on their teacher preparation journeys, educators already in their classrooms, and any other individual seeking reliable, practitioner-friendly tools for behavior management. Tying in our experiences from classroom teaching and preparing undergraduates, we sought to provide a quality textbook that met the unique needs of upcoming educators, either at the undergraduate or graduate level.

The book is hinged on weaving legislation with research, then linking these into practical strategies for classroom management. We sought to produce a text that approaches classroom management from the big picture to the individual student. While this is a large undertaking, we felt it was important to address theory, systems, classrooms, and individuals. First and foremost, we wanted to remind readers that all of our students are complex, with layered identities that hinge on developmental milestones in the areas of cognitive, physical, and emotional domains. Students come to school from a variety of cultural, religious, linguistic, socioeconomic, and racial backgrounds. Then, their identities are layered with individual familial, sexual and gender identity, and personality differences. All this is to say that as authors of this book, we recognize the importance of treating students as the individuals they are, despite the predictability of behavioral theory or research.

With that being said, the theory behind behavior helps to understand the predictable nature of some behaviors. Topics like reinforcement and functions of behavior will help teachers understand the whys of behavior. Laws inform decision making, particularly as it relates to students with disabilities and zero-tolerance initiatives. Behavior-related systems and frameworks provide context for understanding how schools can respond to student behavior in a holistic manner—focusing on prevention, instruction, and climate—rather than knee-jerk reactions after behavior has occurred. Finally, we aimed to address individualized behaviors. While the content covered here about individual behaviors just scratches the surface with the complexities of our students, it is our hope that teachers will be given enough tools to begin to understand how they can support students or, at the very least, understand how they are supported by other professionals, such as behavior analysts.

On the PluralPlus companion site you'll find summary outlines for each chapter, case studies, chapter-by-chapter presentation slides, test banks, further activities, and sample activities. Our goal in writing this textbook was to provide accessible and real examples teachers could use in their classrooms today and in the future. Through linking online content to the pages of text via vignettes and connection boxes, we want to encourage the reader to make sense of the information presented here through a wide lens. Behavior isn't just about theory. It isn't just about the classroom setting. It also isn't just about one student in isolation. Behavior is all of these things and without all the pieces, we don't believe a true "well-oiled machine" of classroom and behavior management can occur.

Acknowledgments

This book would not have been possible without years of ongoing support from Dr. Wendy Murawski. Her encouragement and generosity have opened door after door, including the opportunity to write this book. Her mentorship is unparalleled.

Thank you to the entire team at Plural Publishing. We learned so much from this process and it would have been impossible if not for the patience and support from everyone. Special thanks to Christina who showed us kindness and compassion when it was needed the most.

A special thank you to Dr. Peggy King-Sears. This book would not be the same if it had not been for her keen insight that connected us. Thanks for creating an enduring writing connection and genuine friendship.

—*Colleen Barry and Jennifer D. Walker*

Incredible thanks go to my wife, Laura. She has been the backbone of my writing since my very first (and not so good) paper in my doctoral studies. Your unending patience and positive spirit have not gone unnoticed. Thank you for wrangling Kevin and Bean away from the laptop and your acts of service (chores) that allowed me the headspace to write. I would have never been able to do this without you.

Jen, thank you for being the epitome of a writing partner. You have taught me so much and I am so honored you asked me to join you on this endeavor. Even from halfway around the world, we made an amazing team and certainly maximized the time difference in our favour. We wrote a book!

—*Colleen Barry*

Thank you to my family, including the friends I've chosen as family, for your support while I talked behavior, processed strategies, sat in front of the computer, and lamented for the past year.

I would like to acknowledge the students, teachers, and administrators who taught me so much about behavior during my K–12 teaching career and the colleagues who continue to inspire and share knowledge with me in higher education.

Finally, a huge thank you to Colleen for making writing easy and for being a constant support when I just couldn't put another thing on an overflowing plate. If there was ever an un-lottery to be won, we'd be the people to win it given all the challenges we faced during the writing of this book. Thank you for your sense of humor, which I appreciate more than you know, when I say that one (or many) things that maybe I shouldn't. Thanks for "getting me."

—*Jennifer D. Walker*

Reviewers

Plural Publishing, Inc. and the authors would like to thank the following reviewers for taking the time to provide their valuable feedback during the development process.

Denise A. Soares, PhD
Associate Professor
University of Mississippi
Oxford, Mississippi

Erika Pinter, PhD
Northern Illinois University
DeKalb, Illinois

Cheryl K. Cunningham, PhD
Fort Hays State University
Hays, Kansas

To mom and dad, I know you both would have been so proud. At least you don't have to read it now.

To my wife, Laura, your patience is truly infinite. I hope you enjoy reading every single page.

—Colleen Barry

To Brett, Tatum, Campbell, and Lincoln for teaching me the difference between classroom management and parenting children who need BIPs.

—Jennifer D. Walker

PART I

FOUNDATIONS OF CLASSROOM MANAGEMENT

Chapter 1.   Introduction to Behavior Management

Chapter 2.   Understanding Student Needs

Chapter 3.   Basics of Behavior

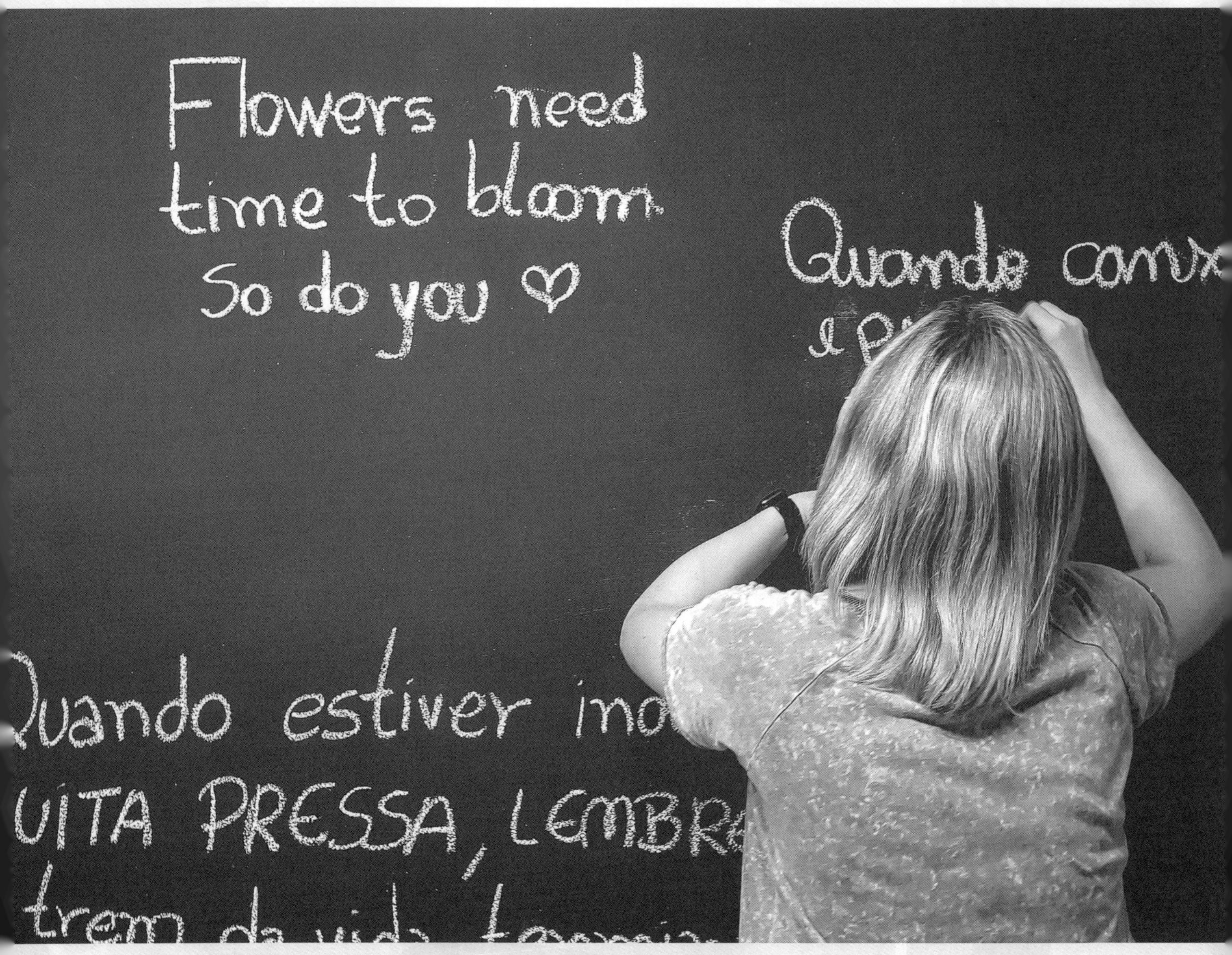
Flowers need
time to bloom.
So do you
Quando
Quando estiver
UITA PRESSA, LEMBR
trem da vida

INTRODUCTION TO BEHAVIOR MANAGEMENT

Learning Objectives

- Explain laws influencing disciplinary procedures
- Identify prominent key figures in the development of behaviorism and foundations for classroom management
- Define terminology in the development of behaviorism and foundations for classroom management
- Define evidence-based practices and high-leverage practices
- Identify where to find information on evidence-based practices and high-leverage practices

Key Terms

Active Listening
Antecedent
Applied Behavior Analysis
Assertive Management Style
Behavioral Intervention Plan (BIP)
Choice Theory
Classical Conditioning
Classroom Management
Conditioned Response
Consequences
Discipline Hierarchy
Functional Behavioral Assessment (FBA)
Hostile Management Style
Individualized Education Program (IEP)
Individuals with Disabilities Education Act (IDEA)

Individuals with Disabilities Education Improvement Act (IDEIA)
Manifestation Determination Review (MDR)
Neutral Stimulus
No-Lose Conflict Resolution
Nonassertive Management Style
Operant Behaviors
Operant Conditioning
Respondent Behavior
Restraint and Seclusion
Satiation
Stimulus Bound
Unconditioned Stimulus
Withitness

Simply put, **classroom management** refers to the ways in which educators implement focused strategies, skills, and techniques to ensure an organized, attentive, and academically productive classroom, free of disruptions resulting from challenging behavior (Davis, 2017). Classroom management is a critical skill for teachers to master and requires specific, direct, and purposeful preparation. This chapter will discuss the foundations of classroom management as well as theoretical models of behavior management and includes a template (Figure 1–1) that will serve as a note-taking guide for you throughout this book. Further, key features of identifying evidence-based practices, strategies, and interventions, along with careful review of legal considerations for behaviors and consequences are discussed.

Figure 1–1. Classroom management planning template.

1. My philosophy on classroom management is:

2. Classroom procedures I want to include in my classroom management system:

3. Expectations I want to include in my classroom management system:

4. Rules I want to include in my classroom management system:

5. Reinforcers I might include in my classroom management system:

6. Consequences I might include in my classroom management system:

7. Classroom arrangement considerations I will use in my classroom:

8. My plan for crisis situations in my classroom include:

9. I will build relationships with parents and guardians using these strategies:

10. I will build relationships with students using these strategies:

11. I might consider the following group contingencies:

12. Some ways I might teach social skills include:

Classrooms are dynamic environments wherein educators are required to maintain a delicate balance of encouragement, challenge, and student engagement. The most vital aspect of a teacher's role is to educate all students to reach their maximum potential and experience success in a safe and comfortable environment. So much of teacher preparation involves pedagogy, content knowledge, and methods; however, without a receptive audience, all of this is for naught. Classroom management is arguably the most important element to learning and achievement as it fosters a coordinated environment and facilitates students' availability to learn (Lester, Allanson, & Notar, 2017). An effectively managed classroom has been shown to have positive, direct effects on children's emotional and cognitive development, as well as a reduction in behavior problems (Ostrosky, Jung, Hemmeter, & Thomas, 2003). It is important to point out that teachers cannot control students, but they can create classroom environments that encourage positive decision making and prosocial behaviors.

Prominent Theorists of Behavior Management

Contemporary classroom management has firm roots in behaviorism, with its fundamental elements linked back to several theorists. The findings from prominent theorists such as B. F. Skinner, William Glasser, Rudolf Dreikurs, and Jacob Kounin are widely recognized as forging the foundation for contemporary classroom management. Although each of these theorists contributed an abundance of ideas that can be used in classroom management development, this chapter highlights some of the most important and relevant contributions for teachers.

> **As you read the information about these theorists, consider what resonates with you as a classroom manager. What traits of each theorist would you like to emulate? Incorporate into your own management plan? Recognize but not use? Discard as not relevant to your situation? It is important to not only learn about theory but also to understand how to use it in your own classroom.**

B. F. Skinner

Much of the early work in behaviorism and human learning did not take place within the context of schools but rather in controlled laboratory settings. B. F. Skinner, one of the most eminent psychologists of the 20th century and known as the father of operant conditioning and the originator of applied behavior analysis, pioneered much of this work. His seminal book *The Behavior of Organisms: An Experimental Analysis* (1938) laid the groundwork for what was to become some of the most influential advances in psychology. Applied behavior analysis was founded on Skinner's principles of operant conditioning, which proposes that consequences of actions may either strengthen or weaken behavior (see Chapters 3, 11, 12, 13). Skinner's body of work sought to fill in the gaps left by the rise in behavioral psychology, namely, the wave of classical or respondent conditioning that dominated the early part of the 20th century. Briefly, classical conditioning focuses on respondent behaviors, or reflexive behaviors (e.g., salivation when seeing or smelling food), being elicited by antecedents, or stimuli that immediately precede them. Russian physiologist Ivan Pavlov was responsible for most of the early work in classical conditioning and is best known for his study examining digestion in dogs. Pavlov hypothesized the dogs would salivate in response to food placed in front of them; however, he noticed the dogs began to salivate upon merely hearing the footsteps of the person delivering the food. He went on to describe classical conditioning as a procedure in which an unconditioned stimulus (food) paired with a neutral stimulus (bell) could elicit a conditioned response (salivating). To clarify, an *unconditioned stimulus* is one that *unconditionally*, or automatically, triggers a response or reflex. Think of these as stimuli that do not require prior learning, such as pupil dilation, jerking your hand off a hot surface, or gasping when you stub your toe. A *neutral stimulus* is one that is simply neutral to the learner; it does not intrinsically produce a response. Examples of neutral stimuli could be a sound or tone. A *conditioned response* may be thought of as a learned reflex. Together, classical or respondent conditioning is thought of in a "stimulus-response" frame, wherein repeated pairing of an unconditioned stimulus with a neutral stimulus results in a conditioned response.

Most psychologists of this era felt that the stimulus-response paradigm did not fully capture the complexity of human behavior or explain behaviors with no apparent antecedent; thus, they sought to describe spontaneous, or "voluntary," behavior of organisms by way of cognition, motivation, and free will. Skinner, in contrast, renounced the concept that internal thoughts, feelings, and motivations could reasonably explain behavior. Rather, he suggested a new type of behaviors known as operant behaviors, which are influenced not by antecedents or preceding events but rather by the consequences following them. Such consequences either strengthen or weaken the future likelihood of a behavior occurring again. Although Skinner's theories did not directly address the classroom setting, many of his foundational theories appear throughout this book.

William Glasser

Among the several other notable theorists who have contributed to classroom management, William Glasser is well known for Choice Theory. Originally called

Control Theory (1950s/1960s), Glasser developed Choice Theory, which states that every part of behavior is a choice. Glasser rejected the notion of outside influences, asserting that no one can make a person do or feel anything (Glasser, 1998). This was further explained as internal control: the belief that we are responsible for our choices, coming from within. Glasser believed people choose how to perceive stimuli, filter information, and respond. Rather than being influenced or shaped by rewards, punishments, or consequences, Glasser believed that only individuals have the ability to control their own behaviors and are motivated by needs. Glasser's Choice Theory included five basic needs of all people: freedom, power, fun, love, and belonging and security. While Glasser believed these needs were constants throughout a person's lifetime, he acknowledged that these needs may change in intensity throughout a person's life. From a classroom management perspective, tenets of Glasser's theory will appear again in later chapters during discussions of motivation and functions of behavior.

Thomas Gordon

Conversely, Thomas Gordon believed that conflicts could be solved through relationships. Like Glasser, Gordon did not believe that rewards, punishments, or consequences were effective because they did not increase intrinsic motivation and relied on relationships of power. Instead, Gordon asserted that individuals could resolve conflict through engaging in identifying ownership of a problem, active listening, I-messages, and no-lose conflict resolution.

When identifying ownership of a problem, Gordon believed that the person who owned the feelings associated with a problem also owned the problem. When children owned the problem, Gordon suggested that adults should provide children with the tools to address these problems, rather than solving the problem for them (Gordon, 2003). For example, if Patty tells her teacher she hates Molly and the teacher is upset by this, then this is the teacher's problem and should be solved by the teacher. However, if Patty might also say this same statement to Molly later and Molly begins rejecting Patty, then this problem is both Patty's and Molly's to solve.

Active listening was suggested as a way to help students find solutions with problem ownership by hearing and acknowledging their own feelings and ideas. Active listening is a technique that encourages the listener to listen for meaning, restate what the speaker is saying, and reserve judgment or advice. Further, active listening may include asking the speaker questions for clarification and more information. By engaging in this process, Gordon believed that teachers could convey the message that students' feelings, opinions, and concerns matter.

When addressing problems, Gordon suggested that I-messages should be used to express feelings in a way that allows the listener to understand how the speaker is feeling without making the listener defensive. I-messages include a brief, factual description of the problem and the way the problem makes the person feel as well a concrete example of the effect of the problem. For example, suppose Mr. Tatum, who is a first grade teacher, is frustrated with Brett calling out in class. During a private conversation, Mr. Tatum could tell Brett, "Brett, I feel frustrated when you call out while I am teaching lessons in class because I am not able to finish the important and fun activities I have planned." Using I-messages places ownership of the problem on the speaker and allows for nonconfrontational conversations. This is also a skill children can be taught as they learn to problem solve and develop problem ownership. Teachers can use I-messages as a way to model ways to deal with feelings in the classroom and express feelings that may interfere with the availability to learn (e.g., anger, frustration, or disappointment). In later chapters about collaboration, it will be important to remember to use these I-messages during difficult conversations.

Chapter 5 will discuss how to effectively work with parents, professionals, and administrators. Don't forget to use those I-messages!

Gordon acknowledged that all problems might not be solved with active listening or I-messages, so he suggested steps for a no-lose conflict resolution (Gordon, 2003). These steps include defining the needs of both the child and the adult, brainstorming solutions, evaluating possible solutions, choosing a solution, implementing a solution, and checking the results. In the classroom, this can take the form of a plan of action or experiment between the teacher and student.

Lee and Marlene Canter

While Gordon's theories and ideas were initially designed for parents and children, from the onset, Lee and Marlene Canter's focus was on the classroom environment. Most well-known for assertive discipline (Canter, 2001), Canter and Canter focused on calm, productive environments where teachers were leaders without hostile or authoritarian discipline. They believed teachers were responsible for a chaotic or caring environment and had the right to teach and expect compliance from students. Although initially more focused on teachers as strong leaders, their theory has evolved to include trust, relationships, positive recognition, and proactive approaches to behavior management. Canter and Canter suggest that teachers use a few clearly stated rules and consistently explain, practice, and enforce those rules. Further, they suggest that positive and negative consequences be developed in a hierarchy of responses that can be used consistently across students. At the same time, Canter and Canter emphasize that teachers should "catch" students engaging in positive behaviors, recognizing the choices you want to see more often.

When developing a discipline hierarchy, Canter and Canter's own hierarchy examples used verbal warnings, time-outs, parent notification, and, finally, class removal. The Canters acknowledged that students may need reminders, but cautioned against putting student names on the board, as this may be used as a means of humiliating students. Verbal reminders may include engaging in the broken-record technique, which is repeating a request for compliance no more than three times before assigning a consequence. Although designed as a hierarchy, students may receive multiple opportunities to make a behavioral change at each progressive level of consequences. For example, a student may be given three verbal warnings before a time-out or two time-outs before a parent is called.

Canter and Canter identified three teacher response styles to classroom behavior. The nonassertive management style teacher engages in ineffective approaches to dealing with student behavior. Teachers who are nonassertive do not follow through with consequences, fail to establish classroom expectations and standards, and generally do not set themselves up as the clear leader in the classroom. A teacher who is nonassertive may repeatedly tell a student to stop talking but never follows through on the consequences of the behavior, or they may continue reminding students of their behavior instead of enforcing rules (e.g., "Jason, why do you keep talking? You know you shouldn't.") Canter and Canter consider nonassertive teachers to be ineffective classroom managers.

Hostile management style includes using aversive approaches to manage the classroom. This includes sarcasm, threats, put-downs, and shouting or yelling (e.g., "Shut up and get to work!"; "There must be something wrong with you if you can't follow directions."; "Clearly your parents didn't teach you any manners.") These teachers do not consider student feelings or dignity and, as a result, damage relationships with students. It should not be surprising that students who are belittled or yelled at in the classroom may not feel safe or secure in the learning environment.

Finally, Canter and Canter identified the assertive management style. These teachers clearly and calmly establish rules, expectations, and consequences in the classroom. Expectations of behavior are expected to be followed and both positive and negative consequences are employed based on the adherence to those expectations. Assertive teachers engage with students in a matter-of-fact, businesslike manner that is explanatory in nature (e.g., "Stan, everyone is expected to remain in their assigned area during this activity."; "You need to raise your hand if you have a question.")

Rudolf Dreikurs

Similar to Glasser's five basic needs, Rudolf Dreikurs also believed that behaviors have roots or causes. According to Dreikurs, students may have "mistaken goals" (Dreikurs, 1968). Mistaken goals include attention, power, revenge, and helplessness or inadequacy and cause behavior. A student who is attention seeking behaves to receive attention. Dreikurs believed this was especially common in younger children who were establishing themselves socially. Power-seeking students want to exert their power over teachers and authority and choose to behave in such ways to prove their power. Dreikurs suggested that this defiance was a way for children to establish their self-worth and importance. Students who lack self-esteem may engage in revenge. The basis for this behavior, according to Dreikurs, was to hurt another person just as the child had been hurt. These behaviors may manifest as threats, yelling, name calling, physical harm, or theft. Finally, students may engage in helplessness or express feelings of inadequacy. These students may feel alone or incompetent and therefore act in such ways to isolate themselves or avoid work. Again, some of Dreikurs' tenets of mistaken goals will appear in later chapters during discussions of functions of behaviors.

Logical consequences were another key feature of Dreikurs' work. Logical consequences are consequences that are directly connected, or related, to the target behavior. For example, if a student tears up a science lab paper and refuses to complete the assignment, then the logical consequence is that the student cannot participate in the experiment related to that assignment. Before using logical consequences, Dreikurs believed that rules must be established and students should be encouraged to participate in development of these rules.

Jacob Kounin

Jacob Kounin's theory of management focused less on student responsibility and more on strategies teachers can use to manage the classroom. He suggested engaging in withitness and overlapping as well as avoiding jerkiness, stimulus bound, thrust, dangles, overdwelling, and satiation. Many of these occur during instruction and are based on Kounin's own observations of the classroom.

Kounin defined withitness as the teacher's ability to know what is happening in the classroom at all times (Kounin, 1977). Teachers who demonstrate withitness seemingly have "eyes in the back of their heads." These teachers are able to engage in instruction and inventory behaviors in the classroom at the same time. Withitness implies that teachers are able to identify where challenging behaviors are originating and address it promptly, without disrupting classroom lessons. Having withitness involves addressing behaviors before they become bigger issues or include additional students. By addressing behaviors promptly, Kounin suggested that a ripple effect occurs, whereby all students recognize their teacher's ability to identify and address behaviors in the classroom, therefore reducing further challenges. In an elementary classroom setting, this may look like a teacher who is teaching a lesson while also walking around the room gently tapping desks of two students who are engaging in a sidebar conversation every time the teacher turns her back. This acknowledgement of the talking allows the teacher to continue teaching but also lets the students know that she is aware of the behaviors. This also connects directly to Kounin's ideas about overlapping, in which a teacher is able to manage more than one task at a time, like instruction and student behavior. He believed that teachers who could focus on more than one task at a time were also more "with it."

During instruction, Kounin asserted that teachers should create momentum in lessons and avoid pitfalls of disrupting student engagement. To avoid disrupting the flow of lessons, teachers should be careful with jerkiness, becoming stimulus bound, thrust, dangles, overdwelling, and satiation. Jerkiness refers to the way in which lessons are delivered and includes poor timing, abrupt topic changes, and overall lack of instructional momentum. Similarly, a teacher who finds themselves stimulus bound is distracted by something or someone in the classroom and instead of using withitness to address the interruption, the teacher loses instructional focus and consequently also pulls students off task. This can also be done by creating a dangle during instruction. A dangle is an instance when a teacher starts an activity or lesson but doesn't finish or bring it to completion. This interrupts instruction, leaving students confused and potentially frustrated, angry, or off task. These behaviors increase opportunities for other noncompliant behaviors because students are no longer academically engaged.

Kounin also warned teachers about overdoing instruction and behavior correction. When teaching, Kounin suggested teachers should also avoid satiation. Satiation happens when teachers remain on a lesson or concept too long. Once students have mastered the content or show disinterest, Kounin suggested showing enthusiasm, positivity, or discussing the challenge of learning something new. As with most of Kounin's ideas, he believed the lesson should maintain momentum. When addressing behavior, Kounin warned against overdwelling. In overdwelling, a teacher continues to dwell on a student's misbehavior long after the student has demonstrated an understanding of their mistakes and need for change. For some students, overdwelling may feel like nagging and can trigger some children and teens back into the conflict cycle.

See Chapter 9 for more information about the conflict cycle.

Curwin and Mendler

Finally, Curwin and Mendler's (1983) theories focus on preserving student dignity and deescalating student behavior. Curwin and Mendler believe that students misbehave because they have lost hope and it is a teacher's job to help students be successful in the classroom through discipline with dignity. Dignity, according to Curwin and Mendler, boils down to respect for the student. They suggested that students misbehave because they are preserving dignity about not feeling confident in academics or feeling out of control in their world. With a goal of effective discipline, Curwin and Mendler focus on seven principles. These include reducing ineffective management strategies that don't work, developing long-term efforts versus short-term quick fixes, treating students with dignity and offering hope, working with individual needs, creating rules that outline what is required in a brief and logical manner, modeling expected behaviors, and giving students choice through responsibility. Curwin and Mendler asserted that behavior management should be situated in a democratic atmosphere where students are involved in the process of rule and consequence development. By giving students a voice in the process, Curwin and Mendler suggested that students would learn to take responsibility for behaviors rather than simply complying based on obedience.

While the ideas and strategies suggested by each of these theorists may work better in particular environments or with some students better than others, it is important for teachers to consider how components of each theory could work in a comprehensive behavior management plan.

What is your management style and how does it fit with the ideas presented here? What pieces of these theories will you take away? Do you want to be a teacher who uses withitness? I-messages? Use your Classroom Management Planning Guide to record some of those ideas now.

Take some time to think about various techniques/approaches you have seen in classrooms that are based on different learning theories. Have you seen multiple approaches (from different theorists) used together in the same classroom by the same teacher?

Identifying and Locating Evidence-Based Practices

Throughout this book we will highlight both evidence-based practices (EBPs) and high-leverage practices (HLPs) in classroom management. Evidence-based practices are educational strategies that are supported by well-conducted research and evidence in the form of research data. These are important to identify because, as educators, it helps us carefully select the interventions that will lead to the biggest impact for our students. There are a number of resources available to help educators identify EBPs, some of which are listed in Table 1–1.

Educators should know that in order for an intervention to be successful, they must implement the EBP interventions with fidelity, meaning exactly as the intervention was designed to be implemented.

In addition to EBPs, HLPs are a concise way for educators to identify practices they should use intentionally and explicitly in the classroom. HLPs are targeted practices that educators, specifically special educators, should master and demonstrate proficiency of in the classroom. While EBPs cover research-based interventions,

Table 1–1. Websites for Locating Evidence-Based Practices (EBPs)

What Works Clearinghouse	Includes ratings of and guides for interventions. Reports for schools outline recommendations for schools.	https://ies.ed.gov/ncee/wwc/
IRIS Center	Interactive module outlines processes for identifying, selecting, implementing, and evaluating EBPs.	https://iris.peabody.vanderbilt.edu/
Promising Practices Network	Provides archived research-based intervention information and includes educational outcomes of practices.	http://www.promisingpractices.net/programs.asp
National Center on Intensive Intervention	Academic interventions are outlined with research quality, results, intensity, and additional research options.	https://charts.intensiveintervention.org/chart/instructional-intervention-tools

HLPs use these interventions and translate them to classroom practice. Through a partnership with the Collaboration for Effective Educator Development, Accountability, and Reform (CEEDAR) and the Council for Exceptional Children (CEC), four primary areas—including collaboration, assessment, instruction, and social/emotional/behavioral—have been identified as practices that improve student outcomes (McLeskey et al., 2017). These practices are further broken down into 22 individual practices. The primary practices included in social/emotional/behavioral HLPs will be of particular interest to the readers of this book. These include a focus on learning environments, student feedback, social behaviors, and functional behavioral assessments (FBAs) and behavior intervention plans (BIPs). Throughout the book, we will identify HLPs for the reader as they apply to the content presented in each chapter. Additional information about HLPs can be found in the text, websites, and videos provided in Table 1–2.

Table 1–2. Additional Information About High-Leverage Practices (HLPs)		
High-Leverage Practices in Special Education	An overview of all HLPs, including practices for specific areas and target ages are presented.	https://highleverage practices.org/
High-Leverage Practices: Social/ Emotional/ Behavioral Practices	HLP7 to HLP10 are outlined in a brief overview of practices for the social and emotional well-being of students.	https://highleverage practices.org/wp-content/ uploads/2017/06/ SEBshort.pdf
High-Leverage Practices Videos	HLPs are demonstrated in videos, including a topical introduction, review of the research, and demonstration of HLPs in action.	https://highleverage practices.org/videos/
Iris Center	Interactive module outlines each HLPs, accompanied by videos, notes, and examples.	https://iris.peabody .vanderbilt.edu/resources/ high-leverage-practices/

Legal Considerations for Behavior and Consequences

In later chapters, we will discuss school systems using positive behavior interventions and supports (PBIS) as well as classroom and individual strategies for classroom and behavior management. While these strategies will help create a positive, safe, and predictable environment, it is important to understand laws and regulations that not only impact decision making about behavior-related consequences but also protect students and the adults who work with them. It is important to understand the context in which behavior-related decisions have been made both historically and currently and how specific groups of students, like those with disabilities, may be directly affected.

In the early 1970s, drug usage and crimes committed by youth came to the forefront in policies about disciplinary issues in schools. The Juvenile Justice and Delinquency Prevention Act (JJDPA) of 1974 specifically addressed both of these issues in the school setting through the coordination of school and outside agency programs. In the 1980s, the focus shifted heavily to drug and alcohol use by youth and these concerns culminated in the Drug-Free Schools and Communities Act. This act created school-based drug prevention programs through the Anti-Drug Abuse Act and required local school agencies to provide drug abuse education and prevention programs. When the JJDPA was reauthorized in the early 1990s, additional policies and programs were added to address the presence of gangs in schools.

The issue of using corporal punishment as a way to discipline students was first addressed in 1977 when the U.S. Supreme Court ruled in *Ingraham v. Wright* that school corporal punishment was constitutional, leaving the implementation decision up to individual states. Corporal punishment is defined as the use of physical force to inflict pain as a way to correct misbehavior (Straus, 2001). In schools, this may take the form of spanking, hitting, paddling, or slapping the buttocks or hands of children. Despite the controversy about corporal punishment, 19 states currently permit school personnel to use corporal punishment (Yell, 2019). The use of corporal punishment has been on the decline since the 1970s (Gershoff, Purtell, & Holas, 2015) and many school districts prohibit corporal punishment, even though it may be legal statewide (Yell, 2019). Even with this decline, it should be noted that racial, gender, and disability status disparities continue to be widespread. African American students, boys, and students with disabilities are disproportionately impacted by corporal punishment (Gershoff & Font, 2016). Further, corporal punishment does not increase compliance (Gershoff & Grogan-Kaylor, 2016) and the more students receive corporal punishment, the more frequently aggressive and defiant behaviors are demonstrated (Lee, Altschul, & Gerhoff, 2013). Corporal punishment has also been linked to higher rates of mental health problems (McLoyd, Kaplan, Hardaway, & Wood, 2007) and lower academic achievement (Berlin et al., 2009). While corporal punishment does still exist as a disciplinary strategy across the United States, it is declining as research continues to accumulate about its impact on students.

In 1994, the federal government passed the Gun-Free Schools Act. This act required school systems to expel any student who brought a weapon onto school campuses. The enactment of this law coincided with the "broken windows" theory of law, which referred to the belief that if small criminal infractions could be addressed early and quickly, then larger, more egregious criminal behavior could be stopped. In line with this thinking, many school districts expanded the zero-tolerance policy of the Gun-Free Schools Act to a broader range of behaviors, including bringing look-alike weapons to school, possessing over-the-counter drugs, fighting, and multiple or accumulated infractions—just to name a few. With this expanded interpretation of the law, school district policies were created that focused on exclusionary discipline, rather than preventative measures. It should be noted that research suggests that zero-tolerance policies can play a role in the perpetuation of the "school to prison pipeline," an increasingly noticeable trend whereby schools may be directly and indirectly funneling students on a path to prison. Zero-tolerance policies call for stringent, consistent, and harsh punitive consequences to infractions and do not consider the myriad of circumstances that may contribute to behavior.

In 2001, the No Child Left Behind Act (NCLB) was passed into law (and subsequently signed in 2002). While best known for addressing disparities among disadvantaged populations by annual accountability testing, this law also set forth provisions for school safety. The U.S. Department of Education (USDOE) promoted NCLB as a way to create safe and orderly schools through enforcement of laws to ensure the safety of children, requiring schools to enforce truancy, suspension, expulsion, and criminal infractions. The law also required states to report on their school safety and develop plans for keeping schools safe and drug free (USDOE, 2007). Further, NCLB also created provisions for parents who wanted to remove their children from schools deemed unsafe, giving them the right to move their children to a designated "safe" school. Unfortunately, during the 13 years NCLB remained a law, the definition of "safe" was never clearly established.

Restraint and Seclusion

Restraint and seclusion was first addressed in 2009 in a report by the U.S. Government Accountability Office (GAO, 2009). The report not only sheds light on the known allegations and reports of restraint and seclusion in schools but it also found that no federal laws restricted the use of these practices. While some state regulations existed across the nations, both the regulations and monitoring of these regulations were inconsistent. In 2012, the USDOE proposed 15 guiding principles for developing policies on restraint and seclusion. To date, restraint and seclusion in school is guided by state laws. More recently, the Keeping All Students Safe Act (2012) was introduced, creating the potential for increased federal regulation. This act proposes protections for students from restraint and seclusion. If enacted, the law would establish federal standards limiting restraint and prohibiting seclusion. While federal regulations and state laws continue to develop, there is no research on seclusion and restraint that suggests that this practice is an effective way to reduce the occurrence of the behavior that led to the seclusion and restraint.

Landmark Legislation, Policies, and Processes

In addition to the aforementioned laws about safety and student discipline, there are also specific laws that address the rights of students with disabilities as it relates to behavior. Students with disabilities have specific rights as outlined in the Individuals with Disabilities Education Act (IDEA, 1997) and the Individuals with Disabilities Education Improvement Act (IDEIA, 2004). Part of the reauthorization of IDEA in 1997 specified that all students with disabilities must receive a free and appropriate education (FAPE) in the least restrictive environment (LRE), using something called the stay-put provision. This is the provision that ensures that a student with a disability is receiving the services outlined in their Individualized Education Program (IEP) and is not removed from the school setting or those services, even when disciplinary issues arise. When a student with an IEP is disciplined for a school behavior with repeated or long-term removal from school (e.g., suspension or expulsion), IDEA states that the school IEP team must determine if a relationship between the student's disability and the behavior that resulted in exclusion from school was related. This process is referred to as the manifestation determination review (MDR).

Manifestation Determination Review (MDR)

According to IDEA (1997) and IDEIA (2004), the MDR is required when a student with a disability is excluded or removed from school for 10 days or more days or is put in an interim alternative placement outside of their typical school setting. This is because, under IDEA, the child is no longer receiving the services as outlined in their IEP since they are not in school. The MDR meeting must take place with all members of the child's IEP team, including parents, special and general education teachers, and an administrator. If needed, other members of the team may include school psychologists, counselors, social workers, other school personnel, and, if appropriate, the child. During this meeting, the team reviews any relevant information about the child and the child's disability as it relates to the behavior that led to the exclusionary discipline.

Ultimately, the purpose of the MDR is to determine whether a child's behavior of concern, the behavior that led to the exclusionary discipline, was caused by or related to their disability. During the meeting, the IEP team reviews all information and the specific incident that led to the meeting and answers two questions. The first question is whether the behavior of concern was related to the child's disability. If the answer is yes, the team is expected to complete a functional behavioral assessment (FBA) and behavioral intervention plan (BIP).

> *Peek ahead to Chapters 12 and 13 for more information on FBAs and BIPs.*

If the FBA and BIP are already in place, the school is required to review and update this document. The child then returns to school without further consequences, except in certain circumstances involving drugs, weapons, or bodily harm to themselves or others. The second question asks whether the student's behavior was a result of the school's or school division's failure to provide all the services outlined in the student's IEP. If the team answers "yes" to this question, the school and school division are responsible for correcting this through a number of avenues, including, but not limited to, compensatory services for the child. If the team answers "no" to both questions, the student receives consequences as any general education student would face. This may include exclusion from school and missed opportunities to complete classwork. When answering "no" to both questions, the law requires the school to do nothing further.

The guidance on conducting the MDR is limited and the process continues to be controversial. There is a lack of research on both the MDR process and the preparedness of general and special educators to make these critical decisions. Administrators and general and special educators may view this as a dual disciplinary model, with a variance of discipline between general and special education students. However, it is important to remember that this process is in place as a way to protect students with disabilities from being unnecessarily, unfairly, and disproportionately excluded from the general education setting. Ultimately, this process protects a student's right to a free and appropriate education with their nondisabled peers. It is imperative teachers come prepared to engage in MDR meetings by reading the student's files, researching the student's disability category as identified in eligibility, and asking questions about the MDR process (Walker & Brigham, 2017).

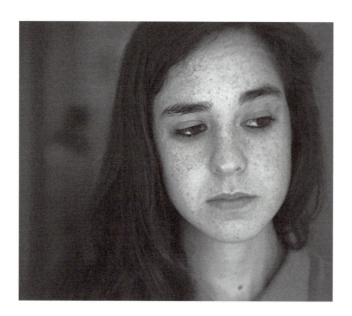

Conclusion

Obviously, the topic of classroom management is extraordinarily vast. Fundamentally, classroom management is an intricate connection of skills, techniques, strategies, and theory that sets up and supports a learning environment free from disruptive behavior, while promoting creative, thriving learners. While there is no doubt this will look differently depending on student age, subject area, and school-/county-wide objectives, the most important single factor is you, the educator. Being a teacher is quite arguably the most challenging, yet most rewarding, career as you bear the ultimate responsibility of infusing your personality, your skill, and your commitment to create students who love to learn.

Chapter Summary

- Classroom management is the way in which educators implement strategies, skills, and techniques in a meaningful way to ensure a productive classroom free from challenging behavior.

- The No Child Left Behind Act (NCLB) sought to address disparities through accountability testing as well as enacted provisions for school safety.

- To date, there is no federal regulations regarding restraint and seclusion in schools; this issue is guided by state laws.

- The Individuals with Disabilities Education Act (1997) and revised Individuals with Disabilities Education Improvement Act (2004) are federal regulations that specify all students with a disability have specific rights and protections. In particular, this law ensures students are not removed from school on the basis of challenging behavior. The process of determining the relationship between a student's disability and the behavior causing exclusion from school is called the manifestation determination review (MDR).

- B. F. Skinner is recognized as the father of operant conditioning and applied behavior analysis, wherein the consequences of behaviors either strengthen or weaken future behavior.

- Ivan Pavlov did extensive work in classical conditioning, wherein learning is dictated by reflexive behaviors being elicited via antecedents. His most well-known study examined digestion in dogs.

- Classical conditioning involves pairing of an *unconditioned stimulus* (i.e., a stimulus that automatically triggers a reflex, such as food triggering salivation) with a *neutral stimulus* (i.e., stimulus that is neutral or does not elicit any particular response) to elicit a *conditioned response* (i.e., a learned reflex).

- William Glasser developed Choice Theory, stating that all behaviors are conscious choices. This theory references internal control, or the belief we are responsible for our choices, and disregards outside influences as capable of making an individual do or feel anything.

- Thomas Gordon asserted individuals could resolve conflict via the following: ownership of a problem, active listening, I-messages, and no-lose conflict resolution.

- Lee and Marlene Canter's work focused on the classroom environment and discipline styles. They identified three teacher-response styles to classroom management: (1) nonassertive management style, where teachers employ ineffective behavior management strategies and do not follow through on expectations; (2) hostile management style, which includes using aversive vocal approaches such as sarcasm, put-downs, and shouting as a response to challenging behavior; and (3) the assertive management style, wherein teachers establish rules and boundaries and enforce consequences fairly.

- A key feature of Rudolf Dreikurs' work is logical consequences, or consequences directly connected to the target behavior.

- Jacob Kounin's theory of classroom management shifted the focus from student responsibility to strategies teachers can use to manage the classroom such as withitness and overlapping.

- Discipline with dignity is an underpinning of the theory put forth by Curwin and Mendler. They suggested challenging behavior resulted from student's attempts to preserve their own dignity and feeling as though their learning was not within their control.

- Evidence-based practices are strategies backed by research and data. High-leverage practices are the basic fundamentals of teaching; these are practices educators should become proficient with as they allow for the inclusion of evidence-based practices into the classroom.

CHAPTER 2

UNDERSTANDING STUDENT NEEDS

Learning Objectives

- Understand how the influence of culture, social, and environmental factors affect student development
- Identify ways in which educators can address the influence of family values, social, and environmental factors to cultivate a culturally responsive classroom
- Identify some of the more prevalent disabilities educators may encounter in their classroom and describe some of the ways in which these disabilities *may* manifest in the classroom
- Define executive functions and describe their link to disabilities one may encounter in the classroom

Key Terms

Attention Deficit Hyperactivity Disorder (ADHD)

Autism Spectrum Disorders (ASD)

Cultural Competence

Developmental Characteristics

Emotional and Behavioral Disorders (EBD)

Environmental Factors

Executive Functions

Family Values

Inclusive Classrooms

Individuals with Disabilities Education Act (IDEA)

Intellectual Disability

Specific Learning Disability

Stereotyped Behaviors

Being an effective educator goes beyond expertise in content knowledge or being able to organize and deliver a lesson. One must hone the ability to connect with and nurture students. In this way, the classroom may be thought of as an ecosystem, wherein a community of individuals interact with one another and operate as a complex, interconnected structure. To harness a healthy and balanced ecosystem, teachers are responsible for knowing each of their students—knowing them in order to *understand* them. Thus, this is beyond simply knowing student preferences and predilections. It is understanding their needs as individuals, learners, peers, and members of the classroom. No matter what type of classroom in which you envisage yourself teaching, know this, you will encounter challenges you've never imagined, disabilities you've never heard of, and social dynamics completely out of your repertoire. The modern classroom continues to evolve and with it, inclusive practices are bringing in students with unique needs. As such, educators are required to be well informed in order to meet these students where they are and provide quality, targeted instruction.

While the topics discussed in this chapter focus on typical developmental patterns, socially constructed disabilities, and theoretical models, it is important to understand that each individual student comes to school with a unique profile. Generalizations about entire groups of students, populations, or learners may actually limit teachers' abilities to work effectively with students, particularly if these preconceived ideas are rooted in biases or misinformation. Given this, teachers should use the information in this chapter to learn about the many facets of a student's layered identity without attempting to box a student into one well-defined category.

Developmental Characteristics

In order to develop classroom expectations and make meaningful connections with students, it is critical that teachers understand the developmental milestones of typically developing children. While not all students will grow and mature at the same rates, developmental characteristics outline the typical developmental milestones at specific ages. Having a general idea of what to expect developmentally will help teachers plan for and manage a range of behaviors. Table 2–1 gives a brief overview of some of the cognitive, physical, emotional, and social characteristics teachers might encounter across age ranges.

This is not an all-inclusive list and does not take into account individual developmental differences due to disabilities, medical conditions, environmental factors, or other unknown or unidentified atypical growth development patterns.

Table 2–1. Developmental Characteristics by Age Range

	Cognitive	Physical	Emotional	Social
Ages 5–6 (K/1st grades)	• Lives in the present • Inquisitive/curious • Developing independence with known tasks • Can follow two-step directions • Developing sense of humor • Maybe impatient	• Developing hand-eye coordination • May still need rest time or naps • High energy • Increased physical ability and coordination • Coordination and control is uneven	• Wants adult praise • Easily scared or uncertain of new experiences • Uses words to express emotions, but may not be consistent • Sensitive to being criticized	• Group play • Exploratory play • Pretend play • Play with same and opposite sex peers * Affectionate with adults and peers • May still have difficulty sharing
Ages 7–8 (2nd/3rd grades)	• Uses basic problem solving • Able to work independently for short periods of time • Increased responsibility • Developing sense of time (past and future) • Able to follow multistep directions	• Increased ability with fine and gross motor skills • High energy • Increased muscle control, less falling and less bumping into objects	• Able to control emotions • Desire for increased independence • Developing more concrete ideas of right and wrong • Consistently uses words to express emotions • Increased self-comparison to peers	• Games, including competition and problem solving • Develops a preferred peer group • May have a best friend • Play shifts to same-sex peers • Understands rules of conversation

continues

Table 2–1. *continued*

	Cognitive	Physical	Emotional	Social
Ages 9–10 (4th/5th grades)	• Uses more advanced problem solving • Works independently • Able to think in the abstract • Can understand sarcasm	• May be entering the beginning of puberty • High energy • May be restless	• Emotions may range as result of puberty • Increased worry and anxiousness • Able to take some responsibility for actions and behaviors • Self-critical	• Interest in being part of a same-sex community or group • Develops close one-on-one friendships • Has a preferred peer group • Interest in specific hobbies increases
Ages 11–12 (6th/7th grades)	• Able to follow complex multistep directions * Independent tasks • Developing strong opinions about range of topics	• Entering puberty • Females may have sudden growth spurts • Hunger and need for sleep may begin to increase	* Self-conscious • Desire for increased privacy • Increased desire to be self-assertive with feelings • Able to show empathy	• Interest in being part of a same-sex community or group • May have an interest in having a boyfriend or girlfriend • Wants approval from others

	Cognitive	Physical	Emotional	Social
Ages 13–15 (8th/9th/10th grades)	• Independent • Can delay gratification • Engages in high level of abstract thinking • Independently plans and organizes	• May appear physically awkward due to sudden growth spurts • Experiencing puberty • Differing rates of growth and development • Increased need for sleep • Increased appetite	• Self-consciousness and self-doubt continue • Over confidence with some tasks • Sensitivity about appearance • Developing sense of individuality	* Interest in cooperative and competitive games and sports • Increased interest in friends over family • Increased identity based on peer group versus family
Ages 16+ (11th/12th grades)	• Develops independent views about the world • Understands personal strengths and weaknesses	• May appear physically awkward due to sudden growth spurts • Males may have sudden growth spurts	• May be critical of parents' beliefs • Develops sense of individuality • Self-reflects on behaviors	• May engage in fads or trends or follow popular media • Separation from home life

This continuum of development is important in the context of classroom management for a number of reasons. First, teachers should know what they might expect from their students in relation to their developmental abilities. If Mrs. Samson is a high school teacher teaching a lesson on current events, she should expect that her students may have some strong, differing thoughts and opinions about the topic. They may also engage in debates or ask difficult questions. It is not that these students are being defiant or oppositional, but rather they are exerting their developing independence and identity as they make sense of the world around them. This is to be expected at this developmental level. Similarly, in a second grade classroom, a teacher should not be surprised to observe that while her students are able to work independently and focus on assigned tasks, they still have high energy levels and need to get up and move around periodically. She would expect that students would begin fidgeting, walking around the classroom, or engaging in play after long periods of stationary, sustained work. This is expected with typically developing second graders. This is to say that certain behaviors, within context of typical development, should be understood and, to some degree, expected.

Understanding developmental milestones is also important because teachers need to know what behaviors they should anticipate for planning purposes. For example, if Mr. Newsome is teaching kindergarten, he would expect that some students in his class might argue over materials in the math center because they may not have mastered the ability to share and cooperate. This behavior would be expected in his kindergarten classroom. Therefore, at an independent work station, he might create separate but identical tubs of materials that alleviate any arguing over preferred items. Alternately, if he is teaching the whole class about counting using manipulatives, he may plan to start the lesson with a brief discussion about sharing since he is aware that some of his students may still struggle with this developmental skill.

All of this is not to say that teachers should ignore or excuse behaviors that are disruptive or unsafe, even when they are developmentally appropriate. Teachers and school staff should always teach students prosocial behaviors and model expectations, regardless of the students' ages or developmental levels. These developmental milestones are markers for understanding students, planning for expected challenges, and teaching behavior in the classroom.

Influence of Cultural, Social, and Environmental Factors

Mirroring our societal makeup, students arrive at school with a myriad of individual influences to include his or her own culture, customs, dress, and values. Beyond understanding how students develop, it is also important to understand how cultural, social, and environmental factors may influence student behavior and how teachers can best respond to and respect those differences.

Family Values

Family values are a family system's beliefs or ideas about what is valued, meaningful, or important. Family values surrounding education and the educational system may influence students' own beliefs about school and subsequent school engagement. Parents' personal experiences with school and learning may also influence how a child perceives school. If a parent had a negative experience with school and found it to be an unsafe or unwelcoming environment, those ideas may be passed on either directly or inadvertently to children who, consequently, may not like attending school or may not understand how or why education is important. Conversely, if a guardian had positive, helpful, and enriching school experiences, a child may hear about the importance of school or the value of an education and develop more positive feelings and attitudes toward school. These differences are important to remember as we work with students who may have varying degrees of interest and investment in school. Classroom management systems can address these differences and challenges by building relationships with students, including hooks in lesson plans that engage students and utilizing motivational strategies.

> *See Chapter 8 for more on motivation.*

Each family unit also maintains values around behavior, including norms and expectations. While one family may interpret a student telling a teacher they don't like an assignment as standing up for oneself or being assertive, another family may perceive this as disrespect. While teachers and school personnel are not in the position to change family values, we can establish expectations and norms for the school and classroom environment and share those with our students and families. Again, teachers cannot ignore behaviors that impede upon learning or safety, but it is important to understand how students' family values may impact a student's classroom behavior. This also includes understanding ourselves as teachers and classroom managers. When thinking about differing values, teachers could ask themselves the following:

1. Student roles: What role do I see students taking in my classroom? Should the relationship be collaborative? Should students comply without question? Should students have a voice as decision makers?

2. Teacher/student relationships: How do I believe students should express disagreements to teachers or adults in school authority? Do I expect students to face me and look me in the eyes when we are speaking? Should a student ever raise their voice at an adult?

3. Differences in values: What behaviors from children do I believe are "crossing the line" with adults? Is cursing, eye rolling, ignoring adults, and/ or sarcasm acceptable communication from children? What are the limits to how a student should defend themselves if they are being bullied or picked on?

After answering these questions, teachers should reflect on the reasons behind their beliefs and how these might differ from some of the students and families they work with. To be an effective classroom manager, differences will need to be reconciled in such a way that students' differences are respected and teachers maintain a consistent and predictable environment.

Make a Connection

How can you create a school and classroom environment that is welcoming to all families, despite the negative or positive feelings parents or guardians may have about school?

Environmental Factors

Environmental factors students may face include poverty, homelessness, and a lack of basic needs, to name a few. In the United States, 21% of children live in households where the family income level is below the federal poverty threshold (National Center for Children in Poverty, 2019). Criticisms of the federal poverty threshold income cutoff assert that families may actually need twice the level of this standard to sustain a household, meaning that even more children may, in actuality, live in poverty. In 2018, the federal poverty threshold was $25,465 for a family of four with two children (U.S. Census Bureau, 2019). While children may live in homes where adults are working, many are earning low wages that do not sufficiently cover living expenses. Trends about children in poverty have not changed drastically over the past five to seven years. Children who are Black, American Indian, and Hispanic are disproportionately overrepresented in poverty statistics. Regionally, poverty rates for southern states trends higher than states in the northern and Midwestern portions of United States. Finally, single-mother families comprise the largest family structure group of children in poverty at 58.2% (Children's Defense Fund, 2017).

Given this, it should not be surprising that most teachers, at some point in their careers, will work with students who may not have stable housing, access to food, adequate clothing, or medical care. Children who live in areas where poverty is highly concentrated have an increased risk of anxiety, antisocial behaviors (Evan & Cassells, 2014), and stress and trauma (Kang, 2016). When students, and families as a whole, lack consistency with having basic needs met, it will certainly impact school behavior. Students who are not living in permanent homes, are in transient living situations, or do not have access to food may be tired, irritable, or have a low tolerance for frustration when they arrive at school. A student who has not had their basic needs met outside of school may be challenged to perform academically or comply with expectations. In fact, the effects of these challenges may contribute to issues with brain development, self-regulation, decision making, and slower cognition, especially when compared to children who are not living in poverty (Blair & Raver, 2016). When working with students with a noticeable lack of food, clothing, or other basic needs, it is important that teachers share this information with their school administrators and support staff to help address these challenges. From a classroom perspective, teachers should be discreet when talking with these students about their needs. Students should never be approached in front of peers and comments should never be made publicly that embarrasses a student.

 High-Leverage Practice Alert!

See HLP3 about the importance of background, socioeconomic status, language, and culture when communicating with families.

Social Factors

Student behavior will also invariably be influenced by their own, and their family's, belonging within a community. How often is the student interacting with other adults outside of school and their home environment? Are they are required to initiate conversations and engage with other adults, developing skills with repeated exposure to novel situations? Are students involved in organized sports where they are learning sportsmanship skills? Is the student part of a club or group where they interact, plan, or organize events with peers? Each of these opportunities to socialize outside of the home and school setting adds to each student's chance to practice behavior and receive feedback. This is something to consider when working with students who demonstrate delayed social skills. When faced with behaviors in the classroom that disrupt the learning process, it is important for teachers to consider whether students have actually been taught the necessary skills to be successful. Further, consider whether students have opportunities to practice the social skills they are taught in school outside of the school environment (Walker & Barry, 2018). This can be especially critical in the early elementary years if a student has not had preschool experiences that mirror the structure of school.

Peek ahead to Chapter 14 for more on teaching students social skills.

Cultural Factors

With increasingly culturally and linguistically diverse schools, it is imperative teachers are knowledgeable about their students and how students' cultures may relate to behavior management. Cultural competence is the ability to interact, understand, communicate, and interact with people across a range of cultures. Without cultural competence, teachers have a difficult time forming relationships with students, managing behavior of culturally and linguistically diverse students, and creating a respectful classroom community (Adkins-Coleman, 2010; Milner & Tenore, 2010). Traditional classroom management often focuses on mainstream norms, like eye contact, compliance, or the dominant culture's definitions of respect, authority, and obedience. These norms do not consider the impact of culture on student, teacher, and parent interactions. Behavior management should consider both the context in which students live and their culture.

Behavior expectations are culturally influenced by the dominant culture and these may be misaligned with the individual norms students bring to school. In light of student differences, some traditional classroom environment norms to consider include collaboration and cooperation versus individualization, conflict and conflict resolution between students, conflict and conflict resolution between adults and students, formal versus informal language and structures, responses to high structure versus low structure, direct versus indirect responses to questions, and expression of emotions. One example of how this may manifest in the classroom with behavior may be in a discussion between two students about an incident about that resulted in conflict. Depending on the students' cultures, one student may be comfortable expressing emotions and viewpoints during the problem-solving process. The student may share openly and without hesitation. Another student may look for a way to compromise in the situation and may only share their perspective if it will move the discussion toward a solution that benefits both students. This student may seek more information or listen to perspectives before sharing. Yet another student may have all the facts and may feel strongly about the situation but avoid conflict at all costs, resulting in a premature and unsatisfying conclusion to the problem solving.

Misunderstanding or misreading the behavior of culturally and linguistically diverse students may lead to unwarranted consequences or punishments. In fact, disciplinary referrals are disproportionately given to students of color and those from lower socioeconomic backgrounds (Milner & Tenore, 2010). More specifically, African American students are four times more likely to be suspended or expelled for a minor infraction in elementary than their peers (Skiba et al., 2011).

To develop a culturally responsive classroom, teachers should first and foremost maintain high expectations for all students, without making assumptions about how students' home life will impact school performance. Teachers should use culturally relevant curricula and purposefully incorporate students' customs and traditions into class routines. This includes selecting a range of texts, examples, and materials that represent a wide range of cultures and perspectives. Not only does this make learning relevant for nondominant cultures but it also enhances the learning of all students through exposure to ideas or cultures that are different from their own.

Learning about students' culture, language, and customs can occur through student questionnaires or surveys, individual interviews, culture quilts, or opportunities to share items or media from home. Teachers can also facilitate conversations that address bias or stereotypes, offering opportunities for students to learn about one another. Classroom climate will be discussed later in the book when we discuss establishing relationships with students and creating an environment built on safety and respect for one another.

Finally, culturally competent teachers should be cognizant about developing an understanding of their own cultural identity. This can be done through reflective practice to include some of the prompts listed in the reflection box (Figure 2–1). This understanding can also be developed through conversations with colleagues

Figure 2–1. Reflection questions for building culturally responsive classrooms.

Reflection Questions

1. Have I learned the correct pronunciation of all of my students' names and do I call them by name?

2. What do I know about my students' cultures, traditions, religions, or customs?

3. How do I learn more about my students' cultures, traditions, religions, or customs?

4. Do I include a range of culturally diverse instructional materials into my teaching to include names, texts, media, topics, and points of view?

5. Do I offer my students a range of ways to learn material? Orally, through stories, games, written expression?

6. Are there incongruities with how I discipline children of different cultures, races, religions, and perceived or actual backgrounds?

7. Do I have expectations of students based on their real or perceived background? Why do I have these expectations?

8. How does the current school or class structure privilege students based on race, socioeconomic levels, culture, religions, or background? How can this be fixed?

9. Do I communicate with parents in a way that engages them? (Native language? Modality of communication?)

10. Do I welcome feedback from my students about my classroom?

and peers. Regardless of how you accomplish this, it is beneficial for you and your students to engage in ongoing reflection about how our cultural identity influences our interactions with students and each other and creates an environment that welcomes all students.

Throughout the book we will continue to address how you can demonstrate cultural responsiveness in your classroom management. This will come up when we discuss working with parents, developing a classroom climate, and building relationships, just to name a few. Cultural responsiveness should not be something that happens in isolation but ingrained in how you manage your classroom every day.

High-Leverage Practice Alert!

HLP7 covers the importance of valuing ethnic and cultural diversity (among other factors) to encourage engagement.

Students with Disabilities

The inclusive classroom is one that actively and purposefully involves all students in learning, regardless of background, culture, race, gender, socioeconomic status, or disability. This section specifically refers to students with disabilities and how certain disability categories may manifest behaviorally within the context of a classroom. The purpose of this information is only to provide an overview of how symptomology of certain disability areas may present in real life, and in no way is this information to be used to diagnose a disability. Profiles of disability characteristics can serve as a reference point to understanding what is common or may be expected with specific disabilities. It should be noted that disabilities do not necessarily cause behaviors, nor are specific behaviors an indicator of a disability. As an educator, if you suspect a child's struggles may be related to a clinical condition, best practice is to first confer with your administration, special education lead, or procedural specialist to approach this highly sensitive topic in a way that aligns to your state, county, and/or district's processes. While this chapter will not go into depth about how to manage such disability areas in the classroom, we will connect these disability areas to evidence-based, functional interventions in Chapter 13.

To begin, a caveat to consider, not every student with a specific disability label will present in the ways discussed here; it is important to be aware that these presentations are being explained in comparison to or in regard to typical development. Additionally, not all students with a diagnosed disability necessarily qualify for or receive special education services. In order to qualify, a student's "educational performance" must be "adversely affected" by one of 13 different disability categories outlined with the Individuals with Disabilities Education Act (IDEIA, 2004; Table 2–2).

IDEA is federal legislation mandating special education and related services be provided to all eligible students. For the scope of this text, we will narrow this discussion to the most commonly encountered disabilities in the classroom. The terms "educational performance" and "adversely affected" are left open to interpretation by states and local legislatures. While specifics vary across states, most agree that "educational performance" spans academic as well as nonacademic areas, such as mobility, social development, and independent living skills. "Adversely affected" educational performance may be measured by poor grades

Table 2–2. Disability Categories Outlined by the Individuals with Disabilities Education Improvement Act of 2004	
Disability Category	**Percent of Total Enrollment 2014–2015**
1. Autism	1.1
2. Deaf-Blindness	~0
3. Developmental Disability	0.8
4. Emotional Disturbance	0.7
5. Hearing Impairment	0.2
6. Intellectual Disability	0.8
7. Multiple Disabilities	0.3
8. Orthopedic Impairment	0.1
9. Other Health Impairment	1.7
10. Specific Learning Disability	4.5
11. Speech or Language Impairment	2.6
12. Traumatic Brain Injury	0.1
13. Visual Impairment	0.1

or low achievement but also may be manifested through behavioral difficulties, impaired social interactions, and difficulty following instructions, as well as difficulty organizing, planning, and prioritizing and regulating emotions.

The percentage listed indicates the proportion of students eligible under a disability category based off of total enrollment in public schools preschool through grade 12 in 2014 to 2015.

The first step to promote an inclusive environment begins with our use of language. Person-first language, wherein the person or student is prioritized over any other distinguishing characteristic such as a disability, conveys value and respect. Person-first language places emphasis on the individual over his or her disability or differences. Thus, we refer to students as "students with disabilities" as they are students first and foremost rather than "disabled students." Person-first language allows the individual to be considered first (e.g., Sam has autism), without being characterized by a disability (e.g., Sam is autistic). It should be noted that some individuals and groups build identities around their disabilities, including the Deaf community. However, disability labels have long been stigmatizing and have perpetuated generalizations, stereotypes, and inaccuracies. To combat this, a conscious approach to gaining knowledge of what disabilities *are* and what they *are not* is critical. Focusing on the individual over the disability will also encourage relationship building; a topic we will discuss more in Chapter 9. The aim of this section is to provide an overall awareness of how disabilities manifest behaviorally and to help foster a sense of expectations around what it means to have a student with a disability in your classroom.

Attention Deficit Hyperactivity Disorder

While not classified as a learning disability, attention deficit hyperactivity disorder (ADHD) is a neurological condition causing symptoms of inattention, poor impulse control, distractibility, and/or forgetfulness. It qualifies as a disability under the "Other Health Impairment" (OHI) category of IDEIA (2004), thus allowing students with ADHD to receive special education services. According to IDEIA, OHI means

> having limited strength, vitality, or alertness, including a heightened alertness to environmental stimuli, that results in limited alertness with respect to the educational environment, that (i) is due to chronic or acute health problems such as asthma, attention deficit disorder or attention deficit hyperactivity disorder, diabetes, epilepsy, a heart condition, hemophilia, lead poisoning, leukemia, nephritis [a kidney disorder], rheumatic fever, sickle cell anemia, and Tourette Syndrome and (ii) adversely affects a child's educational performance. (Sec. 300.8 (c) (9), 2004)

Thus, OHI includes ADHD and other medical conditions including Tourette syndrome, epilepsy, diabetes, and so forth. ADHD is a clinical diagnosis in which a student's social, academic, and/or occupational functioning is adversely affected. There are three presentations of ADHD according to the American Psychiatric Association's (APA) *Diagnostic and Statistical Manual of Mental Disorders* (DSM-5; APA, 2013): predominantly inattentive presentation, predominantly hyperactive/impulsive presentation, and combined presentation. Among the 18 symptoms, nine are related to inattention and nine are related to hyperactivity/impulsivity, and individuals must exhibit at least six symptoms within one and/or both categories in order to receive a diagnosis of ADHD.

Behavioral manifestations of ADHD tend to change over time. With the newest revision of the DSM-5 came a change in terminology to reflect the most current understanding of ADHD. Shifting from the previous "subtypes" of ADHD to "presentations" of ADHD better describes a fluid condition that may change with age and/or settings. Typically, a diagnosis is made in the elementary school years and up to 80% of children will continue to experience symptoms related to the disability into adulthood (APA, 2013). Research indicates boys are nearly twice as likely to be diagnosed as girls. Additionally, around 20% to 25% of all individuals diagnosed with ADHD have a comorbid learning disability (DuPaul, Gormley, & Laracy, 2013).

ADHD Predominantly Inattentive Presentation

Students with this presentation of ADHD are most often overlooked or go unidentified due to lack of overt or disruptive behaviors. Rather, parents and teachers may become concerned about these students due to declining academic performance or difficulty completing schoolwork or homework. These students often daydream, miss some or all of instructions, make careless errors, avoid tasks requiring sustained attention or effort, are easily distracted, and tend to be highly disorganized and forgetful. As such, they may start tasks but quickly divert off task, require adult assistance to ensure they have all necessary materials to complete a task, and require frequent prompts, reminders, and redirection in order to see a task through to completion.

Classroom Example

Sergi, a fourth grade student in Ms. Apple's class, has been having progressive difficulty getting his work completed on time. On Monday, Ms. Apple noted Sergi made several errors when copying math questions from the board, mixing up information from the first and third questions. Two days later, Sergi scored a 20/100 on a science test due to incorrectly transferring responses onto his answer sheet (she let him fix it, of course). Ms. Apple also recalled that Sergi had forgotten his homework at least once a week since the beginning of the year, was unable to attend a field trip because he misplaced the permission slip, often appeared to be staring off into space when she gave instructions, and always struggled to remember what to do when more than two instructions were given. After considering the pattern of behavior observed over time, Ms. Apple contacted Sergi's parents to discuss her concerns.

ADHD Predominantly Hyperactive/Impulsive Presentation

In contrast to students with a predominantly inattentive presentation, students who exhibit hyperactivity and impulsivity are much more likely to be noticed in the classroom context due to higher visibility of symptoms. Hyperactivity refers to a set of behaviors that typically include constant movement (particularly in inappropriate situations or settings), restlessness, excessive fidgeting, and/or excessive talking. Impulsivity is characterized by hasty decision making, taking action with little to no forethought about long-term consequences or potential for harm to self or others, and seeking immediate rewards versus delayed satisfaction. Individuals who are impulsive may demonstrate social difficulties as they tend to interrupt others and say exactly what is on their minds. In the classroom, these students are often seen fidgeting or struggling to remain in a designated area, talking excessively, blurting out answers, interrupting others' activities and/or conversations, and having limited patience. While these students do not have difficulty with inattention per se, their hyperactivity and impulsivity negatively affects their ability to manage tasks and see them through.

 Classroom Example

In elementary school, a student who has been diagnosed with ADHD may be described by parents, teachers, and peers as a child who is "always on the go," "never stops talking," and "can't wait their turn." As this same child enters middle school, emerging difficulties may begin with maintaining friendships. Since one characteristics of ADHD is impulsivity, teachers may need to help students with self-monitoring or self-awareness. In a middle school example of this, Angeline and her friend Ella were approached by Ella's crush James during lunch. Without thinking, Angeline blurted out, "James! Ella really likes you and wants you to ask her to the party on Friday." In the moments that followed, Ella made it clear to Angeline that she was never going to share private information with her ever again and that she no longer wanted to be friends.

ADHD Combined Presentation

As may be inferred, this presentation of ADHD is one in which inattention is present along with hyperactivity and impulsivity. Having this particular presentation of ADHD does not necessarily indicate a more severe or debilitating form of

ADHD. Rather, an individual diagnosed with predominantly inattentive behavior may also exhibit hyperactive or impulsive behaviors but does not meet full criteria to be given a combined diagnosis. Individuals with a combined presentation show six or more symptoms of each presentation and this presentation of ADHD has the largest research base. Those who hold this diagnosis tend to face a different set of social struggles than the other presentations. Inattention plays a huge role in one's ability to attend to others and join into meaningful and relevant conversation. Impulsivity and hyperactivity can lead to social blunders and muddy one's ability to discern and respect individual's boundaries. Such behaviors are also not well tolerated by peers as they can be perceived as annoying, intrusive, and rude. As these students grow older, this can become more significant as social relationships begin to shift and mature, sometimes involving romantic features.

 Classroom Example

Adi, a 15-year-old boy with ADHD combined presentation, enjoys online gaming. Often, he plays on multiplayer online platforms with friends after school and on the weekends. During one particular game, Adi made an error because he was not paying attention and caused his team a massive loss. Immediately, Adi became highly agitated and defensive. He began to throw insults at his fellow players, claiming that he was "tricked" and the game was "unfair." Unfortunately, this was not the first time an incident like this occurred. This massive blowout sparked Adi's friends to remove themselves from his gaming group and this led to social struggles in school.

Executive Function Deficits

Executive functions (EF) are the abilities that allow us to control impulses, problem solve scenarios, and achieve goals through planning and organization. EF span across the cognitive, behavioral, and emotional self-regulation domains. While the other disabilities listed in this section are clinical diagnoses, poor EF is not. Issues with EF indicate a weakness or set of weaknesses in an individual's system of organization, planning, and management. Table 2–3 outlines nine widely agreed upon domains by which the strength of an individual's EF is measured (Gioia, Isquith, Guy, & Kenworthy, 2015).

While we must recognize that students with ADHD exhibit EF deficits, it is not to say that all students with poor EF have ADHD. As you may have gathered, EF skills are not only critical in order to navigate one's educational years but also

Table 2–3. Executive Function Domains with Examples

Domain	Definition	Example: Well-Developed	Example: Poorly-Developed
Inhibit	The ability to resist impulses and stop one's behavior	Steve hit Alvin for taking his ball; Alvin resists hitting back and instead goes to tell an adult.	While working in chemistry lab, Jasmine reaches out and rubs her lab partner's hair because it looks soft.
Self-Monitor	The degree one is aware of how his or her behavior affects others.	While trying to concentrate, Jeremie quietly taps his pencil on his leg during a math test.	Casey hums and reads aloud while working on her English paper.
Shift	The ability to move from one activity, situation, or other circumstance freely.	Matt is not finished with his journal entry but puts his materials away when prompted to move into group work.	Nazaren refuses to leave the classroom when the principal announces an impromptu assembly.
Emotional Control	The ability to moderate or regulate emotional responses to a situation/person.	Sally did not cry, despite receiving a failing score on her exam.	Jeanna screams and curses at the teacher when she gets a tardy slip for being late to class.
Initiate	Ability to independently begin an activity or engage in problem solving.	Scott enters the classroom, puts his belongings away, and immediately begins the morning math warm-up.	When given a long-term group project, Lillian does not know how to begin, how to assign tasks, or what to prioritize.
Working Memory	Ability to briefly remember salient information while completing a task.	Student remembers three instructions delivered at the beginning of a lesson that allows her to complete the task.	After the first block, Fred forgets his science book in his locker because he was trying to remember to also bring his gym uniform and math notebook for the third block.

continues

Table 2–3. *continued*

Domain	Definition	Example: Well-Developed	Example: Poorly-Developed
Plan/ Organize	Ability to anticipate future events, set goals, and gather required materials to action a task or activity.	The night before the first day of school, Mary picks out her clothes, packs her lunch, and makes sure she has all of her supplies in her bag.	Mae sees that the weather is warm, so she wears flip flops to school. She is unable to participate in PE because she doesn't have sneakers.
Task-Monitor	The ability to measure one's own performance during a task or shortly after its completion.	After the quiz on magnets, Brandon reports to the teacher that the section on poles was "hard." A review of the quiz reveals that he answered those questions incorrectly.	When asked about her performance on tests and quizzes, Milly always reports she did "good," regardless of whether she earned a 100% or 50%.
Organi-zation	How one manages orderliness of his or her personal space and keeps track of belongings.	Antwon's locker includes notebooks ordered by period. Notebooks include labeled sections.	Ashley is unable to locate her homework from last night and does not have a pencil in her desk.

throughout one's life span. We rely heavily on EF to organize ourselves, regulate our behavior, pay attention, and remember details. Signs of poor EF mirror those of ADHD quite closely in that these students have difficulty maintaining attention to tasks, have issues with shifting tasks, display limited inhibition or self-control, and have difficulty initiating tasks. Further, problems with working memory are exemplified as difficulty retaining information in the short term and using it to problem solve or complete tasks or by having to manage multiple pieces of information at once.

Clearly, many facets of educational performance may be affected by the previously mentioned issues; however, poor EF also seeps into an individual's social functioning. Those with poor EF tend to be cognitively rigid, which can harm social relationships. Cognitive flexibility is what allows us to shift between different mental processes and adapt through our behavior (Dajani & Uddin, 2015). This flexibility dictates our ability to change in routine, schedules, and procedures. It also allows us to interpret and understand other's viewpoints, which is critical to maintaining meaningful friendships. When one is inflexible, any deviation from the norm can incite an emotional response. Difficulty with controlling impulses may also have dire social consequences. For example, saying exactly what is on one's mind may not always lead to a positive outcome. These inhibitions also manifest as an inability to recognize when one is engaging in social blunders, perhaps until it is too late. Executive function skills develop over time, with differing rates, beginning at around age 2 and growing exponentially until around age 30. Along this course of development, difficulties with EF may present differently, with younger children demonstrating more emotional dysregulation by engaging in tantrums or acting out physically or vocally, while older students struggle with organization from the increased demands of school. Older students may also have difficulty working in groups and find it challenging to manage their time.

Finally, as we've gone through the finer points on what ADHD presentations may look like in the classroom, it is equally important to weigh in on what ADHD *is not*. Students with ADHD are not intentionally ignoring instructions, making mistakes, or being disruptive. Rather, such behaviors and difficulties occur outside of their awareness and self-control. This differs from students who are intentionally defiant, oppositional, or noncompliant; that is, whose behavior would be captured under emotional and behavioral disorders.

 High-Leverage Practice Alert!

Cognitive and metacognitive strategies are covered in HLP14. Check out the information on self-regulation and strategy instruction.

Emotional and Behavioral Disorders (EBD)

Students with emotional and behavioral disorders (EBD) often have difficulty inhibiting or controlling their behavior and commonly lack necessary skills to initiate and maintain social interactions in expected ways. IDEIA (2004) provides specific criteria defining EBD as a condition in which one or more of the following characteristics are evident over a long period of time, which adversely affects educational performance: (a) an inability to learn, which cannot be explained by intellectual, sensory, or other health factors; (b) an inability to build or maintain satisfactory relationships with peers and teachers; (c) inappropriate types of behavior or feelings under normal circumstances; (d) a general pervasive mood of unhappiness or depression; or (e) a tendency to develop physical symptoms or fears associated with personal and school problems. The criteria also includes students who may have schizophrenia but are not socially maladjusted.

Students with EBD typically present in two different subcategories: individuals who exhibit externalizing behavior characteristics and those who exhibit internalizing behavior characteristics. These subcategories are by no means binary, and students may exhibit more behaviors from one subcategory than the other. Externalizing behaviors are challenging behaviors directed outward at the environment, which may include aggression, defiance, stealing, cheating, destruction of property, and noncompliance. Since externalizing behaviors are so visible, they often capture the attention of the classroom, pulling teacher concentration toward management of such distractions. Alternatively, internalizing behavior characteristics are those not readily seen and, as such, can be very difficult to recognize and address accordingly. Depression, anxiety, fearfulness, social withdrawal, and somatic symptoms (Davis, Young, Hardman, & Winters, 2011) are some of the most prevalent internalizing behaviors.

Regardless of presentation, students with EBD experience adverse effects on their learning and social approval. In 2016, students with EBD made up 5.5% of the students with disabilities served through IDEA, Part B. Sadly, this disability area accounts for the largest portion of students who drop out of school, with a rate of at least 30% dropouts per year, as compared to any other disability category (U.S. Department of Education Annual Report to Congress, 2018). These data are not to be taken lightly as dropout rates are correlated with difficulty maintaining employment, high substance abuse rates, and poorer overall social outcomes (Landrum, Tankersley, & Kauffman, 2003).

In the classroom setting, it is important to remember that students who have been identified with an EBD may have difficulty with regulating their emotions and impulse control. While these students may understand the necessary skills to navigate their environment, they may not have the ability to process disappointment, frustration, anger, or sadness in the same way as their more typically developing peers. For these students, what may not seem to be a "big deal" to you, may be overwhelming or troublesome for them. Students with EBD thrive on consistency, clear expectations, and opportunities for breaks. Often, these students have experienced a fair amount of negativity surrounding their school experiences and will need the investment of teachers who will develop relationships with them, provide opportunities for success, reward approximations or progress toward positive behaviors, and celebrate motivation and effort through goal setting.

Specific Learning Disabilities (SLD)

A specific learning disability (SLD) is a neurological condition in which an individual's ability to understand language, either spoken or written, affects one's ability to listen, think, speak, read, write, spell, or do mathematical calculations (IDEIA, 2004). Included within this group are diagnoses such as dyslexia (difficulty in accurate interpretation of words, letters, symbols), dysgraphia (difficulties with spelling, poor handwriting, and difficulty transferring coherent thoughts into written work), dyscalculia (difficulty understanding number and numerical concepts, manipulating numbers, and completing calculations), or developmental aphasia (dysfunction in the development of speech and language expression and/or reception). Disorders not included in this group include issues with an origin in visual, hearing, or motor processes; intellectual disabilities; EBD; or factors related to one's environment, culture, and/or socioeconomic status (IDEIA, 2004).

Often thought of as a discrepancy between aptitude and ability or a gap between what one is demonstrating and how well they are actually performing, SLDs affect the way one learns; yet, do not have an effect on overall IQ. One's IQ may be thought of as what one "should" be able to do; however, an SLD makes it so that one is not achieving at his or her expected level. Such gaps may manifest in the classroom as with the student who is highly proficient in completing algebraic equations yet struggles with the reading comprehension portion of mathematical word problems. Or the student who is able to articulate his answer when speaking to the teacher, but is unable to coherently transfer his thoughts into written work. Students with SLD may appear as though they are not applying themselves fully or are constantly off task. Specific learning disabilities affect executive functions, meaning these students also have challenges with working memory, initiation, and organization—for example. Here is where a teacher may notice students with SLD struggle with multistep instructions, completing assignments correctly, or chronically losing homework.

It is not uncommon for students with SLD to try to silently cope with their learning challenges and hide such difficulties from teachers and classmates. Over time, this may become an overwhelming burden to keep up with and affect student confidence by shying away from participating in class or not wanting to hand in assignments for fear of mistakes. On the other hand, some students may take the opposite approach and engage in disruptive behavior, take on a lackadaisical attitude toward school, or assume the role of class clown.

Autism Spectrum Disorders (ASD)

Autism spectrum disorder (ASD) is a developmental disability in which an individual displays persistent deficits in social communication and demonstrates restrictive, repetitive patterns of behavior (APA, 2013). The federal definition refers to "a developmental disability significantly affecting verbal and nonverbal communication and social interaction, generally evident before age three, which adversely affects a child's educational performance" (IDEIA, 2004). Like most disabilities, autism is a *spectrum* and, as such, presents *very* differently across people. Unfortunately, there are heaps of misconceptions about autism resulting from a general lack of understanding of what the disability is and what it is not. While there is not the space in this textbook to debunk every possible myth about autism, it is important to address those which have had quite a bit of notoriety in mainstream media.

Myth #1: Individuals with autism prefer to be alone and do not want to make friends. This idea is simply untrue. Of course, individual differences influence a person's level of interest in socialization; however, individuals with autism struggle with social skills, making it extremely difficult for them to interact with others and maintain reciprocal relationships. They may seem shy or unwilling to engage or, conversely, be overly familiar with strangers and lack social boundaries. This social "withdrawal" may be a result of long learning histories of failed or awkward social interactions, as repeated difficulties over time usually result in a decrease in a person's willingness to try to engage in socialization.

Classroom Example

Mary is a 12-year-old girl diagnosed with autism and isolates herself from peers in school. Mary's well-engrained learning history stems back to her preschool years wherein she would attempt to play with peers on the playground but ended up being too rough with them, scaring them off. Her elementary years were marked with repeated failed social interactions during lunch and recess where Mary just didn't say the right thing or unintentionally hurt someone's feelings by being too honest. Over time, the consequences to Mary's attempts at making friends were enough to cease her attempts, resulting in what looks like isolation.

Myth #2: People with autism are emotionless, lacking the ability to express or feel emotions. People with autism are first and foremost *people* and absolutely feel emotion. Yet, due to difficulties with expressive language, individuals with autism may convey their emotions differently than their neurotypical peers.

Myth #3: Every person with autism has a savant skill. This is a widely spread misconception regarding the varying levels of functioning of people with autism. Some people with autism do not rely upon vocal language to communicate, but this is not the case for all. Some individuals with autism are very articulate and well spoken. Some individuals with autism will become independent adults, get married, and have children, while some individuals with autism may be dependent on others for daily living skills throughout their lifetime. Some people with autism are proficient in mathematics or have savant-like "splinter skills" in other areas such as music or art; however, not every individual with autism displays such "splinter skills." Each person's pattern of symptoms create vastly different presentations of autism; in fact, individuals with savant abilities represent roughly 30% to 40% of those diagnosed with the disorder (Hughes et al., 2018).

Myth #4: Autism can be cured. While there is no "cure" per se, as autism is a brain-based condition that will be present throughout one's life, early intervention can help children with autism overcome the difficulties they encounter and help them lead very happy lives. Evidence-based interventions, especially when delivered early on in one's life, promote better overall outcomes, improve quality of life, and result in increased independence (Will et al., 2018). Sadly, there is no short supply of new and innovative "therapies," diets, and supplements designed to cure autism, all of which exploit the vulnerabilities of desperate parents, caregivers, and loved ones, luring them with false promises of fast and easy panaceas.

Individuals with autism are entirely capable of learning and are entitled to all of the rights and privileges of their neurotypical peers. As members in your classroom, students with autism present unique learning, communication, behavioral, and social needs. Teachers, therefore, require understanding of the disability in order to guide their practice and support these students to become active participants in learning.

According to the DSM-5, the umbrella diagnosis of ASD requires an individual to display difficulties across two major categories of symptoms: social interaction/communication and repetitive and/or restricted patterns of behavior—both of which may be fairly evident within the context of the classroom. Such persistent difficulties in social communication and social interaction may be evident only once the social and communication demands exceed a student's abilities. So, a child in early elementary school is not expected to engage in perspective taking or understand subtleties in humor or sarcasm; however, by the time that same student enters middle school, most of his or her peers have become more versed in these skills. This may also present as difficulties in modifying one's behavior to suit a social context or inability to maintain an expected back-and-forth conversation. For instance, Christy tells a joke with curse words to friends in the bathroom and notices the positive responses it conjures. Christy repeats the same joke in the presence of the school principal but does not understand why she received a detention. Difficulties with social communication also commonly extend past vocal behavior and can affect an individual's ability to understand the nuances of nonvocal communication. Adding to Christy's example, not only did she have difficulty discriminating that the social context was a less than ideal place to tell a joke but she also was unable to recognize her peers' nonvocal behaviors of head shaking and bulging eyes conveying messages like, "stop talking right now!"

Individuals with autism also struggle with cognitive rigidity, or the insistence on sameness across time, context, and people. Cognitive rigidity in and of itself is not a bad thing, keeping a routine, following rules and regulations, and being able to predict what is coming next based off of circumstances is an adaptive skill in which most if not all humans find comfort. It is when an individual is unable to *shift* and respond in a flexible way to a change that this becomes problematic. Remember those executive functions we discussed earlier? They come into play with ASD as well, particularly those domains of inhibition, self-monitoring, and shifting.

Classroom Example

Rodney is a 10-year-old boy with autism who loves going to school, seeing his teachers, and participating in class. Over time, Rodney has learned to become more flexible to upcoming changes in his schedule through a combination of prewarnings and practiced coping strategies. Unfortunately, Rodney's teacher, Ms. Huffman, has suddenly fallen ill and will been absent from school for an unspecified amount of time. Due

to the abrupt nature of her absence, a consistent substitute has not been secured, causing considerable distress for Rodney each morning before he heads off to school. Due to these circumstances, Rodney's schedule has been shifted slightly each day and he no longer has the reliable routine he did with Ms. Huffman. On the surface, Rodney's now daily fits of crying, work refusal, and vocal protests appear to be oppositional in nature, a product of stubbornness. However, due to the nature of his disability, these behaviors must be understood in context of autism.

Features of cognitive rigidity include literal and concrete interpretation of events, strict adherence to rules and regulations, "binary," or "black and white" thinking in which there is little room for variability, difficulty accepting multiple alternatives, and insistence on maintaining rigid beliefs and expectations. Nearly all situations, particularly social ones, do not follow a prescribed course. Slight fluctuations between circumstances require us to adjust accordingly. However, individuals with autism tend to hold steadfastly to their internal "rules" in an attempt to manage a situation; yet, when these rules are unable to be applied, challenging behavior may occur. You may encounter some students with autism who have a strong tendency toward perfectionism or you may encounter those who see things as "all or nothing" and may not even attempt an unfamiliar task for fear of failure. These related behaviors are a result of distortions in thinking and inflexibility. How would you respond if every time you got on the local bus the fare was different? What about if you had no idea what each day would entail? As humans, we are always looking for patterns. Once we detect the pattern, we can adjust our expectations and modify our behavior to suit. For those on the spectrum, the patterns are always changing; what applies in one setting may not apply in the next. When we understand that these students are merely trying to garner a sense of control of their environment, we are better equipped as educators to approach challenging behavior that may result from this anxiety.

More apparent are the "restricted, repetitive patterns of behavior, interest, or activities" an individual with autism may present. These behaviors, which can vary widely, span across many topographies of behavior, such as repetitive movements, vocalizations, and/or ritualistic or highly routinized behaviors. When asked to think of an individual with autism, some images that may come to mind include spinning objects, lining up toys, or flapping hands. While these behaviors are not seen across all individuals with autism, they are somewhat common and are referred to as stereotyped behaviors, stereotypies, or self-stimulatory behaviors. These types of behaviors are described as nonfunctional and repetitive in nature. There is not a consensus on why these behaviors appear to be common with autism or why a person may engage in them. Some theories suggest these behaviors provide specific and pleasing sensory stimulation (e.g., visually, auditorily, or tactilely) due to a hyposensitive arousal system. Other theories suggest these behaviors serve a calming purpose for hypersensitive arousal systems. To be clear, it is not only individuals with autism or individuals with other disabilities that display such stereotyped or self-stimulatory behaviors. Each and every one of you reading this right now also engages in such behaviors. The difference? Your stereotyped behavior is probably not interfering with your daily activities or preventing you from learning. Twirling your hair, clicking your pen, or jiggling your leg under the desk are all examples of such behaviors. These only come into concern when there is a clinical impairment in social, occupational, or other domains of functioning. Simply, when learning and attention are negatively affected.

Regardless, stereotypies are generally very entrenched behaviors and may very well be present in your classroom. Sometimes, these behaviors do not require any intervention and do not need to be eliminated or reduced in frequency. However, they may also be disruptive, annoying, or socially isolating for the student. Knowing this is part of an individual's autism is only half of the picture. The most common misconception when addressing the topic of such behaviors is "how do I make them stop?" Stereotypies cannot be stopped completely, so the better question is "what is maintaining the behavior and how can we manage it?" Collaboration with behavior specialists and other colleagues can help guide management by teaching students the *proper time* and *setting* in which to engage in stereotyped behavior.

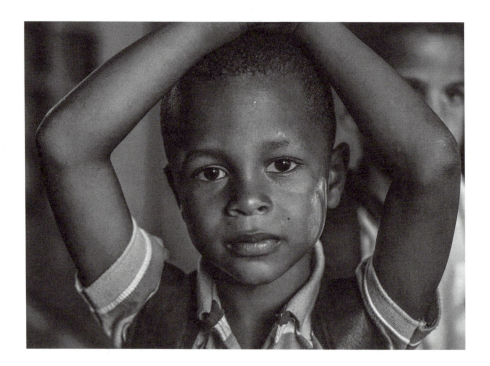

> *Check out Chapter 13 for more information on how a behavior cannot be effectively eliminated; rather, behaviors can be replaced by ones that are more acceptable and efficient.*

Intellectual Disability

An intellectual disability (ID) is defined as a combination of deficits in both cognition and adaptive functioning. Similarly, IDEA identifies ID as "significantly subaverage general intellectual functioning, existing concurrently with deficits in adaptive behavior and manifested during the developmental period, which adversely affects a child's educational performance." An IQ below 70 is one indicator of an ID. For the most part, cognitive functioning is much more straightforward to measure and evaluate, while deficits in adaptive functioning are a bit stickier to discern. Adaptive functioning spans conceptual (e.g., communication, functional academics such as making change), practical (personal info, health and safety, taking public transit, cooking/preparing meals), and social (leisure, interpersonal skills, independent entertainment) domains. Therefore, factors such as dressing oneself, using the toilet, navigating social norms, and engaging in mutual conversation may be used to guide identification of ID along with an individual's strengths and weaknesses. As in autism, IDs also fall along a spectrum, with the severity being dictated by the discrepancy between an individual's capability and expectations of their chronological age. There also exist some genetic conditions in which ID is a cardinal feature, such as Fragile X syndrome or Down syndrome.

While there is no neat and tidy description of how students with ID may present in your classroom, there are some core traits that have a direct effect on educational performance. In addition to slower processing speed, individuals with ID may have difficulty understanding new and abstract concepts, such as telling time or number sense. Most students with ID experience challenges with both receptive and expressive communication. Receptive language refers to one's ability to understand or comprehend vocal language, while expressive language is one's ability to convey language, usually vocally, but also includes modalities such as sign language. As mentioned previously, students with ID usually have slower processing speed, or rate at which they process and respond to information in order to complete a mental task. This lag can create significant issues in the classroom and cause a student to fall even further behind, both in academics as well as general management of oneself. As an example, during a science lesson, Aroha's teacher tasked the class with gathering some materials and setting up a lab before dismissing the class to work independently. By the time Aroha could gather the first of the several materials required, the rest of the class were already at work at their desks. Repeatedly missing critical pieces of information throughout the day can accumulate and present not only as inadequate academic achievement but also may appear as though the student is noncompliance or misbehaving. Perhaps most closely linked with challenging behavior for these students is the inconsistency in their performance from day to day. Difficulties with encoding, or when one's short-term memory does not work as effectively as it could, results in varied ability to answer simple questions or call upon information from memory banks. When this is inconsistent from day to day, it paints an incredibly frustrating scenario: what was fluent yesterday is all jumbled up and difficult to access today.

Issues with adaptive behavior may include limited social and practical skills, such as problem solving, goal setting, and information sequencing. Socially, these students may struggle with peer relationships due to difficulty with controlling impulses and socioemotional understanding. Collectively, this may result in poor peer relationships and may lead to low self-concept and self-esteem for students with ID, who already experience a host of challenges throughout their day.

Conclusion

What is consistent across all students with disabilities is the critical fact that despite the inevitable deficits and difficulties they will face, these students *can* and *will* learn. As you consider how you will develop your classroom management systems it is important to remember the many layers of students' identities. Developmental factors, students with disabilities or medical diagnoses, home life, culture, language, and socioeconomic status all create unique student profiles. As teachers and school personnel, it is our responsibility to understand each of these components and how they influence student behavior. All behavior tells a story.

Chapter Summary

- Having an understanding of developmental characteristics helps to put behavioral expectations into perspective; teachers should know what to expect from their students with respect to their developmental abilities.

- Working in educational environments inherently means coming into contact with a mix of cultures, different value systems, socioeconomic statuses, and an assortment of (possibly conflicting) behavioral and social expectations. Teachers must remain mindful of this and seek out strategies such as self-reflection and relationship building to work with families from diverse backgrounds.

- Inclusive classrooms are those which purposefully involve all students in learning, regardless of background, culture, race, gender, socioeconomic status, or disability.

- Attention deficit hyperactivity disorder (ADHD) is a neurological condition which causes difficulty with inattention, poor impulse control, distractibility, and/or forgetfulness. There are three presentations of this disability: predominantly inattentive, predominantly hyperactive/impulsive, and combined. Roughly 20% to 25% of individuals diagnosed with ADHD also have a co-occurring learning disability.

- Executive functions are the neurological processes that allow us to control our impulses, problem solve, and successfully achieve goals via planning and organization. An executive function deficit is not a recognized disability category; however, there are many clinical manifestations of executive function deficits that come along with disabilities such as ADHD, SLD, and autism (i.e., impulse control, difficulty shifting from one topic or activity to another, poor emotional control, difficulty retaining salient information, etc.).

- Students with emotional and behavioral disorders have difficulty regulating their behavior and lack skills required to initiate and maintain successful social interactions.

- Specific learning disabilities may affect an individual's ability to understand language or affect one's ability to listen, think, speak, write, read, spell, or do mathematical calculations. Specific learning disabilities are discrepancies between aptitude and ability and affect student achievement and performance; however, they do not affect overall IQ.

- Autism spectrum disorder (ASD) is a developmental disability in which individuals have deficits in social communication and demonstrate repetitive, restrictive patterns of behavior. Symptoms of autism are spread over a spectrum and, thus, present very differently across people.

- An IQ of below 70 is indicative of an intellectual disability, which results in deficits in both cognition and adaptive functioning.

- The responsibility falls with the teacher to become familiar with the host of factors students bring to the classroom and understand how these factors influence learning.

CHAPTER 3

BASICS OF BEHAVIOR

Learning Objectives

- Explain classical and operant conditioning
- Understand how the three-term contingency can be applied in classroom settings
- Define reinforcement and punishment
- Discriminate differences between positive and negative reinforcement and punishment
- Identify different schedules of reinforcement

Key Terms

Antecedent
Applied Behavior Analysis
Behavior
Consequence
Contingency
Continuous Reinforcement
Extinction
Extinction Burst
Fixed Interval
Fixed Ratio
Intermittent Reinforcement

Negative Reinforcement
Operant Conditioning
Positive Reinforcement
Premack Principle
Punishment
Reinforcers
Schedules of Reinforcement
Three-Term Contingency
Variable Interval
Variable Ratio

Understanding basic principles of learning and behavior is essential for all educators, across any grade or subject area. Effective classroom management hinges upon the integration of concepts presented in this chapter in order to establish and maintain an organized, supportive learning environment. Educators who are able to garner a solid understanding of basic behavioral concepts and principles are set up to run a classroom backed by empirically supported strategies and approaches. Once adept at understanding why challenging behavior is happening in the classroom, educators are more likely to be proactive and foster positive, enriching environments. The following section will cover operant conditioning, reinforcers, the three-term contingency, positive and negative reinforcement, extinction, punishment, and schedules of reinforcement.

Applied Behavior Analysis

Before we can go into each of the basic principles of learning and behavior mentioned previously, we must first address the science dedicated to their use. Applied behavior analysis (ABA) is the scientific discipline based upon learning theory that looks at how to apply empirical techniques to affect socially significant behavior change (Cooper, Heron, & Heward, 2019). ABA has been studied for decades and sits upon a massive base of well-established research dedicated toward bettering the lives of individuals. The scope of ABA spans widely and, as such, targets a variety of behaviors from teaching basic play skills to learning a new language. Notably, ABA is found at the center of fields such as intensive therapy for individuals with disabilities (primarily autism), general behavior management in classrooms, school-wide behavior systems, and all the way to the industrial organizational level of businesses and large corporations. ABA is discussed again in Chapter 11; however, in order to provide a well-rounded approach to understanding the science of behavior, we must link ABA to its roots in operant conditioning and the ABCs of behavior.

Operant Conditioning

Operant conditioning, as first described by B. F. Skinner, relies upon consequences, which may be either positive or negative, to increase or decrease a behavior. Unlike respondent behaviors in classical conditioning, operant behaviors are learned through what Skinner coined the three-term contingency, also known as the A-B-C contingency or the *ABCs of behavior*. The Antecedent-Behavior-Consequence contingency describes the relationship between the environment and behavior. An antecedent is any stimulus that occurs immediately prior to the behavior of interest. Antecedents may take many forms and may sometimes be difficult to discern; thus, it is important to think beyond what may seem obvious. Antecedents may be the presence of a person, an activity or event, a statement or question, or a physical location—to name a few.

 Make a Connection

Why is it important to acknowledge and recognize antecedents within the context of a classroom? In what ways can altering antecedents change behavior?

Behavior, sometimes referred to as a *response*, is any activity in which a human engages. Behaviors are actions that are *observable* and *measurable*. They influence the environment and include everything we do; talking, running, laughing, smiling, eating, sleeping, and playing sports are all behaviors. If one is unsure if what he or she is observing is a behavior, the cheeky "Dead Man Test" may be applied (Lindsley, 1991). However, for the purposes of this text, we will refer to this as the "Dead Person Test." Simply, if a dead person can do it, it's not a behavior. Can a dead person run? No, so running *is* behavior. Can a dead person *not eat pizza*? Yes, so *not eating pizza* is a "nonbehavior." Other examples of nonbehavior include sitting still, being quiet, and lying down—all very much a part of a dead person's repertoire, right? These are important to consider when we are attempting to define behavior in measurable and exact terms. Before a behavior can be assessed, analyzed, or changed, it is critical to define it in a way that is simple, observable, and measurable (Simonsen, Fairbanks, Briesch, Myers, & Sugai, 2008). Often, we refer to the behavior of interest as the *target behavior,* and a clearly written definition allows for consistency in how the behavior is seen across settings and people. Often, teachers may set out to determine how often something doesn't happen. For example, "I want to see how often Iliza doesn't raise her hand" or "how many times Sally resists shouting out." Applying the Dead Person Test is a great way to determine what to focus on and target for intervention.

For example, if "blurting out" is the target behavior, we could define it as the following:

"Any instance in which Sam engages in vocalizations that are not initiated by the teacher, are out of turn, and/or are unrelated to academic content."

> Also helpful is the addition of examples and nonexamples of the behavior to ensure anyone who observes the behavior is certain.
>
> **Examples**
>
> - Answering questions directed to other students
> - Talking, laughing, or making noises while the teacher gives instructions
> - Talking to a peer when direction is to work independently
>
> **Nonexamples**
>
> - Talking to a peer during group work or free time
> - Making sounds or unnecessary vocal noises during instruction
> - Coughing or clearing throat involuntarily

Finally, consequences round out the last portion of the three-term contingency. Consequences are stimuli that occur immediately following a target behavior. It is important, especially from the perspective of an educator, to note that the use of the term *consequences* is simply *any* event—"good," "bad," or otherwise—which occurs immediately after the behavior. Oftentimes in the classroom, the use of "consequence" is synonymous with an attempt at punishment or as a response to a child's misbehavior; however, this is not the case here. The consequence of putting a dollar in a vending machine is provision of a drink or snack. The consequence of asking for the time is finding out it's 5 o'clock.

Consequences can be reinforcing or punishing. Reinforcement is a consequence applied after a behavior that increases the likelihood of that behavior occurring again in the future (Cooper et al., 2019). Such strengthening of behaviors may be measured via frequency (e.g., number of times a student raises his or her hand), duration (e.g., length of time sitting on the carpet), magnitude/intensity (e.g., Carla scratched Pella, but did not break the skin), or latency (e.g., students lining up more quickly after an instruction). In order to determine if a behavior has been reinforced, more than one presentation of a consequence to a behavior must occur. We need to see what happens again when the same consequence follows a target response. For example, a student raises her hand to answer a teacher's question, and the teacher praises her. One would only be able to identify if reinforcement has occurred if the rate of the student's hand-raising behavior increases the next time the teacher poses a question. Similarly, when one is provided a cookie upon asking, it may be assumed that the future likelihood of asking for a cookie will increase. Both praise and cookies served as reinforcers in the former examples *because they increased target behavior* (i.e., raising hand, asking for cookie). Reinforcers are consequences that increase the future likelihood of a behavior and may be tangible, such as toys, candy, or games or intangible, such as special privileges, extra attention, or positive praise.

On the other hand, consequences can have a punishing effect on behavior. Punishment is a consequence applied after a behavior that decreases the likelihood of that behavior occurring again in the future (Cooper et al., 2019). For example, Paul asks to sit with a group of peers at lunch, who promptly turned him away. For the rest of the school year, Paul sits alone during lunchtime. With knowing just this information, one can assume that Paul's asking was punished by his peers as evidenced by his ceasing to ask again. Just as with reinforcement, it is important to take note of what occurs after behavior over time.

An important clarification must be made regarding the terms *reinforcement* and *reinforcer* (as well as *punishment* and *punisher)* as they tend to be thrown around quite loosely. An all-too-common comment is, "I reinforced Susan, but her behavior didn't change at all!" This is erroneous. Perhaps the intention was to reinforce Susan; but if there was no change in behavior, no reinforcement happened. Reinforcers are individual to a person and *only hold value as a reinforcer based on the effect it has on behavior.* It is this effect on behavior that dictates whether or not reinforcement has transpired. Making sweeping generalizations about what will or will not reinforce a student is the biggest pitfall of all. Not all children will work for stickers, not all kids like attention, and some kids don't know how to play Minecraft® or care about LEGO®. Similarly, be mindful that some consequences that are expected to be reinforcing may in fact be punishing. More on this topic a bit later in the chapter.

Selecting and Using Reinforcers

Let's start with some self-reflection. Make a list with two columns. On one side, write some things (items, activities, etc.) you really enjoy and on the other, write some things you will work for. How are these two lists different? How are they similar? For starters, one of the authors of this textbook really enjoys dark chocolate and coffee. However, she will not wash your car and cut your lawn for dark chocolate and coffee. Herein is the distinction between *liking* something and being willing to *work* for it. Take heed, if you find yourself spinning your wheels while trying to implement a strategy and are not seeing any progress, the first place to look is always to the reinforcer. As you consider reinforcers, consider whether a student might really like something but isn't willing to work for it or isn't willing to work for it in the way the current reinforcer is designed. If behavior change is not occurring, it's almost guaranteed that it's due to ineffective use of, or devaluation of, reinforcement.

Value

In order for a reinforcer to be reinforcing, it must hold value. Part of ensuring this value is making sure the individual/student does not have free access to the reinforcer. Let's pretend you had a tree that actually grew money in your backyard (how fantastic!). The tree grows as much money as you want, with no restrictions or limitations. So, would you still go to work eight hours a day, five days a week? Probably not. Why work when you can just do a bit of gardening and be set for life? How would having unlimited money affect your *motivation* to work? Another reason free access may affect the value of a reinforcer is what is known as *satiety*. Simply, satiety, or satiation, implies that too much of the same reinforcer may reduce its effectiveness (Miller, 2006). If coffee is highly valuable to you, it is almost a certainty that the first cup in the morning is far more satisfying than the fourth or fifth cup. Recognizing that too much of a good thing exists, it is important to rotate reinforcers to keep things not only fresh and exciting but also to prevent satiation on any one thing. Let's examine ways in which we can select and use a variety of reinforcers to keep motivation high and learners engaged.

Reinforcer Selection

Choosing reinforcers may seem overwhelming; however, there are a few methods you may employ to select potent, effective reinforcers. Firstly, consider simply asking a student or the class about what they value. This could be done through discussion or through an exercise similar to the self-reflection described previously. Reinforcer surveys are also another excellent way to gather information on potential reinforcers. These surveys are sometimes preferred by educators due to their ability to be individualized to the classroom and its limitations. If your students are younger, sending home a reinforcer survey at the beginning of the year is a nice way to encourage parent participation and collect relevant advice on what may be effective. Observe students during free time, recess, specials, and so forth. Make note of where, to what, and to whom students gravitate. Do you notice trends or patterns? Do certain children always interact with one another? Are there battles over specific toys or roles in games? Get creative with selecting reinforcers. Ensure you've got lots of choices spanning different forms, such as tangible items, privileges, activities, and even people. By having a variety of potential reinforcers, you ensure that unforeseen limitations will not hinder your ability to reinforce behavior (e.g., if students are working toward earning a picnic lunch and it thunderstorms). Just because you don't like it or think it won't be effective, doesn't mean it won't work! The template included in Table 3–1 on different types of reinforcers may be helpful in organizing your potential reinforcers (see Table 3–1).

Contingency and Immediacy

Once you have gathered potential reinforcers, the next step is understanding how to use them effectively. In order to create a relationship between the reinforcer and the behavior, the reinforcer must be delivered as immediately as possible. If too much time lapses between the behavior and the reinforcer, the reinforcer risks devaluation and more opportunity for inadvertent/accidental reinforcement opens up. For instance, a teacher wants to focus on reinforcing students remaining seated during morning work. If Toni remains seated but receives a sticker 5 min later while she is rocking back and forth and touching peers, the reinforcer has become associated with rocking and touching. Oops. The gap in time between Toni's sitting and receiving a sticker means the reinforcer was not contingent upon the desired behavior. Delivery of a reinforcer must be contingent upon the target behavior, meaning the behavior of interest must be demonstrated in order to receive the reinforcer. Contingency may be thought of as "If . . . , then . . . ." *If* student engages in (target behavior), *then* she can access computer time. Thus, in order to create a strong association between a target behavior and a reinforcer, reinforcement must be promptly and contingently delivered. However, sometimes it is not feasible or possible to deliver a reinforcer right away. For example, your class earned enough points to redeem 10 min of free play, but it's time to transition to specials. A practical option at this point may be to provide the class a behavior-specific praise statement, indicating what has been done well, acknowledging

Table 3–1. Reinforcer Examples

Tangible	Activity	Privilege	People
Games	Run laps around the track	Teacher's assistant	Lunch with teacher
Computer access	Pick-up basketball for 10 min	Free pass to library, music room, etc.	Seat assignment near preferred peer
Stickers	Favorite game for 15 min	Host morning announcements	Positive phone call home from principal

they've earned a reward, and providing specifics around when they will access the reward. Other possibilities for addressing this type of situation are discussed in Chapter 8 under group contingencies.

 High-Leverage Practice Alert!

See HLP8 for information on timely and contingent feedback.

Schedules of Reinforcement

Since we now know what reinforcers are, along with how they are selected and delivered, we need to examine how often they should be provided to reap the biggest behavioral benefits. A schedule of reinforcement is essentially the "rule" stating which instances of a target (correct) behavior receive reinforcement (Figures 3–1 and 3–2). Schedules of reinforcement may either be continuous or intermittent. Continuous reinforcement refers to the provision of reinforcement for every single response. For example (barring nothing is broken), switching on

Figure 3–1. Schedules of reinforcement.

Schedules of Reinforcement	Continuous	Intermittent
Ratio	Reinforcement occurs after every response occurs	Reinforcment occurs after a random or predetermined number of responses occur
Interval	Reinforcement occurs for the first response and then after a specific amount of time elapses	Reinforcement occurs at the first response and then after a random or predetermined amount of time elapses

Figure 3–2. Reinforcement schedules graph.

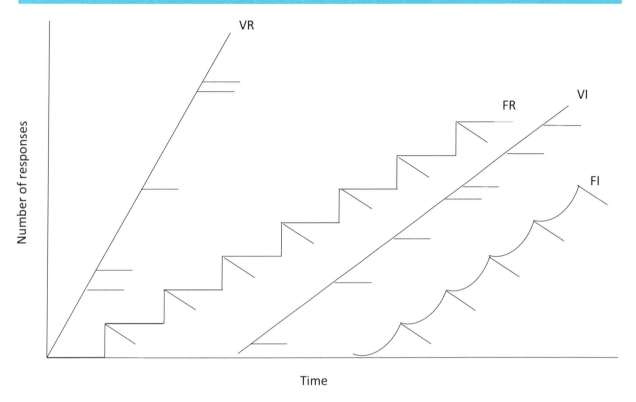

a light, turning on the oven, or putting money into a vending machine produces continuous reinforcement. While not overly common in everyday life, continuous reinforcement is useful when teaching new behaviors and strengthening newly learned behaviors. However, continuous reinforcement is fairly unrealistic in the context of a classroom as it requires constant vigilance on behalf of the educator and poses challenges with reinforcer satiation. If continuous reinforcement is abruptly stopped, the behavior can quickly dissipate. This is not to say that on some occasions, a continuous schedule may be warranted; however, it is not reasonable to maintain long term. Beyond being a bit impractical, using continuous reinforcement widely and/or long term in the classroom may not adequately prepare learners for the real world. Thus, continuous schedules must be faded to intermittent schedules, which allow for more natural spacing between reinforcement and promote excellent long-term maintenance of behavior. Intermittent schedules of reinforcement are characterized by some responses receiving reinforcement and others not. These schedules operate based on either the number of responses (*ratio*) or the time between reinforcement (*interval*). There are four basic types of intermittent schedules, with each one having a different effect on behavior.

Fixed Ratio (FR)

Fixed ratio is a schedule in which a response (behavior) is reinforced after a specified number of required responses. For example, a schedule of FR1 indicates reinforcement delivered after each correct response, while a schedule of FR5 indicates reinforcement delivered after every fifth correct response. This type of schedule produces high rates of steady responding characterized by a brief pause after receiving reinforcer (see Figure 3–2), which is referred to as a postreinforcement pause. A postreinforcement pause is a brief dip in performance that occurs after an individual accesses a reinforcer. To put this into context, consider a student who works diligently all week on a project. Once it comes time to hand the project in, the student's work behavior drops off a bit. The length of this postreinforcement pause is associated with fixed schedules and is dictated by how long the ratio is; large ratios generate large pauses, while short ratios generate short pauses. For instance, people who run marathons likely need a bit longer to rest and recover before heading out for another long run, as compared to a casual runner who completes shorter distances.

Variable Ratio (VR)

The most consistent and stable responding tends to be a product of a variable ratio schedule. These schedules provide reinforcement after an *unpredictable* number of responses, which results in high, steady-rate responding. That is, reinforcement is provided after a variable number of responses has occurred. Variable ratio schedules are characterized by a number representing the average number of target responses required for reinforcement. For example, a VR 7 schedule, every seventh response, on average, is reinforced. This could mean reinforcement occurs after 6, 9, 3, and 10 target responses ($6 + 9 + 3 + 10 = 28/4 = 7$). One of the best examples of variable ratio reinforcement is playing on a slot machine or playing the lottery. Not every response is reinforced and it is impossible to know when a payout will hit; but this schedule maintains behavior fairly consistently over long periods of time. Due to the nature of how this schedule operates, it is quite impractical for use in the classroom; it requires a high degree of monitoring as the teacher would be required to track the number of times a behavior has occurred.

Fixed Interval (FI)

While the ratio schedules depend on number of responses, interval schedules provide reinforcement for a target response after a certain amount of time has passed. A fixed interval schedule of reinforcement provides reinforcement for the first target behavior emitted after a fixed time period. So, if an FI 7-min schedule is in place, reinforcement is provided to the first target behavior following the

7-min time interval. There is a common misconception that the end of the interval signals reinforcement; however, this is untrue. The end of the interval signals reinforcement *becoming available* and more time than the interval may elapse between reinforced responses. This schedule merely indicates reinforcement is available after a specified passage of time. This type of schedule produces high rates of responding toward the end of the interval, which is reflected in a scalloped pattern of responding (see Figure 3–2). A project or paper due date is a prime example of a fixed interval schedule. The student is only reinforced (e.g., graded) if he or she hands the assignment in by a specified due date. Further, a fixed interval reinforcement schedule is seen when students study in the lead up to a test, with the height of studying occurring just before a test. Then, once the test is over, studying drops off quite a bit until the next test. Outside of the classroom, a fixed interval example is observed with a hospital patient using patient-controlled analgesia for pain, wherein the patient uses a button to receive a dose of pain medication. The medication is only administered after a certain passage of time (usually unbeknownst to the patient), as dictated by the doctor; however, as the medication wears off (toward the end of the interval), pain increases and the patient hits the button more often. Once the patient receives the medication, responding drops off a bit until the next interval starts to come to an end.

Variable Interval (VI)

In a **variable interval schedule of reinforcement** the first correct response following the passage of a *variable* amount of time is reinforced. Intervals vary around a mean/average. This implies that the length of time before reinforcement is available differs, appearing to occur somewhat randomly. Just as in fixed interval schedules, variable interval schedules of reinforcement are denoted by the average interval of time. For example, reinforcement is delivered for the first target response following an average of 10 min on a VI 10-min schedule. A pop quiz is commonly used as a way to illustrate a real-life variable interval schedule. In theory, one could have a pop quiz two days in a row, followed by two weeks without a quiz. The random pattern creates uncertainty about when the next quiz will happen. Therefore, students are more likely to engage in study behaviors consistently between instances of pop quizzes.

Positive and Negative Reinforcement

We've looked at what makes up the three-term contingency and how reinforcers may operate as consequences that increase desired behavior. Now, we will examine the distinction between positive and negative reinforcement. The single most important detail to keep in mind when thinking about positive and negative reinforcement is both are reinforcement; thus, we are looking for an increase in behavior.

Positive Reinforcement

Positive reinforcement refers to the *addition* of something to the environment after a behavior occurs, increasing the future likelihood of the behavior. A child learning how to speak says "cookie" and dad immediately provides a cookie. The child now says "cookie" more often. In this way, *positive = addition* because the cookie was *added* to the environment. Take a moment to delete every other synonym for "positive" in your mind (it is **not** preferred, happy, good, beneficial). In another example, a teacher raises his voice to reprimand a student for hitting others. The student begins to hit more often. On the surface, this seems like some sort of punishment or negative scenario. However, reinforcement has actually transpired. Huh? Why?

The teacher *added* something to the environment; he raised his voice. Then, *the rate of behavior increased; the child begins to hit more often.* Think back to the discussion on reinforcers; they're individualized and not every one works for the same thing. Perhaps the attention from the teacher (albeit not "good" attention) was enough to reinforce the student; thus, the increase in behavior.

Negative Reinforcement

And now, the Achilles heel of perhaps all of behavior management strategies: negative reinforcement. Negative reinforcement involves the *removal* of a (usually aversive) stimulus after a target response that increases the future likelihood of the behavior. Negative reinforcement **is reinforcement**. Just as positive = addition, negative = removal. Take another moment to eliminate other synonyms for negative; this is in no way a punishment or aversive procedure. However, for negative reinforcement to occur, there must be a stimulus that is somewhat aversive or annoying present. For example, your alarm goes off in the morning (annoying, aversive stimulus) and you *press the off button* (target behavior) to remove or stop it. The next time your alarm goes off, you are more likely to press the off button. Your behavior *removed* something aversive and *increased* the future likelihood of button pushing: negative reinforcement! Most people *take a pain reliever* (behavior) when they have a headache (aversive stimulus). Pain relievers remove discomfort and increase the likelihood of reaching for a bottle of aspirin next time pain is present: negative reinforcement!

In nearly every situation, there are multiple schedules of reinforcement and types of reinforcement occurring simultaneously. Take for instance the classic "screaming toddler in the grocery store" scenario. You see a tired dad struggling to shush his daughter. He finally caves and grabs a chocolate bar off the shelf, quickly unwraps it, and thrusts it into the child's red, sweaty face. Voila! Silence. Two different types of reinforcement are at play here. First, the child's screaming is being *positively reinforced* because she just received the highest caliber treat of toddlerdom: a chocolate. Second, the dad is being *negatively reinforced* because his actions provided him with his desired (and probably everyone else in the store's) response: silence. Have you ever agreed to do something just to get the requester to stop asking? Your agreement negatively reinforces you because it takes away the nagging request, and, more than likely, the requester is positively reinforced because you've accepted the offer . . . and are now busy on Saturday night.

Another important distinction should be made here between reinforcement and bribery. Bribery is not reinforcement. The best way to think of the difference between the two is that bribery comes *before or during* the behavior. For instance, a grandmother tells her grandson, Perry, "I'll give you $5 **if** you behave in the library." She provides him the hard cash and the two enter the library. Now, what do you reckon happens in the library? Perry has received his reward without having to do anything at all. He's free to act as he pleases, which may include some less than desirable behaviors. Bribery is simply providing the reinforcer at the wrong time. In order to flip the scenario to one of reinforcement, Grandma should say to Perry, "We're going to the library now; if you keep your voice at a whisper and hands to yourself, you'll earn $5." Perry and Grandma go to the library and he does as instructed; Grandma keeps her promise and Perry gets his $5. This order of events is termed the Premack principle, also aptly named "Grandma's Rule." The Premack principle describes how one can use a high probability behavior (getting pocket money to spend) to reinforce a lower probability behavior (keeping a quiet voice and hands to self). The colloquialism of Grandma's Rule makes this easy to remember: "if you eat your dinner, you can have dessert."

Extinction

Extinction is the deliberate withholding of reinforcement in order to decrease a behavior. Extinction occurs when a previously reinforced behavior ceases to be reinforced and a decrease in the behavior is observed, until it gradually stops. Extinction is highly useful across many settings, including classrooms, and does not require the use of aversives to decrease behavior. Extinction can be a highly effective component of an intervention; however, it should never be used in isolation. It is simply impossible to "delete" a behavior without replacing it; hence, extinction must be paired with another intervention aimed at teaching an alternative, replacement behavior to match the same function as the behavior being extinguished. Further, a word about extinction and a fair warning, with any behavior that has been previously reinforced, it can be quite frustrating for the learner who no longer receives the expected reinforcer. Very commonly, an extinction burst is observed in this context. An extinction burst as defined by Lerman, Iwata, and Wallace (1999) is a temporary increase in the frequency, duration, or magnitude of the target response.

More than likely, you consider yourself a reasonable and grounded person, right? And yet, everyone is susceptible to an extinction burst. Let's set the stage for a real-life example:

> You've spent the last three days pulling late evenings and early mornings, studying for a very important exam. You're exhausted, hungry, and irritable. The morning of the exam, you decide to grab an energy drink from the vending machine on campus. You insert your money, you press the magic button, and . . . NOTHING. You press it again, this time a bit more firmly. Still nothing. This is the point at which you begin to panic—how could this be happening? You NEED the caffeine to function at the test. You're running out of time and you're short on cash. It's at this point you begin to slip away from your typical, reasonable self. You grab the sides of the vending machine and start shaking it, hoping to knock something loose. Alas, your reasonable, grounded self is red-faced, sweaty, and frantically shaking a vending machine. In public. This increase in behaviors, some of which may have never been exhibited before, is characteristic of an extinction burst.

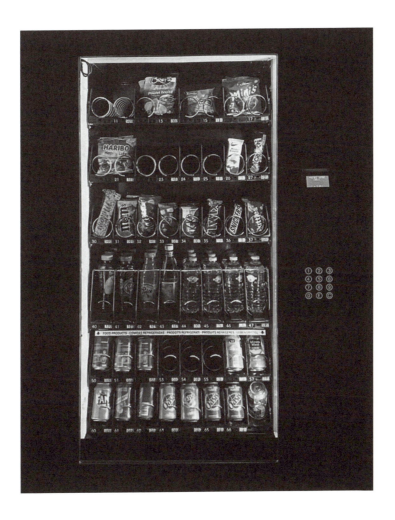

Punishment

Punishment is when a behavior is immediately followed by a stimulus that decreases the future likelihood of that behavior (Cooper et al., 2019). Quite simply, punishment is the opposite of reinforcement; however, that does not mean it is any less important. At its crux, punishment teaches us not to repeat behaviors that lead to distress, pain, discomfort, or loss of reinforcement. Again, it is important to bear in mind that one is usually not able to discern if punishment has transpired without having an understanding of the behavior over time. Very often, it may *look* like punishment in the moment; yet, one will only know if there is a decrease in future behavior. Take the case where a parent scolds his child for hitting. In the moment, the child may cease hitting; however, punishment is only noted if the rate of hitting decreases as time passes. For instance, you arrive late and the teacher calls you out in front of the entire lecture hall. You're never late to class ever again: your behavior was punished. On the other hand, you are late to class and the professor marks your attendance points down. If you continue to arrive late to class, no punishment has taken place; rather, one could argue that your behavior is being reinforced (as the rate is being maintained). An overview of positive and negative reinforcement and punishments are further outlined in Table 3–2. Again, this is where individualization of preferences is key; just as with reinforcers, different actions, items, and so forth may serve as punishers for different people.

Punishment has accumulated flak over the years, and, as such, acquired a fair amount of misunderstandings, misapplications, and blatant untruths. It is often synonymized as a nasty, ugly appellation, calling to mind images of highly unpleasant actions, pain, humiliation, and extreme circumstances. Punishment is pervasive in our culture: prisons punish offenders by placing them in extremely uncomfortable living/social conditions, police officers dole out fines for breaking the law, and countless bullies torment their victims both physically and psychologically. However, these examples are murky, to say the least. Punishment is not about making someone "pay" for their transgressions; it is not about piling on aversive consequences in the hopes someone will correct the errors of their ways. Regardless of what it *looks like*, punishment, in the behavioral sense, is a consequence that has a decreasing effect on future behavior.

Table 3–2. Positive Versus Negative Reinforcement		
	Reinforcement	**Punishment**
Positive	+ Of a consequence that *increases* future likelihood of a behavior Example: Teacher praises a student for raising her hand and student begins to raise her hand more often	+ Of a consequence that *decreases* future likelihood of behavior Example: Receiving a speeding ticket reduces future speeding behavior while driving
Negative	– Of a consequence that *increases* future likelihood of a behavior Example: Clicking the seatbelt in removes the annoying "ding" and increases future chance of fastening seat belt	– Of a consequence that *decreases* future likelihood of a behavior Example: Losing access to video games after hitting a sibling decreases future instances of hitting
	BEHAVIOR INCREASES	BEHAVIOR DECREASES

Just as with reinforcement, punishment may be positive or negative. *Positive punishment* occurs when a stimulus *added* to the environment decreases future likelihood of a target behavior occurring. Remember, the *only* way to determine the effect a stimulus has on behavior is to attend to the behavior over time: what is happening to the rate/duration/and so forth? Perhaps the stickiest wicket when it comes to punishment is its inadvertent use by educators. It is very common for an educator to think he or she is reinforcing a child's behavior, when, in fact, they are punishing it. Take, for example, the use of praise. Now, on the surface, you're thinking, "Of course, praise is meant to be a reinforcer." Not always. Perhaps for some students (more introverted, shy, easily embarrassed, etc.), praise is the most uncomfortable attention imaginable. If such a student musters up the courage to raise his or her hand and answer a question, the simple act of praise could squash all hopes of that child's hand raising in the future.

> *Peek ahead to Chapter 9 on building relationships with students. Know your students and their preferences; connect back to reinforcer preference surveys and how these tools can help foster a productive classroom environment.*

In this way, the addition of an aversive stimulus to the environment that decreases future likelihood of a behavior is *positive punishment*. Such stimuli could include being scolded or told off, being given a detention or extra work, or receiving a parking ticket. On the other hand, *negative punishment* is the removal of a reinforcing stimulus after a behavior that decreases future possibility of the behavior. Some examples could include removal of electronics privileges, deduction of points from a classroom reward system, or being grounded.

A final word on punishment. Despite being a learning tool, punishment should never be relied upon solely within an educator's repertoire of behavior management strategies. Always, always, always exhaust all reinforcement-based strategies and procedures first. After all, there is an abundance of research demonstrating that reinforcement and positive procedures are the most effective, long-lasting, and nurturing ways to bring about behavior change. Punishment is effective; however, its effects are generally short-lived and it only teaches us what *not to do*. Punishment teaches us to escape or avoid undesirable consequences (e.g., "last time I asked the teacher a question, he got cross with me so I won't ask him again" or "last time I was late coming home, mom grounded me for a week"), rather than teaching us *what to do instead*. Reinforcement is what can be used to *teach alternative behaviors* (more on this in Chapter 13). If possible, punishment should not be used at all; however, we recognize there are some circumstances in which its use is required. In this case, it is advised punishment procedures be used under the careful guidance of a professional, such as a board-certified behavior analyst (BCBA).

Unfortunately, there may be unintended effects of punishment, some of which may last longer than the intended effects of its application. As such, these should be recognized and planned for proactively. Most commonly, aggression or retaliation may occur as a response to a punishing consequence. In this, an individual may be observed escalating and/or engaging in new or continued challenging behaviors (e.g., a child who is told "no" then begins to kick, scream, and hit). What is more, the relationship you've worked so hard to foster is at risk of being harmed. The use of punishment may cause an individual to try to escape or bypass the person or setting associated with the punishing consequence. Telltale signs include the individual avoiding you or becoming upset or agitated in your presence, which makes supporting a productive relationship impossible. For example, when Ruth arrived late to class and without her homework, Mr. Keevers reprimanded her in front of everyone. Consequently, Ruth began skipping class to avoid the aversive interaction with her teacher. Additionally, modeling the use of aversives increases the risk of an individual replicating or imitating a punishing consequence. Bullying is a chronic and pervasive illustration of this. Bullying behaviors are learned, with a plethora of research supporting that such behaviors are learned through social exposure (peers, parents, caregivers, etc.; Garby, 2013). Finally, there may be occasions in which the individual providing the punishment is negatively reinforced. For instance, a teacher is reprimanding the class for running down the hallway and the children cease running. This (temporary) cessation in behavior (running in the hallway) negatively reinforces the teacher right away (because the aversive stimuli [running in the hallway] is stopped/removed). Now, the teacher's behavior of reprimanding is being strengthened by the effect it has on the students' behavior.

Conclusion

One of the most chronic issues reported by educators is insufficient preparation for, and lack of support with, implementing evidence-based classroom management practices. Along with a hectic, disorganized classroom environments comes high stress levels and teacher burn out. Thus, purposeful, positive behavior change strategies underpin an educator's ability to effectively lead a classroom. The concepts presented in this chapter are woven through subsequent chapters, highlighting the ways in which they serve both as prevention and intervention methods. Calling upon these classroom management strategies is at the core of student success as creating orderly learning environments is shown to improve students' academic skills and foster social-emotional development (Brophy, 2006).

Chapter Summary

- Antecedents are stimuli that occur prior to a behavior. They may include people, activity, event, comment, and so forth. Antecedents are the first portion of the ABC contingency (three-term contingency). The ABC contingency describes the relationship between the environment and behavior. Behaviors, or responses, are any measurable and observable action in which a human engages. Consequences make up the final portion of the ABC contingency and are identified as stimuli that occur immediately after the target response. Contingencies dictate the future likelihood of behavior; they are either reinforcing or punishing.

- Reinforcement is a consequence applied after a target behavior that increases future likelihood of the behavior. The most effective reinforcement is delivered immediately and contingently (i.e., the target behavior must be demonstrated in order to receive reinforcement).

- Schedule of reinforcement is the "rule" stating which instances of a target behavior will receive reinforcement. Schedules may be continuous (reinforcement after every response) or intermittent (some responses receive reinforcement and others do not).

- Intermittent schedules of reinforcement may operate based on number of responses (ratio) or time between reinforcement (interval). These can be either fixed (constant number) or variable (changing number around a mean).

- Positive reinforcement is the addition of a stimulus after a target behavior that increases the chance of that behavior occurring again.

- Negative reinforcement is the removal of an aversive stimulus after a target behavior that increases future likelihood of that behavior (e.g., a grandmother buys her screaming granddaughter a candy to quiet her down).

- The Premack principle, otherwise known as "Grandma's Rule," is using a high probability behavior to reinforce a lower probability behavior (e.g., **if** you do your homework, **then** you can have computer time).

- Extinction is the deliberate withholding of reinforcement of a previously reinforced response in order to decrease behavior.

- Extinction burst is a byproduct of extinction and is characterized by a temporary increase in the frequency, duration, or magnitude of a target behavior that is a result of deliberate withholding of reinforcement.

- Punishment is a consequence following a behavior that decreases the future likelihood of the behavior occurring. Like reinforcement, it can be positive or negative; positive punishment being the addition of a stimuli after a behavior that decreases future frequency of the target response (e.g., spanking a child for screaming in the grocery store then decreases rate of child's screaming in stores). Negative punishment is the removal of a stimuli after a behavior that decreases future frequency of the target response (e.g., losing access to electronics after lying to a parent decreases future rates of lying)

- Unintended effects of punishment include retaliation or aggression, strained relationships, escape or avoidance of person/setting associated with punishing consequences, modeling of aversives leading to their imitation, and punishment's effects negatively reinforcing the punisher.

- In order for a consequence to qualify as either a reinforcer or punisher, there must be monitoring of the target behavior over time. If the behavior *increases*, the consequence is deemed as a reinforcer; if it decreases, the consequence is a punisher.

PART II

CLASSROOM MANAGEMENT COMMUNITIES

Chapter 4.   School-Wide Systems

Chapter 5.   Classroom Management Collaboration and Communication

Chapter 6.   Setting Up Physical Learning Environments

Chapter 7.   Setting Up the Classroom: Procedures, Expectations, Rules, and Prompt Hierarchies

Chapter 8.   Engagement, Instruction, and Motivation

SCHOOL-WIDE SYSTEMS

Learning Objectives

- Identify different multitiered systems of supports and describe how they support students

- Describe each tier of the Response to Intervention (RtI) framework and how this approach can be applied to support students who are struggling academically

- Define each tier of intervention under Positive Behavioral Intervention and Supports (PBIS) and describe how this framework differs from RtI

- Understand how predictable procedures and routines are embedded within PBIS and how it supports school-wide implementation of the framework

Key Terms

Check-In Check-Out (CICO)

Expectations

Multitiered Systems of Supports (MTSS)

Positive Behavioral Intervention and Supports (PBIS)

Procedures or Routines

Reinforcers (PBIS specific)

Response to Intervention (RtI)

Tier 1

Tier 2

Tier 3

Multitiered Systems of Supports

Multitiered systems of supports (MTSS) is a framework used to support students academically and behaviorally with early intervention and preventative measures. MTSS is not a curriculum or specific set of guidelines but rather a framework of tiers and intervention supports. Generally speaking, MTSS has become a generic term for frameworks that focus on an integrated "whole child" planning. This includes examining academic, social, and behavioral components. Interventions addressing any or all of these areas are meant to complement one another, rather than contradict or conflict. These supports may include Response to Intervention (RtI) and Positive Behavioral Intervention and Supports (PBIS) frameworks. While both RtI and PBIS are key to addressing the challenges a student may be facing with both academics and behavior, this chapter will predominantly focus on PBIS. Both include universal screening with data-driven decision making, a continuum of intervention supports, and progress monitoring, with the difference being a focus on academics (i.e., RtI) versus behavior (i.e., PBIS).

Response to Intervention

Response to Intervention is a framework that uses universal screening assessments to identify students' academic needs. In 2004, RtI was included in the reauthorization of the Individuals with Disabilities Act (IDEIA, 2004) as a way to identify or support students who were suspected of having a specific learning disability (SLD). The framework was intended to provide research-based interventions in a preventive and intensive manner to students who were struggling academically. This approach was intended to occur prior to a referral for special education eligibility and services, but is not required by law. Since RtI is not federally mandated, each state, school district, and school may use the RtI process differently, especially when identifying students for special education services.

Using an RtI framework, a school should ideally screen every student to identify those struggling in reading, mathematics, or writing. Based on the data collected from these screenings, students may be identified and placed in one of three tiers for interventions. Tier 1 includes high-quality classroom instruction for all students. In tier 2, students receive more intensive interventions, typically in a small group. Finally, in tier 3, instruction is individualized and provided with increased frequency and intensity. As students move from tier 1 to tier 3, progress monitoring occurs more frequently. In all tiers, data should be analyzed on an ongoing basis. Students who continue to struggle academically despite intensive, evidence-based interventions or who do not make progress as expected, may be referred for evaluation using the special education eligibility process. Regardless of the tier of intervention, all students should be monitored for progress, both to determine the effectiveness of interventions and to determine if additional supports are needed.

High-Leverage Practice Alert!

HLP6 specifically focuses on using data to evaluate instruction and improve student learning.

Positive Behavioral Intervention and Supports (PBIS)

The Positive Behavioral Intervention and Supports framework was first introduced in 1997 with the reauthorization of IDEA. Although initially focused only on students with disabilities who were exhibiting behavioral challenges, the framework is now used school-wide to support all students on a continuum of needs as well to include students with and without behavioral challenges and those with disabilities. PBIS hinges on prevention through the implementation of behavior interventions rooted in evidence-based practices (EBP).

Go back and review Chapter 1 for more information on EBPs.

The foundation of PBIS consists of rules, routines, and physical arrangements that are designed to prevent the occurrence of challenging behaviors (Office of Special Education Programs, 2014). PBIS is not a curriculum or scripted process, and it is not meant to be implemented without consideration of quality academic instruction. PBIS is a systems approach for managing student behavior, developing individualized supports, and creating a positive school culture (Horner, Sugai, & Anderson, 2010). It requires school teams to use data to identify and develop a continuum of behavioral interventions that address student needs. As it relates to classroom management, PBIS can be drilled down to classroom strategies that mimic PBIS strategies using prevention and reinforcement. When implemented in the classroom, these strategies can reduce classroom disruptions, improve students' behavioral and academic outcomes, and increase teachers' instructional time (Simonsen, Fairbanks, Briesch, Myers, & Sugai, 2008).

To implement PBIS with fidelity, schools be fully invested in the process. Common features of schools who effectively use PBIS include PBIS support teams, buy-in from administration and faculty, a limited number of behavioral expectations that are clearly taught to all students, positive recognition for positive student behavior, correction and redirection of disruptive student behaviors, and ongoing evaluation of behavioral data (Horner & Sugai, 2000). In addition to an investment from teachers and administrators, all school staff and parents should be involved as well.

The PBIS framework includes three tiers of support that include school-wide, classroom, and individual levels of behavioral supports (Horner & Sugai, 2015). Like RtI, behavioral interventions in PBIS are targeted and responsive to student needs. On a more holistic level, the school-wide Positive Behavioral Interventions and Supports (SWPBIS) system requires systematic data analysis, planning, and implementation. SWPBIS is often used interchangeably with PBIS and uses a team approach to develop and monitor every aspect of the PBIS framework, encouraging buy-in from all stakeholders (e.g., administrators, teachers, support staff, parents, community members).

Once schools have established buy-in from administration and staff to participate in PBIS, teams must self-assess current disciplinary systems. In this process, schools critically examine current data to establish areas of need. Using discipline referrals or other behavior related data, teams are tasked with determining where behavioral "hot spots" exist within the school setting. These may include locations like hallways or buses or individual groups like overrepresentation of specific groups, such as fifth graders or students with disabilities. It is through a critical lens of evaluation that schools can determine where to best focus their PBIS planning efforts.

Based on the aforementioned self-assessment, the PBIS team then creates an implementation plan that includes action items and ways to measure success. These plans may include reducing disciplinary referrals, improving social skills of students, reducing absenteeism, or decreasing student disruptions in the hallways. As an example, imagine that a middle school PBIS team analyzes data that show that the majority of their disciplinary referrals happen on buses coming to and from school. The school may create a plan and subsequent target goal that includes reducing disciplinary referrals on buses by half before the end of the school year. Action items might include hosting a breakfast for bus drivers to explain school expectations, procedures, and reinforcers; developing a bus-specific reinforcer that allows drivers to recognize students who follow established bus procedures; or targeting specific grade levels for opportunities to practice bus behaviors. In this way, schools are able to individualize areas of growth and improvement based on need.

Using the principles of PBIS (e.g., individualized supports, positive school culture), schools then design individualized frameworks to address areas of behavioral need, as identified in the action plan. With identified areas of need at the forefront, schools establish specific positive behaviors and expectations for students. These expectations are directly responsive to meeting the goal of improving overall school behavior. In the PBIS framework, school-wide routines/procedures and common language are established for all students and staff. For example, if a procedure for walking down the halls is developed in response to the need for addressing challenges in the hallway, all staff and students would use the same language and procedure. Therefore, if the procedure for walking in the hallways included the phrase "lips zipped" or "make a bubble," then all staff and students would refer to staying quiet in the hallways as "lips zipped" or "make a bubble" and a school-wide, universal understanding of this behavior would be established. Using a middle school example, suppose a hallway procedure was developed that included students using only the right side of the hallway and specific areas were labeled "lanes." In this school, all staff and students would know and understand the language and procedure for using "lanes."

These behaviors and expectations are explicitly taught to students in both classroom and nonclassroom settings (e.g., buses, bathrooms, hallways). Often this is done in the form of lesson plans and students are provided with ample opportunities to practice. As students engage in expected behaviors, they are acknowledged and rewarded. This will be discussed further in the following sections. Each of the PBIS tiers are designed to build upon each other, targeting specific needs for the entire school, small subsets of the school population, and individual students. An overview of PBIS is shown in Figure 4–1 and more information about individual tiers is included later in this chapter.

Figure 4–1. Positive Behavior Intervention Supports pyramid.

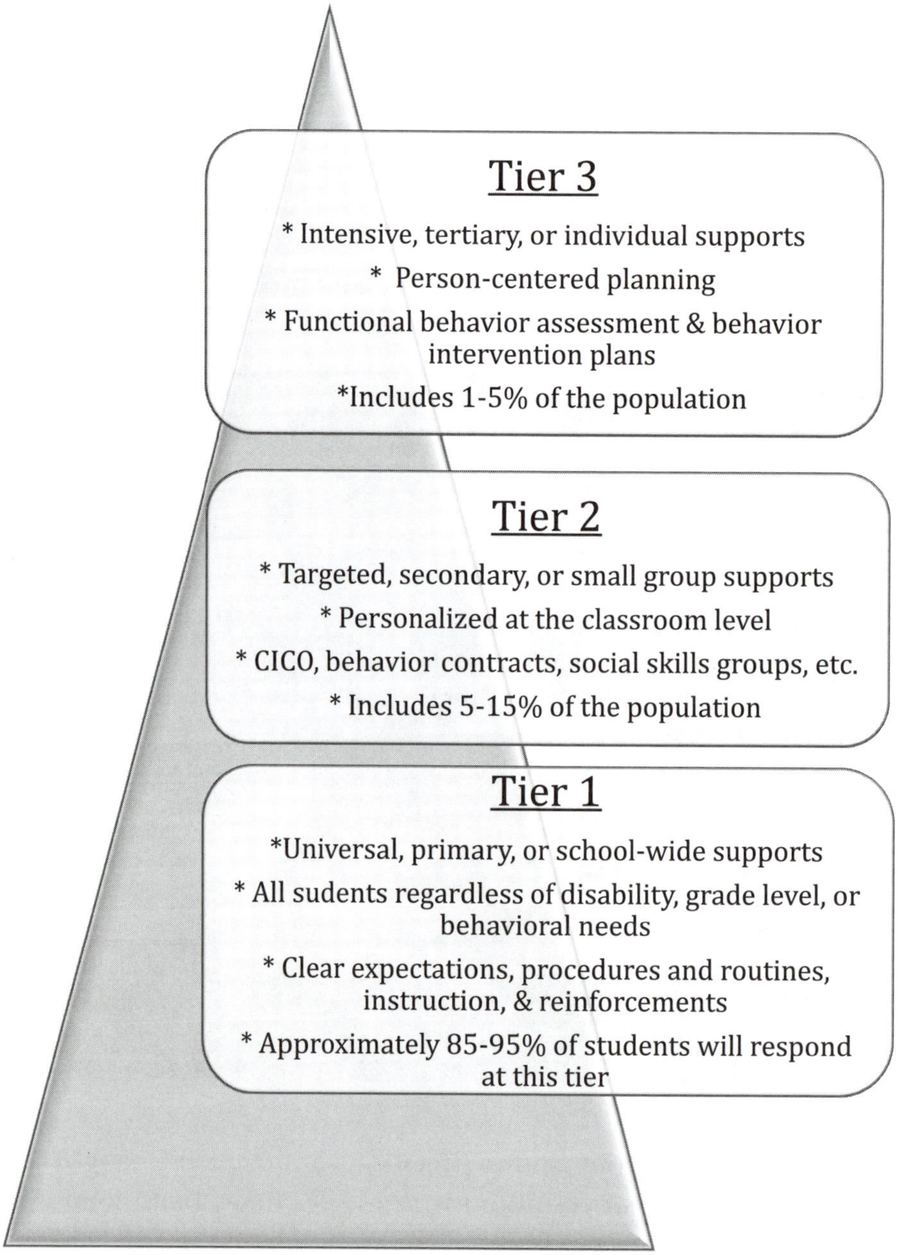

Tier 3

* Intensive, tertiary, or individual supports

* Person-centered planning

* Functional behavior assessment & behavior intervention plans

*Includes 1-5% of the population

Tier 2

* Targeted, secondary, or small group supports

* Personalized at the classroom level

* CICO, behavior contracts, social skills groups, etc.

* Includes 5-15% of the population

Tier 1

*Universal, primary, or school-wide supports

* All sudents regardless of disability, grade level, or behavioral needs

* Clear expectations, procedures and routines, instruction, & reinforcements

* Approximately 85-95% of students will respond at this tier

School-Wide Expectations

After identifying areas of need and creating an action plan, a small, core PBIS team is established to spearhead the development of common or universal expectations for the school. Together, the PBIS team decides on three to five core values or expectations. School-wide expectations communicate to students what school staff expect from students throughout the school setting. Well-designed expectations should be inclusive of all students, displayed visibly throughout the school, known by the entire school community, support academic achievement, create consistency throughout the school, and written to include positive, clear language. These positively stated expectations may be applicable to all times of the school day and to every area of the school, including buses, playgrounds, hallways, locker rooms, and restrooms.

Teams should be knowledgeable about their students and make decisions that are culturally and individually equitable when designing school expectations. It is imperative that PBIS teams demonstrate cultural awareness as they outline expectations. This is particularly true in diverse areas where norms and social interactions may vary among families within a school community. If eye contact is viewed as disrespectful among students within a school community, a school-wide expectation should not list eye contact as a requirement. In addition, schools should also create supports that address the physical and cognitive abilities of all students. For example, if a school's recess expectations involve exiting the building using specific staircases, this may exclude members of the school community who need physical supports from complying with a school-wide expectation. Ultimately, the team should craft expectations that are both practical and achievable for all students. Expectations should be accessible for all students.

 High-Leverage Practice Alert!

Review HLP7, which covers the need for culturally responsive expectations, procedures, or routines.

Expectations should be written in a positive language that outlines what the student *should* be doing, avoiding words like "no" or "don't." Instead of saying, "don't be rude," the expectation would be written as "be kind," since this is the expected behavior. Often these expectations cannot be seen or heard as written and must be further defined within an expectation matrix. Some examples of school-wide expectations may include "be respectful," "show kindness," or "accept responsibility." Sometimes these expectations are tied to school mascots with the intent of making it easier for students, staff, and parents to remember.

For example, as shown in Figure 4–2, the Warrenton Bulldogs may use the word "BARK" to guide school-wide expectations.

B is for "Be safe," *A* is for "Accept responsibility," *R* is for "Respect others, self, and property," and *K* is for "Kindness always." While expectations are typically broadly written, the goal is to use these expectations as a springboard to further describe through objective and observable language the behaviors that match these expectations. Without a doubt, expectations like "be kind" and "be responsible" have many different meanings for a range of individuals, so these must be explicitly described and taught to all students. Procedures and routines help all stakeholders understand how expectations should be seen and/or heard.

As a classroom teacher, these expectations are helpful in defining how students should be behaving across all school settings, including the classroom. One of the benefits of PBIS is that students know exactly what is expected of them throughout the day, in all settings, reducing the need to volley between different expectations in different settings. As a teacher, use these expectations to your advantage and encourage and reinforce students for making good behavioral choices!

Figure 4–2. Example of school-wide PBIS expectations.

PBIS Example: Warrenton Bulldogs

Be safe
Accept responsibility
Respect others, self, and property
Kindness always

School-Wide Procedures or Routines

One of the foundations of PBIS is the development of predictable procedures or routines. Procedures or routines are the "way we do things" in a school, on the bus, on the playground, during an athletic event, or in any location where school is in session. These are the behaviors that are expected of all students and are directly related to the expectations outlined previously. Remember, after an analysis of need, expectations and subsequent procedures target the most challenging areas or times of day in a school. Procedures may include how to use equipment on the playground, the process for late arrivals to school, how to load and unload on school buses, or the way to enter the cafeteria and purchase lunch or find a seat. There is no minimum or maximum number of procedures, but it should be noted that these routines should tie directly back to established expectations and will need to be taught and reinforced to students. One of the easiest ways to accomplish this goal is through a matrix, as shown in Figure 4–3.

For example, the Marshall High School PBIS team is in the process of developing their PBIS framework. They analyze their needs, develop an action plan with goals, and decide their core expectations are to be respectful, be safe, and be ready to learn. Using these three expectations, they begin to develop procedures

Figure 4–3. School-wide behavioral expectations matrix.

Westlawn Elementary School Behavior Matrix
Go Tigers!

	Classroom	Cafeteria	Hallway	Playground
P Prepare for Success	Bring all materials Complete assignments on time	Get all utensils, napkins, and food before sitting down	Go directly to your destination Bring all your materials to your destination	Ask for the rules of a game Play by the rules of the game
A Act Respectfully	Follow teacher's directions Treat peers as you want to be treated Raise hand and wait to be called on	Say please and thank you Chew with mouth closed	Keep hands and feet to your sides to protect bulletin boards Walk quietly	Follow rules of games Show good sportsmanship Keep playground free of trash Use equipment properly
W Work Cooperatively	Share materials Resolve conflicts peacefully Listen to speakers	Help friends if asked Include others at your table	Hold doors for others Keep to the right	Take turns on playground equipment Invite others to play
S Stay Safe	Keep hands and feet to yourself Stay in your assigned area Follow safety procedures	Walk Keep feet under tables Clean up spills Stay seated	Walk single file Keep hands and feet to yourself	Walk to the playground Use equipment correctly Report dangerous activities or equipment Stay on playground or field area at all times

for what those expectations look like in targeted settings in their school. For "be safe," the team decides that safe means keeping hands and feet to yourself in all school settings, remaining in an assigned area unless granted permission to leave, remaining in a seated position on the school bus with your back against the seat, and listening and following teachers' directions during a school emergency situation. The team at Marshall carefully phrases each procedure positively using language that is objective and observable. Much like an operational definition, they make sure each expectation is measurable, objective, and observable (MOO) so that students know exactly what they should be doing.

> ***Check out Chapter 10 to learn how to make a definition MOO.***

Once expectations and procedures have been established, the Marshall team posts them prominently in every area of the school. The cafeteria includes cafeteria expectations and procedures that outline how to be respectful, safe, and ready to learn. The classrooms include posters with the same expectations, only directly related to what those behaviors look like in class. Finally, Marshall's team teaches these expectations to all students, making no assumptions that students are already well versed in the expected behaviors. They encourage their teachers to give students the opportunity to practice and receive feedback on the behaviors, much like writing out a new math formula or speaking a foreign language. Teachers further engage in the PBIS process by developing lessons, actively practicing, and frequently reinforcing school-wide expectations throughout the school year.

While a teacher may add additional procedures to the school-wide expectations in their individual classroom, these additional procedures or routines should never contradict those implemented school-wide. For example, if a school-wide procedure states that juice or sugary drinks should be consumed and disposed of in the cafeteria to avoid bugs and other unwanted visitors in the classroom, a teacher should not make exceptions to this school-wide procedure for an individual class. If the teacher wants to develop a procedure that allows students to bring in refillable water bottles to class because it does not conflict with other school-wide procedures, the teacher should build upon what that might look like under the respectful, safe, and ready to learn school-wide expectations.

Consistent routines and procedures help students establish predictability and develop smooth operations within the school building. When all students and staff know what is expected, there is less room for confusion or disorganization. For new teachers, learning these expectations and procedures may take some time, but it is important to engage in the PBIS framework since the true benefits of

PBIS will only be realized if all teachers and staff are consistent and invested in the process.

School-Wide Reinforcement

A PBIS team is also tasked with developing a system for reinforcing positive behaviors, expectations, and procedures throughout the school. Reinforcers in PBIS frameworks may include verbal praise or tangible items, some of which may be tied to tickets or raffle systems. While the team will generate ideas for reinforcers and staff will provide input, all staff should be involved in reinforcing all students' behaviors. This will be true regardless of whether the student is assigned to the teacher providing the reinforcement or is a student who happens to be walking by a staff member in the hallway. This could include teachers, custodial staff, librarians, bus drivers, or anyone interacting with students throughout the school day. In the initial stages of PBIS and during the first month or so of the school year, students should be "caught" demonstrating desired behaviors frequently to reinforce those behaviors. Students should be praised and reinforced with specific statements about their behaviors (e.g., "You picked up your materials and cleaned your desk just like we practiced—well done!"). When staff notice students who are not following the expected procedures, reteaching is often necessary and students should be given opportunities for practice.

 High-Leverage Practice Alert!

In HLP20, positive and constructive feedback is outlined as a way to promote improved student behavior.

In addition to verbal reinforcement, including specific praise, schools may use tangible reinforcement systems. These systems may include tokens, school "bucks" or money, tickets, positive referrals, awards, or "citizenship coupons," to name a few. Some of these examples are included in Figure 4–4.

Tickets or certificates can stand alone as a reinforcer (e.g., positive referrals or awards) or they can be traded in for other tangible or activity-based reinforcers. Often schools build a menu of items students can buy with coupons or tickets they earned for positive behaviors. Tangible items may include school supplies, books, stickers, activity passes, or toys. Other activity-based reinforcers may include lunch with the principal, free seating in the cafeteria, locker passes, or the use of technology in the classroom. Another option is to use a raffle system where students who earn tokens or tickets may enter into a raffle for a series of select prizes.

Figure 4–4. School-wide behavior token examples.

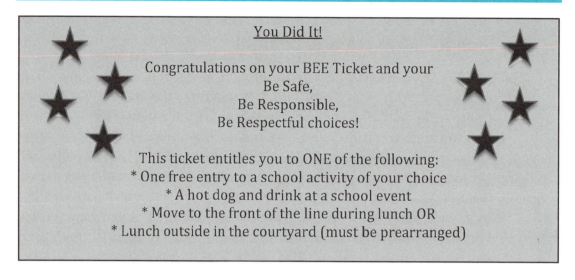

<u>You Did It!</u>

Congratulations on your BEE Ticket and your
Be Safe,
Be Responsible,
Be Respectful choices!

This ticket entitles you to ONE of the following:
* One free entry to a school activity of your choice
* A hot dog and drink at a school event
* Move to the front of the line during lunch OR
* Lunch outside in the courtyard (must be prearranged)

You Demonstrated Your Paw Pride!

Student Name: _____
Referring Staff: _____

Circle one:
   **Bus   Hallway   Classroom
   Cafeteria   Bathrooms   Other**

Drop your ticket in the bucket in the
cafeteria to win a weekly prize!

BEAR BUCK
Fenwick Elementary

Redeemable Fridays at lunch
at the Bear Buck Store

Other schools may use reinforcers to reward entire classrooms or grade levels with weekly or quarterly activities, trophies, or designated honors which are displayed in a central location in the school or outside specific classrooms. As a classroom teacher, these reinforcers can be very helpful during difficult transitions during the day, particularly hallways, recess, and lunch.

Given these lists of ideas, it is still extremely important for school teams to consider reinforcers that are actually rewarding and accessible for all students. If a student isn't invested in the reinforcer, then it is not, in fact, reinforcement. Reinforcer surveys, discussions with PBIS teams, and input from students will help identify options. In addition, teams need to make sure reinforcers are accessible to all students. If a school is planning to reward students with a "field day" that includes bounce houses, relay races, and other team games, there should be discussion about whether students can access this reinforcement. If all students have earned the field day activity, will all students, including those with physical support needs, actually be able to participate in the event? If not, the school team should reconsider this option or expand upon the reinforcer to be more inclusive.

You might be wondering where consequences and punishment fit into the PBIS framework. First, let's take a moment to clarify terms. In the PBIS world, "consequence" refers to an action or event delivered by an educator following a student breach in behavioral expectations. So, in this way, we think of consequences differently than as presented in Chapter 3.

> **Remember, the definition of *consequence* differs depending on the framework from which one is operating.**
>
> **Under the principles of operant conditioning, consequence refers to an event that occurs immediately following a target behavior, which influences the future likelihood of that behavior occurring again.**
>
> **Within the context of PBIS, consequences are administered according to the philosophy of progressive discipline wherein first offenses receive minor consequences, while more severe infractions receive higher level ones.**

Primarily, PBIS focuses on designing positive and preventative strategies using effective interventions. PBIS does not ignore problematic behavior but instead focuses on changing the behaviors to help the student with school success. When students don't respond to the school expectations, correction and reteaching are promoted. Using ideas in the section on tier 3, students can be individually targeted to achieve positive behavioral outcomes. While the PBIS framework doesn't suggest specific consequences, schools can plan for problematic behavior by creating levels of consequences based on severity of behaviors. For example, all students, depending on the behavior, may be given a verbal reminder of rules or a verbal warning. Other students may be asked to participate in a teacher-student conference, problem-solving session, or a conference which includes parents or guardians. In a second tier of consequences, students may be referred to support staff such as a school counselor or they may be asked to take a time-out in an area within or outside of their typical classroom seat or setting. Finally, students may be involved in behavioral contracts or engage in individualized planning for additional supports. Regardless of the specific consequence, they should be delivered consistently across the school and consequence hierarchies should be easily accessible and understood by all staff, parents, and students.

School-Wide Data Collection

Once the framework has been developed, each PBIS team will need to develop a means to collect data. The purpose of data collection is to support PBIS as a cyclical process. Data inform schools about school-wide areas of difficulty that need to be addressed (e.g., frequent hallway disruptions, high levels of truancy), individual student outcomes (e.g., success of social skills groups, disciplinary referrals for students receiving tier 2 interventions), and the fidelity of intervention implementation (e.g., scheduled check-in check-out implementation days and times). Disciplinary referrals are often a common choice for PBIS data collection, but they should not be used solely as counts of behavior. Discipline referrals should be further examined for times of day and days of the week, location of behavior occurrence, people involved, and any other information the school determines critical for analysis. Other sources may include attendance records, behavior rating scales, student progress monitoring reports, classroom management surveys or observations, observational data, or checklists. Ultimately, schools must determine what data collection is appropriate and necessary for their unique situations. Whichever data collection system is selected, as much information as possible is collected to include the location of the incident, person reporting, other people present, and observable and objective reports of behavior. These data allow the PBIS team to identify any pattern of behaviors and subsequently make adjustments with expectations, procedures, and reinforcement as necessary. As discussed later in Chapter 10, data used for PBIS should be valid (e.g., Do the data represent the behaviors you want to measure?) and reliable (e.g., Are the data consistent across data collectors and times?). PBIS teams need to be cognizant about collecting data that are also socially valid. In other words, are the data collected practical and are multiple perspectives represented? Teams need to consider the impact of family, culture, and disabilities on the data collection constructs used for PBIS decision making. Understanding whether or not data sources or tools are truly representative of the needs of the PBIS team helps to maintain a focus on long-term PBIS goals. Finally, teams will need to consider whether the selected data collection methods are efficient for school teams. Given the myriad of responsibilities for PBIS teams, having a data collection method that is actually feasible will keep teams moving forward productively.

> *Read about reliability and validity in Chapter 10.*

PBIS Tiers of Intervention

As previously noted, beyond expectations, procedures and routines, and reinforcements, PBIS includes three tiers of interventions. The tiers include the following:

Tier 1: Universal, primary, or school-wide supports

Tier 2: Targeted, secondary, or small group supports

Tier 3: Intensive, tertiary, or individual supports

These tiers are not meant to function independently of one another but rather build upon the interventions already in place in the previous tier. For example, if Jacks is receiving tier 3 supports (e.g., individualized counseling services and conflict resolution skill instruction), he is also receiving tier 1 (e.g., frequent breaks, behavior-specific praise, and redirection) and tier 2 (e.g., self-monitoring and check–in check-out) supports. Therefore, PBIS is a continuum of interventions designed to improve behavioral outcomes for students. The delivery of individualized interventions is based on data-driven decision making. Just like schools may use a range of data sources for overall data collection (e.g., discipline referrals, records reviews, checklists, rating scales), these same data are used to identify specific students who need additional interventions beyond tier 1 and into tiers 2 and 3.

Tier 1

The goal of tier 1 is the prevention of challenging or problematic behavior through common language and evidence-based practices and interventions. This tier includes positive behavioral instruction for all students, regardless of disability, grade level, or individualized behavioral needs. This includes clearly defining, teaching, modeling, and reinforcing school-wide expectations across all settings, by all staff in a school. In addition, students are provided with positive feedback about desired behaviors and reteaching occurs for behaviors not aligned with school-wide expectations. The clear establishment of school-wide expectations and reinforcements reduces the number of students who will need additional supports in tier 2 because many students just need to know what is expected of them, and, consequently, they will be responsive to those expectations. It is estimated that 80% to 95% of the student population will respond to supports in this tier without additional interventions or supports (Fluke & Peterson, 2013; Sugai et al., 2000). Schools that consistently implement tier 1 interventions with fidelity report a decrease in office discipline referrals (Bradshaw, Mitchell, & Leaf, 2010).

Tier 2

When students are not responding to interventions set forth in tier 1 or have more serious behavioral challenges, additional supports are added in tier 2. In this tier, interventions are more individualized and provided with more intensity and frequency than in tier 1. Although individualized, the interventions are more focused on groups and the delivery of these supports still happens at the classroom level. Students who will benefit from interventions and supports in this tier will include approximately 5% to 15% of the school population (Fluke & Peterson, 2013; Sugai et al., 2000). Some examples of interventions might include Functional Behavior Assessments (FBA), Behavior Intervention Plans (BIP), behavior contracts, targeted academic supports, mentoring, or social skills groups. One additional tier 2 intervention that classroom teachers may be actively involved in daily is check-in check-out (CICO). In CICO, a student, with the support of a targeted adult, sets individualized goals based on the school's PBIS framework. Each morning, a student "checks in" with an adult in the building to discuss their daily goals and receive encouragement. Typically, this adult is someone the student has developed or established a relationship with or is a "preferred" person in the building. This may be a teacher, counselor, support staff, or any number of school personnel. Based on the student's need, a daily point or progress sheet is created. Throughout the day, the student's teachers provide feedback on the student's goals and ideally, the student and teacher should discuss progress as it occurs. Depending on need, the student may "check in" with the preferred adult midday or may wait until the end of the day to review their point or progress sheet through a "check-out" process. This "check-out" process includes reviewing the daily goals, setting new goals for the next day, and, often, taking the daily sheet home for parent or guardian signature. The CICO process begins again the next day with a new "check-in."

High-Leverage Practice Alert!

Check out the information on teaching social behaviors in HLP9.

Tier 3

In tier 3, students receive more intensive supports in addition to those provided in tiers 1 and 2. The number of students receiving these supports would be relatively small, with an estimated 1% to 7% of the school population (Fluke & Peterson, 2013; Sugai et al., 2000). The students who receive these supports are typically not responding to tier 2 interventions or have more chronic or serious behavioral challenges. In some cases, this may mean that the student needs individual counseling services or wraparound services that involve parents or guardians and others in the community. If an FBA and BIP was not created as a preventative measure in earlier tiers of intervention, it would need to be developed as part of these intensive supports.

 High-Leverage Practice Alert!

HLP10 discusses both FBAs and BIPs and the necessary components of both. Further, see Chapters 12 and 13 for more information about these topics.

PBIS is designed to be an iterative process that uses data to inform practice and make adjustments. The PBIS team will need to work with new and existing staff to ensure continued buy-in and data will need to be continuously collected and analyzed. The implementation of PBIS often goes awry when school-wide expectations are not upheld by all members of the school staff or data aren't collected or analyzed to evaluate intervention effectiveness. Based on those data, changes may need to be made or new areas or students of concern may be identified. Interventions will need to be evaluated for fidelity and it is possible that the continuum of supports may need to be expanded or narrowed, based on an individual school's need. PBIS is not a passive process that runs itself and schools may face barriers with developing and utilizing effective expectations, procedures, and reinforcement. However, if schools and staff persist with implementation, the benefits of a consistent and successful system will often feel as if the school is truly on autopilot.

If you are a classroom teacher working in a school where PBIS is implemented, you will be asked to support the framework established by your PBIS team. For fidelity purposes, teachers should make the investment in this process to reap the full benefits of improved school-wide behaviors. Classroom teachers can also incorporate classroom-level routines and procedures that are directly linked to the school-wide expectations and the overall PBIS framework. Much like PBIS, teachers can also use data to make decisions about what groups or individual students need to support them behaviorally. More details about classroom systems can be found in later in this book.

> *Check out Chapter 7 for information on classroom rules, expectations, and procedures.*

School Safety Plans

In this chapter we have been discussing preventative systems to support students academically and behaviorally. Unfortunately, crisis and emergency situations may also arise in school settings and it is important to also develop similar preventative plans to support students and yourself in unexpected situations. Although it is difficult to outline what a specific school safety plan may look like, it is imperative to discuss how teachers can adequately prepare for school emergencies. State-to-state requirements for schools vary as they relate to incidents with students, threat assessments, building security, emergency drills, and active shooters. As you begin teaching in a new school, school division, or state, you should ask for policies and procedures about school safety. While some policies will apply throughout a city or county, division, or state, there will be some planning that will be school specific. These system policies are in place to protect students and staff in the case of an emergency. As you begin a new job or even as a reminder during your 12th year of teaching, you should ask the following important questions:

- What is the policy for supporting students with potential or verbalized mental health concerns (e.g., suicide statements, self-harm)?
- What is the procedure for addressing students who make verbal threats?
- What is the procedure for addressing students who are physically aggressive?
- What is the procedure for reporting suspected physical abuse in the student's home?
- Where do I go and what is the procedure for fire drills?

- Where do I go and what is the procedure for natural disasters?
- What is the procedure for handling student medical or physical emergencies?
- What is the procedure for reporting suspicion or knowledge of weapons or drugs in the school or on the school premises?
- Where do I go and what is the procedure for incidents involving shelter in place?
- Where do I go and what is the procedure if there is a suspicious, unidentified person in the school building?
- Where do I go and what is the procedure if there is an active shooter?
- Does my classroom door lock? Are there locations in my classroom where my students and I cannot be seen from the hallway?
- What supports are available for me after a school-related emergency situation?
- What supports are available for students after a school-related emergency situation?

Conclusion

MTSS provides schools and teachers with a framework for assessing, identifying, and addressing behavioral and academic challenges in the school setting. Preventative supports like MTSS will provide clear expectations, routines, and reinforcements that will address many students' potential behavioral challenges. However, some students will require additional supports for success. Using layers of evidence-based supports and interventions, PBIS can provide schools, teachers, and students with a holistic approach to making positive behavior change. Despite these preventative approaches, it is imperative teachers continue to plan for crisis situations that may not be predicted.

Chapter Summary

- Multitiered systems of supports (MTSS) are frameworks used to support students academically, behaviorally, and socially through a continuum of intervention, progress monitoring, and data-based decision making. Two popular MTSS include Response to Intervention (RtI) and Positive Behavioral Intervention and Supports (PBIS).

- The RtI framework focuses specifically on academics and uses universal screening assessments to determine students' academic needs. The intended use of RtI is to provide research-based interventions for struggling students through a series of three tiers. Tier 1: high-quality classroom instruction; Tier 2: small-group specified interventions for identified students; Tier 3: intensive, individualized instruction with increased frequency and duration.

- PBIS was initially developed to support students with disabilities behaviorally; however, it has expanded to include school-wide supports to all students, with and without behavioral challenges or disabilities. PBIS is rooted in the proactive use of evidence-based interventions, clear establishment of rules, routines, and physical arrangements designed to promote learning and prevent challenging behavior. The three tiers of school-wide PBIS are as follows: Tier 1: school-wide supports; Tier 2: secondary, or small group supports; and Tier 3: intensive, individualized supports.

- School safety plans are important to be prepared in case of crisis or emergency situations. While there are no set guidelines of what must be included, it is important to be proactive and seek out your school's policies and procedures regarding situations you may encounter (e.g., suicidal statements, self-harm, reporting suspected abuse, active shooter drills, etc.).

CHAPTER 5

CLASSROOM MANAGEMENT COLLABORATION AND COMMUNICATION

Learning Objectives

- Identify strategies to work with parents or guardians, including the use of partnerships
- Recognize how differing family structures may affect relationships between parents or guardians and teachers
- Identify strategies to communicate with parents or guardians about behavior throughout the school year
- Be able to explain how school personnel, coteachers, and administrators can work together to address classroom and behavior management challenges

Key Terms

Active Listening
Collaboration
Coteaching

I-Messages
Partnerships

Managing the behavioral needs of the classroom and individual students is certainly not always an easy job, but, thankfully, teachers can rely on other professionals as well as parents and guardians for support. While effective communication is a necessity to make this team approach work, collaboration about our students' needs can lead to increased opportunities for engaging instruction and, ultimately, success for individual students. Collaboration includes shared goals, accountability, resources, and resources all in the framework of trust, respect, and community (Friend & Cook, 1990, 2010). Good collaboration among educators creates cohesive educational programing, supporting all students (Ketterlin-Geller, Baumer, & Lichon, 2015). Using a team mentality, focus on common goals and get those lines of communication open!

High-Leverage Practice Alert!

HLP3 focuses on the need for collaboration with families to meet the needs of all students, regardless of background, socioeconomic background, language, or individualized family systems.

Working with Parents

During the first years of teaching, working with parents or guardians may feel awkward or uncomfortable. While a teacher is well versed in his or her profession, a parent or guardian almost always knows their individual child best, and this may feel daunting, especially to a newer teacher. Often, the best way to work with parents is through a perspective shift. Instead of viewing parents as adversaries, opponents, or a person who is disconnected from the school environment, consider them your partners. Partnerships involve two or more people working together toward a common purpose or goal. When teachers and parents both want success for students, this unified partnership becomes natural. While not all partnerships will yield success, approaching parents as partners will help bridge communication gaps, especially about student behavior. Another perspective shift is to imagine what it might be like to be a specific parent. Imagine the parent or guardian whose child has struggled in school since the early elementary grades, despite outside family and individual counseling, specialized behavior support in the home, and/or positive communication with the school. Imagine the frustration those parents or guardians must feel as they attempt to do "everything right" for their child but to no avail. Imagine how difficult it must be to receive yet another phone call from school about their child's misbehavior. Or, imagine the parent who struggled in school themselves and had many negative experiences with teachers and administrators, but is now being asked to engage in a partnership with you as the teacher. While this doesn't mean a student's behavior should be excused, it should create a pocket of empathy from the teacher while speaking with the parents. As you work with parents or guardians, imagine sitting in their seat and listening to a litany of negatives about their child. In the coming paragraphs, we will outline ways to work with parents with empathy and in partnership.

When considering partnerships, remember that involvement will take on different forms for different parents and guardians. Some families will want to be actively involved by sending emails or notes, volunteering for activities or field trips, or attending every optional school function. Other families may take a passive role and only interact with the school and educators when necessary or when asked specifically to attend or join a function. Still, others may not engage at all, for a myriad of reasons. The level of parent involvement may be based on any number of factors, including availability, their own school experiences and successes, and their perception of how they fit with you as the professional. Some families will view you immediately as their partner, others may see themselves as the expert, while others will defer to you and your expertise in education because they may not feel well versed or confident with educational decision making. Regardless of the level of involvement, treat all parents as if they are engaging in a partnership with you to ensure academic and behavioral success for their child, your student.

It is also important to remember that when discussing behavior, expectations for behavior among family systems vary greatly. This may be due to family preferences, beliefs, family history, culture, or religion. While in some families, parents may expect children to comply with instructions, requests, or demands without talking back to the parent, other families may allow negotiation when these directions, requests, or demands are made. Neither of these approaches are necessarily right or wrong, but if you are a teacher who doesn't want a student to negotiate, this may be a difficult conversation when you speak to parents who believe differently. One way to approach these differences in family systems and expectations is to discuss context and rationale. For example, in the aforementioned scenario about students who may want to negotiate directions, you can explain that while at home with one, two, or several siblings, this may be possible, but it is not feasible in the classroom. Given that there are 20 to 30 students or fewer students who have more intensive needs, it is important to maintain control of the classroom and keep everyone safe and engaged with learning. If every student negotiated a teacher's directions, learning would certainly be disrupted while the teacher had 30 different conversations about whether the direction should be followed or altered. Explaining the rationale for certain procedures, rules, and expectations to parents will help them understand your perspective as a teacher and classroom manager. With all that being said, it is also helpful to affirm and build on each family's strengths since each student's family system is unique and brings value to the classroom community.

As with all behavior management strategies, proactive approaches are best. At the beginning of the school year, share your expectations, procedures, rules, consequences, schedules, and other pertinent classroom management information with parents. The way your classroom runs shouldn't be a surprise to parents, especially a surprise that occurs after their child has experienced difficulty. In the elementary school setting, a quick and easy method for sharing information might be through a flipbook that contains information related to each of these aforementioned topics (Figure 5–1). In secondary settings, this can be shared through syllabi

Figure 5–1. Photograph of welcome packet and explanation of expectations for second grade class.

or information sheets sent home for parents to sign. If your school uses Positive Behavior Interventions and Supports (PBIS), be sure to share that information with parents as well. Since your classroom information should be aligned with the school-wide policies, this will be a natural transition.

> ***See Chapter 4 for a refresher on PBIS in schools.***

To reinforce these expectations or rules while also working on your teacher and parent partnership, take some time within the first two weeks of school to call parents with positive news or send positive notes home. This can be as easy as a call that says, "Good morning Mr. Schied, I was just calling to let you know that Barrett had a great day today. He followed every direction and I really appreciated it because it was a busy day and I knew I could depend on him to be a good listener." This phone call serves several purposes. First, it reinforces positive behaviors. Second, it reiterates classroom and school rules for parents and students alike and bridges the gap between home and school. This call also sets the tone for future conversations, ones that may be more difficult than a positive call home. Finally, it may help begin a parent and teacher partnership by initiating conversations about a student's behaviors.

Communicating about Behavior

Use caution with behavior monitoring systems that are public in nature. While some online and application-based programs exist for monitoring student behavior, not all of these systems support best practice. At no time should all parents be able to see and review every other students' class-wide behavior reports or data. This breaches confidentiality and even if the data are posted or made available with pseudonyms, it could posit the teacher as an adversary who shares individual information and data publicly. In addition, be careful about sharing student behavioral data without explanation. If a teacher is using something like a color-coded behavior chart, like the "stoplight system," and parents or guardians are only receiving a color for their child's behavior, this shares nothing of value. Imagine receiving a note home with your child that indicates they had a "yellow day." As a parent, this doesn't identify the problem, the severity of the issue, what consequences were received, or even how you can support your child with improved behavioral choices. While not every behavioral report needs to come with a detailed assessment or plan, there should be enough information for parents to know what happened and how they can help their child in the future. In the next chapter, we will discuss public displays of behavior in more detail.

Timing is also important as you begin to notice behavioral challenges with students. While it is best not to wait until the parent and teacher conference at the end of the first nine weeks to share that a problem has been occurring daily for the past eight weeks, you also want to make sure you have collected some behavioral data to identify some of the characteristics of the concerning behavior before you notify parents. This includes identifying a target behavior and considering antecedents and consequences. It is always better to share your observations of why and when the behavior is happening versus admiring the problem and telling parents just how bad the problem is without any possible solutions. With enough data and information compiled, it is important to share concerns with parents, especially since some behaviors may be easily addressed with the right teamwork and problem solving. Be prepared to share observational data as well as maintaining consequences with parents, perhaps in conjunction with known or suspected antecedents.

> *Go ahead and peek ahead to Chapters 10 and 12 for more on collecting data, identifying functions of behavior, and using objective, bias-free language for behavior reporting.*

As you begin meeting with parents to discuss student behaviors, it may be helpful to create an agenda to guide the discussion. Even if you plan to meet informally, jotting down ideas and issues you want to discuss prior to the meeting will help keep the conversation focused and on track. Since it is easy to get distracted or off task, the agenda also serves as a way to bring conversations back to the challenges that brought you together. During discussions with parents or guardians about students, maintain professionalism by avoiding assumptions or generalizations about student behavior. Using a solutions-based approach, ask parents what works for them at home, what ideas resonate with them based on their child's personality and needs, and how you can better partner with them. Using I-messages to discuss student behavior is often a helpful approach and avoids parents or guardians feeling as if their child or parenting style is being attacked or put under the microscope. For example, saying something like, "I have a difficult time teaching lessons when Maryanna is out of her seat and walking around the classroom" sounds and feels different than "Maryanna never sits down and walks all around the classroom constantly." The I-message method also conveys why the behavior is a problem and opens up the opportunity for a solution. Another sentence starter that often works well during discussions about behavior includes the phrase, "I've noticed that . . . " With this starter, the student's behavior is an observation and the teacher can convey what has been seen or heard in a factual, nonjudgmental manner. While these ways of discussing student behavior may seem too complicated or watered down, we encourage you, as a partner with parents or guardians, to again remember how a parent might perceive news about their child's behavior, whether it is unexpected and new or for yet another time in the student's school career.

> *Remember our discussion about theorists in Chapter 1? Go back and review those and take note of the connections!*

While the ultimate goal with parents and guardians is partnership, not all situations will lend themselves to easy conversations or productive meetings. If you find yourself in a situation where meetings are not conducive to problem solving, you feel uncomfortable with statements or assertions from parents or guardians, or you feel the situation is more intense or involved than you are prepared for, ask for support. Reach out to administrators, department chairs, or other support staff who may be involved with the student to help provide additional guidance for the discussions. Utilize this support not in an "us versus them" way but as a mediator or liaison to bridge communication gaps.

High-Leverage Practice Alert!

Want to know more about effective meetings with colleagues and families? HLP2 covers ways to support students and meet in such a way that encourages communication.

Keep in mind that some family involvement is either required or best practice when addressing behaviors of students with disabilities. For students with an Individualized Education Program (IEP), discussions about behavior may be directly related to student goals or objectives. If this is the case, the student's case manager, general education teachers, and special education teacher should be involved in those conversations as well. This is especially true if progress is not being made on behavioral goals or placement, accommodations, modifications, or services might be impacted. If this is the case, the team will need to determine whether a conversation about behavior actually needs to be reconvened as an IEP meeting or IEP addendum meeting. It is always best practice to check with your school administrator or administrative designee in these situations. Further, if a teacher believes a student may need a functional behavioral assessment (FBA) or behavioral intervention plan (BIP), it is best practice to bring the student's team together to collect data and develop a plan. Remember, once a student with a disability is excluded from the classroom, even for behavioral challenges, they may not be receiving the services required by law through a free and appropriate education (FAPE) and the Individuals with Disabilities Education Act (IDEA).

Chapters 12 and 13 will tell you all you need to know about FBAs and BIPs. Take a moment to preview those chapters now.

Regardless of the intensity of a student's behavior(s), every effort should be made to maintain a positive relationship with parents and other support staff. Challenging student behaviors can be frustrating and upsetting, but teachers should work to find the balance between feeling safe and supported in their classroom while also respecting students' parents and guardians' family structures as it relates to behavior. This includes asking for support from administration when needed as well as honing in on important communication skills like paraphrasing, summarizing, and monitoring tone and body language. These same communication skills and strategies will also be beneficial to teachers when working with other professionals on individual behavior and classroom management challenges and a few will be further outlined in the subsequent section on coteaching.

High-Leverage Practice Alert!

HLP1 outlines that students' social and emotional learning is best facilitated through collaboration between all staff working with students.

Working with Other Professionals

Teaching should never be done in isolation, and this includes providing instruction to students regarding behaviors. Collaboration among educators involves voluntarily coming together to engage in joint decision making toward goals (Hamilton-Jones & Vail, 2014). If we want positive or prosocial student behavior to transfer from one environment to another or be generalizable, we must have conversations with the other adults who are working with our students. This includes identifying target behaviors in measurable, objective, and observable language; deciding on observation and data collection methods; and identifying strategies for positive behavior change. Without a team approach, a student may receive mixed messages across the school setting.

Students with IEPs will need to have adults who support them collaboratively. Educators must have conversations with one another about the student's behavioral needs, accommodations, or goals. This is particularly true for educators or school staff who may not be familiar with the student. Some of these professionals may include occupational therapists, speech and language pathologists, or behavioral support staff. In some situations, these professionals may work exclusively within your school, but in other situations, they may be employees of the school division or even outside agencies. Given the range of familiarity some of these professionals may have with the student, school, and classroom structures, conversations about students become even more critical if specific behavioral accommodations are needed that may not align with preexisting classroom structures. While some collaboration may need to happen if there are philosophical differences, it is critical that students' IEPs are implemented as written, with fidelity. Given that the IEP is a legal document that was created by a team of individuals responsible for implementation, making changes based on an individual teacher's personal preferences is not permitted. These differences of opinion or mismatches with behavior management philosophies will need to be reconciled within the structure of the IEP team. If you also need to collect behavioral data for a student's IEP or FBA and BIP, these expectations and goals should be discussed early and often with the student's entire team. Providing the team with tools for data collection streamlines the process and allows for quick and accurate identification of an intervention's effectiveness. Such data collection tools can be shared with general and special education teachers as well as with support staff. Efforts should be made to work together to identify an easy and efficient way to collect data.

If you find yourself in an elementary setting where your student is moving from your classroom to lunch, recess, art, music, or physical education, carving out some time for conversations about formal or informal behavior plans with all support staff will ensure student success. Even if a student is only visiting the music room once or twice a week, the music teacher should be made aware of antecedents of a particular child's behavior and how to respond. Without this critical information, the music teacher may inadvertently reinforce a challenging behavior or create a situation that escalates behavior, which is difficult not only for the student but also the teacher and his or her ability to maintain a smooth and uninterrupted lesson. Imagine a team of teachers knows that loud noises are challenging for a first grader named Julia. In fact, when Julia is in an environment with loud noises, she covers her ears, begins crying, and if not addressed immediately, Julia runs away and tries to leave the building. However, if Julia has access to her noise canceling headphones, she is easily able to cope with even the highest noise levels. What would happen if those teachers and school staff on Julia's team didn't share this information with the lunchroom monitor, music teacher, or any other school staff who might work with Julia in situations where the noise level could become problematic? Given that Julia's behaviors could be easily avoidable, a conversation and some collaboration would go a long way!

Secondary settings have a unique challenge when it comes to collaboration about specific students since a single student could have any number of teachers based on their individual schedules. Given this, collaboration is even more important since the student is exposed to so many staff across several classes all day. These collaborative conversations can happen via email, a shared document, or a "mini meeting" that serves the purpose of updating all those who interact with the student in a quick, informational, and direct way. Regardless of how a student's behavioral information is shared, it is not any less important to address in the secondary settings.

Paraprofessionals

In many schools settings, paraprofessionsals are an integral part of a student's educational experience and instruction. Paraprofessionals are found in elementary school through high school and often provide support in special education settings. It is important to remember that not all paraprofessionals have been trained in educational strategies, just as many teachers have not received formal training on supervising paraprofessionals (Douglas, Chapin, & Nolan, 2016). Collaboration with paraprofessionals, just like collaboration with any other professional, will be maximized with respect and shared goal setting (Biggs, Gilson, & Carter, 2016; Knackendoffel, Dettmer, & Thurston, 2018). To best collaborate with paraprofessionals, clarify roles and define the specific tasks that are needed in your classroom. If you need to collect behavioral data on a student, can you enlist the support and help of a paraprofessional to either take that data or teach a small lesson while you collect data? Can the paraprofessional working in your classroom support a student with self-monitoring or provide check-ins for breaks or academic support? What about providing a student with reminders about class rules or expectations, using proximity with students during a lesson, or verbally processing an incident that occurred on the playground? Of course a paraprofessional can provide this support! What is most important is communicating and clarifying roles and needs and taking opportunities to learn together as a collaborative team.

Coteaching Settings

If you are a teacher who gets the pleasure of coteaching, you'll need to find some time to sit down with your coteacher to discuss behavior management. Coteaching involves two teachers working as equals to plan, teach, and evaluate a group of shared students. While coteaching requires collaboration, it is a model of instruction based on parity and shared responsibilities. When two teachers are sharing the same physical space and, ideally, also sharing planning, teaching, and assessing, effective communication is critical. Murawski (2012) suggests discussing the what, how, and who of instruction. This includes what content will be taught, how the content will be delivered, and who in the classroom may need behavioral and/or academic supports. While the level of discussions you will need to engage in will vary based on your individual situation, an overview of questions to discuss is included in Figure 5–2. Use these questions as a springboard for developing a cohesive coteaching classroom management plan.

To make the most of your coteaching experience as it relates to behavior and classroom management, it may be helpful to remember to use active listening

Figure 5–2. Overview of questions and prompts to consider for collaborative coteaching.

Classroom Management Questions and Prompts to Consider with Your Coteacher

1. What are some of your preferred classroom procedures?
    a. The procedures I prefer are . . .
2. What are some of your preferred classroom expectations?
    a. The expectations I prefer are . . .
3. What are some of your preferred classroom rules?
    a. The rules I prefer are . . .
4. What specific classroom policies do you think we should have?
5. What reinforcement strategies do you use?
    a. The reinforcement strategies I use are . . .
    b. How will we both have an equal role in providing reinforcement to students?
6. What consequences do you anticipate using?
    a. The consequences I think are effective and like to use are . . .
    b. How will we both have an equal role in providing consequences to students?
7. What are our roles when a student doesn't follow classroom rules?
8. What are our roles when a student doesn't follow classroom procedures?
9. What are some student behaviors you struggle with monitoring?
    a. The student behaviors I struggle to monitor are . . .
10. What are our roles in a crisis or emergency behavioral situation?
11. How will we convey we are both leaders in the classroom?

strategies, paraphrase what you hear, and summarize discussions at their conclusion. Active listening involves focusing on the speaker, using both verbal and nonverbal acknowledgements of what is being heard. Paraphrasing information from the speaker ensures you are understanding what the speaker is saying and conveys that you are listening. Finally, summarizing discussions to include how each of you will move forward after the conversation outlines any individual responsibilities, addresses any potential misunderstandings, and finalizes the conversation with clarity and closure. Given that individuals often have strong feelings about behavior, it is important to identify how you and a coteacher, or any other professional, can navigate through these potentially difficult conversations.

Working with Administration

Finally, teachers will need to work directly with administrators as classroom and behavior management challenges arise. As mentioned before, an open line of communication will help bring the team together. There are a number of ways in which administrators interact with teachers as it relates to classroom management. These interactions may include, but are not limited to, their role in the development and enforcement of behavior policies; administrative members of an IEP, FBA, and/or BIP team; disciplinarian; and supporter or mediator of difficult situations.

As a teacher new to the field or a teacher new to a school, it will be important to have a direct conversation with your administrators about school policies and expectations around student and classroom behaviors. While all schools or school districts will most likely have codes of conduct, individual schools also have school policies or expectations in place. For example, some schools may have special policies about boarding school buses in the afternoon, using lockers between each class period, playing organized sports at recess, or the use of cell phones during the school day. Knowing these rules, policies, and procedures will ensure that you are helping students make the right decisions and consistently discouraging behaviors that may be problematic. Beyond knowing the policy, it is also necessary to have conversations about procedures for situations that involve infractions.

In light of our previous chapter on PBIS, it is important to know that administrative support is vital to the successful implementation and fidelity of the PBIS framework (Coffey & Horner, 2012; Pinkelman, McIntosh, Rasplica, Berg, & Strickland-Cohen, 2015). For sustainability, a school that is using PBIS should have an administrator who uses data to make PBIS decisions and communicates with school staff, parents, and the community about the PBIS features (Coffey & Horner, 2012). Therefore, if you find yourself in a school practicing PBIS but aren't seeing the follow through from administration, the impact, results, and effectiveness of PBIS will be diminished.

At the classroom level, you will need to decide when, and to what degree, your administration should be involved in an individual student's behavior plans. This may be either a personal decision or your administrators may have clear guidelines on when and how they want to be notified of behavioral challenges. For example, Nikki is repeatedly disrupting Mrs. Wilkerson's fifth period math class by refusing to participate and responding "no" when asked to complete math work. After employing some classroom management strategies to address the behavior, Mrs. Wilkerson might contact her team or Nikki's parents for additional assistance. At what point does Mrs. Wilkerson tell her school administration the behavior is either becoming or has become problematic? While this will be highly variable depending on the individual and school structure, there are some instances that should always warrant administrative notification. If you suspect that a student's behavior may be related to an unidentified disability, you should alert your administrative team of your concerns. If a student has an IEP, FBA, and/ or BIP and the goals aren't being met or you suspect some part of the plan might need to be changed or discussed, a special educator and administrator should be notified of your concerns. If any issues arise with safety, whether this is with the student, other students in the classroom or school, or with your own safety, please notify your administrative team immediately. This is particularly true if students are making verbal or physical threats, engaging in self-harm, or creating situations in which others fear for their own safety. Another instance in which you should provide administration with information is if you find yourself in a situation where a student is so disruptive that instruction is regularly impeded and/or the learning of any of your students is being affected as a result of one student's behavior. If this is happening on a regular and consistent basis, this should be a signal that you need additional support and, at the very least, someone from your administrative team should know this is happening. Finally, seek administration's support if you find yourself in a situation in which a student, or parent, is verbally abusive through threats, name-calling, or bullying. These behaviors are unacceptable and as an educator you have the right to feel safe and respected in your job.

Finally, a word about using your administrators as disciplinarians for challenging behavior. While there will certainly be situations that need immediate attention from your principal or assistant principal, use caution with utilizing the school office as the go-to location for all student disciplinary challenges, especially those that are minor or just annoying in nature. Why? Because the office is a great place to be for a student who wants to avoid the classroom, you as the teacher, peers, and assigned work! It is also a great place to listen in on conversations between adults, front office staff, parents and students, students and principals, and anyone who happens to wander in to have a discussion. Imagine if you were a student in the office how interesting it would be to watch people go in and out of the clinic, listen to phone calls from parents, or hear teachers sharing weekend plans with each other. Of course, there's always the chance you'll be in the office with a fellow student who may or may not have been sent to the office for the same reason you were. You can share stories or lament about how terrible lunch was today!

The front office of any school is a bustling, busy place full of conversation and activity. From a teacher's perspective, think about how much enjoyment a student might get out of being sent to the school's office. Then, once a student move out of the main office area and is with administrators, discussing his or her behavior in individual offices, you are no longer part of the conversation or planning for that student. While this may not be problematic, as a classroom teacher, it's important to know how you can address behaviors in your classroom and without being part of those conversations with the student and principal or assistant principal, you are momentarily, or permanently, out of the loop. To avoid the unnecessary or overuse of your administrators as disciplinarians, communicate about options for challenging behaviors and ask to be part of a team who can help you address the functions of the student's behaviors and teach replacement behaviors. Finally, if you want to be more actively involved in school-wide behavior planning, ask to be part of the Positive Behavioral Intervention and Supports (PBIS) team or inquire about implementing PBIS if your school isn't already using this framework.

Chapters 12 and 13 will dive into identifying functions of behavior and teaching replacement behaviors. Be sure to come back to Chapter 5 to think about how you might use a team approach, to include your administrators, in those important discussions.

Conclusion

Communication about classroom behavior management and individual student challenges may not always happen easily. However, identifying ways to develop partnerships with parents and colleagues will help teachers address some of the more challenging behavior management hurdles. These partnerships can help teachers keep lines of communication open and encourage problem solving from multiple perspectives. Unfortunately, even the best communication cannot address all behavioral challenges in the classroom, so identifying ways to collaborate with colleagues, coteachers, and administrators will also be important. Identifying roles and expectations will provide support and troubleshooting opportunities for the most difficult behavioral challenges.

Chapter Summary

- Instead of viewing parents as adversaries, or opponents, or a person who is disconnected from the school environment, aim to create partnerships with parents and guardians.

- Parent or guardian involvement will take on many forms and be influenced by a number of factors, including family systems, culture, and views on education.

- Communicate privately and often to parents about student behavior. This communication should also include positive feedback.

- Collaboration among educators involves coming together to engage in joint decision making. Collaboration will help develop a cohesive formal or informal behavior plan for students.

- Educators who are in coteaching situations should have direct conversations about all facets of classroom management prior to their coteaching experience.

● Teachers should establish how and when they will communicate concerns about individual or classroom behavioral concerns with administrators. This will be highly variable, dependent on a number of factors.

● Communication with administrators should include school-wide policies and procedures; issues relating to IEPS, FBAs, and BIPs; safety concerns; and incidents involving verbal threats or abuse.

CHAPTER 6

SETTING UP PHYSICAL LEARNING ENVIRONMENTS

Learning Objectives

- Acknowledge strengths and limitations of some classroom layouts and identify ideal physical arrangements to suit student and teacher needs
- List some considerations for student placement and options for how to arrange students for optimal classroom participation
- Identify considerations for movement, access, and safety
- Define learning zones and describe how they can complement classroom management and facilitate student engagement
- Learn how public displays of student behavior can be eliminated

Key Terms

Classroom Climate
Clusters
Horseshoe Arrangement
Learning Zones

Pairs
Rows
Stoplight System

Y ou've been preparing for your new job and have just been assigned your classroom. Maybe you've been teaching for years but are changing grade levels or schools. Now what? As you begin unpacking boxes, it will be important to deliberately plan how your room is physically arranged. The arrangement of your classroom is important for learning, functionality, and safety. Further, these arrangements can also impact the classroom climate and how students relate to one another (McKeown, Stringer, & Cairns, 2015). There are several considerations to keep in mind, including instructional needs, mobility, and routines. The physical space of your classroom can help create an atmosphere that is either inviting or disinviting, calming or chaotic, and organized or disorganized. More importantly, it can encourage better academic and social interactions for students (van den Berg, Segers, & Cillessen, 2012).

Physical Classroom Setup

As you arrange your classroom, you should consider how your students will learn best. If you are in a middle school classroom and you are teaching science, it may make sense to have your students seated at one side of tables so they can see the demonstrations in the front of the room and work with a partner to complete experiments. A high school government teacher may want two clusters of desks facing one another so the class can easily debate and present opposing viewpoints. An elementary teacher will also need to consider where a carpet may be placed in the room or how a reading center will be arranged in a quiet space in the classroom. One of the easiest places to start with classroom arrangement is with the placement of student desks. The following arrangements and individual considerations will help you decide on the best fit for your class.

Horseshoe

The horseshoe arrangement places student desks in a horseshoe or u-shaped formation around the perimeter of the room (Figure 6–1). Depending on the number of students, desks may be in one or two rows or a small row of desks may be placed in the center of the horseshoe, running parallel with the back of the u-shape. Students will either be facing the front of the room or will need to turn sideways to see instruction. This arrangement allows the teacher to access students quickly and directly. In this formation, students tend to talk less to their neighbors because of the openness of the arrangements, but some students may still find facing peers distracting. While partner work can be accomplished easily with a horseshoe, group work will require moving desks. Depending on the size of the room, students may be very spread out, so the teacher may have to work

Figure 6–1. Horseshoe arrangement for student desks.

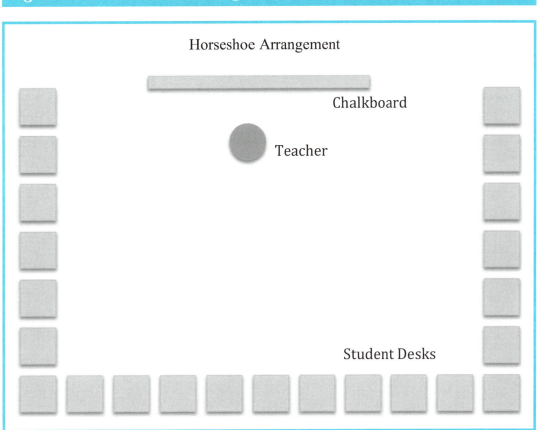

across the room or speak very loudly to reach all learners. Finally, if using this formation, teachers should consider creating openings within the horseshoe for access behind student desks.

Rows

Rows of desks position students' desks side by side, touching one another to form a straight line (Figure 6–2). Desks can be placed facing straight at the front of the room or at an angle. This formation allows all students to face the front of the room while taking up a limited amount of floor space. A benefit of this arrangement is that students are easily able to work with partners, who are sitting nearby. Rows of desks may be a challenge if students have difficulty maintaining personal space or keeping their hands and feet to themselves. The close proximity of desks may also be difficult for some students who are easily distracted by their peers. If desks are placed in rows spaced far enough apart, this arrangement allows teachers easy access to students in a quick and efficient manner. However,

Figure 6–2. Rows arrangement for student desks.

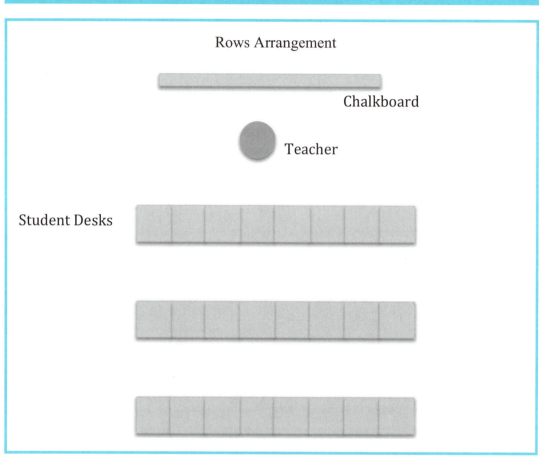

Rows Arrangement

Chalkboard

Teacher

Student Desks

if rows are clustered together, reaching some students beyond the front row may be challenging.

Clusters or Groups

Typically, a cluster or group includes four to six student desks pushed together in a square or rectangle shape (Figure 6–3). In this arrangement, less floor space may be used, which is an ideal arrangement for a small room. This would be conducive to movement around the room, as teachers walk between and within groups. This configuration supports cooperative group work or peer tutoring since students are already seated together. With this configuration, not all students may be facing the front of the room, or some students may have to turn sideways in their seats. Just as group work is made easier with this arrangement, so is socialization and talking. While it is important to consider academics when assigning seating arrangements, it is also important to consider social functioning (Farmer, Lines, & Hamm, 2011).

Figure 6–3. Clusters/group arrangement for student desks.

Clusters/Groups Arrangement

Chalkboard

Teacher

Student Desks

Some students may find facing a peer, or multiple peers, too distracting. During test taking or independent work, teachers may need to have privacy boards to encourage privacy and to reduce distractions.

 High-Leverage Practice Alert!

HLP17 discusses using flexible grouping for instruction and learning. Take this information into consideration when establishing groups or clusters in your classroom arrangements.

Pairs

Student desks can also be placed in pairs versus large rows or clusters or groups. Pairs requires more floor space than rows or clusters (Figure 6–4). In pairs, all students can be seated facing forward with desks either parallel to the front of the

Figure 6–4. Pairs arrangement for student desks.

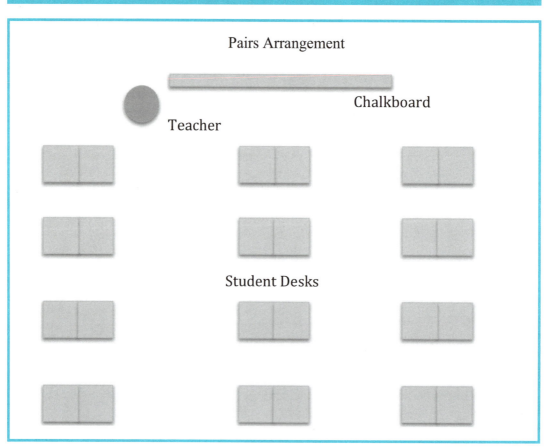

Pairs Arrangement

Chalkboard

Teacher

Student Desks

room or angled to create more space in the center of the classroom. Paired seating is helpful for cooperative learning and if arranged in rows, students can easily turn around to form groups quickly. Students who may need additional supports socially may benefit from sitting with a peer who has mastery of rules and procedures (van den Berg & Stotlz, 2018). The level of peer distraction in pairs will be less than groups, but students will still be seated directly next to peers, so a degree of distractibility may still exist.

Individual Desks

Finally, students may be placed at individual desks in a traditional row arrangement. Teachers have reported that this arrangement is often a starting place at the beginning of the school year so they can establish procedures and routines first (Gremmen, van den Berg, Segers, & Cillessen, 2016). Of all the arrangements, this

requires the most space in the classroom. Given that secondary classrooms typically do not have carpet areas or as many centers, individual desk formations are more feasible. With this arrangement, students have their own physical space and may experience fewer distractions. It should be noted, however, that this arrangement will result in fewer visual interactions with students who are further in proximity to the teacher's instructional area unless there is significant teacher movement around the classroom (Cardellino, Araneda, & Alvarado, 2017). However, teachers are able to move freely throughout the room if desks are arranged in neat rows. This allows for more "withitness" because teachers are able to see what all students are doing. While the opportunities for talking during instruction are reduced, this also means that students cannot easily work together in pairs or groups without moving desks.

> *Go back to Chapter 1 for a reminder about Kounin's ideas on "withitness."*

Tables

Depending on your resources, you may also opt to use tables instead of individual desks. Tables would pose similar benefits and drawbacks as clusters or groups. One additional benefit of tables is the reduced levels of distraction that may result from materials housed inside desks. At tables, students can easily work together in an existing group or move to another table with minimal disruption, since belongings will be kept in another location in the room. Using tables requires storage areas for each students' books and personal belongings; however, this may be ideal for students in secondary settings as they are not required to store materials in each classroom.

Individual Considerations

Although academics is the most common driving force for room arrangements, teachers may also need to consider classroom management needs, students' social interactions, and individual student characteristics (Gremmen et al., 2016). Once you have an idea about the way you want to arrange your classroom, you'll need to figure out how to plan for assigning seats and how you need to address individual student needs. Some students may need preferential seating or seating that supports individualized learning or behavioral needs. For example, Weston may be easily distracted by external stimuli. This doesn't necessarily mean he needs to sit in the front of the classroom but rather in a location in the classroom that doesn't face the hallway, windows, or groups of other students. Given each students' individual needs, arrangements may need to shift throughout the school year. There are a number of classroom design planning tools available online. More low technology options include drawing the classroom dimensions and using differently sized sticky notes for desks and tables, which lend themselves easily to manipulation and movement.

Websites

Classroom Architect: http://classroom.4teachers.org/

Scholastic Tools: http://teacher.scholastic.com/tools/class_setup/

Classroom Floor Planner: https://www.kaplanco.com/resources/floor planner.asp

Virtual Room Designer: https://www.thelibrarystore.com/library_ layouts

SmartDraw: https://www.smartdraw.com/seating-chart/templates/ grade-school-classroom-layout/

Given all of the aforementioned considerations, you may be wondering whether you really want to assign seats or allow students to choose their own seat, particularly in secondary settings. While choice is almost always appealing to students, teachers should make this decision with care and deliberation. Given that students may self-select less than ideal seating for their needs or place themselves near peers who don't support optimal classroom engagement, this may be impractical. However, once the classroom climate has been established and peer-to-peer relationships have been respectfully defined, open or optional seating may be worth exploring.

Finally, if you are coteaching with a general or special educator, it is important to consider where students who receive accommodations and modifications will be seated within the classroom. While a teacher certainly doesn't want to call attention to an individual student, some consideration should be placed on making sure students are easily accessible to receive support. For example, if a student needs frequent check-ins, you should consider a seat at the end of a row or the edge of a horseshoe. If multiple students need support, these students should not necessarily be seated together as a pair or cluster but in proximity to one another (e.g., back-to-back or tables beside each other), so teachers can easily move between pairs or groups.

Considerations for Movement and Safety

Regardless of the arrangement you select, teachers need to consider if and how they can move through the classroom, accessing all students and the classroom door in the case of an emergency. Given instructional needs and potential behavioral challenges, teachers should be able to walk directly to any students' desk without difficulty. As desks and instructional areas are placed around the room, teachers should also be cognizant of movement to the classroom door in case of an emergency. Access should be direct and easy and free of obstacles and clutter.

In addition to being able to physically reach all students, you will also need to consider how students can move around the room. Can all students get to the pencil sharpener, trashcan, bathroom, and the classroom door without bumping into other students' desks or the teacher's desk? Are students able to directly access your desk or your personal items in the classroom? Consider being a student seated in various locations in your classrooms and evaluate their access to key areas in the room.

Learning Zones

In addition to arranging student desks and your own personal space, it is important to design a room that reflects the needs of the classroom. By creating "learning zones" in your classroom, students learn what to expect in each of the designated classroom areas and you can easily organize your materials for specific tasks and instruction. For example, if you create a corner of your classroom for reading complete with book choices and comfortable seating, students will learn that this is the area for the specified activity and, consequently, begin to anticipate the required tasks when asked to go to that area. A reading zone would be a place where you could store books, post strategies for reading comprehension, and set up additional supports like noise-blocking headphones, bookmarks, and flashlights for reading. Developing and explaining the idea that each zone comes with specific expectations and behaviors is one way to utilize an organized and structured environment to support behavioral choices.

Setting up zones in your classroom also allows you, as the teacher, to create rules and expectations for behaviors you expect in that area. If a student is in the reading zone, they should be sitting quietly with a book in hand. If they are at the work table zone, they should expect that they will be working with a teacher or peers on individualized instruction or cooperative group work. These zones also provide students with predictability since students know what to expect when they are in a specific area of the classroom. Finally, zones help students understand and learn about physical boundaries. If a zone is only used with adult supervision (e.g., glass beaker zone in science), then this can be clearly communicated and expectations can be set.

> *In the next chapter you'll learn more about procedures, expecatations, and rules. Keep these zones in mind when reading Chapter 7.*

Zones in your classroom will most likely vary based on whether you are in an elementary or secondary setting, the needs of your students, and the number of students who are in your classroom. Some zones to consider include a group instructional zone, a teacher work zone, work stations other than individual student desks, computer or technology zone, a cooldown zone for students who need space, and a transitional zone for movement in or out of the classroom. Students who may have special equipment may also require storage space in your classroom and this will need to be considered as you design your classroom. Finally, if you are coteaching with another professional, it is also important to create a zone for that second teacher where they can work and store materials.

When thinking about zones in your classroom, you may also need to consider smaller, distinct areas for day-to-day activities. For all classrooms, teachers should consider where students will store their materials during class, where notes or homework can be turned in, how tardy slips will be submitted or stored, and where bathroom passes will be located. For elementary school settings, where will students hang backpacks, complete lunch choices, and store snacks or water

bottles? In secondary classrooms, where will you store materials that must stay in your classroom for each class period?

One way for teachers to check whether clear zones have been established is to invite another professional into the classroom and ask them to identify the activities they believe would occur in each area of your classroom. If another teacher can clearly identify which activities occur where, you have successfully created an environment that supports the learning goals you have designed. Should this be difficult for another teacher to identify, consider that this identification would also be challenging for students and, consequently, students may not know what to expect in your classroom zones.

Additional Considerations

We've all seen photos of imaginative and elaborately decorated classrooms floating around on the internet. Their spinning flowers, cauldrons, and ceiling fixtures are amazing and creative. However, some students will find this elaborate decor to be more distracting than fun or interesting. It's important to remember that any stimuli, whether interesting and creative or messy and boring, can be a diversion for students, particularly those who struggle with attention deficit hyperactivity disorder (ADHD) or those who are easily distractible. Therefore, be selective and deliberate with classroom decorations. Use wall space as a teaching tool. What is the most important for your students to see when they look up from their work for a mental break? What strategies, ideas, or reminders can you post? Consider the meaningfulness of the decorations on your walls, ceilings, and in your classroom space. Some ideas to consider include classroom rules or expectations, school mottos, homework reminders, school news, instructional strategies or templates (e.g., how to write a paragraph, how to format a lab report), resources (e.g., periodic table, multiplication tables), or student work samples.

While it is impossible to keep a classroom organized every single day, consider how a disorganized environment may act as a stressor for your students with executive functioning (EF) challenges, ADHD, and anxiety. For students who have difficulty keeping themselves and their brains organized, a chaotic external environment may only compound their individual challenges. This isn't to say you have to have a perfect room, but organization of materials, papers, books, and supplies must be a consideration as we work with children who may be challenged by external stimuli. The process of arranging a classroom is just that, a process. You may realize you need to rearrange student desks or zones periodically based on instructional or student needs. A list of questions to consider is outlined (Figure 6–5).

Classroom Climate

Classroom climate has been linked to student motivation (Hughes & Coplan, 2017) and student engagement (Wang & Degol, 2016). Therefore, it is worth discussing public displays of student behavior and behavioral progress. Perhaps you've been inside an elementary classroom and seen a system like a "stoplight" or some other variation that involves color coding individual student behavior. Or perhaps there weren't colors involved but instead a scale of words like "excellent," "good," "okay," or "poor choice" with students' names written on clips. Students are often told to "clip up" or "clip down" using these public charts in response to their behavioral choices. In the secondary settings, perhaps you've walked into classrooms where students' names are written on the board; a list of "misbehavers" for everyone to see. Whether it's a traditional stoplight that uses red, yellow, and green indicators of behavior; an ice cream cone with four colored scoops; or a list of student names posted for everyone to see, publicly displaying students'

Figure 6–5. Questions to consider regarding classroom arrangement.

Questions to ask about classroom arrangement:

1. How many students will I have in my classroom? What are my resources? Number and sizes of desks? Number and sizes of chairs? Tables? Carpet area?

2. Do I have special equipment I will need to store for specific students?

3. Can I see my students at all times in every area of the room?

4. Will students be distracted by the amount of materials on the ceiling or walls of my classroom?

5. Does my classroom have clearly identified zones?

6. Is my classroom arranged in such a way that I can easily access the door?

7. Can I move around the room easily to reach every student?

8. Are students' desks distraction free from hallway, bathroom, and outdoor stimuli?

9. Do my students have easy access to necessary materials?

10. Do I have a location to store my students' personal items (e.g., backpacks, lunch bags, notebooks)?

11. Do I have a secure location in my room to store personal items and confidential student information?

behavior is not an effective way to teach students new, more socially desirable behaviors. In fact, there is no clear evidence that suggests that these systems are an effective means of eliciting or maintaining behavioral change. Further, these systems may actually damage teacher-student relationships as both confidentiality and dignity may be violated.

Imagine walking into work tomorrow and your name, along with all of your colleague's names, are posted in the lobby of your building. Further, imagine each rule infraction you have engaged in posted next to your name. Of course, you knew the behavior you engaged in at the time was not okay, but you were having a tough day, or you were sick, or, frankly, maybe you were just done with work that day. Maybe you didn't realize it was a rule at your current work because it wasn't ever explained to you? Perhaps some of your coworkers even knew about your behaviors. Would any of those factors lessen the sting of having your name and the infraction posted publicly? Would it make you want to change your behavior because you learned a new, replacement behavior, or would it be because you didn't want to be embarrassed again in the future? Further, how would you feel about your principal after walking in to see all of your behavioral choices posted for your colleagues and parents to see? While most of us would most likely admit that this would not be a desirable work environment, some educators routinely do this very thing to children who are learning developmentally appropriate norms and seeking opportunities to develop independence with their behavior. Given that when the classroom climate is supportive, caring, and positive, students learn more (Rubie-Davies, 2014), these systems should be used with the utmost caution.

 High-Leverage Practice Alert!

HLP8 and HLP20 note that students should receive constructive, positive feedback to help improve learning and behavior. Given this, carefully consider how public displays of behavioral progress impact student motiviation and engagement.

Rather than displaying individual student behavior in your classroom with lists of names or colored charts with clips, consider alternative methods of discreet data collection and/or positive reinforcement systems. Positive Behavioral Intervention and Supports (PBIS) is a great place to start, focusing on clear procedures, expectations, and rules in conjunction with positive supports. This framework can include ticket systems, class "money," or group rewards. Other options include private systems that focus on discussing behaviors with students, teaching social skills, individual rule infraction cards that can be handed to students, conferences with students, or individual data collection done by the teacher using behaviors that mimic class expectations or conduct requirements on the school report card. Whatever method of behavioral monitoring you select, be sure to maintain a positive classroom climate by considering how displays of students' behavioral choices impact your students' relationships with one another, you, and guests who may enter your classroom.

Review PBIS in Chapter 4 for information on setting up your classroom using a positive framework. Then, peek ahead to Chapter 9 on developing relationships with students.

Conclusion

Carefully considering how your classroom is designed will assist you with not only the delivery of instruction but also with behavior management. Be mindful of how you want your students to interact with you, one another, and the classroom environment as you create seating charts and organize your materials. This is particularly true in light of students' ages, social skills, and instructional needs. Further, creating an environment that is organized and predictable for your students will help them know what to expect in your classroom. Finally, while monitoring student behavior can be a challenge, publicly posting students' behaviors does not actually change behavior and could instead be addressed through other, more private means. Ultimately, your classroom is the place where you and your students will spend the majority of your day, so creating an environment that is organized and positive benefits everyone.

Chapter Summary

- The physical layout of a classroom is an important factor to how students learn; being mindful and planning out the arrangement of the physical space and the placement of students can facilitate participation and support effective classroom management.

- Considerations such as student age/grade, subject matter, instructional delivery, and access to resources factor into classroom layout.

- Individual students must also be taken into consideration when arranging a classroom as some may need preferential seating due to behavioral needs, access to learning supports, or physical needs.

- A well-arranged classroom allows for seamless physical movement throughout, which is required to ensure everyone's safety, support instructional needs, and maintain effective classroom management.

- Creating learning zones helps students understand classroom expectations and physical boundaries, while supporting teachers to remain organized.

- Classroom decor should be kept simple and functional to ensure it is not distracting. Wall space may be used as a teaching tool to post up relevant materials, strategies, and reminders.

- Public displays of student behavior do not teach students new, more desirable replacement behaviors. Student behavior should be monitored and recorded in such a way that maintains confidentiality and dignity.

CHAPTER 7

SETTING UP THE CLASSROOM

Procedures, Expectations, Rules, and Prompt Hierarchies

Learning Objectives

- Define the purpose of classroom procedures and how to identify where and when procedures are required
- Describe how to teach classroom procedures
- Define classroom expectations and identify how they differ from classroom rules
- Identify key tenets about classroom rules
- Describe how to develop and teach effective rules
- Define hierarchy of prompts and understand its link to classroom expectations and rules

Key Terms

Expectations
Gesture Prompt
Hierarchy of Prompts
Physical Prompt

Procedures
Rules
Verbal Prompt

I n Chapter 4 we discussed Positive Behavioral Intervention and Supports (PBIS), which included expectations, procedures and routines, and reinforcement. When the PBIS framework is used school wide, it should also be used in the classroom setting. While PBIS does not only specifically focus on the classroom setting, classroom rules and expectations create specific routines out of overarching and global school-wide frameworks (Gable, Hester, Rock, & Huges, 2009). There are additional supports classroom teachers can use to develop and design their classroom management systems outside of PBIS or in conjunction with PBIS. Given that academic and social behaviors are improved with more classroom structure (Simonsen, Fairbanks, Briesch, Myers, & Sugai, 2008), it's important to outline how this structure can be developed.

 High-Leverage Practice Alert!

The following sections directly coincide with HLP7, covering culturally responsive expectations, procedures, routines, and rules!

Establishing Procedures

When considering time investment in setting up a classroom, one of the primary areas of focus should be establishing classroom procedures. As shown in the time investment triangle, when thinking about procedures, expectations, and rules, the majority of setup should be on procedures. Let's explain. Just like PBIS, procedures, or routines, help students know what is expected of them and how the classroom runs. As a teacher, these procedures make your job easier because students become acquainted with the day-to-day routines and can become self-sufficient. Effective procedures describe the steps necessary for successfully or completely completing a task or routine. In the end, these should begin to establish themselves as patterns of behavior. The goal should be a classroom that mimics an effective and efficient "well-oiled machine," only needing a little greasing, or reminding, now and then but otherwise working so well together that intervention isn't necessary. If all of these procedures are in place, you'll need to spend less time and energy on reviewing expectations and enforcing rules (Figure 7–1).

When thinking about procedures, there is no limit to the type or number of routines a classroom teacher can implement (Figure 7–2 provides examples). Procedures can include daily activities and routines as well as less frequent tasks or events. While each school year may bring new challenges and new procedures,

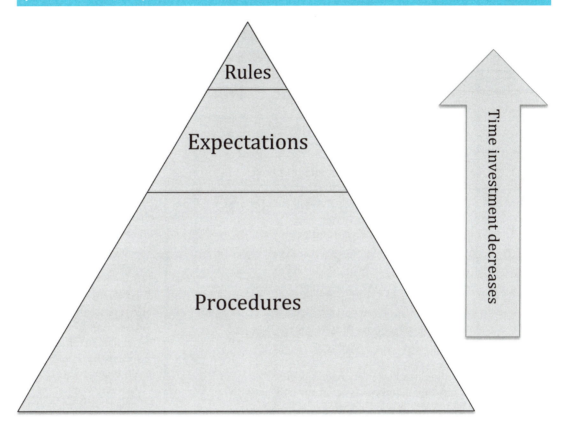

Figure 7–1. Time investment triangle for establishing classroom procedures, expectations, and rules.

many will remain the same from year to year. When thinking about the types of procedures you will need in your classroom, you can approach this in several ways. One way is to think about the procedures you will need in the zones of your room or school (e.g., zones like reading areas, group work tables, desks, storage areas, water fountains, bathrooms, playgrounds, lockers, or hallways). Another way procedures are often developed is by identifying specific areas of need during instruction and transition. For example, how will you gain the attention of the whole class after an activity? How and where should students return completed work? What is the test-taking procedure in your classroom? What happens if a student needs a pencil during small or large group instruction? Finally, procedures are often needed for organizational purposes. These procedures might include how you will take attendance, how students will make lunch choices at the start of the school day, steps for fire or other safety drills, and where students will store personal belongings or school materials in your classroom. The potential procedure list is endless.

Figure 7–2. Sample classroom procedures across settings.

Sample Classroom Procedures for Elementary Settings

* Lining up for transitions or dismissal
* Making lunch choices upon arrival
* Storing backpacks and lunch bags
* Sharing class supplies or toys
* Use of equipment on the playground
* Ending the school day
* Desk organization
* Bringing personal items and toys to school
* What to do with notes from home
* Coming to, sitting on, leaving the carpet area
* Completing classroom jobs
* Getting ready for recess and/or lunch
* How to find games for indoor recess
* When to tell a teacher there is a problem

Sample Classroom Procedures for Secondary Settings

* Going to a locker after class begins
* Coming into the class after the bell rings
* Leaving early for sporting events or clubs
* Ending the class period/class dismissal
* Going to the school library for resources
* Class binder and/or notebook organization
* Cell phone usage
* Makeup work for absences (to include classwork and tests quizzes)
* Policy for staying after school with the teacher
* Using agenda books
* Coming to class prepared
* Movement around the classroom (especially lab areas)

Sample Classroom Procedures for All Settings

* Entering the classroom
* Fire, tornado, lockdown drills
* Using the bathroom during instruction
* Getting the teacher's attention
* Eating and drinking in class
* Asking for, using, and returning supplies (pencils, scissors, etc.)
* Attending to morning and afternoon announcements
* Turning in completed work
* Getting help from the teacher
* Using the pencil sharpener
* Discarding trash
* Expected visitors come to the classroom
* Unexpected visitors come to the classroom
* A classmate or teacher gets sick
* Options for free or down time
* Computer usage
* Emergency situation protocols
* Transitions from one activity to another
* How to engage in group work
* What to do with unfinished work
* Going to the nurse or school clinic
* Regaining students' attention after an activity
* Contributing to a class discussions
* Independent, partner, and group noise levels
* Getting out of assigned seats or designated areas

Should you struggle to figure out what procedures you may need in your class-room, consider one of the following exercises. First, create a schedule of your entire day (Figures 7–3 and 7–4 provide examples). Include transitions like lunch, recess, labs, or locker breaks, depending on your grade level and school schedule. As you review your schedule, ask yourself, what do I assume students will be able to do during these times? Consider how students will move through your room,

Elementary Daily Schedule with Procedures Examples

Mrs. Gail's 4th Grade Daily Schedule	Possible Procedures Needed
8:20 – 8:40 Arrival & Morning Warm-Up	(where to hang backpacks, how to make lunch choices, where to put notes from home, taking attendance)
8:40 – 9:00 Calendar and Morning Circle	(how to come to carpet, where to sit on carpet, how to participate during group discussion)
9:00 – 11:00 Language Arts	(passing out and collecting books, volume level during small groups, how to do an independent station)
11:00 – 12:00 Math	(how to get math manipulatives, rotation of students to the restroom before lunch, clean up of table areas)
12:00 – 12:40 Lunch	(collecting lunch bags from the cubbies, where to line up, order of buyers and packers in the line)
12:40 – 1:10 Recess	(transition from lunch to recess, how to get desired equipment from the storage bin, winter clothing considerations)
1:10 – 1:50 Science	(storage of science materials, safety protocols with equipment, student use of the document camera)
1:50 – 2:35 Specials	(retrieving library books on library day, hallway behavior, using the water fountain in the hallway)
2:35 – 3:10 Social Studies	(recording daily work in planner, group-work responsibilities, interactive notebook setup)
3:10 – 3:20 Pack up and Dismissal	(take home folder pickup, afternoon announcement procedures, bus call)

Figure 7–4. Sample secondary daily schedule with procedures.

Secondary Daily Schedule with Procedures Example

Mr. William's 9th Grade Math Block Schedule	Possible Procedures Needed
10 minutes: Arrival & Morning Warm-Up	(free/assigned seating options, getting forgotten/ missing supplies, how to complete warm-up activities)
15 minutes: Homework Review	(how to make corrections, where to turn in homework, movement around the room during transition)
15 minutes: New Content Instruction	(how to get the teacher's attention, note-taking in math binders, use of technology to include cell phones)
10 minutes: Guided Practice	(use of calculators, process for sharpening pencils, student use of whiteboards)
15 minutes: Independent Practice	(volume level during independent work, what a student can do if they need help, checking in on all students for understanding)
10 minutes: Wrap-Up Questions & Exit Slips	(writing homework in agendas, completing exit slips and turning them in, dismissal from the class)

the materials they will use or need to access, how they will need to interact with other students or teachers, how you will move your students from one activity or location to another, or what ways you will manage instruction.

Another activity that may be helpful is to think about procedures in terms of desired behaviors and signals you will use to prompt students to follow these routines. Using a think sheet (Figure 7–5), walk through deciding on a desired behavior, creating a procedure, outlining how it can be taught, and then developing a signal to assist with the procedure completion. This process could be used for any number of sticky situations in your classroom and allows you a chance to imagine how it could and would look in your classroom setting.

Once procedures have been identified as necessary, the next step includes identifying, step by step, what that procedure looks like. This includes steps that students need to accomplish to be successful. For example, suppose Mrs. Stribling

What Do I Want Students to Do?	What Procedure Do I Need?	How Will I Teach the Procedure?	What Signal Can I Use for This Procedure?
Example: *Students need to line up at the door in a straight line, facing forward.*	*Put adhesive dots on the floor for each student to stand on. Call each table group to the line to stand on dots. Hands should be to the sides of each student's body. Students should be facing the door.*	*Show students each dot. Explain how tables will be called. Explain how students should walk to the dots on the floor. Show students how to stand, facing forward, with arms at their sides. A few select students stand in line for modeling purposes.*	*Put one hand up in air to get students' attention. Say "line up time." Teach students to chorally respond, "Line up? Okay." This is the cue for students to stop talking and listen for table numbers.*
Example: *Students need to label papers with names and period numbers before turning them in to the homework bin.*	*Create two homework bins. One bin will be for papers with names and periods and one bin will be for papers without names and periods.*	*All students will be shown the two bins in the classroom. They will be instructed to select one bin per homework submission. Each student will be called up to practice selecting a bin.*	*Label each bin. On one bin create a label that says, "Homework with Names and Periods Labeled." The second bin will be labeled, "Homework Without Names or Periods Labeled."*

notices that her students have difficulty lining up when it's time to go to recess. Since the students are currently all running to the door to be the first to go outside, she knows a procedure is necessary. She wants her students to wait to be called to line up and decides on the following steps to accomplish this task:

1. Mrs. Stribling will give the 2-min warning that the line-up transition is coming.

2. At 30 s, Mrs. Stribling will begin counting backward.

3. At the 30 s countdown, students should begin putting materials in their desks or baskets.

4. Students should sit quietly, with hands on their desks when they are ready to go outside.

5. Mrs. Stribling will call tables who have materials put away and are sitting quietly.

6. When tables are called, students should quietly stand up.

7. Students should push their chair completely under their desk.

8. Students should quietly walk to the blue line in front of the classroom door.

9. Finally, students should quietly stand in line, hands to their side, facing forward until the whole class is lined up.

While this may seem like a lot of steps for a simple activity, imagine the order it will restore in Mrs. Stribling's classroom at recess time. Once these steps have been established and described to students, they will need to be explicitly taught, practiced, and reinforced to be effective.

In the secondary setting, students may need a procedure for entering class. While the process of developing, teaching, practicing, and reinforcing may be the same, the steps may be fewer but more detailed. For example, a procedure for entering class may include the following:

1. Walk into class quietly.

2. Find your seat and sit down before the bell rings.

3. Place all books and materials under your desk and out of the aisle.

4. Start warm up on the corresponding day labeled in your composition notebook.

As you decide how these procedures will look in your classroom, keep the creative juices flowing and make those procedures fun. If you need 10 min each morning without any interruption from students so you can submit attendance and lunch counts, create a procedure that includes wearing a crown for "King Time" or "Queen Time." The crown can be your signal that you should only be interrupted for absolute emergencies. Or, if you are a middle school teacher and you want to give your students opportunities to not be called on during class discussions, provide stickers or place cards for desks that have smiles or frowns that only the teacher can see from the front of the room. If you're not particularly creative, ask your students how they might want to complete a routine or create a procedure for everyday activities. By creating a procedure they enjoy or have created, students will also be more invested in the process.

Like most new information you introduce in the classroom, you will need to teach these procedures to your students. It is not uncommon for teachers to spend the first few days, or even the first week of school, directly instructing students on the "how to" of the classroom. Although it may feel tedious or unnecessary, writing out the steps for procedures that students may not have practiced before will ensure success. This investment in time up front will save you time in the long run as students engage in classroom procedures and routines independently of your instruction or supervision. To keep these procedures intact, it will be necessary to positively reinforce students as they practice and successfully complete each routine in the classroom.

In conclusion, as you begin to think about setting up your classroom, or as you think about starting your 18th year of teaching, you can ask yourself the following questions:

- **Do I need a procedure?**
- **Why do I need to create this procedure?**
- **Where would this procedure apply?**
- **When would the class need this procedure?**
- **What is the procedure? What are the steps to completing the procedure successfully?**
- **Who will teach this procedure?**
- **Who will need to learn this procedure?**
- **When will this procedure be taught?**
- **How will I know the class has learned this procedure?**

Establishing Expectations

When reviewing the triangle on time investment, the next area of focus after procedures should be expectations. Expectations are reasonable and necessary desired behaviors or outcomes in an environment. They identify, define, and operationalize concepts of desirable behavior. While procedures outline how to navigate routines in the classroom, expectations quantify or qualify the degree to which those procedures, and other requirements, are expected. Expectations are the standards to which students and teachers are held. Imagine you are going to a restaurant to eat, the procedure for entering the restaurant includes a sign that states, "Please wait for the hostess to be seated." Therefore, you know that this restaurant's routine is for customers not to seat themselves and instead wait to be seated. An expectation, however, is that you are not standing in the front of the restaurant repeatedly yelling, "Hostess, come seat me! Hostess!" This expectation was most likely taught to you as a child by parents, guardians, or other role models. You may have also learned it by observing others in the restaurant, watching how they stood quietly, waiting for the hostess to return. In this manner, you picked up on the social norms. In the classroom, we don't want to assume that students will just "pick up" social norms or that they instinctively know what is expected of them. This is especially true given the wide range of backgrounds of our students and their individual exposure to a range of familial, cultural, and/or gender-based expectations. While each teacher should examine their own biases in respect to culture, expectations can be established universally in the context of school success. In other words, while we must be aware of our students' backgrounds, we can also require and expect that all students will be kind to one another, without yelling or name calling, so that the classroom can be a safe and welcoming environment.

To further understand expectations, consider the repercussions of not following or meeting an expectation. If you were in the restaurant, you probably wouldn't be asked to leave if you only yelled out to get the hostess' attention. Most likely, the entire restaurant would be looking at you or perhaps a manager would tell you not to yell. Similarly, if a student in your classroom didn't meet your expectation to be kind to other students, you would most likely give them a reminder, ask them to practice kindness, reteach them necessary skills, or redirect their behavior. Expectations are different than rules, which we will talk about in the next section, because there aren't necessarily enforceable consequences for not meeting expectations. Often, not meeting expectations is met by social isolation or exclusion, disappointment from adults or peers, reminders, or redirection. Expectations might include nonobjective or nonobservable behaviors that need to be operationalized for students. For example, Miss Layne might tell her students she expects them to "be respectful" of each other. Since the definition of respect will vary widely among her students, she will need to explain what respect looks like and sounds like.

> *See Chapter 12 for more on operational definitions.*

Some examples of other expectations might include being honest, coming to class prepared, treating each other kindly, or being a responsible learner.

By teaching expectations, we can anticipate that students will be more academically engaged and have fewer incidents of disruptive behavior (Lane, Wehby, & Menzies, 2003). To teach expectations, we need to explain to students what is expected of them in our classrooms. An easy way to introduce expectations to students in your class is to explain that expectations are what students need to do to be successful. Given our need to be culturally sensitive to differences, one way to start the conversation would be to ask students how students and teachers should treat each other. Once this question is posed, teachers can allow students to brainstorm ideas while the teacher creates a comprehensive list. Finally, as a class, ideas can be condensed and refined until the class has developed a list of expectations. Like everything we've discussed in this book, these expectations will need to be taught, practiced, and reinforced, especially at the start of the school year.

 High-Leverage Practice Alert!

See HLP9 for teaching social behaviors, including those that align with behavioral expectations.

Establishing Rules

Finally, after time and focus has been spent on developing procedures and expectations, teachers should establish rules. In the PBIS framework, enforceable rules are explicitly taught to students (Reinke, Herman, & Stormont, 2013). Rules should be few in number (Simonsen et al., 2008) and should be stated positively (Gable et al., 2009; Hester, Hendrickson, & Gable, 2009). Ideally, four rules are easiest for students to remember (Cowan, 2001) and these rules should be consistent with school policies. While this may not seem like enough, it's important to remember a few key tenets about rules. First, rules are a way for students to monitor their own behavior (don't overwhelm them with more than they can keep track of on their own). Second, rules are reminders for students about expected behavior (keep procedures and expectations in the forefront of your time and teaching). Finally, if rules are broken, there should be consequences; otherwise, why do we have rules we don't enforce? It would seem like a rule without a consequence is really a classroom expectation. Are you wondering, why does it matter? Isn't this just semantics? It matters because as teachers, we should be focused on reinforcing positive behaviors and managing our time in such a way that we aren't spending our day doling out consequences without teaching the behaviors we want to see. While some behaviors certainly require us to address them in the moment and provide subsequent consequences, it is a much more effective use of time to determine what behaviors absolutely require consequences versus those that are really expectations and can be addressed through nonverbal or verbal reminders or opportunities to practice new skills. With all that being said, let's talk about how to develop and construct rules.

Often it is helpful to think about rules in terms of absolutes. What is absolutely not safe in your classroom? What absolutely disrupts the learning of all students in the class? When you think in terms of optimal safety and learning, you'll find that rules like "keep hands and feet to yourself" and "stay in your assigned area" might come to mind. These are rules that would require consequences if broken. A student cannot push, pinch, or kick another student because this violates other students' safety and most likely the school's overall conduct plan. Leaving a classroom or the building without permission also creates safety and learning concerns and will need to be addressed. These are great examples of enforceable and realistic classroom rules. While seasoned teachers may have a general idea of rules they want in their classroom, new teachers may not know where to begin. As new teachers think about the rules, it may also be helpful to think in broad categories. What rules might you want that include the use of materials, respectful behavior, work completion, classroom engagement, participation, and student responsibility? In the end, all rules should still come back to learning and safety, with enforceable consequences. Another way to think about rules is to think about behavioral pairs (Kauffman, Mostert, Trent, & Pullen, 2006). Teachers can identify a behavior of concern demonstrated by students or the class and then identify an incompatible positive behavior. That positive behavior, a replacement behavior, can become a rule.

Like expectations, involving the class in rule development promotes buy-in from students and increases the likelihood that they will be invested in the process because they understand the value of the rules they helped create. Prior to this class discussion, you may want to personally and privately identify some rules that address safety and learning. Keeping those in mind, open up a classroom discussion about what rules students feel are necessary for creating an environment that promotes learning and safety. Using your own list as well as the ideas from students, you can begin to craft classroom rules as a group.

When creating rules, there are a couple key points to remember, the "rules of rules," if you will. First, be positive. Rules should be written in such a way that tells students what they should be doing or what is expected. For example, instead of a rule that says "Don't run," rephrase it positively to tell students what you do want them to do. A better rule would include the word "walk" since this is the desired behavior. Next, be specific. If walk is better than run, then "walk inside the building" is even better. Finally, make sure the rules are measurable, objective, and observable (MOO). Students should be able to see the rule and know exactly what is expected of them. Going back to our example, "walk inside the building" could also include "walk inside the building with hands to your sides."

At this point it should be well established that rules should be taught systematically and explicitly. In fact, clearly communicated rules promote desired behaviors (Tanol, Johnson, McComas, & Cote, 2010). There are several ways to accomplish this goal. One way to encourage buy-in from students and help them understand the importance of rules and their role in following them is to construct a rights and responsibilities grid (Figure 7–6).

Using each rule, ask students the following prompts: "Because we have the rule <insert rule here>, I have the right to . . . " and "Because we have the rule <insert rule here>, I have the responsibility to . . . " For example, if the class decides that a classroom rule should be "take turns speaking" then a student may respond by stating, "Because we have the rule to take turns speaking, I have the right not to be interrupted when I am talking" and "Because we have the rule to take turns speaking, I have the responsibility to raise my hand." This exercise helps students understand why the rule is important (right) and their role in following that rule (responsibility). Other ways to teach rules are to provide students with case scenarios, alternating between following rules and not following rules and asking students to decide if rules were adhered to. True and false or smiley or sad faces could also be used in conjunction with scenarios, stories, or pictures.

When thinking about developing classroom rules, it's important to acknowledge that rules will certainly be different for elementary school versus middle school or high school students. While elementary students may need rules about

Figure 7–6. Rights and responsibilities grid.

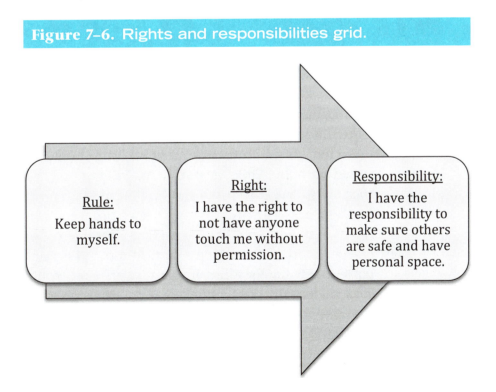

walking in the hallways, high school students may need rules about displays of affection in class. Further, rules will most likely be consistent from class to class in middle school and high school settings, but the rules needed for different grade levels in elementary school may vary greatly. A kindergarten class may need rules about sharing, but by fifth grade, the majority of students will have developed sharing skills and will most likely not need this type of rule any longer.

Hierarchy of Prompts

The focus on procedures, expectations, and rules assumes that students may need some level of reminders or prompts to comply with these established structures. It's important to remember, however, that prompting should be done in the least intrusive manner possible. While most students will respond best to a hierarchy of prompts, others may need errorless prompting. A hierarchy of prompts includes no prompting, a visual or gesture prompt, verbal prompts, and, finally, physical prompts. Initially, a student should be expected to complete the task, expectation, or request independently, without a prompt. At most, this might also include an expectant pause immediately following reminders that would be given to the whole class. If a student still does not respond, prompting should be done visually or with a gesture. A gesture prompt is one that students can see as a reminder. For example, if Mr. Wayne directs the class to open their books and Stacey still does not respond accordingly after the whole group direction, Mr. Wayne could pick up his own book and point at it while looking at Stacey. Or, he could make eye contact with Stacey and use two hands to create the visual of a book opening. If Stacey still doesn't respond, Mr. Wayne could then give a verbal prompt. This might be done indirectly, with a whole-group reminder (e.g., "Remember everyone, your book should be open.") or to Stacey directly (e.g., "Stacey, open your book"). While in this situation Stacey most likely knows how to open her book, there may be situations where modeling is the next phase of the prompting process. Perhaps students in Mr. Wayne's high school biology class have forgotten or aren't correctly completing the procedure for moving around the lab in a safe manner. After moving through the hierarchy of gesture and verbal prompts, Mr. Wayne may model, or demonstrate, how students should be walking through stations and around lab equipment. Finally, if modeling is not effective, teachers may use physical prompting. In Stacey's case, this may mean walking to her desk and physically opening her book, or in the lab, this may mean that Mr. Wayne is blocking one end of the classroom as a physical reminder that everyone should be moving clockwise when carrying equipment to avoid spills. While Stacey may be responsive to a hierarchy of prompts, Jordan, another student in her class, may need errorless prompting. Errorless prompting is providing a prompt that directly tells the student how to respond, skipping the hierarchy, but ensuring a correct response. In the lab example, Mr. Wayne would tell and show Jordan how to hold and manipulate his equipment. While Jordan may initially need this support to be successful in the lab, the ultimate goal would be to fade errorless prompting and utilize a hierarchy of prompts instead. When thinking about prompting students, the ultimate goal is always independence. It should be noted that using this hierarchy of prompts also assumes that students are not engaging in behaviors that are unsafe or disruptive and need immediate attention.

 High-Leverage Practice Alert!

Scaffolded supports to help student become independent are covered in HLP15.

Conclusion

While creating procedures, expectations, and rules may seem daunting and time consuming for first-year teachers, the payoff is worth the time. When a classroom teacher establishes how their classroom will run, the expectations of students, and the rules that keep everyone safe and engaged with learning, the entire classroom climate can shift positively. While it is best to create these structures prior to the start of school or early in the year, it is never too late to make adjustments. A simple conversation that begins with, "I've noticed we might be struggling to complete this activity, so let's come up with a procedure so everyone can keep learning and not be disrupted" can address those unexpected hiccups along the way.

Chapter Summary

- In conjunction with supports outlined in the PBIS model, classroom procedures, expectations, and rules all work together to enhance classroom management systems.

- Classroom procedures provide students with predictable structure and are used to communicate what is expected of students for routines, daily activities, and/or less frequent tasks or events. They are also useful for administrative and organizational purposes.

- While procedures help students navigate classroom routines, expectations are the desired behaviors required within such procedures. Expectations quantify or qualify the degree to which such behaviors are required.

- Always "check your lenses" and consider culture and background when establishing and enforcing expectations to create a safe, welcoming, and inclusive classroom.

- Expectations differ from rules in that they don't necessarily include enforceable consequences for not meeting a stated expectation. Rather, social consequences such as isolation or exclusion are much more likely.

- Positively frame classroom rules to communicate what *should be done* by students rather than what should not be done (e.g., "Walk" instead of "Don't run"). Key tenets of classroom rules are as follows:
  1. rules are a way for students to self-monitor;
  2. rules serve as reminders for expected behaviors; and
  3. if rules are broken, there should must be follow through regarding consequences.

- Provide students with specific, objective, and measurable criteria to teach procedures, expectations, and rules as often these may include nonobjective or nonobservable behaviors such as "being respectful" or "showing kindness."

- As a natural byproduct of procedures, expectations, and rules, students will require prompts and reminders to help them follow through. A hierarchy of prompts serves as a guide to ensure teachers are prompting in the least intrusive way possible so as to not create learned helplessness or reliance on prompts.

CHAPTER 8

ENGAGEMENT, INSTRUCTION, AND MOTIVATION

Learning Objectives

- Differentiate between intrinsic and extrinsic motivation
- Be able to generate a SMART goal
- Define group contingency and describe how these may be used within the classroom
- Identify each type of group contingency and describe how and when to use a group contingency in applied classroom settings
- Acknowledge limitations of group contingencies and how to address them

Key Terms

Dependent Group Contingency
Differential Reinforcement of Low Rates (DRL)
Good Behavior Game
Good Student Game
Group Contingencies

Inadvertent Reinforcement
Independent Group Contingency
Interdependent Group Contingency
Motivation
SMART Goals

Effective behavior management is required for a classroom to operate successfully, engage students, and promote positive experiences in a calm, organized environment. Igniting a student's motivation to learn and maintain it over time is a hurdle faced by educators every single day. As such, teachers hold a challenging responsibility to harness student interest and foster enjoyment of learning and school.

 High-Leverage Practice Alert!

HLP8 specifically discusses providing students with feedback to increase motivation and engagement. These topics will also be covered in the following sections.

Students who are motivated and engaged in their learning demonstrate better overall performance in academics and behavior and are consequently happier and more self-reliant than their unmotivated, disengaged peers. This chapter will discuss what motivation is and some ways in which you may foster it in the classroom. We will also address how to design, implement, and assess various types of group contingencies along with considerations and common traps to avoid.

Motivation

Motivation is the drive to act or accomplish; it is derived from the word "motive," and is the push behind our needs, wants, and desires. Motivation is what stimulates us to get up and go and is the overarching psychological factor that directs us toward the big picture: achievement in school, postgraduation aspirations, job satisfaction, healthy relationships, and the desire to be happy. Much of education rests on the student's willingness to be invested in the content in order to produce work. So how do we approach motivating our students? We can start by tapping into what sparks our student's interests, then look to see how and when we can embed these interests in the classroom. Motivation can be divided into two main branches: intrinsic and extrinsic.

Intrinsic Versus Extrinsic Motivation

Intrinsic motivation may be thought of as internal motivation that guides an individual toward doing for the sheer satisfaction it brings rather than for an external source. Intrinsically motivated students pursue something for the sheer interest, enjoyment, or challenge it produces, and their actions have no link to external pressures or rewards. These students read for pleasure and to satisfy curiosity, write because it makes them feel good, and solve equations for mental stimulation. Behaviors resulting from intrinsic motivation are longer lasting and generally more robust; however, behavior change can be rather slow and promoting this type of motivation can be challenging since it is so highly individual.

Meanwhile, extrinsic motivation is the drive to accomplish something in order to earn a reward or avoid an aversive consequence. External motivation relies heavily on external outcomes to drive someone toward doing. Such outcomes may include studying to good grades, satisfying expectations from teachers and parents, or needing to achieve a certain grade to avoid being kicked off the swim team. Extrinsic motivation generally produces a more rapid change in behavior as compared to intrinsic motivation, albeit these gains are more susceptible to dropping off and are not sustained long term once external consequences are removed. As you may assume, there is criticism around extrinsic motivation and how teachers should be focused on fostering student's intrinsic desires to learn. Such criticisms include the short-lived effects and concerns that extrinsic motivators cause dependency on reward (e.g., "What do I get if I do this?") and reliance on the opinion of others (e.g., "Will my dad be disappointed I got a B– in chemistry?")

Regardless, extrinsic motivation is not necessarily all bad; it all boils down to finding the right balance. It is simply impossible for an individual to be intrinsically motivated in every aspect of life, or in the case of our students, in every subject area and social domain. Not to mention, much of the time, motivation is not purely one or the other; adults who have passion for their careers (intrinsic) subsequently earn a paycheck, even if it's a modest one, for going to work (extrinsic). In life, there are heaps of tasks that are unpleasant yet necessary. Extrinsic motivation works to aid in the drive to get things done and teaches us about what reinforces us. Ultimately, the use of extrinsic motivators can hook learners into content and expose them to material that may eventually serve as an intrinsic motivator. As such, there are some ways in which educators can inspire intrinsic motivation in students, while also providing external motivation for new or developing skills.

Intrinsic motivation is highly individual, and while we cannot change the individual preferences of a student, we can employ strategies to motivate them to become engaged in their learning. Aim to be an enthusiastic educator and serve as a role-model to foster student interest by taking an honest look at how you are delivering content and how much effort you are extending into lessons. This does not mean spending hours poring over creating a perfect set of visuals or writing the most comprehensive lesson plans; it's as simple as asking yourself, "am I making this lesson engaging by showing *my interest* in the content?"

Next, take some serious time to get to know your students. This may seem obvious, but is often overlooked as a critical element to a well-run classroom. It's too easy to get caught up in what content needs to be covered and pacing lessons rather than making time to check in with students and really get to know them. Incorporating simple activities or games designed to spark conversation about personal interest into lesson plans can help zero in on what makes your students tick. Certainly, this poses a challenge for middle school and high school educators, as the sheer number of students and intermittent contact creates a barrier; yet, dedicating one class period to getting to know student backgrounds, personal interests, and abilities can pay off in the long run.

Refer to Chapter 9 for a list and description of classroom activities that foster relationships in the classroom.

Using the information gleaned from student preferences can help design instruction. Link student interests to content and deliver instruction through a variety of teaching activities. Connect students with similar preferences for group work, focus on problem solving, and provide connections of concepts and materials to real life. Providing choices within lessons is another great way to harness student engagement. In addition, be flexible with students and give them ownership of their work and classroom. Allowing students to have some control over their learning promotes creativity and prevents boredom. Also, look for ways in which you can assess student learning outside traditional exams or presentations and maintain a reasonable emphasis on grades. Students are already exposed to numerous external pressures to do well and succeed, which may hinder intrinsic motivation; highlight that tests are merely ways they can demonstrate what they *do* know.

Other strategies to motivate students include teaching students how to set measurable and realistic goals, both of academic and nonacademic nature. Goal setting is a skill that should be practiced as it helps to develop healthy practices students will need throughout school and into their careers. Achieving goals creates momentum and improves motivation while encouraging a growth mindset. Carol Dweck, a prominent researcher on the powerful topic of growth mindset, maintains that talent is something capable of being developed (Dweck, 2014). She asserts that combining this mindset with a strategized approach to goal setting is incredibly powerful as goals provide motivation to persevere. It should be noted, however, that the research on the effectiveness of growth mindsets on academic achievement has been mixed. Caution should be used on using the growth mindset framework as a solution for lower achieving students, but this framework deserves some attention as a way to motivate some, but not all, students.

SMART Goals

Originally coined in business management literature, the SMART goal has become the preeminent method to goal writing in education (Doran, 1981). The clever acronym is well suited to the classroom and emphasizes making goals **s**pecific, **m**easurable, **a**ttainable, **r**ealistic, and **t**ime-bound (Figure 8–1). Creating a SMART goal is free and can be done by anyone for any type of goal, and by focusing on these key elements, one greatly improves his or her chances of successfully reaching a goal.

Specific

The first aspect of a SMART goal is to be specific about what the intention of the goal. With the student, identify the *area for improvement* and include *who* will be involved. Then, define *what* is it that is to be accomplished and, if needed, *where* will this occur. Finally, specify the *why* behind the goal; what benefits will come about from accomplishing this goal and why is it important?

Measurable

How will the student know if he or she actually attains the goal? Making the goal measurable aids in this assessment and is an indicator of progress. Questions like "how much?" or "how many?" help to guide students toward identifying when the goal has been achieved.

Figure 8–1. SMART goal guidelines.

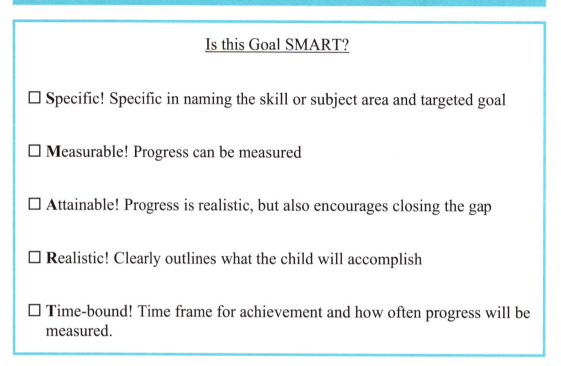

Is this Goal SMART?

☐ **S**pecific! Specific in naming the skill or subject area and targeted goal

☐ **M**easurable! Progress can be measured

☐ **A**ttainable! Progress is realistic, but also encourages closing the gap

☐ **R**ealistic! Clearly outlines what the child will accomplish

☐ **T**ime-bound! Time frame for achievement and how often progress will be measured.

Attainable

This one can be a bit tricky. Keep in mind that attainable goals are not necessarily easy to achieve nor too lofty. Rather, the student must have the basic set of abilities and access to resources in order to facilitate success. Then, it's about finding the balance between knowing what he or she needs to achieve a goal and outlining the steps that need to be taken.

Realistic

Ensure the goal is clearly within reach and relevant to the student's circumstances. Consider what resources the student has ready access to and determine what can be realistically achieved with those in mind.

Time-Bound

To garner motivation and to ensure the goal being set will be achieved, support the student in identifying an end point or a clear targeted deadline. Help the student to set a timeline, with checkpoints along the way to keep him or her on track and moving in the right direction. Once goals are achieved, they can be extended, modified, or changed altogether to suit the student and his or her growing needs.

So, for example, a goal written without the SMART formula may read something like the following: Kayla will get better grades.

Now, applying the criteria described previously, we can transform it into a SMART goal:

> Kayla will raise her classroom participation grade at least five points by the end of the semester by raising her hand and making at least one comment per class and handing in all relevant assignments by the indicated due dates.

Using SMART goals encourages students to make and meet personal goals, motivating them to accomplish new or challenging tasks they may have otherwise avoided.

 High-Leverage Practice Alert!

Teaching students strategies to support self-regulation of learning is covered in HLP14. This includes monitoring and evaluating performance on goals.

Group Contingencies

With motivation comes action. Through motivation, educators provide students fuel to accelerate learning. Managing this as a whole-class endeavor can seem quite daunting, but strategies such as group contingencies can be easily applied to educational settings to manage behavior and enhance motivation. As discussed in Chapter 14, behavior contracts work to establish a connection, or contingency, between behavior and reinforcement. An extension of this is what is known as a group contingency, which can serve as a pragmatic and effective approach to managing behavior of several students at once. Group contingencies are a behavior management intervention that provides a reinforcer (and sometimes an aversive consequence) to an entire group of people based on either the behavior of one individual within the group, the behavior of a portion of people within the group, or the behavior of the entire group.

Individual contingencies or behavior plans can be time intensive and require dedicated attention from the teacher. In turn, this can pull teacher attention away from other students in the class. Group contingencies can alleviate some of the challenges associated with individual plans while also extending benefits to targeted and nontargeted students. Group contingencies are commonly found as part of school-wide Positive Behavioral Intervention and Support systems as they are effective with a wide range of age ranges and abilities (Molloy, Moore, Trail, Van Epps, & Hopfer, 2013). In short, group contingencies are effective behavior change interventions that can be applied across a variety of different behaviors, students, and environments. They are one of the best ways in which to reduce challenging behaviors, reinforce desired behaviors, and teach skills. These interventions also hold several advantages, with the most evident being that they are economical, practical, and time efficient. As mentioned, group contingencies streamline consequences to the entire group, eliminating the administrative power required to monitor and attend to individual students. Group contingencies do not require much time to prepare, can be easily implemented by just one teacher, and are useful when trying to manage behavior quickly.

Perhaps the most distinguishing characteristic of group contingencies is the use of peers as agents of change. Peer pressure is not uncommon in any classroom by any stretch of the imagination; so, rather than fighting against this, group contingencies leverage it to promote desirable behavior and facilitate positive working relationships among students. In these cases, carefully structuring group contingencies will offset any potential social issues, such as scapegoating or bullying, which will be discussed in the following text.

Group contingencies are most often used as a class-wide behavior management system, but its uses extend far beyond just that. Group contingencies are well suited for gaining traction with new routines, new rules, and any time other basic expectations need to be established. They are helpful when trying to increase participation in an activity or when there is a new or challenging portion of content that may require additional instruction, sustained focus, or increased effort. Group contingencies are also quite handy when teachers need to attend to a smaller group of students, while needing the larger group to maintain engagement with independent work. For example, Ms. Atkin is administering reading benchmark tests to each of her first-grade students. Using a group contingency can facilitate management of the larger group, while her attention is directed toward individual students. Additionally, group contingencies capitalize on the use of peers as change agents by promoting them as role models for target behavior, which can foster positive peer interactions and class-wide cooperation. Let's now take a look at the three types of group contingencies: dependent group contingency, independent group contingency, and interdependent group contingency (Figure 8–2).

Figure 8–2. Comparison of group contingencies.

Dependent Group Contingencies	Independent Group Contingencies	Interdependent Group Contingencies
Least commonly implemented.	More popular and more commonly used.	Most commonly used group contingency.
Reward of the group depends on behavior of one individual or small group.	All individuals within a group who meet criterion earn a reward.	All members of the group must meet the criterion, both individually and as a group.
May work best for students who respond well to peer attention.	Works well in conjunction with systems that are already in place.	Capitalizes on joining students together to achieve a common objective.
Sometimes referred to as the "hero procedure."	Teachers must be mindful to monitor which students are not consistently earning the reward.	Teachers must be mindful about negative social pressures and scapegoating among students.

Dependent Group Contingency

The dependent group contingency is possibly the least commonly implemented of the three types. Within this type of group contingency, the reward for the entire group is dependent upon the behavior of either one individual or a small portion of the group. This is useful when trying to motivate a particular individual or small group who may not consistently perform well. For example, if Ms. Atkin wants to target chronic messy desks, she can implement a dependent group contingency like, "if the front row has their desks tidy by 3 p.m., the whole class will earn 15 minutes of free time." In this way, all students have access to the reward under the exact same terms and no one is penalized for the behavior of others. If the identified group or individual does not meet the criterion for the reward, no reward is given. Students who respond well to peer attention may benefit from this approach. As such, this type of contingency is sometimes referred to as the "hero procedure" to describe when a student or group of students earn the reward for the whole class. Likewise, negative social attention is a potential outcome if the student or group do not meet criterion to earn the group's reward. In order to address this, the teacher may randomize some or all of the contingency components. Randomly selecting the target behavior or randomly selecting students/ small groups to meet the contingency's criterion can offset negative peer pressure as anyone within the group can be selected at any time to meet criterion.

Independent Group Contingency

In contrast to dependent group contingencies, independent group contingencies are quite popular and very commonly used. In this type of contingency, all individuals within a group who meet the specified criterion earn the reward. The most universal example of this is a grading system; all student who score a 90 or above earn an A, while those who score below a 65 receive an F (Skinner, Cashwell, & Dunn, 2008). This emphasizes each student's responsibility for his or her own behavior. Students working within an independent group contingencies are all held to the same set of expectations (e.g., target behaviors, specified criteria) and earn the same reward, which, in practice, makes this a relatively easy system to manage. These systems are also well suited to pair with existing behavior management tools already in place, such as token economy systems. Provided a set of expectations or target behaviors, students earn points or check mark that can be cashed in for a reward once they meet a minimum requirement. For instance, a teacher may state the expectation of "all students who hand in their classwork on time will earn extra credit." This places the onus on the student to self-monitor and learn about goal-setting and attainment. Independent group contingencies are an excellent way for educators to clarify what is expected and provide structure to students.

As no system is perfect, there are risks to using independent group contingencies such as limiting and withholding reinforcers and inadvertently creating undesired classroom inequities. Naturally, some students will meet criteria and earn the reward and some will not. How a teacher manages this will dictate the success of the contingency. When rewards are tangible and able to be distributed individually, there should be systems in place to ensure those who did not earn do not achieve unwarranted access. Similarly, if the reward is more activity or privilege based, the teacher needs to remain mindful that he or she is still required to supervise those students who will not be participating. Independent group contingencies are not sensitive to individual differences, and as a result, teachers should remain vigilant in noting which students are consistently earning the reward and which are not as this can contribute to a "social class" system within the classroom. In addition, teachers should be diligent about examining whether gender, class, or race inequities are occurring based on who is consistently earing or not earning rewards. To address this, teachers can ensure that there are a variety of target behaviors that are representative of a variety of strengths (e.g., have some academic targets, some social targets, some creative targets, etc.) so as to mitigate any sense of "have" versus 'have not' (Skinner et al., 1996). Alternatively, using an interdependent group contingency can offset any issues with some students receiving a reward and others not.

Interdependent Group Contingency

An interdependent group contingency involves the requirement of all members of the group meeting the set criterion, *both individually and as a group,* before earning the reward. This is the most commonly used of the group contingencies as it holds some distinct advantages over the other two methods. Interdependent group contingencies capitalize on joining students together to achieve a common objective and appropriate naturally occurring peer pressure within the classroom to encourage cooperation. So, for an interdependent group contingency to work, a target behavior is set for all members and the reward is only provided given all individual members of the group satisfy the expectation. This is an all or nothing approach and is well suited when the goal is to increase accountability of actions among a group. For instance, Ms. Atkin states that all students must turn in their homework every day for one week in order to earn a class party. Further, this approach may prove to be more time effective in that group rewards are easier to manage and distribute as it eliminates the need for record keeping and having to dole out rewards to different students at various times. Because the whole group is working toward the reward, interdependent contingencies encourage students working together as they may not typically would have, which can foster respect for individual differences and diversity.

Interdependent group contingencies can be managed in a variety of ways. The first variation is when the entire class or group meets the specified criterion (e.g., everyone turns in their homework), they earn the reward. Sometimes the nature of the task could lend itself nicely to the group having to meet a predetermined criterion or group average. For example, if Ms. Atkin's students achieve a mean math test score over 85%, they will earn a reward. Alternatively, if Ms. Atkin's students are earning points for demonstrating target behaviors during a lesson, the class can earn a reward once a predetermined number of points is earned cumulatively. Due to the interdependent nature of this contingency, if one student fails to meet criterion, none of the students get the reward. As can be expected, some potential cons of this approach include student sabotage to withhold the reward from the whole group or undue negative social pressure or scapegoating. Just as with the dependent group contingency, these consequences can be mitigated by random selection of behaviors, rewards, or students. This can be done throughout the day, week, or school term, depending on feasibility and need. Teachers can randomize behaviors that access the reward or randomize the reward so that students are not privy to what it is before they earn it.

Good Behavior Game

The Good Behavior Game is a form of an interdependent group contingency that uses a point system to reduce challenging or disruptive behavior (Barrish,

Saunders, & Wolf, 1969). Let's use Ms. Atkin's class again as an example. Ms. Atkin decides she will implement the Good Behavior Game during the language arts block and independent seat work times and identifies and operationally defines the following disruptive behaviors based off of recent data collection: calling out and out-of-seat behavior. Additionally, Ms. Atkin decides upon some reinforcers, both daily and weekly, that will serve as the reward for winning the game. Then, the class is divided into at least two teams and points are given to a team if anyone on that team engages in the defined behaviors (i.e., calling out or leaving one's seat). The team with the fewest points at the end of the independent seat work time is the winner. This type of procedure is known as differential reinforcement of low rates of behavior (DRL). A DRL is procedure used to reduce (but not eliminate) behaviors which are occurring too frequently by delivering reinforcement when behavior levels fall below a predetermined criteria, or in this case, the lowest team's score. Ms. Atkin records points up on a whiteboard, visible to all students. She is also careful to minimize any undue attention when giving points, remaining matter-of-fact and neutral. It's also recommended for teachers to keep a running record of points not only to monitor daily and weekly rewards but also to look at progress over time (minding that the teams remain consistent). Potential obstacles to the Good Behavior Game are similar to those found with other group contingencies, primarily sabotage and scapegoating. If one or more students deliberately engaging in challenging behavior to earn points for their team, consider regrouping the teams and putting these students into their own group, or, alternatively, consider another variant of an interdependent group contingency—the Good Student Game.

Good Student Game

While the Good Behavior Game (Barrish et al., 1969) targets a reductive behavior change and points are given for rule breaking, the Good Student Game relies upon self-monitoring strategies and points are given for rule following. Ideally, the Good Student Game should be played during times where students are working independently and students may play on small teams or as individuals. The primary distinctions between the Good Student Game and the Good Behavior Game lie with the recording of target behaviors and the shift of focus from negative to positive behaviors. Rather than the teacher recording points for behavior infractions, as in the Good Behavior Game, students self-monitor and record their own points for following behavioral expectations in the Good Student Game when prompted to check-in by the teacher (Babyak, Luze, & Kamps, 2000). These check-ins also serve as an opportunity for teachers to praise positive behavior. The shift to student recorded data eases some implementation burden from the classroom teacher while simultaneously teaching students how to observe, evaluate, and record their own behaviors. Further, this focuses on positive behaviors instead of negative ones.

Considerations

The effectiveness of a group contingency rests upon careful planning and vigilance to potential issues. Here are some helpful tips to take on board when implementing a group contingency in the classroom.

Choose Relevant Reinforcers

Remember, since these group contingencies involve many students, the system must be flexible yet sensitive to individual differences. Ultimately, there will be some rewards that serve as strong reinforcers for some students but be weak for others. More so, some rewards could even function as potential punishers for some students, depending on their learning history and experiences (e.g., an ice cream party may be punishing for a student diagnosed with diabetes; going on a class outing in the middle of winter could be punishing for a student who can't afford proper winter gear). To address this, recruit student input for ideas of what will be motivating and keep these choices available in a menu. Frequently revisit the list of potential rewards to keep it updated and relevant to all students. If you suspect potentially sensitive issues related to rewards, solicit student input from an anonymous checklist or survey and assure students that the results are confidential. Maintaining a growing and flexible list of rewards is also helpful as preferences shift over time. You may come to discover after a few weeks of the same or similar rewards, behavior change starts to stall, but having a variety of options available helps to maintain positive changes and keeps behavior change momentum moving forward.

Prerequisite Skills and Attainable Criterion

Employing a group contingency also requires students to have a basic set of prerequisite skills. Teachers must ensure that target behaviors selected or criteria required to access the reward are all within the reach of each student involved. If in question, data are helpful in this situation (of course!) Finding the average of student performance can help to determine the appropriate criterion for a group contingency. For example, Ms. Atkin calculates the class average from the last spelling test (e.g., 80%) and uses that to set the criterion for an independent group contingency, meaning all students who score 80% or above receive the reward.

Alternatively, Ms. Atkin could refer to the highest or the lowest test score and use that to set group contingency criterion (e.g., the highest score of 90% sets criteria at 90% or above; the lowest score of 70% sets the criterion at 70% or above). Of course, knowing your students well will help in the selection of appropriate criterion. If Ms. Atkin had several students consistently scoring in the mid-70s on the spelling tests, choosing a high-score criterion would not be suitable.

Potential Risks with Group Contingencies

A potential drawback to the use of group contingencies is inadvertent reinforcement of undesired behavior. There is a risk students may alter (either intentionally or unintentionally) behaviors other than the target behavior. For example, Ms. Atkin's is targeting academic achievement quantified by scores on spelling tests and so forth. While her students may be putting forth extra effort in this area and improving their test scores, there may be an increase in undesirable behavior, such as calling out or bickering between students. This puts Ms. Atkin at a disadvantage; students meet the criterion and get the reward but are engaging in challenging or undesired behavior, which also inadvertently receives reinforcement. A simple way to address this is for the teacher to randomize the target behavior tied to the contingency. For example, Ms. Atkin can have a jar full of slips of paper, each indicating a different target behavior (e.g., quiet voices during instruction, raising hand to answer, score at least 80% on Friday's spelling quiz, etc.), which can encourage students to maintain more consistent behavior (Kelshaw-Levering, Sterling-Turner, Henry, & Skinner, 2000).

Unfortunately, the very nature of group contingencies leaves them susceptible to the potential for students to engage in challenging behavior in order to escape the contingency or throw the system for others. While there are several reasons why a student may engage in purposeful sabotage, one of the most common is retaliation due to not meeting criterion for rewards. While this is not unexpected, it does indicate the student is (or at least was) motivated by the potential reward (a good thing gone bad). This tends to be the case with regard to larger rewards that may take several days or even weeks to attain. To offset this, teachers may offer smaller rewards along the way to maintain positive momentum toward the larger goal. If problem behavior continues to occur, teachers may need to reevaluate criterion and adjust to ensure that it is within all students' capabilities or change the nature of the group contingency (e.g., from an independent to dependent). As stated previously, teachers may also institute a randomization of group contingency components to neutralize this limitation. Selecting different students for dependent group contingencies and randomizing reinforcers can enhance incentive as students are unaware if what they are working toward is a high-quality, powerful reinforcer. As a last resort, teachers may offer students an opportunity for restitution. This is not ideal, as changing the criterion reduces overall effectiveness and may be viewed by other students as preferential treatment; however, it may be just the nudge some students need to get back on track.

Conclusion

Motivating students will always be an ongoing, dynamic process. With some intentional planning and commitment to finding out what works for your students the benefits, both immediate and long term, are endless. Motivated students exhibit greater social competence, retain information longer, and show better critical thinking and problem-solving skills. Using positive behavior strategies such as group contingencies can increase student motivation and enhance effective classroom management. These systems also help to promote student cooperation, which can be more influential than individual learning (O'Donnell, Reeve, & Smith, 2009).

Chapter Summary

- Motivation is one's drive to act. There are two main categories of motivation: intrinsic and extrinsic. Intrinsic motivation refers to one's internal drive toward accomplishment and resides in the satisfaction gained through action. Extrinsic motivation relies on outside influences, either to earn a reward or avoid an aversive consequence.
- SMART goals are goals that are specific, measurable, attainable, realistic, and time-bound.
- Group contingencies are behavior management interventions that provides a reinforcer to an entire group of people based off of one of the following types:
  - Dependent: the reward for the entire group is dependent upon the behavior of one individual or a small group of individuals.
  - Independent: all individuals within a group who meet a specified criterion earn the reward.
  - Interdependent: requires all members of the group to meet the set criterion both as an individual and as a group to earn the reward.
- The Good Behavior Game is an interdependent group contingency in which a group is divided into at least two "teams" and a behavior is targeted for reduction (e.g., calling out). Teams receive points for whenever anyone in the group engages in the target behavior and the team with the lowest score at the end of a predetermined interval "wins" the reward.

● The Good Student Game is an offshoot of the Good Behavior Game and relies heavily on self-monitoring. Students can work in small groups or independently and record points for following preset behavior expectations.

● Differential reinforcement of low rates (DRL) is a procedure to reduce behaviors which are happening too frequently by delivering reinforcement when behavior levels fall below a prespecified threshold.

● Considerations for group contingencies include choosing relevant and salient reinforcers, ensuring all students have prerequisite skills for the target behavior, and setting attainable criterion. Common risks include inadvertent reinforcement of undesired behavior and potential retaliation or sabotage.

PART III

MEETING INDIVIDUAL NEEDS

Chapter 9. Establishing Relationships with Students

Chapter 10. Behavioral Data Collection

Chapter 11. Graphing and Data Analysis

Chapter 12. Functional Behavioral Assessment

Chapter 13. Behavioral Intervention Plans

Chapter 14. Teaching New Skills

ESTABLISHING RELATIONSHIPS WITH STUDENTS

Learning Objectives

- Describe how positive, healthy relationships can affect overall student performance and identify best practices for building these relationships
- Understand the benefits of behavior-specific praise and describe the conditions under which it should be delivered
- Describe how to acknowledge and manage conflict among students
- Identify relationship-building activities and any potential considerations to keep in mind

Key Terms

Behavior-Specific Praise	Relatedness
Conflict Cycle	"Saving Face"
Power Struggles	Tootling

The student and teacher relationship is an important one. These relationships are frequently tied to students' academic achievement and engagement (McGrath & Bergen, 2014). To take it a step further than just building relationships with others, students who feel supported by their teachers also have fewer behavior problems and do better academically (Maldonado-Carreno & Votruba-Drzal, 2011; Strom, Thoresen, Wentzel-Larsen, & Dyb, 2013). When talking about relationships, relatedness refers to having safe and satisfying relationships with others (Hughes & Chen, 2011). More broadly, school connectedness includes relationships between students and school personnel (Blum, 2005), significant others at school (Rasmussen, Damsgaard, Holstein, Poulsen, & Due 2005), and peers (Santos & Collins, 2016). Given the aforementioned research, it should not be surprising that students who have strong connections to their schools also experience more self-efficacy (Murphy & McKenzie, 2016) and improved school outcomes (Nasir, Jones, & McLaughlin, 2011). Further, when students are asked what they value in teachers, they report compassion, a willingness to help, and taking the time to know them and their personal situations (Hoy & Weinstein, 2006). Clearly, all relationships in the school setting—including those between teachers, students, and school staff—matter!

 High-Leverage Practice Alert!

HLP7 describes positive and respectful relationships as one way to establish a positive classroom climate.

Best Practices for Positive Relationships

Given what we know about the importance of relationships, teachers should be reflective about how they interact with students. This includes, but isn't limited to, considerations like using students' names, avoiding sarcasm and power struggles, focusing on relationship building, and knowledge of community and cultural norms. In addition, teachers should also carefully monitor the relationships between students, serving as a moderator when necessary and ensuring that bullying is not taking place between students. In the following section, some key relationship-building considerations are outlined and detailed.

Names

Learning your students' names is one of the easiest ways to develop rapport with students. When you learn your students' names, you are conveying to your students that they are important and you care enough to get to know them. In elementary settings, learning student names is easier since you have fewer students. However, using your students' names, and even learning them, isn't impossible in secondary settings where you have several sections of classes. Using "cheat sheets" or strategies for name recall are excellent ways to address students by name. On the first day of class, have students create name tents for their desks or tables. As you progress through the year, phase out the name tags as you learn their names or use them all year long as a quick and easy way to take attendance. Collect name tags after each class for students to pick up as they enter the next day; leftover name tags allow for quick marking of absent students. Another strategy includes using a labeled seating chart to reference prior to calling on students. Some memorization techniques include taking pictures of your students and practicing names outside of class, having students share personal information or preferences and using a name/preference association (e.g., Rosie likes running, Siad swims), or learn student names in chunks, one group at a time. Although it may be awkward at first, try addressing students by name every time you speak to them. Whatever method or strategy you use, practicing students' names will promote memorization.

Finally, make sure you pronounce your students' names correctly. If calling students by name demonstrates that you are invested in the relationship, pronouncing their name correctly is even more powerful. If you are uncertain about pronunciation, ask the student for the correct pronunciation and then practice to perfection. Often, writing out the phonetic spelling is helpful to learn an unfamiliar or new name. Under no circumstances should a teacher create a new name or nickname for a student based on their own comfort level with the correct pronunciation. Further, if a student uses a nickname or goes by a preferred name (e.g., Grace for Grayson), always call the student by their indicated preference.

In addition to calling students by name, students should also be called by their preferred gender pronoun. Whether a student prefers she, he, ze, hir, or they, the preferred pronoun should be respected and used. If you are unsure about a student's preferred pronoun, ask all students to complete basic information sheets that include their preferred names and pronouns, along with other pertinent information like seating preferences, favorite books or magazines, or any other school related information. If you are unsure about which pronoun to use, using a student's name is always an option. Most importantly, remember that outward appearances do not dictate pronouns, so avoid assumptions about gender pronouns and under no circumstance refer students to students using "it" because you are unsure. Like names, using preferred gender pronouns demonstrates respect and is important in the teacher-student relationship-building process.

Sarcasm

While sarcasm may be widely used among families and friends, exercise caution when using sarcasm while working with students. It's important to remember that some of your students may have disabilities or barriers that hinder their ability to understand subtle cues of language or tone, or perhaps comprehend language in a more literal manner, missing the intended humor of sarcasm. Similarly, other students may be learning English or be at the beginning stages of understanding how English is used in a school context. These students may be listening for comprehension and not be able to differentiate between what is literal, implied, or said in sarcasm. Ultimately, sarcasm can fracture relationships with students who lack full understanding of its intricacies, and, consequently, sarcasm can be perceived as mean spirited or hurtful to those who don't understand its intended meaning or humor. It should also be noted that simply because a student is older (middle school or high school aged), this still doesn't mean they understand or appreciate sarcasm more than a younger student.

Power Struggles

As a teacher, you may have, or have had, students who don't follow directions, blatantly refuse to comply with instructions, or demonstrate behavior in opposition to requests. During these situations, it is easy to get into power struggles with students for the sake of being "right." In the framework of relationship building, power struggles break down these relationships because it pits you, the teacher, against the student, and the only way the power struggle ends is if someone "wins." While a teacher always wants to have control over their classroom and maintain expectations, a power struggle does not solve problems or ultimately change behavior. In fact, power struggles take the focus off of learning and can create a learning environment where students feel unsafe because trust may be compromised.

If you find yourself in a power struggle with a student, offer the student a choice and provide wait time. Acknowledge the student's feelings, and, if necessary, take an adult time-out from the situation. Above all, maintain composure and make statements in a nonjudgmental but matter-of-fact manner. For example, imagine this dialogue between Miss Campbell and her fourth grade student Lincoln:

> **Miss Campbell: "Lincoln, put your notebook in your desk. Math time is over."**
>
> **Lincoln: "No, I'm not done."**
>
> **Miss Campbell (tone becomes sharp): "Lincoln, I said put it away."**
>
> **Lincoln: "I said no, I'm not done."**
>
> **Miss Campbell (beginning to talk louder): "Put it away right now or else."**
>
> **Lincoln (yelling): "You're stupid. You didn't give me enough time."**
>
> **Miss Campbell (yelling): "You can't call me stupid. Give me the math notebook."**
>
> **Lincoln: "No."**

As you can imagine, this bickering between teacher and student could go on endlessly and would most likely end with an escalation in Lincoln's behavior and a frustrated and angry Miss Campbell. All the while, Miss Campbell is directing her sole attention toward Lincoln, leaving the rest of the class in the midst of an instructional transition to a science activity. In this scenario, both the teacher and student most likely perceive the other as the opponent. This will certainly strain their relationship. If we revisit this situation but take away the power struggle, the interaction may look like the following:

> **Miss Campbell: "Lincoln, put your notebook in your desk. Math time is over."**
>
> **Lincoln: "No, I'm not done."**

> Miss Campbell: "I understand that you are not done and that might be frustrating. Right now, your direction is to put it away, when you are ready to follow directions, let me know so I can help you transition."
>
> Lincoln: "You're stupid. You didn't give me enough time."
>
> Miss Campbell: "If you cannot follow directions, there will be consequences. Let me know when you're ready."
>
> Lincoln: "I really don't like you."
>
> Miss Campbell: "Let me know when you're ready."
>
> Lincoln: "I hate you!"
>
> Miss Campbell: "Let me know when you're ready."

At this point, Miss Campbell has clearly laid out her expectations and is no longer engaging in the back and forth dialogue. Often, this is called the broken record since the teacher says what needs to be said and nothing more other than a repetition of the same statement. As a teacher, it's important to remember that you are not "losing" the discussion, control of the class, or direction over that student. Instead, you are preserving the relationship by not arguing. Once the student has regained composure and is ready to engage, you can revisit the incident and have a conversation about what is and is not acceptable or permissible in the classroom and at that time, if consequences are warranted, discuss them. By waiting until the student has moved past the conflict cycle, the teacher is able to have a reflective and proactive conversation versus a situationally reactive interaction. We will talk more about the conflict cycle in the coming sections of this chapter.

"Saving Face"

Along the lines of breaking from power struggles, it's important not to create situations where students feel they need to "save face." This is a term that broadly means to help the student not feel embarrassed, humiliated, or disrespected in front of their peers. During power struggles, students may take the interaction one step too far (e.g., name-calling) and while some students may not show immediate remorse, others may realize they have taken the situation too far. If we—as adults and teachers—continue to engage in a power struggle with the student, we don't provide room for them to "save face" and exit that struggle without feeling disrespected. For example, revisit the exchange with Miss Campbell and Lincoln about the math notebook. What if at the end of that exchange Miss Campbell, who is already very upset and feeling challenged, says to Lincoln, "I'm stupid? Who can't even finish the math during the math block?" Miss Campbell has set Lincoln up to defend himself from being "stupid" in front of his classmates. In this situation, it would be expected that Lincoln would respond with additional name-calling or even outward anger. Miss Campbell just created a situation where Lincoln cannot "save face" in front of his peers. While this might be an extreme example, it is not uncommon for power struggles to end in forcing students to make decisions about making an uncomfortable or challenging situation worse. It is our job as teachers to guide that interaction to the greatest extent possible.

Conflict Cycle

If you find yourself in the middle of a power struggle and realize a situation with a student has moved into a negative, unproductive place or perhaps even a crisis situation, remove yourself from entering into a conflict cycle. In a conflict cycle, student and teacher behaviors can become cyclical, escalating behaviors and emotions repeatedly over time. Once emotions and tensions rise, the best response is to step away from the situation, providing space for both the student and teacher. Teachers should aim to minimize further escalation or avoid creating another stressor for the student; this can be done by waiting until emotions have cooled before discussing the concerning behaviors. Use a calm, quiet voice and allow students the opportunity to share their beliefs, perceptions, and emotions about the incident that caused the student's heightened reaction. Remember, not all students have the language to process their emotions or may have skewed perceptions about events, so listen and provide perspective. What is most important about the conflict cycle and the reason it is called a "cycle" is the teacher's role in **not** exasperating an already emotionally heightened situation. During the height of a student's crisis situation, the last thing a teacher should do is begin doling out consequences or asking students to problem solve. When a student, or anyone for that matter, is emotionally charged, it is extremely difficult to think clearly and rationally. Therefore, students should be given space to emotionally and mentally exit the crisis situation and return to a calm emotional baseline before any consequences, conversations, or problem solving take place. Sometimes this can happen quickly, other times it may take an extended amount of time for a student to cool down and be ready to discuss their behaviors or crisis situation. As teachers, we have the unique power and position to either calm a student or escalate them further with our words and actions. Don't be the reason a student reenters a conflict cycle.

Behavior-Specific Praise

Undoubtedly, we all enjoy hearing positive affirmations about our behaviors over negative critiques. Students are no different. However, did you know that some types of praise are actually better than others? While general praise will work for some students, behavior-specific praise (BSP) is a more effective evidence-based strategy that can actually improve overall behavior (Royer, Lane, Dunlap, & Ennis, 2019; Sutherland, Wehby, & Copeland, 2000), on-task behavior (Hollingshead, Kroeger, Altus, & Trytten (2016), and engagement (Rathel, Drasgow, Brown, & Marshall, 2014). In fact, BSP can increase positive behaviors in the classroom (Allday et al., 2012) and improve academic outcomes. In relation to this chapter, BSP also improves teacher-student relationships and creates a positive classroom climate. With BSP, students are given explicit feedback on observable behaviors in such a way that tells students exactly why they are receiving praise. BSP are free, portable, and super simple; these statements are designed to reinforce desirable or successful student behaviors. For example, general praise for Maria might be a statement like, "Good job Maria!" In this example, Maria doesn't know what she did that was "good." To make this behavior specific, the teacher could say, "Maria, good job raising your hand and waiting to be called on!" While this phrase still uses the words "good job," it also adds the specific details about what Maria did to earn her this praise.

When providing students with BSP, deliver it in a timely manner, as immediately as possible after the student has demonstrated the desired behavior. To connect student behavior to the praise statement, BSP should be delivered within seconds of the target behavior. This not only clarifies the behavior that is accessing the praise but also eliminates the chances of inadvertent reinforcement of another less desirable behavior. Ideally, if a teacher hopes to change a student's behavior, six BSP statements should be delivered for every 15 min of class time (Myers, Simonsen, & Sugai, 2011). While this may seem extreme, consider the time it would take to redirect or correct undesirable or disruptive behaviors. Perhaps this reallocation of time is worth the investment! Behaviors can be reinforced for academics or social behaviors, so the opportunities for BSP are endless. Another way to enhance the effectiveness of BSP is to use the student's name while detailing the observable positive behaviors. Although this may be obvious, praise should always be positive. Instead of saying "Vickie, I appreciate that you weren't yelling across the room" it would be better to say "Vickie, thank you for walking across the room to talk to your friend quietly."

If you haven't traditionally used BSP in your classroom, it may take some time and practice to deliver it in a genuine and natural way. Consider keeping a list of behaviors you want to target for reinforcement and use language that mimics your classroom or school expectations (Ennis et al., 2018). Then, practice your delivery of BSP both individually and class-wide to promote success. If nothing else, keep in mind that four positive statements to every negative statement (a 4:1 positive to negative ratio) will promote school success in your classroom (Myers et al., 2011), so use those BSP statements liberally!

 High-Leverage Practice Alert!

HLP20 outlines providing students with feedback to meet goals. This could certainly be directly related to behavioral goals as well!

Relationships Between Students

While the student-teacher relationship is an important one, creating a safe environment where your students will interact with one another is equally important. As a teacher, it is your job to facilitate student-to-student classroom interactions in a positive and proactive manner. Positive peer relationships are a positive predictor of school adjustment and school success (Steedly, Schwartz, Levin, & Luke, 2011). Relationships with one another also help students feel connected to one another and the school community. While individual student characteristics certainly affect the development of these relationships, they are also influenced by the classroom management system and a teacher's responsiveness to social dynamics and peer groups.

First and foremost, create behavioral norms and expectations that promote prosocial behaviors and respectful interactions. Highlight social acceptance, including discussions about the importance and value of having individual differences. Role model how students should interact by using the words and tones you expect students to use when talking with one another. Encourage these positive interactions by frequently regrouping students in seats and academic groups, increasing the opportunities to get to know one another and work with a range of other students.

In addition, supervise and monitor student interactions to include academic work groups, recess for younger students, and hallway behaviors for older students. By actively watching and noticing student interactions, potential disagreements, conflicts, and bullying behaviors, disruptive peer-to-peer issues can be squashed before they even begin. While it may be initially easier to avoid or ignore student-to-student negative behaviors, doing so will only create larger and deeper problems in the long run. Choose to stand up for all students, especially those who may be targeted because of disability, culture, race, language, gender, or other differences.

In elementary settings, consider that developmentally, students are still highly egocentric and working on skills like sharing, negotiating, and creating friendships. To assist with this, teachers may need to explicitly explain how students should interact while playing a game or working in a small group. To encourage inclusion, it may be beneficial for teachers to establish policies with parents that state that the distribution of invitations to private, out-of-school events must include all students if they will be given out at school. Should a parent or child want to invite only select students to a private event, then these individual students should be contacted outside of school. While the aforementioned events would happen out of school, a policy such as this lessens the potential exclusion of specific students based on any number of known or unknown factors and ultimately maintains a welcoming classroom environment.

As students get older, it is important for teachers to also closely observe peer affiliations or cliques. Support peer interactions and avoid feeding into hierarchies of social networks or groups. For example, some groups of students may be identified by themselves or others as "popular." As a result of their perceived or actual social status, these students may convince classmates that they should select project topics first, have preferred seating or activities assigned to them, or create workgroups to the exclusion of others. As a teacher, it is vital to treat all students as if they are in the "popular" group, not allowing students to establish hierarchies that place other students in disadvantaged or unsafe academic or social situations. It is sometimes easy to allow these affiliations or cliques to go unchallenged because it avoids potential pushback from students, yet this avoidance doesn't create a positive climate of inclusive relationship building.

Conflict between students is to be expected, and, in some cases, it is developmentally appropriate for students to begin navigating their rights within relationships. However, these conflicts need to occur in respectful and productive ways. For older students, model ways to share their perspectives and to come to resolutions about misunderstandings. Younger students may benefit from having an adult work with them to resolve conflicts. One way to facilitate conflict resolution is through teacher-led prompts (as outlined in Figure 9–1). Using active listening, a teacher can also rephrase or restate what students are sharing to help students make sense of the situation. Students should be encouraged to use I-messages and avoid name-calling. Sometimes, conflict may arise because students are lacking specific skills or do not understand how to execute skills in certain social situations. If this is the case, the teacher should work with the student through instruction, role-play, and practice to acquire the necessary skills to overcome this skill deficit.

Visit Chapter 14 to learn more about social skills.

Finally, conflict may be more prevalent in the younger grade levels in the form of tattling, "snitching," or gossiping. While some students see tattling as well-meaning efforts to encourage rule following and compliance, other students engage in tattling in attempts to get other students "in trouble." When presented with this challenge, consider turning tattling upside down and encourage "tootling" instead. Tootling is the opposite of tattling; rather than reporting negative behaviors, tootling promotes reports of positive behaviors (Skinner, Cashwell, & Skinner, 2000). Students can be taught how to deliver BSP, and tootles can be done verbally or on paper. This also opens up the opportunity for group contingencies by encouraging a specific number of tootles for rewards or reinforcement

Figure 9–1. Sample problem-solving prompts.

Problem-Solving Prompts
1. "Both of you will be given the chance to tell me your side of the story. Then, we will talk about any misunderstandings and come up with a solution."
2. "Student #1, tell me what happened."
3. "Student #2, tell me what happened."
4. "Students #1 and #2, what differences do you notice between your stories about what happened?"
5. "Why do you think these differences exist?"
6. "How could this situation been handled differently?"
7. "What will you do in the future to avoid this problem?"

activities or prizes. The best news about tootling is that it not only replaces tattling behaviors, but research also suggests that it reduces disruptive behavior (Lambert, Tingstrom, Sterling, Dufrene, & Lynne, 2015; Lum, Tingstrom, Dufrene, Radley, & Lynne, 2017) and increases appropriate behaviors (Lambert et al., 2015; McHugh, Tingstrom, Radley, Barry, & Walker, 2016).

> *Check out Chapter 8 for more information on group contingencies.*

Recognizing Diversity and Cultural Differences

As discussed in Chapter 3, it is essential teachers understand how students' culture, religion, background, or differing value systems might impact relationship building. Teachers should consider the ways in which students interact with both teachers and peers under a variety of situations and how teachers can create a culturally responsive environment. While it is impossible to know the profiles of students in your school from year to year, there are certainly some considerations that would apply to any classroom.

Students may come into your classroom with many assumptions about your role as the teacher. For example, some students may see teachers as authority figures who are held in high regard. These students may not value a close, personal relationship with the teacher outside of adhering to classroom expectations and procedures. Conversely, other students may not come from a home where education is valued and the teacher may be viewed as someone who holds them accountable in an undesirable way. For these students, the teacher may be viewed as an adversary and a person to keep at arm's length. In both examples, it may be difficult for the teacher to establish a close relationship with the student. However, this doesn't mean the students shouldn't be included in relationship-building activities and shouldn't be treated as warmly as the students who are engaging and open with the teacher. Help them to understand you better by creating a list of facts about yourself or asking students what they might want to know about you.

There will also be students in your classroom who look to you, as the teacher, as a parental figure, friend, or confidant. Just as a teacher needs to be aware of students who may be resistant to building a relationship, a teacher also needs to be aware and cautious of students who may need additional boundaries to maintain a professional teacher-student relationship. It may be helpful to explain your role as a teacher to establish and uphold clearly defined boundaries. With this being said, teachers should commit to avoiding stereotypes of students and not expecting them to fit into social boxes or expected relationships.

When working with students from a variety of backgrounds, it is important to realize that not all students (or adults) have experience with diversity. While staring or insensitive comments are undoubtedly hurtful, the root of these behaviors may be because of fear or confusion about the unknown. Instead of ignoring differences, invite students to share about their culture's traditions, clothing, food, holidays, or customs. Create opportunities for students to bring items to school that are important to their heritage, language, religion, or culture and allow them to teach others about these items. Select culturally diverse texts and books that are inclusive of a range of students' backgrounds and life circumstances. Use these texts to explore differences with positive and inclusive language. If you have students who have language barriers and are nonnative speakers, encourage them to teach peers vocabulary in their native language, or invite native speakers to create pictures or tools to support nonnative classmates.

Similarly, these same opportunities can be created if you have students who have visible or invisible disabilities. Look for ways to open the door for sharing and communication. Finally, create respectful environments that foster communities of learners by establishing, maintaining, and enforcing respectful treatment of all individuals. Ultimately, highlight differences among students in such a way that encourages uniqueness and individualization rather than isolation.

As a teacher, it would be virtually impossible to know the subtleties of all cultures and/or disabilities, so ask questions of your students to demonstrate you care to know more about them. Further, create opportunities for students to share privately with you any instances where the student has felt that peers or adults have not been sensitive or understanding. This may provide a teachable moment for the teacher or other students, or it may be a key to avoiding an adults' misinterpretation of that students' behavior because it is not understood. Remember that respecting each students' social identity will demonstrate that you, as a teacher, care about that student and want them to feel safe in your classroom. It is through knowledge that we become more comfortable with the unknown and more accepting of individual differences.

High-Leverage Practice Alert!

In HLP18, one way to promote student engagement is through knowing your students and making those personal connections through learning. Relationship building in the context of diversity is a perfect place to start!

Relationship-Building Activities

One of the ways teachers can encourage relationship building between themselves and students, as well as among students, is through a variety of activities in the classroom (Figure 9–2). This list is certainly not comprehensive and can be applied to both elementary and secondary settings. It should be noted that teachers should establish expectations for interactions and discussions prior to engaging in these activities. It is necessary for the teacher to create an environment that is safe for sharing and welcoming to all students. No relationships can be built in a classroom where students cannot openly participate in these activities without fear of being made fun of, bullied, or worse.

These activities can be done at the beginning, middle, or end of the year, depending on the cohesiveness of the group or the needs of individuals. These activities don't have to be time consuming but instead done as quick transitions as students enter or leave the room or wait for dismissals or assemblies to start. As you engage in these activities, consider how the information your students share can change how your learning environment is structured. Further, how could an atmosphere of trust and respect be further developed or enhanced? It is never too late to build relationships with students or between students.

Figure 9–2. Relationship-building activities. *continues*

Relationship-Building Activities

- **All About Me Posters.** Either provide students with templates or have students design posters about themselves. For younger students, this can include a finite number of sentence starters such as "My favorite color is . . . " or "I like to play the game" Students can also draw or attach photos. These posters can be displayed around the classroom and/or presented to classmates on a rotating basis. Older students can select from a bank of questions or prompts (e.g., What is your favorite sports team? My favorite books are . . .) or generate their own topics. While traditional posters could certainly be developed by middle school and high school students, they could also incorporate technology by developing digital posters that could be shared on a class web page or blog. Whether using this relationship builder with elementary or secondary students, teachers should be sensitive to the types of questions students are asked to answer. Prompts like "My favorite vacation . . . " may not be answerable by students who do not have the financial means to vacation and "What is your favorite activity to do with your dad?" would not be sensitive to students who do not have a father or father figure in the home. While a teacher certainly cannot know every student's challenges, being sensitive to these possibilities is an important factor when developing prompts.

- **Brown Bag/Warm Fuzzies.** Using a simple brown paper bag, students can fill the bag with five items from their home or school that describe themselves or gives them the "warm fuzzies." As a teacher, it is often helpful to complete this exercise first as a model. Showing students your own bag of items also encourages relationship building and opens the classroom up as a safe place for sharing. For example, in Mr. Ray's bag he might include a book because he likes to read, a bottle of sunscreen because summer is his favorite season, a clipping from a magazine that says "France" because he hopes to see the Eiffel Tower one day, a piece of candy because he loves sweets, and a photo of his dog because he adores his pet. Students can be invited to share with the whole class, small group, or a partner. This can be done one day or for many days, rotating partners. Teachers who use this relationship-building activity may want to set ground rules about only bringing nonperishable items and items that can fit in the small brown bag.

- **Student of the Week.** Either in conjunction or separately with the All About Me Posters or Brown Bags, students can be assigned as the star student or student of the week. While older students may not want to be called a "star," these students could still engage in sharing All About Me portfolios, artwork, sporting trophies

Figure 9–2. *continues*

or ribbons, photographs, or favorite items. Younger students can participate in a daily or once a week show and tell. This could even be expanded to inviting family members or friends to school as special guests or readers.

- **Five Items.** Much like the Brown Bag or Warm Fuzzies activity, students are asked to identify items that describe them as a person. Instead of finding items around the home or school, students are asked, "What are five items you could buy at the local store that describe you?" In this activity, teachers can limit the discussion to a type of store (e.g., grocery store, bookstore, convenience store, etc.) or select a local store all students have a general knowledge about. Again, modeling this activity would be helpful for students.

- **Five Things in Common.** This activity is a good fit for students who are older, have been together for many years, or know one another well. For this activity, students are placed in small groups of three or four. Groups larger than four may become too challenging to work effectively. With this activity, groups are asked to generate a list of five things they have in common. The caveat of this task, however, is that the five things cannot be something that everyone in the room would also have in common with the group. For example, if a teacher is using this activity with tenth graders, a small group could not say, "We are all tenth graders" because that would apply to every person in the room. Another example might be a group of students who use the commonality, "We all have two arms." If everyone in the room does indeed have two arms, this could not be used as a common fact. In fact, it is often more fun if students attempt to find the more original or obscure commonalities. This relationship-building exercise can also be rewarded with a prize for the most obscure or odd commonality among group members.

- **Money.** For this relationship-building activity, each group is allocated a specific amount of money. Directions can either include creating an island to live on and detailing how they are to spend the designated money or receiving a grant in their community and detailing how it would be used. Any responses are acceptable, but the groups must come to a consensus.

- **This or That.** The This or That activity gets students up and moving around the room but may not be an activity all students are comfortable participating in early in the school year. For this activity, the teacher states two choices, such as "chocolate ice cream or vanilla ice cream," and when stating each choice, points to one side of the room or the other. Students must select one of the two choices based on their preference. While some students may not like ice cream at all, all students should pick one of the two choices as the preferred or better choice.

Figure 9–2. *continued*

When first introducing this activity, it's important to keep the choices nonthreatening and impersonal. Questions such as beach or mountains, early riser or night owl, tea or coffee, or football or soccer are all easy ways to start this activity. Students can also be prompted to submit their own questions as a way to find other students who have common interests. This can be done in writing and submitted directly to the teacher.

- **Two Truths and a Lie.** In this activity, students share three facts, two of which are true and one of which is a lie. Other members of the class are responsible for determining which of the three statements is not true. Given that some students may overshare or give out personal information that is not appropriate for school, it is important for teachers to preview the three facts prior to sharing. Asking students to write down each of their statements, starring the statement that is not true, is an easy way to review what students want to share. It is then up to you, as the teacher, to make sure students aren't sharing overly personal information. Once the student has revealed the statement that isn't true, the class may ask questions about the two truths to get to know the student better.

- **BINGO.** There are many variations on this activity and it could be done as an introduction or a midyear recap of personal classroom information. In this activity, students are given a BINGO board with a variety of statements about classmates. Some statements may include "Find a classmate who has a sister" or "Find a classmate who likes to eat broccoli." As students find classmates who meet these criteria, they have the identified peer sign their name in the corresponding box. Therefore, if a student asked me if I liked broccoli, I would say yes and sign my name in the box that said "Find a classmate who likes to eat broccoli." To use this activity later in the school year, a teacher could write one fact about each student in each box. For example, "Find the student who got a puppy this fall" or "Which classmate lost a tooth during math this year?"

- **I Trust.** In an older elementary or secondary classroom, one way to get students thinking and talking about relationships with you as the teacher and with their peers is to consider what respect for one another looks and sounds like. First, ask students to finish this sentence: "Because I trust <fill in the blank with someone you trust>, I . . . _____." The word trust can also be replaced with respect. Students should be encouraged to include thoughts, behaviors, words, expectations, and/or feelings. Then, ask students to complete a second sentence starter: "Because I want someone to trust me, I . . . _____." Again, the word trust could be replaced with respect and responses should include thoughts, behaviors, words, expectations, and feelings. These two prompts can be used as a discussion starter between you and your students.

Conclusion

With all this being said, it's also important to remember that there is a limit to the amount of personal information that should be shared with students. While sharing photos of your pets or your favorite foods are completely reasonable, sharing information about your interactions with your spouse, what you did in Las Vegas, or stories of the "good old days" may not be appropriate. Remember, a great relationship with your students still means that you want your students to view you as their teacher, leader, mentor, and, most importantly, the professional that you are.

Chapter Summary

- Using names, avoiding sarcasm, avoiding power struggles, and focusing on relationship building, while maintaining sensitivity to student background, are some of the ways in which best practice guides educators toward building healthy relationships with students.

- Behavior-specific praise (BSP) is an evidence-based strategy that can improve overall classroom behavior while promoting positive relationships among all class members. These statements provide direct and immediate feedback to students on what behavior accesses praise and helps to strengthen compliance with expectations and norms.

- Student conflict is to be expected. Educators can be prepared to handle this via active listening, encouraging I-messages, and helping to rephrase or restate the situation to bring about clarity. For younger students, "tootling" may be used as a strategy to counter conflict by having students deliver positive praise to peers.

- Remain sensitive with regard to cultural diversity within the classroom. Create opportunities for students to share their background and ensure material used for learning is diverse and inclusive of various backgrounds, abilities, and life circumstances.

- Relationship-building activities are one way teachers can encourage and foster positive relationships in the classroom. This chapter provided several examples of such activities.

CHAPTER 10

BEHAVIORAL DATA COLLECTION

Learning Objectives

- Identify target behaviors and create corresponding operational definitions
- Identify and select a method for collecting behavioral data using dimensions of an identified behavior
- Define and understand how to collect frequency counts, duration recording, rate, time sampling (including whole interval, partial interval, and momentary time sampling), latency, magnitude, topography, and permanent products
- Describe the importance of setting data collection timelines and identify factors that influence timeline decision making
- Identify digital or physical tools that can be used for a variety of data collection
- Define and explain the importance of validity, accuracy, and reliability as it relates to data collection

Key Terms

Accurate
Antecedent
Duration Recording
Event Recording
Force
Frequency Counts
Latency
Magnitude
Momentary Time Sampling
Operational Definition
Partial Interval Recording

Permanent Product
Planned Activity Check (PLACHECK)
Rate
Reliable
Target Behavior
Termination Criteria
Time Sampling
Topography
Valid/Validity
Whole Interval Recording

Even with a classroom management structure in place, you may find that individual students require additional supports. While some solutions and strategies may be easy to identify, some situations may require additional information. Often, teachers need to observe students and analyze data to best understand the complexities of student behavior. Data collection is a first step to working with individual students on behavioral challenges.

Behavioral data collection is a critical component of developing functional behavioral assessments (FBAs), behavioral intervention plans (BIPs), and monitoring goals on Individualized Education Programs (IEPs). Briefly, an FBA is a thorough assessment aimed at sourcing the function, or the reason, of why a person is engaging in a specific behavior (e.g., is the reason for Patty's screaming in order to get attention or to avoid doing a particular task?) Once this function is determined, the next step is to develop a BIP, which seeks to decrease a challenging behavior while teaching an alternative, more prosocial replacement behavior.

> *Review Chapters 12 and 13 for a thorough discussion on FBAs and BIPs.*

Not only is data collection important for monitoring components of interventions related to challenging behavior, it is also a daily classroom necessity as it relates to routine academic assessments, grading, and general skill acquisition. Yet, while this is the case, the majority of this chapter will be focused on data collection as it relates to challenging behavior. Behavioral data collection is an integral component when determining appropriate behavioral interventions and monitoring progress (Mandinach & Gummer, 2013; Sulzer-Azaroff & Mayer, 1991). Evidence suggests that most classroom data collection practices are nonsystematic, incomplete, or inaccurate (Sandall, Schwartz, & Lacroix, 2004). It should be no surprise that data-based decisions are challenging for teachers (Dunn, Airola, Lo, & Garrison, 2013; Newton, Horner, Algozzine, Todd, & Algozzine, 2012). If data are inaccurate, incomplete, or do not reflect the target behavior, educators face a greater chance of selecting an intervention that is unsuitable and, consequently, ineffective (Lerman, Hovanetz, Strobel, & Tetreault, 2009). Further, if IEP goals include behavior components, not monitoring the IEP with accurate data collection could result in an insufficient IEP, ultimately denying a free and appropriate education (FAPE; Yell, Katsiyannis, Ennis, Losinski, & Christle, 2016).

Consequently, effective data collection is necessary to support informed decision making and progress monitoring. Specifically, data collection is a critical component of behavioral intervention selection, implementation, and progress monitoring with the goal of gathering information about conditions under which a behavior occurs and to generate hypotheses about why such behaviors are occurring (e.g., function of behavior). Once this is achieved, teachers or specialists are able to select and implement interventions specifically aligned to functions.

While data collection may become cumbersome if not streamlined, developing a data collection process can help gather a sufficient amount of information to analyze for assessments and goals. While indirect behavioral data collection—such as interviews or rating scales—has advantages (McIntosh et al., 2008), direct behavioral data collection—such as recording rate or duration—greatly reduces respondent bias (compromised data as a result of inability, unwillingness, or inaccurate responses to questions). Once direct behavioral data are collected, its analysis can be used to detect patterns or trends to guide decisions about interventions. It is important that both independent (intervention implementation) and dependent (student behavior) data are collected (Gresham, Gansle, & Noell, 1993) for data driven decision making.

Identifying and Defining Target Behaviors

Before any behavior change measures are taken, a target behavior, or the behavior selected for change, must be identified and deemed significant enough for such a process. It is critical that the behavior selected be one that, if changed, provides the student with both immediate and long-term benefits. Choosing a behavior to change is a highly personal, intimate process. Unfortunately, the nature of challenging behaviors can sometimes lead individuals in this role to select behaviors that are self-serving, rather than those which will improve the quality of life for the student. For example, Mr. Brown has decided to target Peter's incessant pacing. Peter frequently gets up in the middle of lessons to pace up and down the back portion of the classroom, which happens to be directly in Mr. Brown's sightline. With just knowing this bit of information, we can pose some questions to help us discern if pacing is an appropriate behavior to target. First, does Peter's pacing affect his learning? Keep in mind that one does not need to be sitting square on their bottom with eyes on teacher to "pay attention." Also consider that movement is necessary for some learners to focus, which may be the case with Peter. Next, are other classmates being affected by Peter's pacing? If Peter is in the back of the classroom and moving quietly, his peers may not even notice his movement. Finally, does the pacing render Mr. Brown unable to deliver a lesson and/or are there no other ways in which this can be dealt with? If the answers to these questions are "no," this may not be the most significant behavior to target, despite its somewhat disruptive nature to Mr. Brown. In other words, reduction of pacing will not likely lead to an improved quality of life for Peter or provide him with any short- or long-term benefits. In fact, if the pacing is targeted and Peter is no longer permitted to engage in this specific behavior, Peter may replace the pacing with a more distractible or dangerous behavior like tapping on his desk or leaning back in his chair. On the other hand, let's say Peter's pacing is not only distracting classmates but is also affecting Peter's ability to attend and retain information, as evidenced by falling test scores and his inability to answer questions in class discussions. If this is the case, perhaps targeting pacing may hold more benefit. Teachers should be reflective about the behaviors they are targeting. Is the behavior disrupting the learning of the student and/or others? Is the behavior unsafe? Is the behavior serving a function for a student that needs to be met?

Once a behavior is selected, but prior to data collection, it is imperative that the target behavior is defined in such a way that is measurable, observable, and objective (Gage & McDaniel, 2012), which is often referred to as an operational definition. A good operational definition is one that considers multiple dimensions of the behavior to measure, namely how many instances of behavior (i.e., frequency), for how long (i.e., duration), and at what point in time these instances occur (i.e., latency). Sometimes, dimensions such as magnitude (or force) and topography (or the physical form of the behavior) are helpful in describing the target behavior. Since a team of school personnel should be involved in data collection and subsequent behavioral planning, each person should be in agreement with the definition of the behavior. This provides team members, including teachers, with a clear picture of the behaviors that will be monitored and measured. This is particularly important at the middle school and high school levels where students have multiple teachers and behaviors may be inconsistent in different settings and throughout the day. If the behavior is not clearly defined, different team members may collect data or measure the behavior(s) in accordance with their own definition, yielding inaccurate or inconsistent data that does not sufficiently represent the target behavior, and thus does not produce effective behavior change.

In order to create objective and observable definitions, it is helpful for the team to describe exactly what they would see and hear if the target behavior were to occur. One easy way to remember how to write clear, concise operational definitions is to "make it MOO," or make sure it is *measurable*, *observable*, and *objective*. Creating T-charts to describe "what the behavior looks like" and "what the behavior sounds like" is also useful to hone in on subtleties of the behavior, which can affect how data are collected.

An objective definition includes language that all team members agree upon. If a behavior such as "disrespect" is being measured, then it is essential that all team members have the same definition of what disrespect looks and sounds like. For some people, this may include eye rolling, but for another person, it may be a student who talks out of turn during lessons. It is especially helpful if words like "expected," "disrespect," and "disruptive" are defined in observable and objective language since they tend to lend themselves to interpretation and may be linked back to an individual's personal values.

A definition is observable when it can be seen or heard by observers. Behaviors like "focused," "attentive," or "engaged" may not look the same for all students. In fact, one student's "focused" appearance may look identical to another student's "unfocused" appearance. Further, other behaviors like "on task," "distracted," "calm," or "annoyed" may not even be physically noticeable when exhibited by some students because there is no outward display or manifestation of the behavior. When creating observable definitions, be sure to accurately and completely describe what the behavior would look and sound like. Assumptions about the student's feelings cannot drive a well-crafted operational definition.

When behavior definitions are objective and observable, they can be measured. Measuring behavior can be accomplished via an observation using means such as frequency, duration, latency, or other concrete measures (which will be discussed in the following sections). The easiest way to know if the definition is suitable for data collection is to simply ask, "How and what would I measure if I used this definition?"

Using an example as an illustration, assume a teacher has concerns about a student who is "disruptive." To better understand what the target behavior looks and sounds like, the teacher would need to describe what the student is doing. Based on her observation, "disruptive" involves walking around the classroom. After further reflection, the teacher decides to label the target behavior "out of seat" since the term "disruptive" is subjective and does not accurately capture what the student is doing (or not doing). She further defines the behavior in the following measurable, observable, and objective terms: "Out of seat is standing up from an assigned seat, walking around the room, or standing at locations in the classroom other than an assigned seat during times when all students should remain in their assigned seat." In this way, the behavior is measurable (how many times does the student get out of his seat), observable (physical movement from the seat), and objective (free of any additional interpretation). Further, the teacher can also provide some nonexamples of when other teachers would expect to see the student out of his or her seat, such as sharpening a pencil or turning in completed work. Finally, the definition of the target behavior should be revisited after team members conduct a trial data collection session. This is one of the finest ways to determine if the definition is discrete enough for data collection. Once a behavior has been adequately defined, the next step is to decide on a data collection tool to use for data collection.

Methods of Behavioral Data Collection

Once the target behavior has been clearly defined, decisions around how to collect data are necessary in order to determine which dimensions of the behavior to measure. Such dimensions are comprised of frequency, duration, and latency, with magnitude and topography as supplements helpful in defining target behaviors. For example, if Thuy is talking during instruction, the teacher must decide whether the larger concern is the number of times Thuy is talking (i.e., frequency) or the total time spent talking during instruction (i.e., duration). Usually this decision is guided by the teacher or team's concerns about how the behavior is manifested with relation to impact on classroom disruption, academic engagement, and/or the student's or other's safety. In order to do this, the teacher may need to estimate either the frequency or the duration of the target behavior (e.g., once per hour, more than 10 times per hour, less than 1 min, greater than 5 min, etc.). As a starting point, collecting a simple rate or duration baseline (or preintervention measure of behavior) can be helpful to understand next steps for data collection. An overview of different types of measurements and related behaviors is presented in Table 10–1.

Table 10–1. An Overview of Different Types of Measurements and Related Behaviors

Data Collection Method	Behavior Type
Frequency	• Behavior is infrequent • Behavior is easy to count/discrete • Length of observation time is consistent
Rate	• Length of observation time varies • Behavior does not occur too often
ABC	• Behavior is infrequent • Behavior is easy to count/discrete • Length of observation time is consistent
Duration	• Behavior occurs for long periods of time, with clear start and stop • Infrequent, long-lasting behaviors
Latency	• Objective of data is to know how long it takes for student to begin a behavior after presented with opportunity
Interval	• High-frequency behaviors • Short duration • Behavior is constant
Scatterplot	• High frequency behaviors • Short duration • Behavior is constant
Time Sampling	• High frequency behaviors • Short duration • Behavior is constant • Observer needs to record multiple behaviors of multiple students at once
Permanent Product	• When documentation of an intervention is needed • If extra data are needed to support primary method of data collection

Frequency Counts

Using the aforementioned talking example, the teacher might suggest frequency counts, or event recording, to collect data on the number of times Thuy talks to peers. She may also suggest duration recording to record how long she talks to others. Frequency data collection simply reflects the count of behaviors across the unit of time measured, or behaviors per unit of time. In this way, the terms frequency and rate are used interchangeably. Ensuring that time is measured in addition to the frequency of behavior is critical, as without this information, data are skewed and misinterpreted. For example, consider the following reports on Thuy's behavior: "Thuy talked out of turn 12 times yesterday"; versus "Thuy talked out of turn 12 times between 1:00 p.m. and 2:00 p.m." The former statement is much less descriptive, while the latter gives information about rate per hour as well as guidance to look at what else is happening between 1:00 p.m. and 2:00 p.m. that may be contributing to Thuy's behavior. Referencing the time measured along with count of behavior is also important when comparing sets of data for interpretation. One could say that if Lola and Sian both typed 50 correct words per minute, their performance is comparable; whereas, if we only knew Lola and Sian are able to type 50 correct words, we are prematurely assuming they are of the same skill level (perhaps Sian took 3 min, while Lola only took 45 s). Knowing the unit of time measured is integral in being able to accurately evaluate and compare data.

Frequency data collection lends itself to discrete behaviors, or behaviors that have a clear "start" and "stop." For instance, raising a hand, moving out of an assigned seat/area, throwing an object, or requests for help would all be behaviors that could be recorded with frequency. Behaviors such as crying or "tantrums" are not suited to frequency counts as they have a more ambiguous start and stop. Such behaviors are more appropriately measured via duration recording and require specific definitions of what constitutes a discrete instance of the behavior (e.g., a clear start and stop).

Using a frequency data collection method can also aid in evaluating skill development as it allows for correct and incorrect responses to be calculated. Consider if one were to only measure correct responses; it would appear as though performance is improving. But what if incorrect responses were also increasing? Take for instance a teacher recording correct responses of hand raising to replace Thuy's calling out. As Thuy learns the hand-raising skill, she begins to demonstrate more hand raising (e.g., correct response). However, if Thuy's teacher were to also record instances of calling out (e.g., incorrect response) and notice that she is still calling out at the same rate as baseline, the data indicate Thuy is not progressing as intended. There are countless ways in which one may collect frequency data. Pragmatically, teachers may use simple tally marks (Figure 10–1), physically move objects from one pocket or space to another, or use handheld click counters.

Figure 10–1. Frequency count data chart.

Behavior of Concern: Out of seat or assigned area				
Monday	Tuesday	Wednesday	Thursday	Friday
|||	||	⊥⊥⊥⊦					||||

Duration Recording

Using the aforementioned example, if Thuy's teacher was most concerned with how long Thuy talked out during instruction, she might select duration recording as the best method for data collection. Duration recording includes recording the length of time the behavior occurs. This may be helpful for nondiscrete, or continuous, behaviors, such as tantruming, independent or parallel play, sleeping, or refusal to do work. It is important to include termination criteria along with the operational definitions of behaviors to be measured via duration. Termination criteria provide clear parameters for when one behavior terminates, or is "complete," and another one begins. For example, tantrum behavior may be defined as a student engaging in any/all of the following for at least 1 min: screaming, kicking, hitting, or lying on the floor. The termination criteria would indicate the episode concludes when there is an absence of screaming, kicking or hitting, and/or lying on the floor for two consecutive minutes.

Duration data collection can be done using a wall clock, stopwatch, or any number of tablet applications or online counters. Regardless of the data collection method, it is important that the individual who is recording is able to attend to the observed behavior to accurately capture beginning and end times. In the example with Thuy's talking, the teacher decided to simply attach a sticky note to the back of his employee badge and used a classroom wall clock to record beginning and ending times when Thuy talked out during instruction.

Time Sampling

When it is impractical to constantly observe behavior or if behavior is occurring at a very high rate (e.g., more than x times per x), another practical option for collecting behavior data is to use a time sampling method. Time sampling indicates whether or not a behavior occurred during a particular period of time. There are three main variations of time sampling: whole interval recording, partial interval recording, and momentary time sampling. While this data collection method provides approximations, it is practical for classroom use, as it does not require the intensity or long-term commitment that a traditional frequency count would require. Time sampling does require periods of brief focused attention to monitoring time, so having some support in the classroom to collect these data may be beneficial.

Whole Interval Recording

Whole interval recording is well suited for continuous behaviors or ones in which it is difficult to discern a beginning and end point (e.g., tantrums, tics, self-stimulatory behaviors, etc.). For this method of data recording, an observation period is divided into equal parts. For instance, a 10-min observation block may be divided into ten 1-min intervals. It is important to have rough baseline estimate of how often the target behavior occurs in order to appropriately designate an interval. Too short of an interval may become cumbersome, while too long may not capture the desired data. Once this is determined, the observer records data at the end of each interval. An affirmative or positive interval is indicated if the target behavior occurred *throughout the entirety* of the interval. If the behavior does not last the duration of the interval or if the behavior ceases and then starts again during the interval, the interval is marked as a negative. Data gathered via whole interval provides information on the total duration of behavior; however, due to the nature of whole interval sampling, behaviors tend to be underestimated (Alberto & Troutman, 2013). For example, if a student was out of his or her seat for 58 of 60 s, this interval would be marked as a negative because the behavior did not occur for the entirety of the interval, thus underestimating overall out-of-seat behavior.

Assume a student exhibits self-stimulatory behavior where he emits loud humminglike vocalizations. These vocalizations do not interrupt the student's work, but are reportedly disruptive to other students. The teacher has defined the behavior and based off of initial baseline measures, has decided to use whole interval recording. Data will be collected for 10 min during independent work-stations. The 10-min period is divided into ten 1-min intervals. Using his tablet timer, the teacher begins the interval and waits for the student to display the target behavior. If there is any portion of the interval in which the student *does not* emit the vocalization, the interval is marked as negative. However, if the student vocalizes throughout an entire interval, it is marked as positive. The percentage of time spent vocalizing is obtained by dividing the number of positive intervals by the total amount of intervals (e.g., 10) and then multiplied by 100.

Partial Interval Recording

Partial interval recording is best for behaviors that occur quickly, do not last for long periods of time, or situations in which other data collection methods (such as frequency or rate recording) are not feasible. While not concerned with the frequency or duration of target behaviors per interval, partial interval recording is well suited for very high rate behaviors and reflects whether the target behavior occurs at *any point* during the interval. Just as with whole interval recording, an observation period is divided into equal intervals and an observer marks an affirmative, or positive, in the presence of the behavior. If the target behavior does not occur during the interval, a negative, or absent, mark is recorded (Ayres & Ledford, 2014). As such, partial interval recording provides a glimpse at the minimum rate of responding per observation period.

Partial interval recording may be easier to execute for a teacher who is actively engaged in instruction since he or she is looking for a discrete behavior to occur in any part of the interval. Further, partial interval recording lends itself to being able to measure multiple behaviors of multiple students concurrently. For example, a teacher has 1-min intervals set up to record target behaviors of three students (hand raising, being out of seat, and throwing items). The teacher observes student 1 for the first minute, marking a positive or negative for behavior, then moves on to student 2 for the second minute, and so on. Because behavior may occur multiple times within the interval but is only recorded once, partial interval recording tends to overestimate behaviors; information gained from this method provides the proportion of observation periods the behavior occurred (Alberto & Troutman, 2013; Cooper, Heron, & Heward, 2019).

In order to collect data at a scheduled interval, it is necessary to have a timer to repeatedly remind the observer of the scheduled intervals (e.g., 10 s, 2 min, etc.). Several online timers have features that allow users to loop countdowns with each culminating with a quick alert. Several phone or computer apps also include this feature and allow the user to predetermine intervals. Whatever the method, the timer should be easily accessible and not be a distraction to the teacher or students.

Both whole and partial interval data are reported with regard to the percentage of total intervals in which the behavior occurred. A simple formula of

$$\frac{\text{\# of intervals behavior occurred}}{\text{\# of intervals behavior occurred} + \text{\# of intervals behavior did not occur}} \times 100$$

Consider the example in Table 10–2 of partial interval recording for throwing items, where each interval is 5-min.

If the desired goal is to estimate the frequency of the target behavior, one may divide the number of positive intervals by the total number of intervals, which would indicate that throwing items occurred in 75% of the intervals observed.

Table 10–2. Partial Interval Recording for Throwing Items				
Thursday, 4th of April	Interval #			
10:00 a.m.–10:20 a.m.	1	2	3	4
+/–	+	+	–	+

Momentary Time Sampling

Momentary time sampling is another way for teachers to provide snapshots or approximations of behavior. This method, while also having some limitations, provides opportunities for longer observation periods and more data points. Since the observation periods may be longer than interval recording, this method is slightly easier for teachers to manage during instruction. During momentary time sampling, the target behavior is only observed and recorded at the end of the interval period versus during the entire interval period, like in interval recording. With this data collection, the behavior is only counted if it is happening at the exact moment the time interval ends. For example, given a 1-min interval and a target behavior of "attending," the behavior would only be counted if the student is attending to a task at the end of the 1-min mark, 2-min mark, and so on. Even if attending were to occur at the 30-s mark and 45-s mark, it is only recorded if it happened at the identified interval's end (i.e., 1-min). Because it only requires a moment to record data, this method frees the teacher for instruction and allows him or her to maintain "withitness" (Kounin, 1970) in the classroom, versus focusing solely on the student with challenging behavior. Yet, since data are only taken at brief moments of time, there are many opportunities for target behaviors to be missed, which can result in an underestimate of behavior. As such, this method is best suited for continuous, or ongoing, behaviors rather than lower frequency, discrete behaviors.

> *Review Chapter 1 to read more about Kounin.*

Perhaps one of the most practical and valuable variations of time sampling is known as a Planned Activity Check, or PLACHECK for short. PLACHECK allows teachers to observe and measure group behavior quickly and easily. PLACHECK requires the teacher to decide upon a target behavior, ideally one that is continuous or high frequency in nature, and an interval for recording. Just as with momentary time sampling, once the specified interval is over, the teacher scans the room and tallies how many students are engaged in the target behavior. Overall, data are recorded as the percentage of the group engaged in the target behavior for each interval. Because this data collection method is helpful for monitoring group behavior, a teacher may use it to determine if students are remaining engaged throughout a lesson. The teacher needs to simply decide on an interval and set up a timer. The teacher then begins the lesson and waits for the timer prompt, at which time he scans the classroom and records how many students are engaged in the lesson (according to his operational definition of "engagement," of course). These steps are repeated for each interval and then graphed.

Review Chapter 11 to read more about data graphing.

Latency

Collecting data on latency provides information on how much time elapses between a prompt, or opportunity to engage in a target behavior, and initiation of the behavior. For example, if Ms. Nancy gives an instruction for a student to begin work, latency would be measured from the time she gave the instruction until the student began working. This type of measure is helpful when determining if a student is becoming more fluent, or faster, with behaviors such as starting tasks, transitioning between activities, recalling facts, and so forth. Alternatively, latency data also may be used in the prevention of challenging behavior by measuring the length of time between a trigger, or antecedent, (e.g., "Get out your math book and do questions 20–40") and challenging behavior (e.g., student throws books on floor). This information can help the teacher know exactly *when* to prompt the student with a new, more functional behavior (e.g., student asks for help) to precede the challenging behavior. As with duration, a timer is required for recording and these data are typically reported by average latency, which can be calculated by adding together each latency and dividing by number of opportunities measured. For example, if a student took 1 min, 4 min, and 90 s to begin their assigned work, we would add 60 + 240 + 90 s and divide by 3. This would inform us that the student took an average of 130 s, or a little over 2 min, to begin assigned work. This form of data collection may also warrant another individual to assist, as it does require careful attention and observation.

Magnitude (Force)

Behavior may also be measured by its magnitude and its topography. Both are important features, yet these are meant to be supplementary measurements to the dimensions mentioned previously as they do not indicate the occurrence of behavior. Magnitude, or force, is the degree of intensity a behavior emits (Cooper et al., 2019). Applying too much force on a pencil on paper will result in a broken pencil, while if one does not apply enough force to a stapler, nothing will get stapled. Classroom instances in which measuring magnitude may be beneficial include addressing voice volume, opening or closing materials, throwing a basketball into a hoop, and so forth. Because the behavior being observed is one that is dependent on a certain magnitude, or range of magnitudes, one can measure this with direct observation or a scale based off of specific descriptions of the target behavior. For some behaviors with a permanent product, direct observations are effective measurements and can be as simple as a yes/no indicator of "did the paper get stapled?" or "did the ball approach the height of the hoop?" If the target behavior is continuous, one may devise a scale based off of what the target behavior looks and sounds like. For example, if the target behavior is "tantruming," then a teacher or team might define "tantrum" with a range of behaviors to include sulking without engaging with others, yelling, kicking, or stomping. In addition, the magnitude of the behavior could also include whether the student remains in his or her seat and has a tantrum or ends up lying on the floor having a tantrum. Table 10–3 is an example of creating a scale for magnitude of tantrums.

Topography

Topography refers to the physical form of the behavior, or what the behavior looks and sounds like. Topographical descriptions are often part of quality operational definitions as they are objective observations of the target behavior. This is

Table 10–3. Sample Intensity of Behavior Scale

Intensity	Behaviors
1	In seat; crying, sulking, whining, vocalizations, etc.
2	In seat (crying, sulking, whining, vocalizations, etc.) AND slamming fists on surface, stomping feet, pushing items
3	Out of seat (crying, sulking, whining, vocalizations, etc., slamming fists on surface, stomping feet, pushing items) AND throwing self on floor, punching, kicking

especially important if the behavior involves social constructs or other subtleties in need of clarification. Topography helps teachers break down terms like "disruptive" and focus on which observable behaviors "disruptive" encompasses, bearing in mind these will differ across individual students. A topographical description of behavior is one that is free of emotion, assumption of intent, and simply describes the outward appearance of behavior. What topography does not capture is the "why" or function of the behavior. Topography is often of most importance for behaviors that rely on some sort of artistic ability (e.g., handwriting, coloring within the lines, etc.) or specific physical capabilities (e.g., holding a pencil, running, specific sport skills, etc.).

> *See Chapter 12 to read more about functions of behavior.*

Permanent Products

While the aforementioned methods for data collection are conducted in real-time, some behaviors allow for data to be recorded after they have taken place. A permanent product is a concrete artifact or an observable outcome of a behavior. For example, a permanent product could be submitted homework, tests, or projects. Measuring permanent products is a fantastic option for teachers as it does not require the recorder to be present, freeing up precious instructional time. Some behaviors have naturally occurring permanent products (e.g., a clean room, a writing sample); however, for behaviors that do not leave lasting effects on the environment, one may contrive a permanent product. Audio and video recordings of individuals yield a permanent product that allows for observation and measurement of target behaviors. In this way, permanent products also allow for more careful and accurate measurement as the observer is afforded multiple opportunities to listen, watch, pause, and rewind the segment and capture aspects that may have been missed in a real-time observation. This is also helpful when measuring complex series of behaviors or if the environment in which the behavior occurs is quite active or fast paced. When considering the use of permanent products for data collection, Cooper et al. (2019) put forth two basic "rules" to determine if the behavior is appropriate for this type of measurement. First, the target behavior must produce the same permanent product each time (e.g., producing a work sample, completing a typing task, etc.). For example, consider tidying up one's workspace. A permanent product measure may be the number of items left on the desktop or work surface (with the objective of having zero items remaining). Next, the permanent product is only produced by the target behavior. If one were to measure number of items left on the desk, the observer would need to be assured that no one else contributed to the tidying up (LeBlanc, Raetz, Sellers, & Carr, 2016). As such, a possible disadvantage to using permanent product data collection is not being certain a particular individual produced the product. Further, without direct observation in real time, it is impossible to know if there was interference from other factors that affected the product's production (e.g., if a fire drill went off during the typing task).

Setting Data Collection Timelines

After determining the method for data collection, it is now time to decide where, when, and for how long to collect data. Settings are critical to understand the antecedents, or triggers, that precede target behaviors. In order to gain a more complete picture of the target behavior, it is beneficial to consider not only where it occurs most often but also where it is less likely to occur. Settings may include specific classrooms, transition areas such as hallways, restrooms, the cafeteria, or the bus. Further, they can be more specific and focus on areas within a classroom (e.g. reading table, carpet, front row of seats) or specific seats on a bus. To ensure a complete capture of target behavior, one must consider factors beyond just the physical location in which the target behavior is occurring, such as the following:

- Who is around while the target behavior occurs?
- Does the target behavior occur with specific staff or peers?
- When does it occur?
- Does this vary across time?
- Are there activities during which the behavior occurs *or does not* occur?

Check out Chapter 12 for a detailed description on Antecedent-Behavior-Consequence (ABC) data collection, which includes considerations on settings of challenging behaviors.

Collecting data can seem like a daunting task for a teacher, especially considering the multitude of other responsibilities being juggled. A common misconception is that data collection must occur all day every day, which is simply not true. With some careful planning, data collection need not be time consuming or overwhelming. While some data collection sessions may need to occur for extended periods of time due to the nature of the target behavior (e.g., infrequent or long duration), short intervals of data collection may only need to happen for 10 to 20 min, depending on the severity of behaviors. To establish a baseline, educators should collect a minimum of three to five data points over the course of several days or weeks. Ultimately, baseline data should be stable, with more data points collected yielding more reliable data. However, this can be shortened if the target behavior is dangerous or if it is unethical to withhold an intervention for a period of time. Regardless of the time of day or location, the more opportunities there are for data collection, the more accurate the results of the data analysis. Therefore, a team should invest in the time to collect many samples of data across settings, time of a day, people, and days of the week. One such approach could include a staggered two-week plan as outlined in Table 10–4.

Collecting data during different times of the day with different school personnel is beneficial since behaviors may increase or decrease given any number of factors (e.g., hunger, alertness, etc.). Student behaviors may affect different school personnel (e.g., administrators, teachers, etc.) differently, reinforcing the need for multiple data sources across individuals (Crone, Hawken, & Horner, 2015). Depending on the target behavior, these specifics may contribute to a clearer understanding of the behavior and whether or not they may be time or person specific.

When collecting student data, it is important to attempt to be as discreet as possible in order to preserve the integrity of the data collection. If the student is aware of the data collection, he or she may react or alter his or her behavior as a response. If another staff is completing the data collection session, it is helpful to prepare an explanation of why they are there that does not indicate data are being collected on a student, which could be as simple as "I'm observing your teacher today to see how he delivers this lesson" or "I wanted to watch your class read this portion of Romeo and Juliet, it's my favorite." Scanning the entire room, as in a whole-class observation style, or even using peripheral vision while writing or reviewing notes will reduce the focus on particular students.

Table 10–4. Staggered Data Collection Times

	Monday	Tuesday	Wednesday	Thursday	Friday
9:00 a.m.–10:00 a.m.					
10:00 a.m.–11:00 a.m.					
11:00 a.m.–12:00 p.m.					
12:00 p.m.–1:00 p.m.			X		
1:00 p.m.–2:00 p.m.		X		X	
2:00 p.m.–3:00 p.m.	X				X
	Monday	Tuesday	Wednesday	Thursday	Friday
9:00 a.m.–10:00 a.m.			X		
10:00 a.m.–11:00 a.m.		X		X	
11:00 a.m.–12:00 p.m.	X				X
12:00 p.m.–1:00 p.m.					
1:00 p.m.–2:00 p.m.					
2:00 p.m.–3:00 p.m.					

While self-monitoring is an important skill for students to learn, a teacher who is collecting data about a student should utilize discretion to best understand the target behavior (Table 10–5).

Table 10–5. Data Collection Solutions	
Method or Program	**Types of Data Collection**
Handheld golf counter	Frequency
Sticky note on badge, pen	Frequency, duration
Stopwatch	Duration, latency
Super Duper Data Tracker	Frequency

See Chapter 14 to read more about self-monitoring.

Data Collection Tools

The next step in the process is to decide on the type of data collection sheet or strategy for the data collection. Data collection tools should be compatible with the type of data being collected (Yell et al., 2016). Data collection can be done by hand using sticky notes, simple grids or charts, or apps on tablets or phones as referenced in Table 10–6. There are also websites that provide additional data collection tools and some of these options are listed in Table 10–6. The means of collecting data may be highly individualized, but no matter what method is used, the collector should be comfortable using the tool and should understand the organization of the data collection.

Considerations for Data Collection

Thus far, we have discussed the importance of identifying target behaviors, creating accurate and measurable definitions, choosing appropriate data collection methods, and deciding which tools to use for data collection. However, in order to be useful, the data collected must be valid, accurate, and reliable. Measurements hold validity when the dimension of the data being measured aligns with the intended target behavior; in other words, is the data collection measuring what it is intended to measure? For example, every Friday Ms. Kate gives her class a timed 20-question quiz on multiplication tables. If she wanted to measure student fluency with multiplication tables, a valid measurement would be number of

Table 10–6. Websites for Data Collection

Website	URL Address	Description
PBIS World	http://www.pbisworld.com/data-tracking/	Using a tiered intervention framework, this website provides data collection templates and spreadsheets to organize behavior tracking.
Chartdog 2.0	http://www.jimwright online.com/php/chartdog _2_0/chartdog.php	Chartdog allows users to input their own parameters and plot behavior data over time.
The Curriculum Corner	http://www.thecurriculum corner.com/thecurriculum corner123/2014/07/student-data-binder/	Website includes a student data binder that tracks progress in editable downloads.
University of Nebraska–Lincoln Student Engagement Project	http://k12engagement.unl .edu/databasic1	Provides downloadable tools for student data collection including anecdotal reports, student engagement monitoring, work completion, and student goal tracking.

correctly answered questions in the time allotted, without extended time or opportunities for corrections. Measurement is accurate when the observed value of an event matches the true value of the event (Johnston & Pennypacker, 1993). This brings us back to making sure behaviors are operationally defined and all those collecting data are truly watching for the same behaviors. Consider the scoreboard for a basketball game; the score posted for each team *accurately* reflects the number of points earned by each team. If a student's target behavior has been defined as "out of seat," then no behaviors that are related (e.g., using the water fountain) or unrelated (e.g., forgetting homework) should be recorded. Only recording when the student is out of his or her seat accurately reflects the number of instances the behavior occurs. And finally, measurement must be reliable, meaning the measurement produces the same value over repeated measurements. For instance, the dimensions of a desk are measured multiple times, these data are reliable if each measurement yielded the same information. A reliable measurement of tantruming would mean that if all members of a student's team watched a video of the tantrum's intensity, they would all score the tantrum the same way, using the predetermined measurement scale.

Together, when measurement is valid, accurate, and reliable, the data are trustworthy and may be used to guide intervention plans. However, when data measurement is lacking in one of these three conceptual areas, the data are flawed in some way, and may erroneously guide a data-based decision. It is safe to say that accuracy and validity, above all, are the most important concepts for data measurement. If what is being measured is not valid, then there is no point to it being accurate. If what is being measured is inaccurate, the data will always be incorrect. Reliability is a bit of a funny concept as it refers to the degree to which a data collection method produces consistent results; reliability does not reflect accuracy in the data. Think of reliability as a "double-check" on data; measuring the same behavior more than once and looking for consistency. Bear in mind, however, one may repeatedly measure inaccurate data, yet still obtain reliable results.

As you would expect, there are a variety of factors that post threats to validity, accuracy, and reliability. Indirect measurement, or when the target behavior is measured via a proxy or intermediary means (e.g., a description from a substitute teacher after the fact, other student reports, etc.), is a threat to measurement validity. Indirect measurement threatens validity because it forces the observer to rely on secondhand information to infer aspects about the target behavior and its relationship with the environment. Self-reports or satisfaction surveys are some examples of indirect measurement as the target behavior is not being directly observed. Another common threat to validity, particularly amongst classroom teachers, is measuring the wrong dimension of the target behavior. Simply put, will the aspect of the target behavior being measured provide valid information on what is being sought by the measurement? If you want to know more about how heavy different cell phones are, then measuring weight would provide valid data. Further, ensuring the correct unit of measurement (e.g., grams, ounces, pounds, etc.) is also important when comparing the data across samples. If one were to measure each cell phone's length and width, those measurements may be accurate and reliable; however, those data are irrelevant to the original question. If a teacher wanted to create math groups based off of math fact fluency, measuring just number of correct responses provided by a student would be insufficient. The teacher would also need to collect data on how quickly the student provided the correct response, as fluency is not only about accuracy but also about speed.

As stated previously, reliability refers to consistently obtaining the same result across multiple measurements. For the simple fact we are measuring behavior, the most significant threat to this is human error. These errors may come about from a variety of factors such as having an overly complex measurement system, inadequate training for observers collecting the data, or unintended bias from an observer. If an observer is not naive to the intent of the data collection, observer expectations may seep in. For example, knowing the intent of a reading intervention's effect on reading accuracy may affect an observer's count of words read per minute. Similarly, if a teacher expects a student who exhibits challenging behavior to be "bad," he or she may count more instances of challenging behavior potentially due to this underlying expectation. Additionally, reactivity on behalf of the observer is another threat to reliable data collection. Observers aware the data being collected will be used and possibly compared to other observer's reports may tinge what is recorded.

Conclusion

Beyond a strong foundation in classroom management, educators must understand how and when to collect data on behavior in order to effectively support specific students. Behavior is multi-faceted and dynamic, which requires educators to adopt a streamlined approach to data collection. As such, the development of effective data collection processes not only helps to clarify the events surrounding challenging behavior, but also provides insight on how educators can improve their practice. Finally, information gathered from these data are critical to inform decisions that affect both the individual student as well as the classroom community.

Chapter Summary

- The importance of behavioral data collection extends beyond classroom management. Behavior data must be captured accurately and efficiently in order to choose appropriate function-based interventions as well as satisfy measurement criteria in documents such as IEPs, FBAs, and BIPs.

- Behavioral data are vital in supporting data-based decisions as it informs patterns or trends in behavior that can guide interventions.

- Choosing a salient target behavior is of critical importance. Evaluate the effects of the behavior not only on the student but also on classmates and the teacher as well as evaluate its effect on classroom climate (e.g., teacher unable to deliver an effective lesson).

- Operational definitions allow for multiple dimensions of behavior to be measured accurately. Involving multiple members of a school team ensures a more accurate description of what the behavior looks and sounds like.

- Operational definitions must be *measurable, observable,* and *objective.* Measurable behaviors are those that can be counted (e.g., frequency, duration, etc.), observed (e.g., physical movement, sound, effect on the environment, etc.), and objective (e.g., free from feelings or assumptions).

- Frequency counts/event recording examines the number of times a behavior occurs across time. This form of data collection is suitable for behaviors that are discrete in nature (behaviors with a clear "start" and "stop").

- Duration recording examines how long a target behavior occurs. This data collection method is best suited for nondiscrete or continuous behaviors. Include termination criteria along with these operational definitions to ensure clarity on when one behavior is "finished" and another one begins.

- Time sampling is a data collection method that indicates if a behavior did or did not occur within a specified interval of time. There are three main types of time sampling: whole interval recording, partial interval recording, and momentary time sampling. This method is best suited if it is impractical to constantly observe a behavior or if a target behavior occurs at a very high rate.

- Whole interval recording is suited for continuous behaviors without a clear start and stop. Divide an observation period into equal parts based off of baseline measures of behavior. A positive interval is noted when the target behavior occurs throughout the entire interval. A negative interval is noted if the behavior does not last throughout the interval or if the behavior stops and restarts within an interval. This method underestimates behavior.

- Partial interval recording is suited for behaviors that occur quickly, are short in duration, or occur at high rates. Set an observation period divided into equal parts; a positive interval indicates the target behavior occurred, while a negative interval is the complete absence of the target behavior within the interval.

- To calculate whole or partial interval data, use the following formula:

$$\frac{\text{\# of intervals behavior occurred}}{\text{\# of intervals behavior occurred} + \text{\# of intervals behavior did not occur}} \times 100$$

- Momentary time sampling involves observing the target behavior only at the very end of the interval. The behavior is only counted if it is occurring at the precise moment the interval ends. While this method allows for teachers to be unencumbered by data collection, it tends to under report estimates of behavior.

- PLACHECK (Planned Activity Check) is a way to measure group behavior quickly and easily. It is best suited for high frequency or continuous behaviors. Using a momentary time sample interval system, the teacher scans the room at the end of each interval and marks/tallies students engaged in target behavior.

- Latency refers to the elapsed time between a prompt and an individual's response.

- Magnitude refers to the force or degree of intensity emitted by a behavior. This can be measured via permanent products (i.e., artifacts of an observable outcome of behavior), specific descriptions of the behavior, or a teacher-created scale with specific behavioral references.

- Topography looks at the physical form of behavior; what a behavior looks and sounds like.

- Preceding triggers or environmental changes to behaviors are known as antecedents. These can include places, people, materials, or other factors that affect the individual engaging in the target behavior.

- In order for data to be useful, it must be valid, accurate, and reliable. A measurement is valid when the data collection is measuring what it is intended to measure. Accurate data are when the observed value of an event matches its true value. And reliable data produce the same value over repeated measurements.

- Indirect measurement is a threat to validity as it relies upon secondhand information. Additionally, measuring the wrong dimension of behavior will threaten validity.

- Human error, unintended bias, and reactivity all threaten reliability.

CHAPTER 11

GRAPHING AND DATA ANALYSIS

Learning Objectives

- Understand the importance of visually displaying data and learn how data in this form can assist in classroom decision making
- Describe the basics of single-subject design and how to use visual analysis on these data
- Discriminate between single-subject and group design and understand conditions under which each one is to be used
- Describe the different types of single-subject designs discussed and identify strengths and weaknesses for each
- Identify basic elements of graphing

Key Terms

Applied Behavior Analysis (ABA)	Replication
Baseline	Reversal Design
Dependent Variable	Scatterplot
Experimental Control	Single-Subject Design
Independent Variable	Trend
Level	Variability
Multiple Baseline Design	Verification
Prediction	Visual Analysis

The previous chapter spent quite a bit of time discussing the details involved in collecting accurate, valid, and reliable data; however, that is just the first step. For a moment, let's recall the *why* behind data collection by asking, what is the purpose of taking these extensive steps to gather information on a student's hand raising, truancy, or screaming? First and foremost, the data collected informs a teacher or school team about baseline levels of behavior and helps guide which intervention to apply. Next, as interventions are being applied, data collection is vital because it reveals what is happening over time: Are behaviors improving? Getting worse? Unchanged? This vital data collection results in data sheets with heaps of numbers representing frequency, duration, or any other dimension measured but which are not easily interpretable. Herein is where visual displays or graphing of data are a teacher's best friend.

Graphs are simple visual displays of data that help us efficiently make sense of data gathered. Graphic displays of data provide quick summaries and highlight relationships among the data. They provide loads of information in a tiny space and, since they use nearly zero text, they are inherently more accessible to individuals who may not be well versed in data analysis, such as parents or even the students themselves. Before we dive into the "how-tos" of graphing behavioral data, let's first explore the underlying structure of single-subject experimental designs and how they fit into the field of Applied Behavior Analysis (ABA). Note that this chapter will not cover every single-subject design as it is meant to provide an introductory overview. The intent of this chapter is to demonstrate how these designs link with behavioral interventions and guide practitioners on how to implement interventions with purpose and evaluate results.

 High-Leverage Practice Alert!

HLP6 focuses on using student data to make adjustments in instruction and improve student outcomes. This entire chapter specifically targets the information outlined in HLP6.

Applied Behavior Analysis

Applied behavior analysis (ABA) is the scientific discipline that relies upon theories of learning and behavior to improve socially significant behaviors. ABA has replaced the former term *behavior modification,* which insinuated that individuals who were the focus for the intervention had no input or even knowledge about their behavior being altered. ABA aims to replace challenging behaviors with positive, prosocial behaviors. ABA is a science, and, as such, it relies upon experimental design to demonstrate a functional relation between independent variables (i.e., the intervention) and dependent variables (i.e., what is being measured). Now, we know what you're thinking, "what does *any of this* have to do with my classroom or my students?!" As discussed in Chapter 10, data are gathered in order to learn more about a set of circumstances; for instance, if a point system (the intervention or independent variable) increases student participation in classroom discussion (what is being measured or the dependent variable). If we want to know if the point system is having its intended effect (e.g., more student participation), we need to show experimental control, or a predictable change, in behavior after systematic manipulation of variables. Plainly, experimental control is simply asking if what we did worked. So, we want to determine that the point system *alone* increased participation and that a change in student participation was not brought about by any other means. This is the *analysis* part of ABA. Think about it this way: without analyzing the data you collect, you have no idea, *quantitatively speaking,* if the interventions are doing what they are intended to do. We tend to think or feel certain things about our students and what is happening in our classroom (i.e., subjective opinions), but there are numerous cognitive biases that impact the accuracy of our thinking and decision making, which is why data collection (i.e., gathering objective facts) is so important for making accurate, factually-informed decisions.

> *For a refresher on data-based decision making, data collection is more deeply covered in Chapter 10.*

Single-Subject Design

In order to determine if the intervention is working (e.g., demonstrating experimental control), ABA utilizes a type of experimental design referred to as single-subject, or single-case, designs. Single-subject designs are named as such *not because there is only one subject or participant (although this can be the case), but because each participant serves as his or her own control.* Single-subject designs typically employ a small number of participants who are similar in some way (e.g., students in Ms. Green's classroom, a group of first grade teachers, students in a guided reading group, etc.). These types of designs are not just limited to ABA but also are used in applied settings such as education and human resources.

Within single-subject designs, each participant is exposed to some sort of baseline (e.g., preintervention) and intervention conditions, during which his or her performance is continually measured and then graphed for visual analysis. Single-subject designs seek to determine if an individual's behavior changed in any way throughout baseline and intervention. This comparison of one's performance across conditions is what is meant by each participant "serving as his or her own control" and in no way is an individual's performance compared to a group or average. For instance, Ms. Westin is providing points for participation in class. If we were to look at Jimmy and Anita's performances, we would compare each student's data against his or her own. So, we would compare Jimmy's participation prior to the point system to his participation during and after the point system, and then the same would be done for Anita. In no way are the student's data combined or compared between individuals.

The single-subject approach differs vastly from group designs, which are what you may be most familiar with. Group designs are often seen in fields such as medicine, marketing, and health, just to name a few. Group designs involve large groups of individuals placed into conditions, or *groups,* such as "treatment," "comparison," and "control." The highest standard of such designs are referred to as randomized control trials, wherein participants are randomly selected for each group/condition, which serves to reduce bias and increase rigor within the study. In group designs, comparisons are made within or between groups to establish the presence of a relation between the independent and dependent variables. The major difference here is the application of statistical tests to do such comparisons (e.g., correlation coefficient, independent samples *t*-test, etc.), which are not used in single-subject designs. Thus, single-subject designs are sensitive to individual differences rather than averages of groups, meaning that single-subject designs do not inherently permit for the same degree of generalizability to the broader population as group designs do. Instead, these designs allow for a detailed examination of *how* an intervention affected individual behavior (i.e., the behavior increased or decreased, or there was no change).

Now that we have built up a bit of background on single-subject designs, let's look at some specific types of commonly used single-subject designs that you will most likely use in the classroom. These approaches are meant to be used with a small group of individuals (usually around 6 to 8), such as those receiving targeted intervention or for those students who have behavior goals set forth in their IEP. These small groups of students may also be part of a small targeted group within a PBIS framework, receiving either Tier 2 or Tier 3 interventions.

Want more information about PBIS? Review Chapter 4 for more on tiers of intervention!

Single-subject designs can also be used to look at the effect of an intervention on a group of individuals, such as an entire classroom of students. In this way, data are collected and graphed as an aggregate, rather than collecting and graphing each student's data as this is not really practical or time efficient. Note, this does not allow for any one student's behavior to be analyzed as it just provides information about the group as a whole (e.g., did the point system increase student participation in Ms. Westin's class?).

To begin such a vast discussion around experimental design, it is important to go over some basic concepts and terms that you will encounter throughout this and other chapters. Single-subject designs may be simply thought of as experiments. Please, however, do not think of this in a clinical or laboratory fashion, especially within the classroom. We are not performing "experiments" on our students (or anyone) for that matter! Rather, an experiment is a carefully monitored comparison between a dependent and independent variable. Again, dependent variables are simply whatever is being measured; think of these as the *target behaviors* that we are hoping to influence with the independent variable, or the intervention. The independent variable is what is introduced and what is expected to produce a change in performance. Examples of independent variables include a token economy system (e.g., point system), reading interventions, behavior-specific praise, or self-monitoring. Baseline, or preintervention, is a condition in which there is no independent variable at play. This is the period in which a target behavior is being monitored and data are being collected in the *absence* of the intervention. For example, number of words read incorrectly per minute prior to the introduction of a new reading program. In this sense, the baseline condition is not a condition in which the student is not being taught or the absence of any instruction, it is merely the absence of the new reading program. So, that's it; we are looking to see if the intervention affects performance. And how do we know if this is happening? Well, it's all about how we setup the "experiment."

Within single-subject designs exist three components of experimental reasoning: prediction, replication, and verification. Prediction is just as it sounds; what is the predicted or expected outcome of future measurement? What do you think will happen to the rate of screaming after the intervention is put into place (hopefully a reduction in screaming . . .). Replication refers to the repetition of conditions within an experiment that contributes to the reliability of outcomes. Think of replication as the *believability* of an experiment. Finally, verification is showing that the dependent variable (target behavior) would not have changed without the independent variable (intervention). These three elements are used together to determine if the results from the experiment are reliable. It all starts with a question: what do you want to know about how *x* will affect *y*? Will a new online math program increase number of correct responses on the weekly math quiz? Does putting a 15-min break between social studies and science lead to increased participation during the science lab mini-lesson? Will a point system decrease calling out during circle time?

Teachers should consider factors such as time constraints, number of students participating, and the nature of the intervention to determine which design to select. But prior to this and perhaps the most overlooked aspect of properly executing a single-subject design is the establishment of a steady baseline measure. The baseline measure is the level of behavior in the absence of an intervention. In the previous example, the baseline measured the number of words read incorrectly per minute, prior to introducing a new reading program. The baseline condition is the key factor to determining if an intervention is having the desired change; it is the *control condition* to which all other conditions will be compared. It is also critical to establish that the baseline is stable before the intervention is introduced as an unsteady or volatile baseline may indicate the presence of other factors at play that may be influencing the dependent variable.

Beyond this, baseline data are also beneficial as other factors may be highlighted, particularly related to the environment or other individuals. For instance, Ms. Bally reprimands Ron every time he fidgets in his spot during circle time. If each instance of Ron's fidgeting is followed by some form of teacher attention, these data indicate the need for an alternative response on Ms. Bally's part. Additionally, baseline data may also provide a more accurate illustration of what is happening in a given situation. When asked about Ron's fidgeting, Ms. Bally responds that he fidgets "all the time; he never stops and distracts everyone." Upon taking baseline measures, the actual occurrence of Ron's fidgeting is roughly once every 6 min, hardly an "all the time" situation.

> *For a review of target behaviors and the importance of social significance, review Chapter 10.*

Establishing a steady, reliable baseline is ideal in order for the most accurate assessment of an intervention. This steady pattern will allow for a clear demonstration of change between baseline and intervention conditions. Ideally, a minimum of three data points is required to identify a steady trend. However, your classroom is in the real world and this is not always the case. A few variations of baseline data may present challenges prior to intervention. If baseline data are on an upward or ascending trend, a downward or descending trend, or highly variable, it is nearly impossible to garner an accurate assessment. Think about the following scenario, a teacher collects some baseline data on Lily's calling out during discussion. Figure 11–1 shows Lily's callouts per minute. Notice how over the course of a few observation sessions, Lily's callouts are decreasing in frequency.

Figure 11–1. Lily's callouts; example of decreasing baseline.

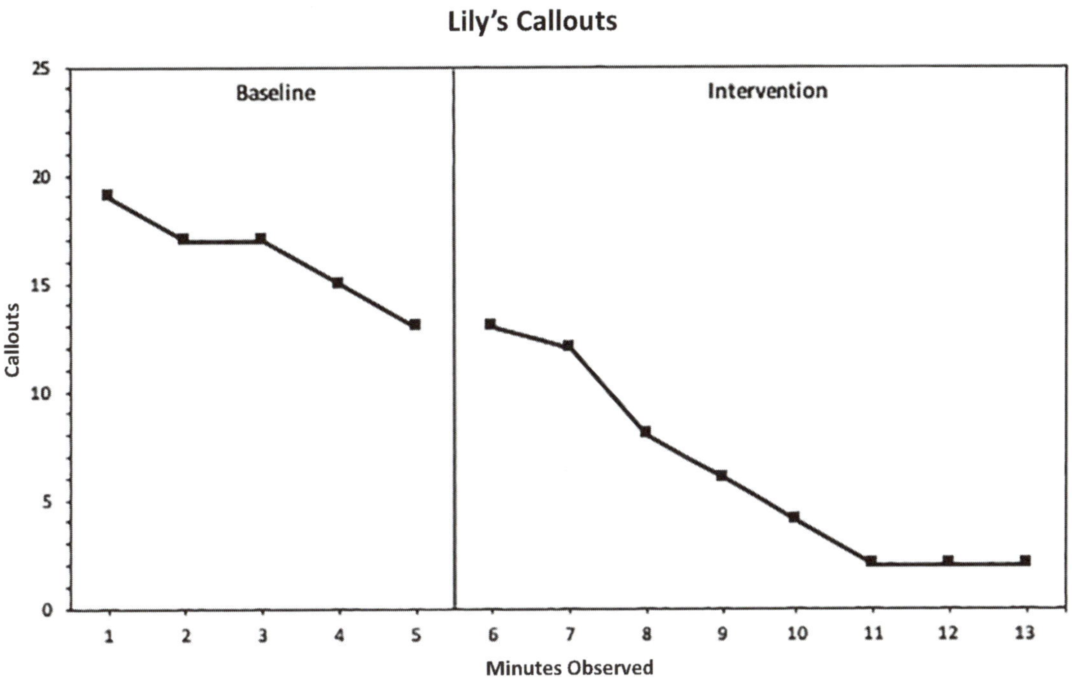

Lily's Callouts

Now, if the teacher were to begin implementing an intervention targeting reduction in callouts, what do you think the data will infer? Further reduction in the frequency of Lily's callouts per minute may make it is *appear* as though the intervention is having the intended effect, but we must remember that the frequency already appeared to be decreasing prior to the intervention, which begs the question, "why?" Although we don't necessarily know the answer, we can conclude that some other factor (independent variable) is likely influencing the behavior (dependent variable).

Flat and consistent baseline data are pretty data. If and when you find yourself with some not-so-pretty baseline data, it may be necessary to extend baseline measurement to gather more data points. More data points increase the likelihood of detecting a stable pattern. Now, this is ill-advised if the target behavior is one that poses threat to the student or others. If this is the case, immediate intervention is usually warranted and a design option (B-A-B) is discussed in the following section.

A-B Design

The A-B design, the simplest of all single-subject designs, consists of two conditions: the baseline condition, A, and the intervention condition, B (see Figure 11–2 on sight word recognition). This design may be used to quickly assess the effects of

Figure 11–2. Line graph of an A-B design; sample data on sight word recognition.

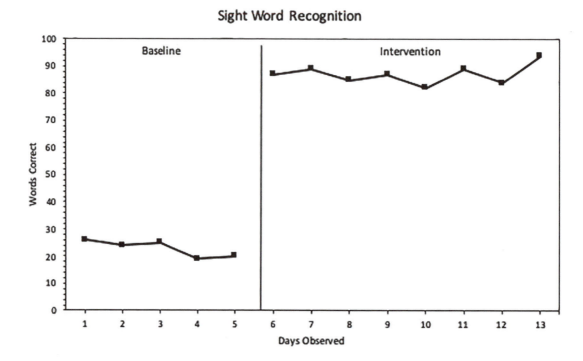

an intervention. Yet, due to only having two conditions, this is the weakest of all single-subject designs because of a lack of replication and verification. That is, there is no way to ensure with certainty that the change in performance between A and B is *solely* due to the intervention and not a confounding variable or some unplanned factor that could affect the dependent variable. In order to address this, a reversal design can be used, which involves returning to original, baseline conditions (A).

Reversal Designs

A-B-A Design

Similar to the A-B design, the A-B-A design simply has one more phase—a return back to the baseline condition. This return to baseline condition is done via removing the independent variable, or the intervention that was in place during the B condition. Let's recall Ms. Bally who typically reprimands Ron's fidgeting behaviors (e.g., bouncing on bottom, flicking carpet pieces, etc.) during circle time. As shown in Figure 11–3 on Ron's fidgeting, an intervention using an A-B-A design is planned wherein Ms. Bally will ignore Ron's fidgeting.

The baseline condition (A) entails collecting data on Ron's fidgeting with *no change* in Ms. Bally's behavior (i.e., it's "business as usual" and she will continue

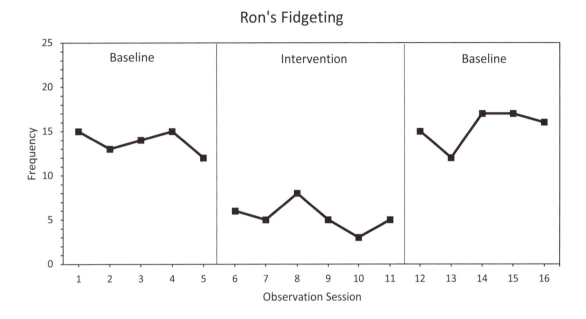

Figure 11–3. Line graph of an A-B-A design; sample data on Ron's fidgeting.

to provide reprimands as she has done thus far). Then, during the intervention (B), data are again collected; but this time, Ms. Bally ignores all instances of Ron's fidgeting. Finally, the reversal occurs, we return to baseline conditions (A) wherein Ms Bally reverts to reprimanding Ron and data are taken once more. The prediction here is that during the initial baseline (A), Ron's rate of fidgeting would be rather high; then, during the intervention (B), we anticipate a drop in fidgeting; finally, during the reversal (A), fidgeting rates creep back up toward initial baseline levels.

The advantage here is the last condition: the return to baseline conditions, which is known as replication and allows for a stronger assessment of the intervention. However, there are a few issues to note with the A-B-A design. Firstly, it is not ideal to end on a baseline condition, especially if the intervention proved to be beneficial in some way. Next, it is not advised to use this type of design with interventions that may have irreversible effects. For example, consider a reading program. Once you introduce such a program, say for comprehension, it is not possible for the students to "unlearn" what they have already learned. Thirdly, this is not a viable design for interventions that may be targeting dangerous or harmful behaviors. Namely, if a student is hitting others, it would be unethical to (a) take baseline data on hitting without intervening in some way and (b) provide an intervention targeting reduction in hitting and then take it away! In such cases, *sometimes* a B-A-B design, where an intervention is provided right away and then removed for a short time before being reintroduced, is preferred. These designs are not as strong because there was no assessment of preintervention levels of behavior; yet, they may prove to be beneficial when there is limited time in which to show improvement in behavior as it eliminates the need to establish a steady baseline.

A-B-A-B Design

The strongest and most reliable of all reversal designs is the A-B-A-B design. As you may gather, this design has four conditions, where the final one is a return to the intervention. This is displayed in Figure 11–4.

This is preferred because the student comes back into contact with the intervention, which not only verifies the effects of the intervention but also promotes desirable behavior change. As with the A-B-A design, the A-B-A-B design may not work as well with behaviors that do not return back to baseline levels, such as those which cannot be "unlearned" or completely removed from one's repertoire or that pose a risk.

Multiple Baseline Design

Perhaps the most widely used design in single-subject research is the multiple baseline design. Multiple baseline designs are characterized by a staggered introduction of the independent variable for at least three different points in time and take one of three basic forms: across individuals, settings, or behaviors. In a

Figure 11–4. Line graph depicting A-B-A-B design; sample data on student performance.

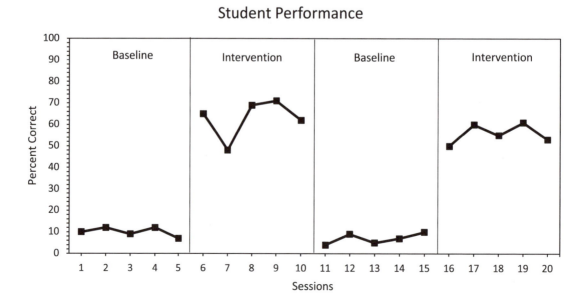

multiple baseline across behaviors, two or more dependent variables or behaviors *of the same individual* are intervened upon. For example, see the graph using a video feedback intervention to improve Scott's dribbling, passing, and free throw shots (i.e., dependent variables) in P.E. class (Figure 11–5).

Figure 11–5. Multiple baseline design across behaviors; sample data on Scott's basketball skills.

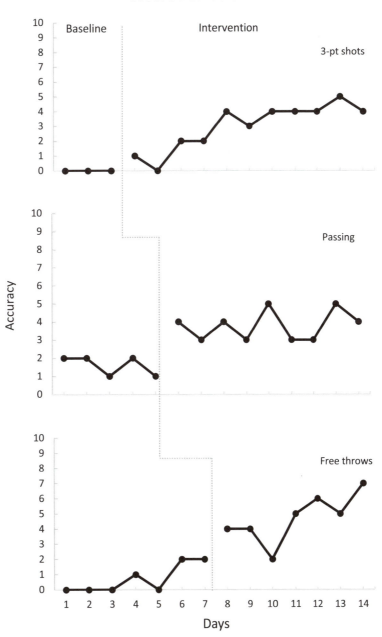

Scott's Basketball Skills

In a multiple baseline across settings design, *only one behavior* of a person is targeted in *two or more settings*. This could look like Ms. Bally providing the planned ignoring intervention to Ron's fidgeting in morning circle and again in afternoon circle. Or, she could provide the intervention for Ron in the classroom, library, and then computer lab. Finally, a multiple baseline across individuals targets one behavior for two or more individuals. This is the most commonly used form as it allows teachers to intervene on one behavior (e.g., calling out) across several students; for instance, a token economy intervention introduced to Emma first, then a few days later to Sam, and then finally to Mahala. Essentially, multiple baseline designs are several "stacked" AB designs replicated within the same study. Each tier represents an individual, a behavior, or a setting. In any of those possibilities, the multiple baseline design is employing the same intervention across time.

The first phase of a multiple baseline design is a baseline condition. Once a stable baseline is established across all tiers, the intervention (independent variable) is introduced to the top tier only, while the others remain in baseline. This allows for one to see an immediate change between the conditions. Once stable responding is achieved, the independent variable is then introduced to the next tier, and so on. We can assume the intervention worked (or experimental control is demonstrated) when there is a change observed after the application of the independent variable across tiers.

While this type of design does require more time and resources to implement than other single-subject designs, there are still several distinct advantages to multiple baseline designs. Part of the appeal is there is no need for the removal of the intervention to demonstrate a functional relationship among variables, which is particularly useful for behaviors that are dangerous or pose risk. Herein there is the consideration for this type of design as there can be ethical issues related to extending baseline. This can be advantageous in a school setting because you do not have to reverse an intervention and this may be more amenable to teachers and parents. Additionally, this design resonates well with teachers because it resembles typical practice of staggering intervention (e.g., think of guided reading groups or social skills instruction) and lends itself to be used with more than one student at a time. Further, teachers are continually charged with having to teach multiple students across settings and therefore can reap the benefits of interventions across students, settings, and behaviors.

Visual Displays of Data and Visual Analysis

During a single-subject intervention, data are continuously collected throughout each condition, which is not a task to be taken lightly! Once all of that glorious, hard-earned data are collected, what do you do with it? Perhaps fold it up and stuff it under that uneven desk leg? Place it far into the depths of your filing cabinet? Alas, all joking aside, this is often and unfortunately the case. There is a staggering gap in the number of teachers, both general and special educators, trained to actually *do* something with these data. As educators, we have a duty to uphold, to the highest degree, the intent of improving the lives of our students. Our work goes beyond teaching spelling, math, and reading. We are charged with fostering and nurturing the future members of the community. With particular focus on managing challenging behavior, it is simply a disservice to implement an intervention without further showing *evidence* that it is working (or not working). Parents entrust their children to us, just as they do with other professionals (e.g., doctors). They expect doctors to prescribe the correct medicine for their child and will simply not accept a doctor' saying, "Well, I think this should work but I don't have evidence to support it." Therefore, it is reasonable for parents to expect us as teachers to provide evidence that supports the actions and decisions being made in schools and classrooms that can impact their children. Thus, the integrity in single-subject design rests on making use of the data collected by graphing it, analyzing it, and acting upon it.

Graphing

Graphic displays of data allow for quick conclusions to be drawn from a set of information. Such displays provide information about the relation between dependent and independent variables and provides a quick "summary" of progress. Such conclusions are valuable when determining if an intervention is having the intended effect, if a student is making progress toward an IEP goal, or overall academic growth. Further, this "summary" of information may also be used as a valuable source of feedback to students about their performance. Several types of graphs may be used to display data:—namely, line graphs, bar graphs, and scatterplots, with line graphs being the most common type used to evaluate behavioral data. While there are several styles and appearances of line graphs, they are all made up of the same basic elements: specifically, *x*- and *y*-axes, condition change lines, labels, data points, data path, and a figure caption.

Line Graphs

The *x*-axis, or horizontal axis, is the horizontal line across the bottom of the graph that represents time or the value of the independent variable. While it is ideal to use equal intervals to represent time's passage across the *x*-axis, these need not be represented by minutes or seconds; rather, these can be expressed in number of sessions. The *y*-axis is the vertical axis on the left-hand side of the graph and represents the value of the dependent variable. Such values may be expressed by percentages, number of responses, duration, and so forth. Examples of dependent variable measurements include words read per minute or duration of problem behavior (minutes). As with the *x*-axis, the values along the *y*-axis should be divided into equal intervals for accuracy. The point at which the *x*- and *y*-axes meet is the origin and is generally represented with a zero value. Figure 11–6 provides an example of a basic line graph.

As we know, single-subject design features repeated measurement over time and the manipulation of the independent variable across conditions. As represented on a line graph, a condition change line is required to demarcate changes between conditions. This is simply a vertical line extending upward from the *x*-axis that indicates the point in time a change in condition occurred. These condition changes generally include moving from baseline to intervention and/or when there is an introduction and subsequent withdrawal of

Figure 11–6. Example of a basic line graph.

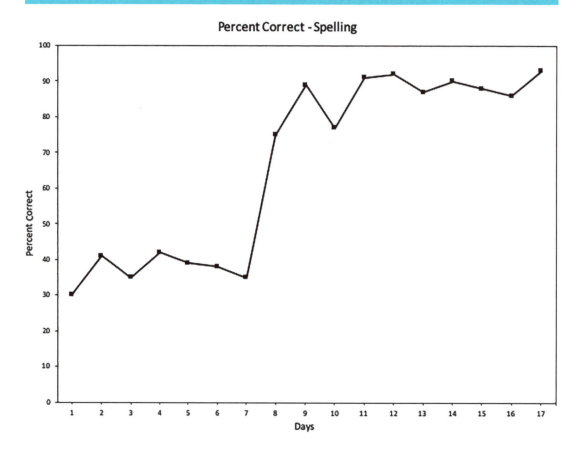

intervention, as with an A-B-A-B design. Required along with the condition change lines are condition labels for each condition. Just one or two words centered within each condition along the top of the graph provides the reader necessary information on what the condition entails (e.g., "baseline," "planned ignoring," "tokens").

We've discussed much of what goes into a line graph; however, a line graph is not of much value without data points. Data points are indicators of the value of behavior at a specific point in time. Connecting several data points graphed across time with a straight line reveals the data path, which provides reference to the level and trend (discussed in the following section). Line graphs depict individual data points over time. Data points are only ever connected *within conditions* (never across) to create a path, which is the focal point for visual analysis. In general, more data points are associated with a stronger certainty about the information displayed by the data. Finally, the figure caption, the last element, is meant to be a placeholder for a title and succinctly describe what the data display in about one sentence. Also specified within the figure caption is if there are any undefined elements within the graph, such as symbols or unplanned events that resulted in outlier data point(s). Figure 11–7 provides a sample line graph with all the graphing elements labeled.

Figure 11–7. Sample line graph with graph elements labeled.

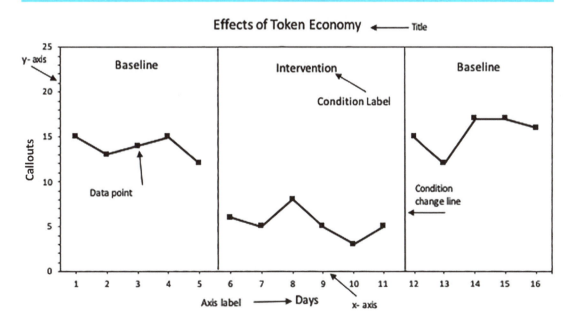

Bar Graphs

Bar graphs, or histograms, are another excellent way to display data for quick and easy analysis. Bar graphs are also made up of both *x*- and *y*-axes, just as in the line graph, but do not display individual data points. Rather, instead of indicating rate, duration, or frequency of a behavior, bar graphs use vertical or horizontal bars that represent one condition or variable. The height of the bar represents the value along the *y*-axis. These types of graphs are excellent for comparing performance/ behavior across conditions, as in number of callouts in Classroom A versus Classroom B or comparing the performance of groups, as in percentage of homework passed in for November as compared to December (Figure 11–8).

Figure 11–8. Example of a bar graph (histogram); sample data on classroom callouts.

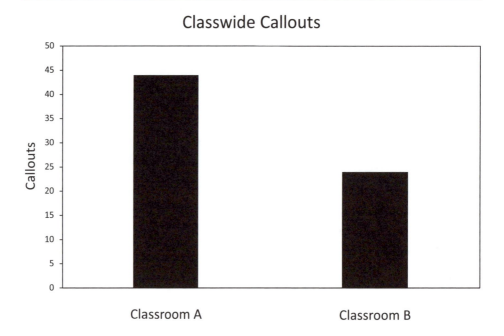

Scatterplots

Scatterplots are visual displays of data that help to reveal relationships between two or more variables; they show changes in the value of one variable on one axis with respect to the other axis. In this way, scatterplots can show how data are *correlated* with one another (but remember, *correlation does not equal causation!*). Data points on the scatterplot represent variables; for example, gender or age-range, while the axes represent what the data are being correlated to; for example, scores of math tests or participation rates. Data points on a scatterplot are never connected and may be represented with different shapes or colors for clarity in the visual analysis. Interpretation relies upon looking for clusters of data points and the use of a trendline is often helpful in determining how the data are related. Among the several ways to fit a trend line over data (e.g., formulas, computer programs, etc.), the freehand method is quite common with scatterplots. This method simply involves visually inspecting the data and drawing a straight line through the most tightly clustered points. Sometimes, the data come close to forming a straight line, which is indicative of a strong correlation between the variables (Figure 11–9). Lines originating at the origin driving out toward the high y-values indicate a positive correlation—that is, as one variable increases, so does the other—while data originating at high y-values and dropping down toward lower x-values are said to have a negative correlation (Figure 11–10). Finally, no correlation exists

Figure 11–9. Sample scatterplot with positive correlation.

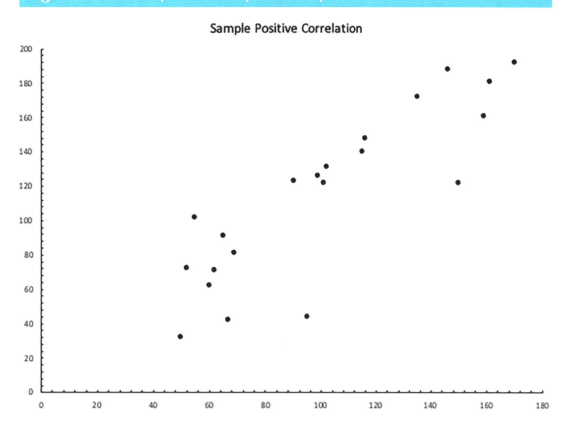

Figure 11–10. Sample scatterplot with negative correlation.

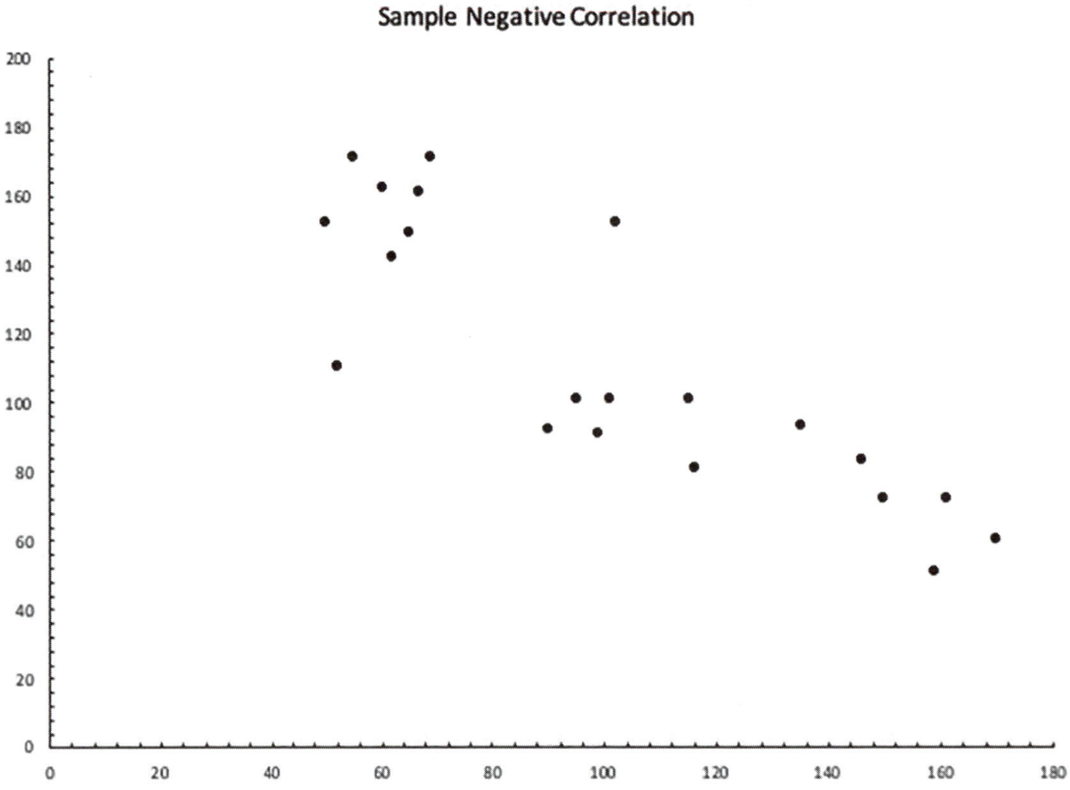

Sample Negative Correlation

when data points are scattered throughout the *y*- and *x*-axes without any discernable upward or downward trend (Figure 11–11).

While these displays are quite handy in revealing relationships among many types of variables—for example, comparing gender and rate of hand raising in class—scatterplots are excellent tools to show relationships between behavior and time. This involves dividing the day or observation period up into equal intervals along the *x*-axis and frequency of behavior along the *y*-axis. Data are recorded according to the interval in which they occur. Over time, these data are examined for patterns, and if detected, these patterns can be traced back to environmental events that occur during those identified times. Such patterns may be detected across the day, week, or even month. For example, clusters of data points related to shouting toward the beginning of the week may indicate events occurring over the weekend that may contribute to increased likelihood of challenging behavior (e.g., later bedtimes, transitions between single-parent homes, etc.). Alternatively, clusters of data at certain portions of the day may indicate something specific about that point in time, such as increased demands in a particular

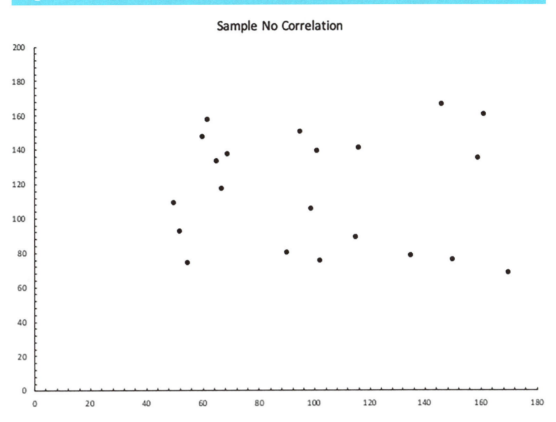

Figure 11–11. Sample scatterplot with no correlation.

class or presence of specific individuals. Conversely, a sparsity of data points at a particular point in time may also be helpful in determining factors that contribute to decreased levels of behavior, be it desired (e.g., sharing materials) or undesired (e.g., calling out).

For example, Cheryl's scatterplot data (Figure 11–12) shows a lack of leaving her seat daily from about noon to 1:00 p.m. (i.e., science) versus a cluster of Cheryl being out of seat daily around 9:00 a.m. (i.e., math). While these data cannot tell us any underlying cause to Cheryl's behavior, it can lead us toward clues. Perhaps the more hands-on lessons in science satisfy Cheryl's need to move about; or maybe she is more actively engaged with the specific peers or teacher in science. Other factors could pertain to her general preference for the subjects, her level of fatigue first thing in the morning versus after lunch, or simply the physical layout of one classroom versus another lends itself to getting up out of her seat. In all, scatterplots are tools that may help direct teachers toward specific times, which can then be further assessed with more in-depth data collection methods (e.g., A-B-C assessment).

Scatter Plot for Behavior

<u>Student</u>: Cheryl

<u>Date of Observation</u>: 2/3/2020 – 2/7/2020

<u>Observer</u>: Ms. Jones

<u>Target Behavior</u>: Any instance in which Cheryl leaves her seat for longer than 5 consecutive seconds without teacher permission

Time	Class	Mon	Tues	Weds	Thur	Fri
8:00-8:30am	Assembly	/	X	/	/	■
8:30-9:00am	Circle	X	/		X	/
9:00-9:30am	Math	■		/	■	/
9:30-10:00am	Math	■	/	■		
10:00-10:30am	Inquiry	/	X	X	X	X
10:30-11:00am	Lab	/	/	/	X	■
11:00-11:30am	P. E.					
11:30-12:00pm	P. E.					
12:00-12:30pm	Science	X	X	/	X	X
12:30-1:00pm	Science	X	X	X	X	/
1:00-1:30pm	Lunch					
1:30-2:00pm	Recess					
2:00-2:30pm	Inquiry	X	■	X	/	■
2:30-3:00pm	Pack up					

Key	Target Behavior
	No data
X	Did not occur
/	Occurred 1-2 times
■	Occurred 2+

Visual Analysis

Once your data are neat and tidy on a graph, they are ready to be analyzed. The best part of single-subject design (in the author's humble opinion) is the simple, straightforward interpretation of data accomplished through visual analysis—no calculators or highly sophisticated software required! Visual analysis is made up of three main features: variability, trend, and level. Taken together, these features tell a story of what is happening across conditions. A sufficient quantity of data points is desirable as too few may not show clear patterns (yet fewer data points are acceptable if there are multiple conditions/reversals, etc.). Variability is the degree to which the data are spread out across time. High variability looks like the data are "jumping" around on the graph. Variability indicates that there is not much control within the condition. See January versus September math scores in the graphs in Figures 11–13 and 11–14. January's data points are far less variable than those data points collected in September.

Figure 11–13. Example of high variability in a line graph; sample data for September's math scores.

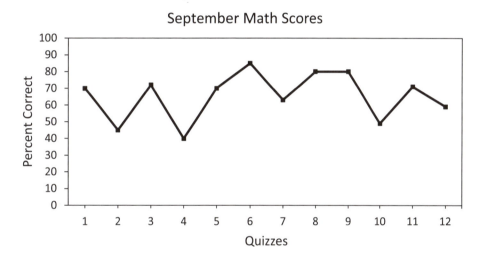

Figure 11–14. Example of low variability in line graph; sample data for January's math scores.

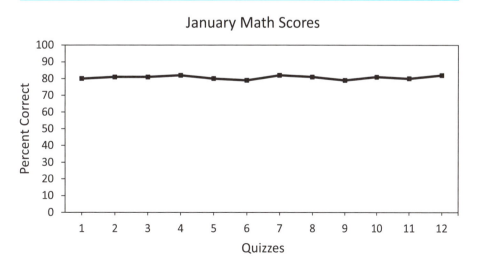

In general, if variable data are present, more data points are required in order to detect a pattern. Herein is an illustration of the flexibility within single-subject designs; if more data points are required, collect them! Level refers to value or placement of data on the vertical axis, or *y*-axis. As you can see in Figures 11–15 and 11–16, with Matt's quiz scores, Matt's baseline data are highly variable with a low level on the *y*-axis, whereas his intervention data have low variability with a high level on the *y*-axis.

In general, a larger change in level indicates a more powerful effect from intervention. Finally, trend is the direction in which the data are tracking. Trends describe the direction of the data and are labeled as either increasing, decreasing, or zero-trend. A quick and easy way to demarcate trend is to freehand a line through the cluster of data in a condition (never across conditions!), known as a trendline. While there are many other, more sophisticated methods to finding trendlines, for the sake of this text, we recommend the freehand method (Lindsley, 1985). A steep upward trend shows strong evidence for increasing behavior, while

Figure 11–15. Matt's quiz score data with highly variable, low level baseline data compared to low variability, high level intervention data.

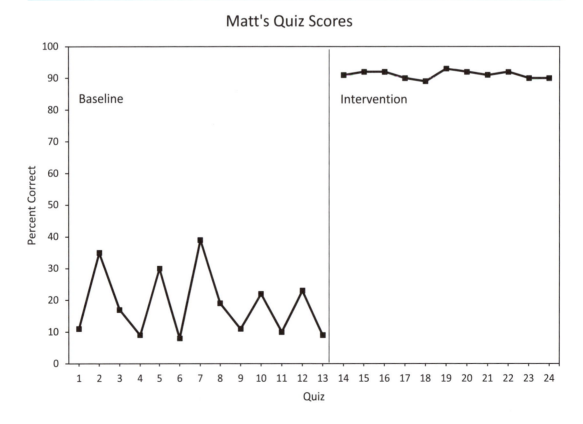

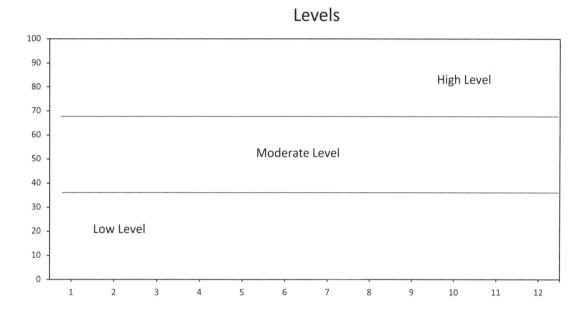

Figure 11–16. Illustration of data levels.

a steep downward trend indicates the opposite. See the graph in Figure 11–17 to see an example of an upward trend. A note about trend, just as with baseline data, it is important to observe a steady, stable trend before changing conditions (e.g., moving from baseline to intervention or vice versa).

Conclusion

We know data collection is important. As educators, we gather incredible volumes of academic data both formally, through tests and quizzes, and also informally, via observations and anecdotal evidence. Further, we understand the importance of collecting data on social skills and behaviors, which may be more ambiguous but are just as integral for students' overall learning and development. Data act as a fundamental tool for decision making on both micro (i.e., classroom) and macro (i.e., school wide, county wide) levels. Yet, as this chapter highlights, it is more than just *having* the data, rather it is more about what you *do* with those data. Through graphing and subsequent visual analysis, teachers are equipped with information on student strengths and needs and are better able to take meaningful action in the classroom. In this way, data provide teachers with a "report card," highlighting areas of strengths and needs and allowing them to improve instruction and classroom management.

Figure 11–17. Scatterplot with trendline; sample data for quiz scores by gender.

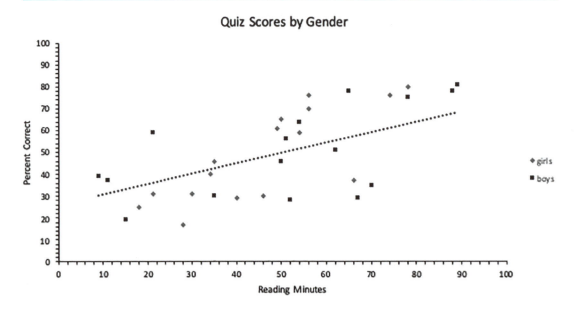

Chapter Summary

- Graphs are visual displays used to assist in making sense of data collected, which is meant to inform decisions and further action.

- Applied behavior analysis (ABA) is the scientific approach to understanding behavior. ABA applies principles from learning theory and behavioral science to improve socially significant behaviors and improve quality of life.

- Experimental design demonstrates a functional relation between an independent variable, or the intervention, and the dependent variable, what is actually being measured.

- Experimental control is achieved when there is a predictable change in behavior after systematic manipulation of variables.

- Single-subject designs are the most commonly used experimental design in ABA. These are designs in which a small number of participants are exposed to baseline (i.e., condition wherein there is no intervention occuring) and intervention conditions, with performance continually measured throughout. Single-subject designs are unique in that each participant serves as his or her own control and data are not compared across individuals, as in group designs.

- Single-subject designs rely upon three components of experimental reasoning: *prediction*, or what is the expected outcome of future measurements;

replication, or repetition of conditions to enforce reliability of results; and *verification*, or showing the dependent variable changed as a result of the independent variable and nothing else.

- The A-B Design is the most simple yet weakest of single-subject designs. It involves two conditions, baseline and intervention, and does not allow for replication or verification.

- Reversal designs are extensions of A-B designs and involve additional conditions. A-B-A returns the participant back to baseline (replication), but it may not be ideal to withdraw intervention. An A-B-A-B design allows for the participant to go back to intervention and this design satisfies the requirements of replication and verification.

- Multiple baseline designs are widely used and are characterized by a staggered introduction of intervention for at least three different points in time and can be across individuals, settings, or behaviors. Part of the appeal of this design is there is no need to withdraw intervention to demonstrate functional relations among variables. Multiple baseline designs allow one to intervene with one participant (as in across behaviors) or across several participants (as in across settings and people).

- Graphic displays of data allow for quick conclusions to be made between the dependent and independent variables. These displays can support decisions for students with regard to IEP goals, academic growth, or behavioral changes.

- Line graphs are comprised of an *x*-axis (horizontal), which represents units of time or value of the independent variable and a *y*-axis (vertical), which represents the value of the dependent variable. Line graphs display individual data points connected within conditions (e.g., all baseline data points connected, all intervention points connected) but never across conditions.

- Bar graphs display data along *x*- and *y*-axes but do not display individual data points; rather, data are displayed using vertical or horizontal bars extending up out of the *x*-axis.

- Scatterplots are visual displays of data that show relationships between two or more variables. Scatterplot data show how data are *correlated* with one another. Data points on a scatterplot are never connected and are typically represented by different shapes or colors. Interpretation of scatterplots looks toward clusters of data points and encourages examination of what events or variables occur at those intervals.

- Visual analysis is the visual interpretation of data that looks at variability, level, and trend. Variability refers to the data spread out across time; level is the placement of data on the vertical axis (particularly between conditions); and trend is the direction in which the data track.

CHAPTER 12

FUNCTIONAL BEHAVIORAL ASSESSMENT

Learning Objectives

- Understand the purpose of conducting a functional behavioral assessment
- Identify the ways in which a functional behavioral assessment may be conducted; understand what circumstances dictate each one's use
- Describe different types of data collection methods
- Describe the difference between functional assessment and functional analysis and identify factors involved in the use of functional analysis
- Identify the functions of behavior and understand how this links to effective intervention

Key Terms

A-B-C Chart	Functional Behavioral Assessment
Antecedents	Indirect Assessment
Behavioral Intervention Plan	Interviews
Consequences	Locus
Direct Assessment	Rating Scales
Functional Analysis	Setting Events

s educators, one of the few absolutes we can predict is the certitude of dealing with challenging behavior. Knowing the function of behavior, or what purpose a behavior serves, is the first step in helping facilitate positive behavior change. For instance, a student having difficulty with word problems in math tears his papers into shreds, refuses to participate, and is generally disruptive. While not a very positive way to deal with frustration, this student's behavior served a purpose: a way to avoid or delay doing word problems. Functional assessment is a systematic approach used to help educators ascertain the function of behaviors. Results from functional assessments assist with making important decisions regarding interventions to help students replace challenging behavior with more positive, prosocial means.

> ## ⚠ High-Leverage Practice Alert!
>
> **HLP10 specifically covers the importance of both functional behavioral assessments and behavior support plans. This HLP outlines the necessary components of an FBA and the importance of determining functions of behavior and formulating a hypothesis about the student's behavior.**

Functional Behavioral Assessment

A functional behavioral assessment (FBA) is a process designed to identify the variables controlling and maintaining specific target behaviors, leading to the development of a behavioral intervention plan (BIP), also sometimes referred to as a behavior support plan (BSP). There are three specific methods to conduct a functional assessment: indirect informant methods, direct observation, and functional analysis. Within these methods, data are collected via indirect and direct methods and then analyzed to determine the function of the behavior, which is used to inform intervention methods.

Although an FBA is considered good practice when working with any student with a challenging behavior, there are instances in which it is required by law. Although the aforementioned legal requirement falls under the Individuals with Disabilities Act (IDEA, 1997, 2004), this is a topic all school personnel, including both general and special educators, should be knowledgeable about. An FBA is required by law when a child with a disability has violated the code of conduct in a school division and is removed from their current educational placement. In this situation, the law states that if the student is in an alternative educational setting for more than 10 school days, they should receive, as appropriate, an FBA and BIP to address the behavior which resulted in the removal from their current placement. The law goes on to say that after 10 days, if the student's Individualized Education Program (IEP) team finds that the student's behavior was a manifestation of the student's disability, then an FBA and BIP must be conducted and implemented, if it has not been previously completed. As discussed in Chapter 1, this type of meeting/hearing is known as a manifestation determination and considers two main questions: First, are the behaviors a result of, or manifestation of, an inappropriate educational placement or program? Second, are the behaviors a direct result (manifestation) of the student's disability? If the answers to these questions are "yes," the student may not be expelled (but his or her placement/program may be changed). Further, if the student's behavior is found to be a manifestation of the student's disability and a BIP has already been conducted, the BIP must be reviewed, updated, or modified to address the behavior which resulted in removal from the current educational placement.

> ### *See Chapter 10 for more about data collection.*

While the law is written as a reactive approach to behavior, this is not best practice (O'Neill et al., 1997). The FBA and BIP process is meant to be preventative and individualized, not reactive to days missed from school in an alternative educational setting. Waiting until a student has been removed from school for more than 10 days may indicate that preventative measures were not taken and that the behavior was not addressed during early stages. Further, data collected in an alternative setting may not be accurate or reliable given that the student is not in their typical setting where the behavior has historically occurred.

> **For example, Patty is a student who is receiving special education services through an IEP. Recently, she was suspended for pushing a peer. While she was standing in the hallway after asking for space to calm down, she was repeatedly asked by a teacher to go to the office. Patty became so upset that when another student yelled at her to just listen to the teacher, Patty pushed the student. Patty did not currently have an FBA or BIP, but she was found eligible for special education under the disability category, emotional behavioral disability. Initially, Patty was suspended for five days, but the school realized a manifestation determination review must be held because Patty had already been suspended for two days for leaving school without permission and four days for individual**

incidents of taking others' property without permission. Therefore, this series of suspensions was a change in placement under IDEA. Patty's IEP team met the day after the pushing incident to discuss the most recent suspension. Her parents, special education teacher, general education teacher, and administrator were all present. Patty was brought into the meeting briefly to share her perspective of the pushing incident. After all information was shared and Patty's file and disability eligibility information reviewed, the team answered the two aforementioned questions about Patty's pushing behavior. First, they decided that the behavior was not a result of an inappropriate placement or delivery of services. However, they did determine that the behavior was directly and substantially related to her disability. Therefore, the team immediately scheduled a date for an FBA review and BIP development since this was required by law based on the manifestation determination decision.

The purpose of conducting an FBA is to help understand what is driving a student's behavior. This process allows a team to dive into behavioral data and critically analyze the data to discover patterns and functions. Since all behavior serves a purpose, or *function*, a team cannot support a student with behavioral challenges until they understand why the behavior is occurring. Through this understanding of function, teams can develop plans to support students with making positive choices and developing necessary skills to be successful. Ultimately, this process is designed to assist the team with developing a behavioral intervention plan (BIP), which will be discussed in the next chapter.

Review Chapter 1 for a refresher on manifestation determinations.

Components of FBA

Data collection is the crux of the FBA process and requires teams to work together to collect as much data as possible to design interventions in the BIP process. As mentioned, there are three *methods* to conduct an FBA (i.e., indirect, direct, and functional analysis), and, further, an FBA is comprised of the following main *components* (Figure 12–1).

The first component of an FBA is an operationally defined, socially significant target behavior. As outlined in Chapter 10, the data collection method selected for this behavior should be carefully aligned to behavioral dimension and accurately reflect factors that influence the behavior. These data, which comprise the

Figure 12–1. Visual breakdown of FBA methods and components of FBA.

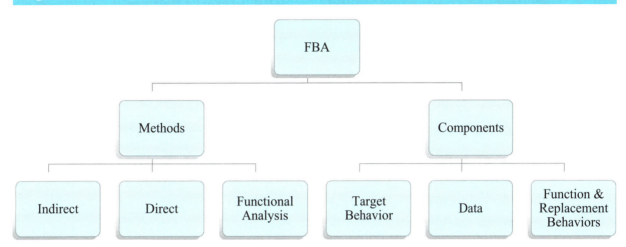

next component of an FBA, are used to determine triggers, events, and conditions under which the target behavior does or does not occur. This also includes data on consequences maintaining the target behavior. Lastly, an FBA is complete when the data identify the function(s) of the target behavior and which replacement behaviors will be used to serve the same function in a positive, prosocial way. Once these components are fully addressed, practitioners are able to generate a working hypothesis regarding the function of the target behavior. This may read something like, "Given demands in math, Kevin is more likely to engage in vocal disruption in order to delay or escape the task." Next, we will discuss each method of the functional assessment process.

 High-Leverage Practice Alert!

HLP4 stresses the need to develop a comprehensive profile of students based on multiple sources of information. Read the following sections to determine the best way to collect student information for individualized profiles.

Indirect Assessment Strategies

Indirect assessment, or indirect measurement of behavior, involves obtaining data through means other than direct observation of behavior. Examples of indirect assessments include record reviews, surveys, checklists, and interviews. This type of assessment has some great advantages as they are relatively easy to complete, can be done quickly, and do not require many materials or other individuals. Further, indirect assessments do not require direct participation of the student, which is helpful if the target behavior is one that poses risk (or occurs at a very low rate). However, a distinct disadvantage of indirect assessment is the reliance on secondhand information, which is fraught with subjectivity, bias, and/ or inaccurate recollections or perceptions of past events. Results from this type of data collection may be skewed due to a recency bias, the phenomenon whereby a respondent recalls and reports on events that occurred most recently versus those that occurred further in the past. For example, if a student exhibited a recent spike in challenging behavior that has caused significant distress, the respondent may be more inclined to report dimensions of behavior incorrectly (e.g., higher frequency, greater intensity). Further, results from indirect assessments may identify environmental factors related to the target behavior but do not provide any causal information as the behavior in question is never directly measured. While indirect assessment has the capability to yield a lot of information quickly, it should never be used in isolation. When used in conjunction with more direct methods, discussed in the following sections, indirect assessment can add valuable information to an FBA.

Records Review

The FBA process can be quite overwhelming at first, so starting with a records review is a good way to gain important information about a student's history. Records available for review will vary by student, but may generally include IEPs and other educational documentation, medical documents, psychological testing and reports, mental health records, preexisting or existing FBA/BIP, discipline referrals, and any specialist assessments (e.g., speech and language pathologist, occupational therapist, etc.). When conducting a records review, it is often helpful to have a document to organize the copious amounts of information (Figure 12–2). If previous behavior plans are available, a thorough review and read through may reveal valuable information not only on strategies that were successful but also on those that were not. Keep in mind that such strategies may or may not have been successful because of the individuals implementing them, changes in the student's life or the environment in which the student was participating at the time the plan was created.

While a records review is straightforward and can be completed quickly, it has its limitations. All records refer to prior behavior and do not reflect the student's current status. Even if the behavior(s) outlined in prior records are the same as the current issues, changes in the student's environment, educational placement, supporting individuals, social and home-life factors, and the passage of time all must be considered as supporting information and only used to supplement current hypotheses.

Figure 12–2. Sample of a records review for FBA data collection. *continues*

Records Review

Student: _____   Review Date: _____

Team Member Reviewing: _____

Mark an "X" by each document reviewed and summarize significant details.

☐ **Medical Documents/Health History:**

_____

_____

_____

_____

_____

☐ **Psychological Reports:**

_____

_____

_____

_____

_____

☐ **Academic Reports:**

_____

_____

_____

_____

_____

Figure 12–2. *continues*

☐ **Mental Health Documents:**

_____

_____

_____

_____

_____

☐ **Discipline Referrals:**

_____

_____

_____

_____

_____

☐ **Attendance Record:**

_____

_____

_____

_____

_____

☐ **Previous FBA/BIP:**

_____

_____

Figure 12–2. *continued*

_____

_____

_____

☐ **Previous Behavioral Interventions (e.g., token system, contracts):**

_____

_____

_____

_____

☐ **Educational Plans & Programs (e.g., IEP, 504 Plan):**

_____

_____

_____

_____

☐ **Specialist Assessment or Report (e.g., speech therapy, occupational therapy):**

_____

_____

_____

_____

Interviews, Rating Scales, and Checklists

Interviews are another indirect measure used to gain perspective on a student's behavioral concerns. Key people such as parents, caregivers, teachers, specialists, and—whenever possible—the student should all be considered as sources. The purpose of gathering interview information is to determine events related to when the behavior does and does not occur. Further, interviews can solicit information about student's preferences, strengths, and—importantly—conditions under which the behavior does not occur. Honing in on situations in which the target behavior does not occur (or is less likely to occur) can help tailor interventions, as knowing such conditions can predict desired behavior and promote positive behavior change.

There are several published interview forms that can be used to assist with this portion of the FBA. The Functional Assessment Interview (O'Neill et al., 1997) is a comprehensive structured interview covering 11 sections of behavior. Additionally, there is also a form of the Functional Assessment Interview that allows the student to respond for himself or herself. Included within the student informant version are questions related to the student's schedule as it relates to challenging behavior, questions about factors outside of the school environment (e.g., sleep, family home life, etc.), behavior intensity rating scales, and questions related to the student's environment and situations (e.g., bullying).

Also included under the umbrella of indirect assessment are rating scales and checklists. The aim of rating scales is to estimate the extent to which the target behavior occurs across different conditions using a Likert-type scale (e.g., never, sometimes, often, always). A brief description of commonly used interviews, rating scales, and checklists is presented in Table 12–1.

Some well-established rating scales include the Functional Analysis Screening Tool (FAST; Iwata & DeLeon, 1996), Motivation Assessment Scale (MAS; Durand & Crimmins, 1992), and the Questions about Behavior Function (QABF; Paclawskyj, Matson, Rush, Smalls, & Vollmer, 2000). Similarly, behavior checklists usually include a Likert-type scale used to gauge information about a set of specific antecedents, behaviors, and consequences. Commonly used published checklists include the Functional Assessment Checklist for Teachers and Staff (March et al., 2001), the Child Behavior Checklist (Achenbach & Edelbrock, 1991), and the Problem Behavior Questionnaire (Lewis, Scott, & Sugai, 1994). Data gathered from these types of indirect assessment aid in development of hypotheses around the function of what is maintaining the target behavior.

Direct Assessment Strategies

While indirect measures add richness to functional assessment, these measures can be quite limited and rather subjective. Direct assessment strategies, however,

Table 12–1. Commonly Used Tools for Indirect Assessment

Measure	Format	Purpose/Use
Child Behavior Checklist (CBCL)	Checklist	Covers 11 sections related to behavior and has a form that student can fill out about self
Functional Assessment Interview (FAI)	Interview	Seeks to identify routines and activities linked to target behavior
Functional Assessment Checklist for Teachers and Staff (FACTS)	Interview	Can be completed in about 15 min by teachers, school staff, and/or families
Functional Assessment Screening Tool (FAST)	Checklist	Identifies factors that influence problem behaviors; 16 questions answered Yes/No or N/A
Questions about Behavior Function (QABF)	Rating Scale	Assesses potential functions via 25 questions on a 4-pt Likert Scale
Motivation Assessment Scale (MAS)	Rating Scale	Assesses function of problem behavior across 16 questions and four subscales
Problem Behavior Questionnaire	Rating Scale	Designed to be used by teachers for behavior issues in general education settings

are used in conjunction with indirect assessment strategies to add objectivity and accuracy. Direct assessments involve direct observation of the student in the environments in which challenging behavior is most likely to occur as well as those environments in which the target behavior does not occur or is less likely to occur. This provides a distinct advantage over indirect methods as it provides an objective report of the target behavior. Further, when a teacher is dedicating time to observing and collecting data, he or she is removed from their usual classroom duties and may see things from a different perspective. It is worth noting that direct strategies are not in any way foolproof. Often, low-frequency behaviors make data collection difficult if observation periods do not capture any direct observation of the target behavior. This then extends the timeline of the process, thus delaying intervention. Additionally, direct measures are also vulnerable to subjectivity, particularly in anecdotal recordings, as described in the next section.

For instance, it is entirely possible for practitioners and teachers who become acclimated to challenging behavior and sometimes learn to avoid presenting certain events that may lead to behavior. Strategies included in direct assessment are anecdotal observation and Antecedent-Behavior-Consequence analyses.

Anecdotal Observation

If the team decides that a written description of a behavior would be helpful, anecdotal notes, or observations of the behavior and the environment, may be written down. In this context, anecdotal notes are a running log of observations as they occur. While this type of data collection is certainly an option, this will only describe what is happening and not necessarily result in the identification of patterns. Therefore, it is recommended that this method only be used in conjunction with other direct methods such as A-B-C recording, described in the next section. Observers should record events exactly as they occur using objective, detailed, and descriptive language. Any and all opinions and evaluations of the behavior should be omitted, even if the observer believes they understand why the student is behaving in a certain way (e.g., to get adult attention).

Antecedent-Behavior-Consequence Recording

An Antecedent-Behavior-Consequence recording, or A-B-C chart, is one way in which to organize anecdotal observations. This type of direct observation relies on continuous monitoring and descriptions of behavior, including time, setting, antecedents, behaviors, and consequences. The data garnered from this kind of monitoring can either help identify possible behaviors to target or hone in on already known target behaviors. In this way, A-B-C recording allows for a flexible approach to data collection. In some instances, the team may already know the target behavior in question. For example, a teacher using an A-B-C chart to record events around Johnny's vocal interruptions during group instruction. Other times, A-B-C data collection can be used to bring clarity to behaviors described as "disruptive" or "noncompliant," such as the case with a behavior specialist observing a math lesson wherein Sammy's "disruption" entails numerous callouts and wandering the classroom.

Regardless of how you intend to use A-B-C recording, the components remain consistent. First, let's take a look at antecedents. The antecedents are the first portion of the three-term contingency and are comprised of actions or events that occur immediately before the target behavior; they are the stimuli that trigger behavior.

Go back to Chapter 3 to review three-term contingencies!

Determining what the antecedents to behaviors are is important because once identified, the environment may be altered to change the course of the target behavior or encourage and foster new replacement behaviors. Keep in mind that antecedents are *specific events immediately prior to a behavior* and will vary from student to student and it is also important to consider contributing factors such as the following:

● Context of setting, locations, subjects, materials, and activities

● Presence or absence of specific people, such as peers, teachers, support staff

● Changes in the environment or transitions between environments, people, activities, and so forth

Just as important, but often much less visible are what is known as setting events. Setting events are distinguished from antecedents as they occur *before* the antecedent and alter the effects of antecedents, making challenging behavior more likely to occur. Because setting events are temporally separated from the actual occurrence of the target behavior, they are usually more difficult to detect, especially for teachers, since many occur before the student even arrives to school. Keep in mind that *setting events are not antecedents*; they merely *set the stage* that an antecedent will trigger a behavior. And further, despite the name, they are (almost always) unrelated to the actual setting in which the target behavior occurs as they often occur well before. The following are some commonly occurring setting events to consider:

● Internal factors like tiredness, hunger, thirst, medication effects, illness

● Outside school factors like issues on the bus, home life, morning challenges

> *Peek ahead to Chapter 13 to read more on setting events.*

Next in the A-B-C recording is the actual target behavior. As mentioned, the target behavior in an A-B-C recording may the behavior that has been identified and operationally defined by the team. At other times, an A-B-C recording may be completed in order to provide clarity and identify target behaviors (e.g., teacher reports student as "defiant" but is unable to articulate exactly what the student is doing). When recording behaviors on the A-B-C chart, remember to make the behavior MOO—ensure it is **m**easurable, **o**bservable, and **o**bjective. This ensures that any observer or team member would be able to see and understand the behavior the same way. To facilitate completion of an A-B-C recording chart, one may find it helpful to take detailed observation notes, noting time, setting, and individuals present. Because A-B-C recording requires the full attention of the observer, it is not possible for a classroom teacher to conduct a lesson and take data concurrently. However, with that said, one needs about 20 min of dedicated time over the course of a few days to commit to this form of data collection. A-B-C data collection should occur in this manner until patterns emerge. In order to collect the most accurate data, ensure everything the student says/does is recorded along with all events before and after the behavior. Setting, time of occurrence, and duration—if applicable—are also important to capture the most accurate picture of the behavior. It may also be helpful to abbreviate certain terms for expediency, such as the use of "bx" for behavior or initials instead of names.

While antecedents and setting events occur prior to behavior, consequences are events that occur immediately *following* a target behavior. Consequences have the power to influence future likelihood of a behavior occurring again in the future. Consequences can be *reinforcing* or *punishing,* and are critical to understanding what is driving the function of the behavior. Often, the word "consequences" conjures up negative images related to punishment or general unpleasantries; however, this is not always the case. As mentioned, consequences serve to either reinforce, or punish, the continuation of the target behavior. If an event following a behavior increases the likelihood of it occurring again, reinforcement has transpired; if the likelihood decreases, the behavior has been punished. Possible consequences to behavior are infinite, but may include receiving or avoiding attention from peers or adults, avoiding academic tasks, being removed from a classroom or undesirable situation, receiving or avoiding sensory stimulation or input, engagement in desired or undesirable tasks or activities, and so forth. Keep in mind, as mentioned in Chapter 2, one cannot determine how a consequence operates until future behavior is observed; thus, this is the ultimate purpose of accurate and comprehensive A-B-C data collection. Also bear in mind that consequences cannot be assumed because of what *should* happen. For example, the teacher that "reinforces" a student's hand raising by using public praise. If that student does not respond positively to public praise and ceases to raise her hand, that teacher inadvertently punished the behavior, even though "kids like praise and praise should make her raise her hand more." See the A-B-C data recording for an example of how this data might be collected (Figure 12–3).

In addition to the antecedents, behaviors, and consequences, recording where a behavior is and is not occurring is also important when understanding behavior. Setting, or locus, describes where a behavior occurs, typically naming the environment or a specific location. If a student is only wandering around while in the music classroom, the locus of the behavior would be the music room. This could also be specific to certain locations within a larger area as well. For example, a student may only engage in a behavior on the carpet in an elementary school

Figure 12–3. Example of antecedent-behavior-consequence data sheet.

Student Name: <u>Blake</u>   Observation Start: <u>11:34</u>
Observer: <u>Colleen</u>   Observation End: <u>12:00</u>
Location: <u>Room 34; science</u>   Date: <u>10/26/19</u>

<u>Target Behavior</u> (if known): Physical Aggression

<u>Operational Definition</u>:
Hitting- any instance in which Blake uses an open or closed hand to make forceful contact with another person or any object.

Kicking- any instance in which Blake's foot or leg makes forceful contact with another person or any object.

Time	Antecedent	Behavior	Consequence
11:36am	J sitting in B's chair	B struck J on back of head w/ open hand; B said "get out of my seat!"	J cried; teacher reprimanded B
11:47–11:50am	Teacher direction to get materials for worksheet	B kicked table, knocking materials on floor	Peers shout at B; teacher reprimands & requires B to clean up

room or at a worktable in a high school classroom. Both of these specific locations would describe the locus of the behavior and this is important because it helps to explain where a behavior is most or least likely to occur.

To gather the most accurate data, an A-B-C chart should not just be completed on one single occasion. The more data collected, the more confidence the team will have about accurately identifying the function of the behavior. Additionally, more data will help identify patterns of behavior and since the observations are done in the presence of the challenging behaviors, it is more likely to deduce causal relations between events.

Functional Analysis

Very often, the terms functional assessment and functional analysis are mistakenly used interchangeably. Functional assessment is the overarching umbrella under which functional analysis sits. Differing from the direct and indirect methods, a functional analysis is an active process whereby a teacher/practitioner manipulates antecedents and consequences of a target behavior in order to "test" what is causing the behavior to occur. Functional analysis is the most direct form of functional assessment and seen as the gold standard as it is the only one of the functional assessment methods that can reliably predict behavior. A note here, functional analyses are not to be taken lightly and require a behavioral expert, such as a Board-Certified Behavior Analyst (BCBA), ideally one with school-based experience. Functional analyses should never be undertaken by individuals without explicit training. The description presented in this text is intended to inform about the process rather than guide it.

The basic procedure of a functional analysis involves systematic manipulation of antecedents and consequences in each one of the four test conditions: contingent attention, contingent escape, alone, and control (play). Each condition of a functional analysis is set up to represent an individual's environment, with each condition providing potential antecedents and possible sources of reinforcement for target behavior. For example, a series of task demands (i.e., antecedents) are presented to a student in the contingent escape condition. If the student engages in the target behavior, let's say screaming, the student gets a break from the task (i.e., reinforcement). If we see higher rates of the target behavior in the contingent escape condition, we can be fairly certain that demand conditions elicit problem behavior and escape from demands reinforces problem behavior. This is even more evidenced when the occurrence of target behavior is low across the other conditions and when repeating the contingent escape condition provides similar results. To note, the assumption underlying the alone condition is that if the individual engaged in high rates of the target behavior within this condition, the behavior is automatically maintained. Additionally, the control/play condition assumes low levels of target behavior observed as there are no demands and all forms of reinforcement (i.e., tangible, attention) are freely available. Table 12–2 provides a breakdown of functional analysis conditions and what each condition entails.

Something to consider for conducting a functional analysis is to have a practitioner who is well versed in functional assessment provide supervision to the process, guide the team, and provide input; *functional analysis should not be a solitary venture, especially within the school setting.* Whenever possible, it is best to have an observer available for data collection. The actual implementation of a functional analysis need not be time consuming (such as with a brief functional analysis), with each condition lasting about 5 min to 10 min, followed by a 5-min break prior to moving on to the next condition. Moving between conditions quickly and repeating conditions that evoke problem behavior will garner more accurate and reliable results. Of course, all relevant parties should be notified and proper consents obtained from parents or caregivers.

Table 12–2. Functional Analysis Conditions

Condition	Antecedents	Consequence for Challenging Behavior
Contingent Attention	• Practitioner gives student moderately preferred items and instructs him or her to play with no further instructions given • Practitioner ignores all attention seeking attempts by student	• If student engages in challenging behavior (i.e., target behavior), practitioner responds with attention, usually in the form of a reprimand or a calming statement
Contingent Escape/Avoid	• Practitioner provides student with a series of task demands	• Practitioner provides a break from task demands if student engages in challenging/target behavior
Alone	• Student left alone with very low levels of environmental stimulation present; no toys, no activities • No instructions given	• No programmed consequences provided
Control (Play)	• Preferred items available • No demands given • Practitioner provides attention for any behavior other than challenging/target behavior	• Challenging behavior is ignored or redirected

Table 12–3. Functional Analysis Conditions with Student Examples (Katie)

Condition	Antecedents	Consequence for Challenging Behavior
Contingent Attention	• A teacher provides Katie with a few toys and activities and tells Kate that she can engage with them if she'd like • Teacher then puts her feet up and starts to read a magazine, ignoring Katie	• Kate does not engage in any screaming
Contingent Escape/Avoid	• Teacher provides Katie with an instruction to sit down at the table • Teacher gives her a math worksheet and says, "Here, you need to do the first five problems" and proceeds to sit down next to Katie	• Katie screams and the teacher removes the math worksheet from her workspace
Alone	• Katie is left in a quiet portion of a classroom with some toys and activities with no explicit instruction to do anything • No instructions given	• Katie does not engage in any screaming
Control (Play)	• Katie is provided with a variety of preferred toys and items in which she is freely able to play • The teacher sits with her and engages with her, talks to her, and no demands are given	• No screaming observed

Nonetheless, caution must be used with this type of functional assessment in particular as ethical issues may arise. First and foremost, bear in mind what the functional analysis is doing: actively manipulating an environmental condition in order to bring about challenging behavior. Precautions must be taken if behavior you are trying to replace is one that has the potential to cause harm to either the individual engaging in it or others, such as aggression or self-injury. In these cases, it may be best to defer to a different form of functional assessment or consult with a trained professional. Also consider the alone condition. Most school districts will not allow for this to occur as it can be interpreted as seclusion, as the child is in a room alone with no toys or activities. In most clinical settings where functional analyses occur, an observer is placed outside the room and watches the child either via a one-way mirror or video camera.

Once information has been gathered via direct and indirect methods, the next step to conducting an FBA is to examine those data and develop a hypothesis regarding the function of the challenging behavior. As we know, all behavior serves a function (or sometimes more than one); once we sort out what the function is, we are able to provide proper intervention to replace the challenging behavior and improve quality of life. Specifically, identifying the function allows teachers and school personnel to support the student by providing consequences and reinforcers that facilitate alternative, positive behavior that serves the same function. Let's now take a deeper look into what functions drive behavior.

Functions of Behavior

At first glance, "function of behavior" may sound rather cold and clinical; however, it is a simple way of framing what the behavior does for the individual, or the reason why a person is behaving in such a way. Remember, all challenging behavior is being reinforced by *something* and that something is efficient and effective for that individual.

> "The function of a behavior refers to the source of environmental reinforcement for it" (Tarbox et al., 2009, p. 494).

Oftentimes the means to access an outcome may be the easiest, fastest, or only way an individual knows. Let's put this into context. If you were presented with the same outcome, say a delicious donut, but had two ways in which to access it, either by making it from scratch or by grabbing one on your way into work, which would you take? More often than not, one would likely choose the least time-intensive, fastest, easiest way. Despite the seemingly endless number of behaviors one may possibly engage in, the function of such behavior can be captured into one of four main categories: attention, escape/avoidance, access to tangibles, and automatic. Generally speaking, none of the functions are "stronger" or more reliable than another; this is truly where individual differences influence what controls specific behaviors for specific individuals. And, of course, functions of behaviors can shift and change over time to suit the individual. Considerations for each function as well as behaviors with multiple functions are discussed in the following sections.

Attention

Attention from others is a very common consequence that maintains many behaviors. Of course some of the behaviors maintained by attention are positive and socially acceptable, while others can be maladaptive. Consider a student raising her hand to ask for help from the teacher. Now consider the student ripping up worksheets and throwing supplies. Both behaviors result in attention being given but in very different ways. A common misstep when looking at attention as a function is to dismiss behaviors that receive "negative" forms of attention (e.g., being told off, sent to principal's office, detention, etc.). You may hear things like "There's no way Anthony is pushing kids for attention; they always tell on him and he always gets sent to the principal's office." However, attention that is maintaining behavior need not always be what is considered to be "positive"; there are often many times individuals engage in behavior to solicit negative attention from others. Behaviors such as self-injury, property destruction, and other forms of disruption result in almost immediate attention. While attention is most likely given with honest intention, it may be inadvertently reinforcing (i.e., maintaining) the behavior.

Escape

Behavior that causes something aversive to be removed from the environment is maintained by an escape function. Just as with any other function, escape maintained behavior can be adaptive or maladaptive. When presented with something uncomfortable or annoying, such as the beep from a smoke detector battery, individuals engage in behavior to escape or cease the annoying stimulus. Sometimes the behavior is adaptive, such as changing the battery. Other times, it is maladaptive, as in ripping the smoke detector down and smashing it on the floor. Additionally, avoidance is often lumped in as a function along with escape-maintained behaviors, yet these two terms are not synonymous. Escape indicates that there is an aversive/annoying stimulus that the individual is actively experiencing, whereas avoidant behaviors operate prior to an individual experiencing an aversive stimulus. In other words, avoidance relies upon an individual's learning history—something like, "When I encounter X, Y happens"; "I don't like Y, so I'll avoid X . . . " For instance, students are required to run the track for a fitness test in P.E. Peg starts running but quickly tires, feigns illness, and sits out the rest of class. This is an example of escape. In contrast, Joe, knowing the fitness test is during his third period P.E. class, lies and tells the coach he forgot his sneakers and sits out. This is avoidance. Peg experienced discomfort from running and then engaged in a behavior to escape it, while Joe, who likely has a learning history of antipathy toward running, engaged in behavior to get him out of running prior to P.E. Just as with attention maintained behaviors, it is important to remain completely open minded and unbiased to whatever an individual may be escaping/avoiding. Remember, we all have very specific learning histories and what is tolerable for some, is absolutely unbearable for others.

Access

Some behaviors are maintained by an individual's access to items, privileges, opportunities, or activities, which act as reinforcers to such behaviors. This function is also known in some spheres as "tangibles" or "access to tangibles"; however, this is a bit misleading, as it indicates that behavior is reinforced by access to *stuff*. As we know, this is not always the case as individuals seek to access many intangible things as well. A student cutting to get ahead in a classroom lunch line, the child screaming at the checkout for a candy, or an employee working overtime to get a promotion are all examples of behaviors that operate with an access function. As you can see from these examples, engaging in behaviors to access to items, materials, opportunity can be highly detrimental and/or highly beneficial. A quick note here, as sometimes the access function gets a bit murky. Very often, "control" is discussed as a function of behavior as in something like, "Ella just screams and tantrums to control the situation." *Control is not a function of behavior.* Most of the time, this is a semantic misunderstanding and data will often indicate that Ella screams and tantrums to, in fact, gain access to a specific outcome, privilege, or activity. Placating a screaming toddler with a candy might be a fast and easy fix, but carries with it many unintended consequences that extend well beyond the grocery store checkout (do you think that parent really wants to buy an extra sugar-loaded treat every grocery store trip?!). On the other hand, an individual's motivation to access a promotion, with all of the benefits associated (monetary, responsibility, status, influence, etc.), serves that individual, and very likely others, in many positive ways. Perhaps the most universal tangible that individuals seek to access is money. Because we (authors) are optimists, we presume most people access money via positive, prosocial behaviors such as working in fulfilling careers; however, real life (and reality television) reveals this is not always the case.

Automatic

Perhaps the least understood, or rather the function with the most circulated misinformation, is the automatic function. This category is quite different from the others as it is tied to an individual's sensory receptors. Automatic reinforcement is unique in that only the individual experiences the effects, and as such, it is impossible to observe. "Automatic reinforcement occurs independent of social mediation by others" (Cooper, Heron, & Heward, 2007, p. 267). Thus, automatically reinforced behavior is behavior maintained only by an individual's actions, entirely independent of the social environment. In contrast with the other functions that are socially mediated, automatically reinforced behaviors are said to be "nonsocial" or not mediated by social contingencies. For example, putting seasoning on your food to enhance the taste, exercising to experience an endorphin high, or engaging in self-stimulatory behaviors (such as pencil tapping, hand flapping, or hair twirling) may be maintained by an automatic reinforcement.

Conclusion

Functional assessment is a process which allows educational teams to support students with behavioral needs by uncovering variables contributing to challenging behavior. Data collection is one of the most important components of intervention planning. By creating an effective data collection plan, teams are more likely to meet the needs of students experiencing behavioral challenges. Understanding antecedents and consequences of behavior not only informs individual assessments but also contributes to educator's wider scope of practice. By skillfully choosing a data collection system and evaluating data, educators can detect patterns and trends of student behavior and are then better equipped to adjust their teaching to match student need. Becoming familiar with the various methods and practices presented in this chapter is essential for gathering the information required to inform pragmatic, effective behavioral intervention plans.

Chapter Summary

- A functional behavioral assessment is a systematic process by which the variables that maintain problem behavior are identified. This information is then translated into a behavioral intervention plan (BIP), which is a plan designed to teach prosocial behaviors to replace the challenging behavior. The FBA to BIP process is intended to be individualized and proactive to best support students.

- There are three ways to conduct an FBA: direct, indirect, and functional analysis.

- An FBA itself is made up of three components:
    1. Operational definition of a socially significant target behavior
    2. Data collection
    3. Function of behavior

- Indirect assessment is a means of gathering information through means other than directly observing the target behavior. Rating scales, record reviews, interviews, and checklists are some examples of indirect assessment.

- Direct assessment is gathering of information via directly observing the student and collecting data on the target behavior. Common methods for collecting such data include anecdotal notes (e.g., written descriptions of behavior) and A-B-C (e.g., organizing observational data into antecedents-behaviors-consequences).

- Antecedents are actions or events that occur immediately prior to the target behavior; these are what triggers the target behavior to occur and typically involve changes to the environment, people, demands, or transitions.

- Setting events occur *prior* to antecedents and are factors that alter the effects of antecedents. These can be difficult to detect because they may occur well outside of an observation. Setting events typically involve states such as hunger, fatigue, and pain.

- Consequences are the events that occur immediately following a target behavior and influence the future likelihood of that behavior occurring again. These events are critical to understanding the pattern of the target behavior. Consequences may include access to an item or privilege, access to attention, avoidance or escape from demand, or receiving sensory input. Consequences may be reinforcing (i.e., increases the likelihood of target behavior occurring) or punishing (i.e., decreases the likelihood of target behavior occurring again).

- Functional analysis is considered to be the gold standard of functional assessment; it is an active process by which the teacher/practitioner purposefully manipulates antecedents and consequences of the target behavior to "test" the variables that contribute to it. Precautions must be practiced here as the challenging behavior is being evoked and can cause distress or stress for the students and as such are not typically carried out in school settings.

- The function of a behavior is the underlying reason an individual engages in a specific behavior; it frames the "why" behind behavior. The four functions of behavior are attention, escape, access, and automatic.

CHAPTER 13

BEHAVIORAL INTERVENTION PLANS

Learning Objectives

- Describe how an FBA translates to a BIP
- Define replacement behaviors and understand their importance in the FBA process
- Identify considerations when selecting functionally equivalent behaviors
- Explain how to construct a BIP (competing pathways model)
- Identify essential components of a BIP and how to implement them in applied classroom settings
- Discriminate between reinforcement and extinction

Key Terms

Behavior Skills Training
Behavioral Momentum
Competing Behavior Pathway
Extinction

Functional Communication Training
Noncontingent Reinforcement
Replacement Behavior

s the previous chapter details, the role of a functional behavioral assessment (FBA) is to identify how environmental variables are related to behavior. Once these variables are made visible, they become available to interventions intended to shape them and bring about a positive behavior change. While we have dedicated separate chapters to FBAs and behavioral intervention plans (BIPs), it cannot be stressed enough that these two processes are intimately coupled and operate as complements to one another. This chapter will outline and describe the link between FBAs and BIPs and how teachers can use information gleaned from the FBA process to design effective interventions targeting challenging behavior.

High-Leverage Practice Alert!

HLP10 specifically covers the need to conduct FBAs to plan for BIPs. These processes should not be done in isolation. Further, HLP10 addresses the need for addressing setting events, replacement behaviors, behavior skills training, and collecting and analyzing data for decision making.

Replacement Behaviors

We've looked at the steps to take when conducting various types of FBAs and discussed how to analyze data to reveal function; yet, this only goes so far. Good assessment results are only as good as what is done with them. The purpose of an FBA is to find the root cause of the challenging behavior in order to find a functionally equivalent behavior with which to replace it. It is impossible to delete a behavior from an individual's repertoire; *all behaviors must be replaced with another behavior.*

Let's consider some examples you, or someone you may know, might have experienced. Someone seeking to lose weight and decides to cut out drinking soda altogether. While this sounds great on the surface, if someone is highly accustomed to drinking soda, this change is likely to be very short lived. What *is likely* is the individual, who is off soda but craving sugar/caffeine, will look for an alternative—perhaps energy drinks, coffee, or fruit juices. These replacements, while not soda, are likely to have the same amount of sugars and carbohydrates (unless the coffee is straight black) as soda, thus, inhibiting weight loss. Quitting something "cold turkey," such as cigarettes, also sets the stage for a behavioral rebound. One of the authors decided to go without cigarettes and use sheer will power to overcome her addiction. She was successful in that respect; however, she began to replace cigarettes with cupcakes, chips, and anything else to keep hands/mouth busy, thereby trading one "bad" habit for another. The point here is that we must shift our mindset to one of adding functional skills to an individual's repertoire rather than aiming to squelch a behavior altogether.

Constructing a Behavioral Intervention Plan

To help us organize the way we approach functional assessment, we will refer to something called the competing behavior pathways model (Horner, Sugai, Todd, & Lewis-Palmer, 2000; O'Neill et al., 1997) (Figure 13–1).

The competing behavior pathways model provides a link between the FBA and how to develop a sound BIP. The model relies upon learning theory and maintains many behaviors may serve the same function. Thus, if we can identify a positive, alternative behavior for an individual to engage in that also produces the same reinforcing consequences as the challenging behavior, we can reasonably *replace* challenging behavior. Moreover, if we can select a replacement behavior that is more efficient or requires less effort, we further increase our chances that behavior will take hold in the individual's repertoire.

Data from the FBA are entered into the chart in order to generate a new pathway to the maintaining consequence. In other words, we want to replace the challenging behavior with an alternative that provides *the same maintaining consequence*. In this way, "maintaining consequences" refers to the function, or what keeps the behavior going. So, if the maintaining consequence of screaming is to access attention, the replacement behavior must also allow the individual to access attention but in a more positive, prosocial way, such as raising a hand or asking for help. In all, we want to replace the challenging behavior with a stronger, more powerful alternative; a behavior that successfully *competes*. Figure 13–2 provides a sample portion of a competing behavior diagram for the following case example on Alice.

To begin completing the competing behavior pathways diagram, information taken from the FBA data are entered into the first four sections: (1) label and definition of the challenging behavior, (2) antecedents to challenging behavior, (3) consequences to challenging behavior, and (4) setting events to challenging behavior. Together, these elements fit into a hypothesis statement, which provides context for the behavior's function. Hypothesis statements simply connect each portion of the antecedent-behavior-consequence chain and put it into context. A hypothesis statement may read something like, "Given (setting events/antecedents), Alice is more likely to engage in (challenging behavior) in order to (consequence)," or "Given low medication levels and demands in math, Alice is more likely to throw personal materials in order to avoid the task." This statement is a summary of the factors leads us directly to the function of the challenging behavior.

Figure 13–1. Competing behavior pathways chart.

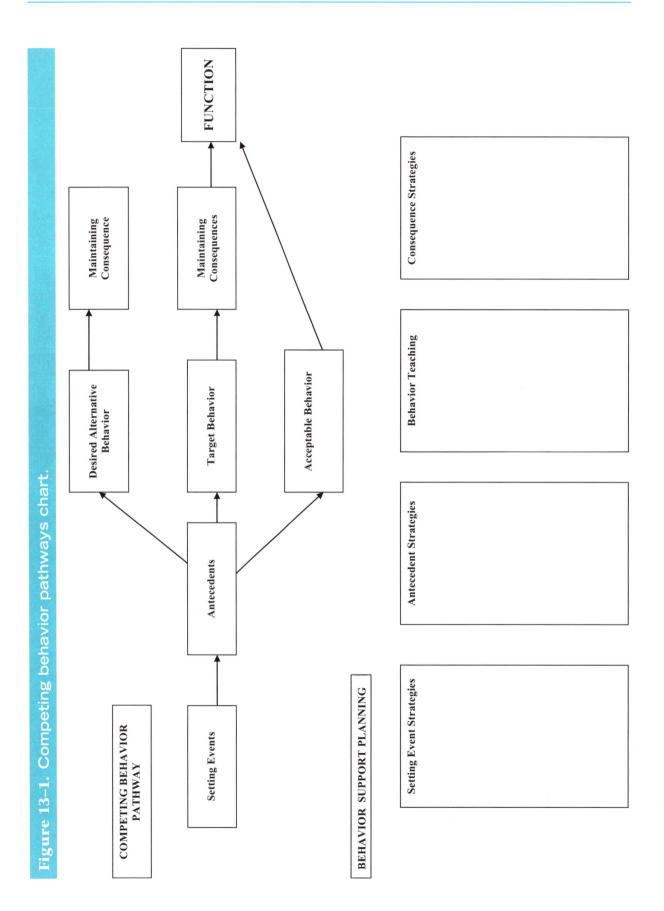

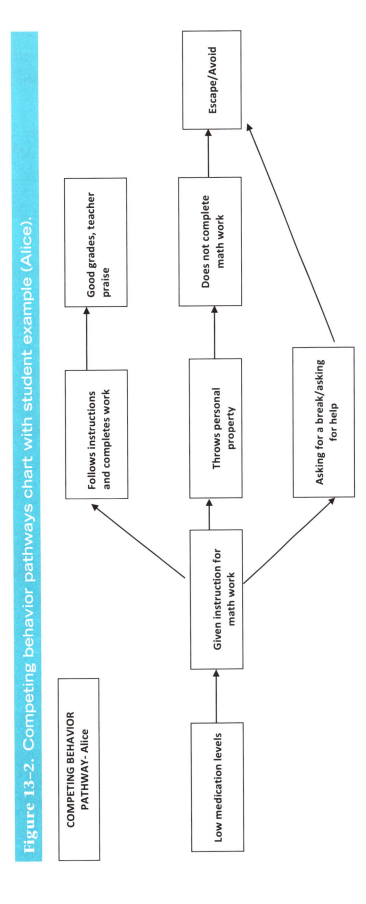

Figure 13–2. Competing behavior pathways chart with student example (Alice).

Review Chapter 12 to refresh your memory on antecedents, setting events, and consequences.

The next portion of the competing pathways behavior diagram is intended to prompt dialogue among the team of professionals working together. The last sections include the following: (5) desired behavior alternative, (6) consequence for desired alternative, and finally, (7) positive replacement behavior. Individually, the desired behavior alternative (5) is simply the "in a perfect world, what behavior would we want to see?" This is not the replacement behavior! For example, if the challenging behavior is Alice throwing personal property when given a math instruction, the desired behavior would be "Alice completing her math work and following instructions." It is important to think about the alternative behavior in this way in order to identify the maintaining consequence, or what reinforces that behavior, as this is the key for identification of an acceptable replacement behavior. Next, we look at what consequences would maintain the desired alternative behavior (6). For instance, what naturally occurring consequence might maintain a student's completion of assignments? Often, we can assume good grades, bonus points, and/or teacher praise would reinforce completing school tasks.

Finally, the key element to the competing pathways diagram is the identification of the *functionally equivalent* replacement behavior (7). What is another behavior Alice can engage in *that meets the same needs as throwing her items around the classroom?* If Alice gets to avoid a demand when she tosses her materials, what else could she do to successfully avoid a task in a positive, socially acceptable way? While you may wonder why a teacher would ever allow a student to successfully avoid a task, it's important to remember that no behavior just disappears without new skills, antecedents, or consequences. For change to occur, the function of the behavior must be addressed. A functionally equivalent replacement behavior could be Alice asking for a break from work, thus avoiding work briefly. See Table 13–1 for possible replacement behaviors by function.

Considerations for Selecting Replacement Behaviors

This may seem obvious, but when considering what replacement behavior(s) to use, it is ideal to select a behavior that is already in the student's repertoire. By selecting something the student is capable of doing and may already be doing (just not at the right time or in the correct context), it eliminates the need to teach a brand new skill, which takes time and effort beyond what is already being used in dealing with challenging behavior. In this way, the BIP will be used to teach to a

Table 13–1. Examples of Replacement Behaviors According to Function

	Function	Possible Replacement Behaviors
Access	Attention	• Raise hand • Say/use teacher or peer name • "Excuse me" • "Come here/play with me"
	Tangible	• Request item (e.g., "Can I have a turn?") • Request more of an item (e.g., "One more minute;" "May I have more time with?")
	Sensory	• Request a break to engage in sensory seeking activity/self-stimulation • Teaching competing leisure/play skills • Finding other acceptable ways to access same sensory input
Escape	Escape (from demand, task, etc.)	• Ask for a break • Negotiate a delay • Ask for help • Appropriate rejections
	Automatic	• Request a break • Communicate discomfort (e.g., "I don't feel well"; "My head hurts"; "It's too loud"; "I'm tired")

performance deficit, versus a *skills deficit.* However, if required, it is entirely possible to teach a replacement behavior.

Peek ahead to Chapter 14 where we discuss teaching new skills. Then, come back to this chapter after reading about skill instruction to better understand the differences between performance and skill deficits.

Also consider the level of effort required for the individual to use the replacement behavior. If the replacement behavior requires a significant amount of time or effort, especially if this is more than the challenging behavior, the student is less likely to use it. The replacement behavior should be far easier, faster, and more reliable than the challenging behavior. Think about all of the effort, both physical and mental, that goes into throwing a tantrum to gain attention—quite a bit, right? We could choose a replacement behavior such as requesting "play with me" or "come here," which not only takes less effort but is also much faster than throwing oneself on the ground and screaming for minutes on end. Now, let's extend this a bit further. What if we are working with a learner that does not communicate vocally? Or what about those students whom we know so well and can "read" and respond to their idiosyncrasies? We must take every effort to ensure the replacement behaviors selected translate across environments. The replacement behaviors must be easily understood by most people in most situations in order to successfully compete with the challenging behaviors. Finally, we must hook into the power of reinforcement in order to shift the balance away from the challenging behavior and to the replacement behavior. The replacement behavior needs to access *more reinforcement, more frequently* in order to compete and replace the challenging behavior. Reinforcement of the replacement behavior must be built into the BIP.

Behavioral Intervention Plans

Now that the competing behavior model is complete, the team is tasked with strategizing each portion to create a comprehensive intervention plan. The lower portion of the competing behavior pathways chart breaks down BIP components into setting event strategies, antecedent strategies, behavior teaching, and consequence strategies.

Setting Event Strategies

Recall from Chapter 12 that setting events are global influences on behavior that occur beyond the scope of immediate antecedents and consequences. Setting events momentarily alter the value of a reinforcer or punisher and can be environmental, social, or physiological. While these lists are far from inclusive, the following are some examples of setting events:

- *Environmental setting events:* noise levels, heat/cold, physical environment, crowded spaces
- *Social setting events:* family discord, changes in family structure (e.g., divorce, birth of a baby), negative social interactions, losing a game

● *Physiological setting events:* fatigue, hunger, pain or discomfort, allergies, medication levels and/or side effects, menses, or low mood

Setting events may explain why a student's behavior varies from one day to the next. While not widely known by the term, setting events are actually quite visible in everyday life. One such example references the word "hangry," which was added to the Oxford Dictionary in 2018 (Hangry, n.d.). Consider a student who is generally compliant with academic tasks; now that same student may respond very differently to those same academic tasks when she has missed breakfast and is feeling the effects of low blood sugar. Now, if we can surmise from our data collection when a setting event is occurring, we can program for and provide a number of strategies for intervention.

Setting event strategies mostly involve finding ways to try to minimize the likelihood of a setting event occurring. Obvious interventions are providing care for illness or injury or any other type of physical discomfort. Recognizing signs of discomfort early on, such as one rubbing his or her eyes or temples at the onset of a headache, can help mitigate the effect of the setting event on behavior. There are, of course, some setting events that are unable to be manipulated or changed. Take for instance, the addition of a new baby to a household. A new baby may cause a shift in the dynamics of the family and also adds a degree of stress to the household via sleep deprivation, additional responsibilities, and quite often numerous visits from extended family members and friends. While the school team cannot change the fact that a baby has come into the home, they can still intervene on setting events that are likely working against the student's favor. Considerations for a student who might be coming to school fatigued may be to adjust the expectations for academic output, perhaps decreasing the amount of school work or providing extended deadlines for completion. Additionally, allowing the student some quiet down time or time to take a short nap may be helpful.

Next, there may be times in which the setting event has occurred and strategies are required to neutralize its effects. This involves providing access to preferred activities in order to alter the response to an antecedent (trigger). For example, if Raj engages in challenging behavior to delay a writing task, a teacher may sit down with him and discuss some choices of activities prior to writing time. Allowing Raj some time with his choice activity not only provides him something enjoyable but also gives him a sense of control.

As mentioned previously, setting events may also stem from failed or faulty social interactions, and as such, increasing opportunities for positive social interactions may foster better behavior overall. Something as simple as connecting with a preferred adult upon arrival at school can neutralize (socially related) setting events. Done proactively, these interventions are intended to try to offset any challenging behavior resulting from negative social interactions that may occur prior to the start of school. This can be done by finding activities that are motivating and foster communication and choice making as well as increase opportunities to contact positive social interactions.

> *Remember check-in check-out from Chapter 4? This is an example of connecting with a preferred adult upon arrival to school! Go back and review how this intervention also fits into the PBIS framework.*

Antecedent Event Strategies

While setting event strategies addresses events that affect the likelihood an event will elicit a problem behavior, antecedent interventions address physical, social, and biological events that actually trigger challenging behavior. Setting event and antecedent event strategies are usually used in conjunction with one another, as is often the case when a setting event cannot be eliminated or sufficiently neutralized.

Antecedents are events that occur immediately prior to challenging behavior. These could consist of the presence of a person, an activity, time of day, physical environment, a social interaction, and/or demands or instructions to complete a task. Alternatively, antecedent events could indicate the absence of something, such as being left out of a social interaction or being ignored. Just as with setting events, careful data collection is required in order to identify such antecedents in order to effectively address them by either removing the trigger, modifying the content, or adjusting the presentation of content.

Sometimes, it is possible to eliminate the antecedent, or trigger. If a teacher has identified a student's seat placement close to the noisy hallway is a trigger to problem behavior, he or she could move the student to a quieter location, further from the door. Similarly, if a student engages in challenging behavior to escape having to read aloud in class, the teacher may offer an alternative way for the student to show understanding that does not involve public reading. Other times, it is simply not possible or not appropriate to remove the trigger, as may be the case if problem behavior is triggered by math instruction. While one could *technically* remove math instruction from the curriculum to remove the trigger, it's just not reasonable. There are a few options to address this type of issue. One option could be to have the student sit out of math instruction for a designated amount of time in order to reduce the frequency of challenging behavior. Once the behavior has reduced, the teacher may slowly reintroduce instruction bit by bit. Challenging behavior in this context may also indicate some sort of unmet need. Perhaps the student is not fully grasping the content and requires some accommodation or modification to instruction.

Perhaps the student from the previous example finds math work irrelevant or boring. Modifying the math content to include student interests can help to make the work more exciting and salient. There is also a strong link between task difficulty and the occurrence of challenging behavior. One may address this by manipulating the difficulty of the task and incorporate more support around tasks known to be challenging. Further, one can create a higher likelihood of compliance to a task or instruction by using a concept called behavioral momentum. Behavioral momentum involves using a series of high-probability requests or tasks to increase compliance with lower-probability requests or tasks (Ray, Skinner, & Watson, 1999). To use, present the student with "easy" or "throw away" requests (i.e., high-probability behaviors) and be sure to provide lots of reinforcement for compliance. These demands, which are purposefully chosen to be those completed quickly and easily, help to build up success, or "momentum," so that more challenging questions/requests can be presented after. For example, if Ms. Williams wants Steve to clean up his workspace, she could present some high-probability requests such as having him go get his backpack and give a high five (high probability behaviors) followed by the instruction to tidy up his workspace (low-probability behavior). For older students, this could look like interspersing easier tasks within a longer, more difficult task to increase engagement and motivation. Incorporate the use of student-specific, high-probability requests and vary these when using this strategy.

Other antecedent strategies aimed at decreasing challenging behavior include adjusting the length of tasks or providing breaks throughout work time. Presenting larger assignments or tasks in smaller chunks can foster a student's success by reinforcing smaller goals. Additionally, the order in which activities occur can influence the likelihood of positive behaviors occurring. Many schools are known to order the recess to follow blocks of work as having a high-energy activity *before* academics may increase problem behavior. Further, providing choices is also shown to have positive effects on student performance. Offering an option of doing one task before or after another, even when both tasks are less preferred, can be beneficial.

Within a smoothly run classroom system, you're bound to find antecedent strategies disguised as "general classroom management." The use of visual schedules, from sophisticated full day details to simple bullet points for what will be covered in second period, offers predictability and routine. Taking some time to model and practice classroom routines can smooth out transitions between topics, activities, or places that may otherwise be tricky without preemptive planning.

> *Refer to Chapter 7 for an in-depth look at establishing classroom procedures.*

Behavioral Teaching Strategies

The purpose behind the team completing an FBA is to gather enough relevant information about the student's challenging behavior to create the BIP. The focal point of the BIP is the identification of the alternative behavior that will be used to replace the challenging behavior. Thus, the objective of the BIP is to *teach the student how and when to use the replacement behavior*. The antecedent strategies discussed previously only go so far in dealing with challenging behavior, and while they can be highly effective, they must never be used without behavioral teaching strategies.

Behavioral teaching strategies may be thought of in two categories: interventions to teach to a skill deficit or interventions to teach to a performance deficit. The former, teaching to a skill deficit, indicates that the replacement behavior is not currently in the student's repertoire. For example, a student who is nonvocal and does not have a means to communicate may be taught some simple sign language to request items. This would be different from a performance deficit, wherein the student who is nonvocal knows a wide variety of signs but does not use them in the appropriate context to access an item. Another indicator of skill versus performance deficit may be a student who does not have any de-escalation/coping strategies to deal with changes in routine versus a student who inconsistently uses coping strategies. The inconsistency of coping strategy use indicates the skill resides in the student's understanding, but is not under sufficient control of the surrounding events.

 High-Leverage Practice Alert!

The need for teaching social behaviors and addressing functions of behavior is outlined in HLP9.

Behavior Skills Training (BST)

BST is a simple, four-step method that may be used to teach a new skill (Miltenberger, 2004). BST can be used to teach most any skill and allows for practice opportunities to create fluency with the new skill.

Prerequisites required for BST simply state that the skill should be a chain of behaviors that can be role-played or modeled. The four steps are (1) Instruction, (2) Modeling, (3) Practice, and (4) Feedback (Figure 13–3).

During the instruction stage, the student is provided with a description of the skill. It may be beneficial to also write this down to use as a visual aid. Along with the description of the skill, and perhaps the most important of all, is to provide a rationale for its use. Why is it important for the student to learn the skill? How will it improve daily life? How will it make life easier? (Remember, just because you've identified a replacement behavior that ticks all the above boxes, it is useless without relevance to the learner!) Once you've established the description and importance of the skill, it is time to model the skill for the student. This occurs as many times as required for the student to see all aspects of the behavior chain completely. Real life modeling is best, but the use of video models suffices, if necessary. Additionally, consider using a few different models (e.g., other staff, peers, etc.) to incorporate a bit of generalization at the outset of skill instruction. Next, it's time to practice. This is critical! Allow sufficient time over many days to have the student practice the skill. During the practice sessions, staff has the

Figure 13–3. Behavior skills training steps.

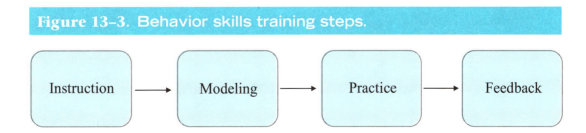

opportunity to provide immediate feedback to the student. Feedback may take the form of praise and reinforcement or could include corrective feedback, explaining exactly what is required and how to change the behavior.

 High-Leverage Practice Alert!

Feedback in the context of learning and behavior is covered in HLP8. As mentioned previously, the forms of feedback may vary, but it should be timely and contingent on the execution of desired target behaviors.

BST may also be used to target those behaviors that are already in a student's repertoire, albeit with some minor adjustments. Since the behavior chain is already known to the student, BST can facilitate opportunities for role-play and feedback. For example, let's look at the chain of behaviors required for "asking for help." This specific skill may be broken down into three basic parts: (1) Find someone that can help; (2) Get the person's attention; and (3) Say something like "I need help" or "Can you help me?" If Cora only asks for help by yelling across the classroom, this needs to be adjusted so she doesn't disrupt instruction. Therefore, Step 2 can be expanded upon, covering the wide variety of ways to ask for help (e.g., raising hand, approaching, eye contact with gesture, etc.). The provision of the skill's importance and rationale is still relevant in this case; the objective is to accumulate as much buy-in as possible from the student. Depending on the learner and the complexity of the skill, modeling may or may not be used. Next, offering plenty of practice opportunities spanning a variety of scenarios is ideal. Within these sessions, the teacher or staff may help the student by providing a prompt for her or him to engage in the target behavior (i.e., asking for help). Prompting is a strategy to increase the probability of a correct response. Keep in mind that any prompt you use to teach is temporary and must be faded to ensure the student's mastery of the skill. Without fading a prompt, the student may become dependent on it and you will find yourself in the same place as when you started. To make this as easy as possible, start by using the least intrusive prompt for the situation. In our example of Cora asking for help, this may look like the teacher giving a discreet hand signal. Throughout practice opportunities, the teacher also practices fading the prompt by giving less and less of the hand signal—perhaps fading from a fully raised hand, to a hand raised to midsection, to raising one finger, and, finally, no prompt.

Functional Communication Training

Another incredibly powerful and well-established intervention for challenging behavior is functional communication training (FCT). Again, as with many concepts presented throughout this text, there is no way to fully provide the level of depth and detail FCT deserves. This text aims to identify FCT as a viable intervention that may be used in the classroom and to provide a brief overview.

FCT is a form of differential reinforcement that teaches a communication response to replace challenging behavior. Initially described by Carr and Durand in 1985, the communication response is an alternate response to challenging behavior and is one that is reinforced by the same consequence as the challenging behavior. In this way, this newly taught communication response becomes more valuable and, in turn, replaces disruptive, inappropriate, or otherwise challenging behavior. So, rather than Max tearing up papers and shouting during instruction (attention-maintained behavior), he is taught a more socially acceptable way to communicate his needs, such as asking the teacher for help. There are three main steps in an FCT procedure, with the first being a thorough FBA to determine what is reinforcing the challenging behavior (i.e., function). Next, a socially appropriate, alternative communication response is chosen. FCT creates a new behavioral pathway by strengthening the alternative communication response with the same reinforcers that once followed the challenging behavior. Lastly, the intervention is delivered across multiple settings and across different people.

Frequently, FCT is quite successful with attention-maintained behaviors; however, it can be used to address challenging behaviors that stem from a variety of functions. While FCT can be used to address a wide range of behaviors across various individuals, most of the research on the topic relates to individuals with developmental disabilities displaying aggression or self-injury (Tiger, Hanley, & Bruzek, 2008). It's also important to note that the alternative communication response may take any number of forms, such as visuals, gestures, vocal speech, sign, or picture exchange. Further, the effectiveness of FCT is enhanced when it is used in conjunction with other strategies, such as prompting, extinction, or redirection.

The form of the communication taught (e.g., vocal, gesture, picture exchange, etc.) in FCT is not the emphasis; rather, the focus should be on the function of the response. FCT is dependent on accurate identification of the challenging behavior's function. In order to effectively intervene on challenging behavior, the function of the communication response must match the function maintaining the challenging behavior. Once the function of the challenging behavior is identified, a hypothesis statement can be formed, just as described previously. For instance, "Given an instructional block, Max is more likely to engage in challenging behavior (e.g., tearing papers, shouting) in order to gain attention from others." From this statement we can see that the function of Max's behavior is to *communicate* that he needs some sort of attention. In order to address this, the BIP must reasonably provide Max with that same consequence, albeit, a more socially acceptable one. Here is where the FCT procedure seeks to identify some acceptable ways in which Max can access attention. Rather than shouting and interrupting instruction, Max can raise his hand to make a comment or request help. Once the communication response is established, the focus then shifts to the teacher. In this way, the teacher is responsible for prompting and teaching the communication response, while no longer honoring the challenging behavior (usually through planned ignoring); this reinforces Max for engaging in the desired behavior and/ or the absence of challenging behavior. These communicative responses must be reinforced continuously at the outset of the intervention in order to shift the power away from the challenging behavior.

Of course, it should go without saying that FCT is in no way a rapid solution for management of challenging behavior. It takes numerous iterations of prompting and reinforcing to diminish the frequency of challenging behavior with the alternative communication response. Keep in mind that this is just an overview of the FCT process in its most simplified version. There are many variations of FCT that extend beyond the scope of this text. It should also be mentioned that while it may increase the effectiveness of FCT, using extinction to remove reinforcement for the challenging behavior may prove difficult in the classroom. Not only can extinction produce some unpleasant side effects (see Chapter 3), but because the teacher is only one person in a busy environment, there is the potential for him or her to miss opportunities to prompt the communication response and/ or inadvertently attend to the challenging behavior. In all, using FCT to teach students alternative ways to appropriately meet their needs can be highly beneficial. Recruiting the expertise of behavior specialists within your school or district is a first step to developing and implementing this powerful, effective intervention.

Consequence Strategies

The preceding sections focused on setting events and antecedent strategies aimed at adjusting the environment to neutralize or eliminate triggers and behavior teaching strategies to teach a replacement to challenging behavior. Yet, using setting event and antecedent manipulation long term will not set the student up for generalized success across environments and across people. Imagine a case wherein a teacher has put into place a morning check-in (setting event strategy), preferential seating assignments, and visual schedules (antecedent strategies) for one of her higher needs students. Using these strategies can be very advantageous and likely produce lower levels of challenging behavior, but how will that student function when she is no longer in that environment with those supports? Even with teaching a replacement behavior, the BIP is incomplete without consequence strategies. As discussed, consequences are the events occurring immediately following a behavior that increase or decrease the likelihood of the behavior occurring again. Tying this into the BIP, consequence strategies are those that will strengthen the use of replacement behaviors, giving them more power over challenging behavior.

Consequence interventions serve two main functions: first, to decrease the amount of reinforcement the challenging behavior receives, and second, to increase reinforcement for the replacement behavior. Remember the overarching goal of the BIP is to teach the student a new skill that provides the same outcome as the challenging behavior. Yet, putting a BIP in place does not preclude the student from continuing to engage in the challenging behavior that has served them for so long; thus, the need for consequence interventions. Several considerations go into programming consequence interventions; namely, ensuring they are rooted in positive behavior supports rather than relying on punishment as it is well established that punishment-based systems produce only short-term change and may lead to increases in challenging behavior. Here, we will discuss the most common consequence interventions: extinction, positive and negative reinforcement, noncontingent reinforcement, and redirection.

Extinction

As Chapter 3 outlines, extinction is withdrawing or ceasing reinforcement that is maintaining challenging behavior. For behaviors maintained by social attention, planned ignoring can be a highly effective way to terminate reinforcement. In this way, if attention is providing fuel to a challenging behavior's fire (i.e., positive reinforcement), ignoring is the water dousing the flames. Extinction for escape-maintained behaviors consists of not allowing the student to avoid or escape the demand when they engage in the challenging behavior. If whining allows a student to avoid work (i.e., negative reinforcement), the teacher would continue to present the work until the student complies, despite the whining. In other words, escape-maintained extinction is discontinuation of negative reinforcement for a challenging behavior. Whenever an extinction intervention is implemented, there is always a risk for an extinction burst: a temporary increase in the behavior's frequency and intensity before decrease.

> *Go back and review Chapter 3 for more on extinction, extinction bursts, and reinforcement. Further, peek ahead to Chapter 14 to preview how to use reinforcement in the classroom setting.*

Reinforcement

Reinforcement is always required in order to establish the replacement behavior as superior to the challenging behavior. Recall from Chapter 3 that reinforcement needs to be just that . . . *reinforcing.* A personalized approach will ensure the positive consequences following a desired behavior are relevant and motivating. Positive reinforcement strategies include token economies and behavior-specific praise, while negative reinforcement strategies may consist of homework passes or early recess.

Noncontingent reinforcement is a strategy wherein reinforcement is regularly provided for any behavior excluding the challenging behavior. So, if Robin's calling out behavior is maintained by social attention from teacher, the teacher provides Robin with quality attention throughout the day so long as Robin is not calling out. The underlying premise is that the student is less likely to engage in challenging behavior if he or she accesses the reinforcer (attention) on a regular basis.

The BIP is successful when challenging behavior is put on extinction and the replacement behavior is reinforced. Another strategy to build a positive climate and add reinforcement is to monitor the events that surround the nonoccurrence of target behavior. While much discussion around challenging behavior involves data collection on its frequency, intensity, duration, and so forth, it is just as feasible to note what activities, people, and so forth are occurring while the student is not engaging in challenging behavior. Once this information is gathered, teachers or staff can help to replicate these activities, events, and so forth to closely resemble environments in which challenging behavior is less likely to occur.

Redirection

Redirection involves strategically refocusing a student toward a positive interaction or activity. Sometimes referred to as an *antiseptic bounce,* redirection is used as a temporary strategy to remove the student from triggers that may escalate to challenging behavior. This strategy is to be used at the first sign of a student's distress, prior to any challenging behavior (e.g., fidgeting, increase in vocalizations, etc.). For example, a teacher can redirect a student from some instructional time by asking him or her to pass out some papers, go to a neighboring classroom to retrieve a box of tissues, or give a note to the front office staff. Using redirection, teachers create opportunities for student's to engage in in a positive, alternative activity. This takes the student out of the potentially triggering situation and also provides a model of an acceptable, alternative behavior. As mentioned with the other consequence strategies, the function of the target behavior must be taken into consideration if redirection is to be used. If a student engages in challenging behavior to routinely avoid instructions, this may not be the best strategy to employ. Further, use redirection sparingly as is also meant to accompany reinforcement and extinction, as detailed previously.

Safety Plans

The foundation of this chapter is focused on building an effective BIP through identification, teaching, and reinforcement of replacement behaviors. However, it would be remiss to address those circumstances in which a teacher finds him or herself in the midst of dealing with crisis level behaviors. Safety planning is a necessary consideration for those children who require BIPs. As a general rule, not all BIPs require a safety plan, but all individual student safety plans require a BIP. For example, you may have a student for whom you want to target socially appropriate attention seeking and replacing calling out with hand raising. This would likely not sound any alarm bells and require safety planning, as calling out is more of a disturbance than a risk concern. A safety plan would be required if one were targeting a student's aggression toward peers.

A safety plan is exactly as it sounds: a plan designed to maintain the safety of the student and others by implementing strategies to neutralize or de-escalate challenging behaviors. While safety plans include proactive strategies to minimize triggers, the primary purpose is to mitigate factors that maintain challenging behavior. As such, safety plans *do not teach replacement behaviors* and therefore should never be used without a supplemental BIP (because those *do teach replacement behaviors!*). The safety plan may be thought of as a means to create an environment in which the student is available for learning.

For more on classroom safety plan considerations, refer back to Chapter 4.

Team Process

While the FBA/BIP process focuses attention on the student's challenging behavior, it is actually the responsibility of the teachers, staff, parents, and other support members to implement the BIP in order to achieve behavior change. So, even though Christy's name is on the top of the FBA/BIP documents, *the plan is for her team* to take steps to modify her environment, teach replacement skills, and provide reinforcement for new skills. A collaborative team approach should always be the first step in FBA/BIP planning. This team should be made up of relevant individuals to include the student (if appropriate), teachers, principal/ administration, related service providers, parents, and behavior specialists. This ensures that all aspects of the FBA/BIP planning reflect the values of the student and school, that selected interventions are evidence-based, and that all members have an active role in the implementation of the plan. Further, if this plan is attached to the student's Individualized Education Program (IEP), all members of the IEP team are required to be invited and/or present at the development of the FBA/BIP.

Clear, consistent communication among the team is imperative to the success of the plan. This communication may also need to extend out to ancillary individuals, such as teachers in nearby classrooms, cafeteria staff, or front office staff. Take for instance a student whose problem behavior is maintained by social attention. What if that student engaged in challenging behavior in the middle of the front office during the morning rush? Well, it is *highly likely* that a well-meaning administrative assistant would engage with that student and inadvertently reinforce problem behavior. With some careful planning, these potential situations can be accounted for and proactively addressed. Further, a collaborative team approach allows for division of responsibilities and provides structure for regular meetings to analyze data and make necessary changes. This is not to say that the roles and responsibilities within the team are absolute; ideally, *everyone* is providing support in teaching and reinforcing replacement behaviors through a variety of interventions as this will help to generalize the skill for the student.

The collaborative team approach is also responsible for progress monitoring of the BIP. Once in full implementation, a measure of progress to determine whether to continue, change, or end the intervention is required. The BIP is not a document that is completed and filed away in the school office. It is a living document, a work in progress. The team must determine and clearly state how often data are to be collected on both the challenging behaviors and the replacement behaviors and by whom data will be collected. Then, the team is responsible for holding regularly occurring data review meetings to analyze what has been collected and discuss what is working well, what may not be working well, and any observations or additional input. These data are then used to determine what, if any, changes are required. These meetings are also important to determine when the goals have been met and when the student meets criteria that no longer requires the BIP.

Conclusion

As you can see, the relationship between the FBA and BIP is continually evolving as each process informs the other. Purposeful coordination and collaboration among team members is vital to progress from the FBA all the way through to implementation of the BIP. Effective plans are those that clearly connect function to behavior and identify suitable replacement behaviors. The BIP is intended to be a working document that puts strategies into practice within applied settings with the ultimate goal of helping students.

Chapter Summary

- The desired outcome of an FBA is to determine the function of the target; this information is then used to select a replacement behavior to replace the challenging behavior. Replacement behaviors are positive, prosocial behaviors that are functionally equivalent to the target behavior. It is best to select a behavior that is already in a student's repertoire, is efficient, and requires the same or less effort than the challenging behavior.

- The competing behavior pathways model is a way to organize one's approach to functional assessment and provides a series of connections between the steps of the FBA all the way through formulation of the BIP. It breaks down the BIP into setting event strategies, antecedent strategies, behavior teaching, and consequence strategies.

- Setting event strategies involve finding ways to neutralize or minimize the likelihood of a setting event, which may include things like ensuring a comfortable classroom temperature, providing snacks and a drink before a lesson, or providing an area for some quiet down time.

- Antecedent event strategies target the antecedent, or events immediately prior to challenging behavior. Strategies in this area focus on how to mitigate or neutralize the trigger(s) to challenging behavior, which could be moving a student's seat, decreasing the number of math questions required, or modifying academic content to reflect interests of the student.

- Behavior skills training is a four-step method to teach a new skill, or in the case of a BIP, the replacement behavior. It is comprised of (1) Instruction, (2) Modeling, (3) Practice, and (4) Feedback. In order to use BST, the target behavior should be a skill made up of a chain of behaviors capable of being modeled and role-played.

- While setting event and antecedent strategies are useful in shaping new behavior patterns, consequence strategies are integral in strengthening the use of replacement behaviors while reducing the likelihood of challenging behaviors.

- Extinction is the purposeful withdrawal of the reinforcing variable maintaining challenging behavior.

- Reinforcement is required to establish the replacement behavior as the preferred behavior in which the student should engage. Reinforcement is the provision of a consequence following a behavior (e.g., the replacement behavior) that increases the future likelihood of that behavior occurring again in the future. If a behavior does not increase in frequency following reinforcement, it is not being reinforced!

- A successful BIP puts a challenging behavior on extinction while reinforcing a functionally equivalent, prosocial replacement behavior. A collaborative team approach is required for successful planning and implementation of the FBA/BIP process.

CHAPTER 14

TEACHING NEW SKILLS

Learning Objectives

- Explain how and when to use a behavior contract
- Identify what a token economy is and understand how it can be applied in a classroom setting
- Understand the importance of social skill instruction and identify how to approach teaching social skills
- Define character education and identify approaches teachers can take to integrate it into the curriculum
- Explain steps to implement self-monitoring interventions and understand how these interventions can recruit student participation, promote responsibility, and increase independence

Key Terms

Backup Reinforcer
Behavior Contract
Character Education
Response Cost
Self-Monitoring

Social Competence
Social Skills
Social Skills Instruction
Token Economy

Previous chapters covered details required to design comprehensive, accurate functional behavioral assessments, as well as explored the development of behavior intervention plans as outlined through the competing pathways framework. We introduced behavior skills training (BST) as a teaching procedure to address skill and performance-based deficits within behavioral intervention plans (BIPs) in order to teach replacement skills. Consistent with skill development and teaching, this chapter focuses on several behavior change strategies that may be applied both on an individual as well as class-wide levels. These strategies are well established in the literature and are powerful elements that may be included within the context of general classroom management spanning all the way to tier three interventions/BIPs.

High-Leverage Practice Alert!

HLP7 covers the need for classrooms to have procedures, expectations, and performance feedback. The following section on behavior contracts allows teachers and students the opportunity to review these expectations and receive feedback.

Behavior Contracts

Behavior contracts are simple interventions that establish a specific contingency, or relationship, between a behavior and a reward. They can be used to target a wide variety of behaviors from completing a routine or transition to reduction of challenging behavior. Firmly rooted within the framework of positive reinforcement, there are three components within behavior contracts that specify exactly what each member of the contract is to do in order to access reinforcement: (1) definition of the task; (2) description of the reward/reinforcement; and (3) task record. To help illustrate these components, let's use Ellen as an example. Ellen is a student in Ms. Woolworth's sixth grade class who has a behavior contract for work completion. We will talk more about Ellen in the following sections.

Definition of Task

If behavior contracts are seemingly straightforward, it's because they are. The task portion of a contract specifies the *"who," "what," "when,"* and *"how well"* details of the behavior contract. The *"who"* is fairly straightforward: it's the student or students for whom the contract is required (i.e., Ellen) and the individuals who are entering into the contract alongside the student (i.e., Ms. Woolworth). The "*what*" is an observable, measurable, and objective description of the behavior being targeted by the contract. For Ellen, Ms. Woolworth wants to target work completion and turning in assignments. Next, the "*when*" is the point in time at which Ellen will engage in the task. In this case, Ms. Woolworth expects work completion and assignments turned in daily, no later than 3:00 p.m. Finally, "*how well*" Ellen completes her work is critically important. Because behavior contracts are linking behavior to reward, ensuring the "*how well*" aspect is well-defined is the difference between Ellen indiscriminately scribbling answers on her work versus her taking the time to read each question and answer thoroughly.

Definition of Reward

Similar to the task definition, the definition of reward includes the "*who,*" "*what,*" "*when,*" and "*how much*" details of the contract. The *who* involves individuals responsible for determining if the student has met the criteria specified in the task and providing the reward. In our case, this is Ms. Woolworth; yet, this does not always need to fall with the teacher. Behavior contracts are very flexible and can be molded to suit the circumstance. Parents can be involved by providing contingent rewards at home as long as there is a strong relationship and clear communication between home and school (e.g., Ms. Woolworth reporting to parents that Ellen can collect her reward as she completed and turned in her assignments). However, caution should be used with relying on parents or guardians to provide rewards. Given a student's hard work, what would happen if the parent decided the student shouldn't earn the reward, the parents got busy and didn't give the reward, or they changed the reward after it was earned? Only rely on parents or guardians if you are certain they will follow through with the predetermined reward. Next, the "*what*" refers to the actual reward with clearly defined specifics around what exactly may be accessed. Consider the difference between Ellen having free time versus Ellen earning computer time in the library. The "*when*" is the point in time Ellen can receive her reward. Of course the "*when*" requires that Ellen receive her reward after she completes her task; however, behavior contracts allow for flexibility here in that the reward may or may not be immediately following the behavior. Lastly, "*how much*" indicates exactly how much of the reward is earned (e.g., Ellen earns 10 min of computer time to be spent using the school's digital drawing program). This is also a space where bonuses can be added in, if desired. "If Ellen completes and hands in her work Monday through Friday, she can have earn 30 min in the computer lab with a friend of her choosing."

Task Record

The task record, or the physical contract, is a means of recording both completion of contract components and reward delivery. In Ellen's case, the task record would span each weekday and a + (plus) would denote that she completed her portion of the contractual agreement for that date. Each instance of rewards are noted on the task record as well. As with all other aspects of the behavior contract, the task record is flexible and can be adjusted to suit the needs of the individual. A notes section may or may not be included, along with space for the teacher to write some positive words. The task record is an excellent way to keep track of progress across time and keeps all data in one place. A sample behavior contract is included in Figure 14–1.

Guidelines and Considerations

When determining if a behavior contract is an appropriate intervention for a student, consider the student's current skill set. It is important to target only those behaviors which are already well-established in the student's repertoire. A behavior contract is not an intervention tailored to *teaching a skill*; rather, its purpose is to

Figure 14–1. Example of behavior contract for Ellen.

Ellen's Contract

Task: Ellen will:
- complete all daily work tasks assigned for the day
- turn all tasks in to Ms. Woolworth before 3:00pm every day

Reward: Ellen earns 10 minutes of computer for each day she turns in her completed work by 3:00pm. Computer time must be cashed in after 3:00pm and may be spent on any application loaded onto classroom laptops.

Bonus: If Ellen completes and turns in work five consecutive days, she earns 30 minutes in the computer lab with one friend of her choosing.

Signature: _____   Date: _____
Signature: _____   Date: _____

Task Record
Indicate + for each day Ellen completes her task successfully. Indicate – for days Ellen does not complete task successfully.

	Monday	Tuesday	Wednesday	Thursday	Friday
+/–					
Notes:					

create contingencies between behaviors and rewards. Additionally, choosing a behavior that results in a permanent product (e.g., tidy desk, work handed in) or behaviors that occur in the presence of other individuals involved in the contract (e.g., raising hand, walking in line) suits best here. Reading is not a prerequisite to use a behavior contract as they can be adapted with visuals, photos, audio clips, and/or video clips to convey the contract.

In order to maximize success with a behavior contract, it is important to ensure the contract is just like a genuine contract. Contracts should be clearly written, explicitly stating expectations for each party and promote fairness to ensure the effort required garners an appropriate reward. And consistent with formal contracts, be sure to include a signature section for all parties to complete.

Perhaps the most common issue encountered with implementing a behavior contract is simply if the system fails to work. Several factors may contribute to ineffective behavior change with a contract. Firstly, it is imperative that the contract be constructed collaboratively with the student. This active role not only creates buy-in from the student, but also affirms what types of rewards will be reinforcing. As we know from Chapter 3, reinforcement is only reinforcement if there is a change in behavior; without the change, *we are not reinforcing*. Ongoing student input can help to accurately identify those rewards that reflect current preferences and will be motivating enough to change behavior.

Consistent with the conditions required for effective reinforcement, if rewards are not occurring frequently enough or, conversely, if they are occurring too often, motivation may wane and the plan will stall. This issue is most commonly seen in the early stages of implementation but may occur at any time. In order to find the best balance between task completion and reward, take a look at current rates of behavior and reward. If Ellen's baseline revealed she handed in one assignment on time per week, setting the bar at completing and handing in work for five consecutive days is too far of a reach. Aiming for roughly a 10% to 20% increase at the outset will ensure the goal is manageable and provides the student with access to reinforcement more immediately. Once the student is having consistent success, the terms of the contract can be altered to increase time between rewards and/or adjust the amount of rewards earned. While certainly not required, bonus clauses may be implemented to provide extra incentives for students to abide by the contract obligations. Bonus clauses are usually additional reinforcement (e.g., in duration, amount, variety, etc.) that may be accessed when the student consistently achieves his or her contract targets.

What is not uncommon, particularly at the outset of implementation, is for disagreements to arise around the interpretation of the contract or among parties involved. If this does occur, it is best to address it straightaway and have a discussion to clarify terms, definitions, meanings, and so forth. If arguments persist, the teacher or staff may want to consider adding in a term to the contract stating the student (or any other party) may not contest any aspect of the contract. Be sure to give implementation enough time to catch some momentum (at least two to three weeks) before adjusting too much. However, with that being said, a behavior contract may not be a suitable fit if the student is consistently combative over its use.

Token Economies

Similar to behavior contracts, token economies are positive, reinforcement-based interventions. Token economies are suitable for students with diverse needs as they can be easily adapted for a variety of ages, abilities, and behaviors. Token economies are extremely versatile and can be implemented individually or across entire classrooms or larger. In its most basic form, a token economy mirrors a consumer economy wherein monies are traded in for goods. Token economies allow students to visualize their progress toward behavior change while promoting self-management. Token economies are comprised of three main elements: specific target behavior, tokens, and backup reinforcers.

Target Behaviors

Token economies are attractively flexible in that they can target a vast array of behaviors ranging from following simple, routine instructions to addressing academics, self-care, or challenging behaviors. As discussed in Chapter 10, a target behavior is the observable, measurable behavior required to access reinforcement or, in this case, a token. In order for a token economy to be successful, the target behavior must be specific and clear to everyone involved so that there is no question about what behavior is being reinforced. All aspects of the target behavior should be specified at the outset of the token economy implementation. This is especially true if the target behavior involves multiple aspects, such as "Student will complete daily math worksheet within the time frame allotted **and** hand it into the teacher before 3:00 p.m. the same day." All too often, teachers get caught in the trap of providing tokens contingent upon students "being good" or "behaving"; however, this is not systematic and can lead to blurred understandings of what specific behaviors are acceptable and will access reinforcement.

> *Review Chapter 10 if you need a refresher on identifying and defining target behaviors.*

Tokens

Next, tokens are used as a physical symbol that can be exchanged for backup reinforcers. Tokens can be thought of as the "currency" of a token economy, and just as with a consumer economy, they are used to "buy" goods, materials, and privileges. Tokens may be something as simple as a hole punch card or teacher initial on a sheet of paper, buttons, coins, poker chips, teacher created "money," and so forth. Importantly, the token itself must not hold any inherent value to the students; they are merely placeholders, representing upcoming reinforcement. If the tokens are valuable, the integrity of the token economy would diminish as the student would not be as motivated to continue collecting tokens to exchange. In addition to choosing tokens that are simple, inexpensive, portable, and reusable, consider using tokens which cannot be easily counterfeited.

Backup Reinforcers

Since the tokens do not hold any value, the items for which they can be exchanged must be valuable in order to serve as a reinforcer/reward. Token economies should offer a variety of different backup reinforcers to capture student's interest and motivation. Having a menu of items from which to choose enhances this and can also tap into student's ability to self-manage by planning and saving up tokens for larger ticket items. Backup reinforcers can be tangible items or materials, such as toys, games, art supplies, and so forth or privileges like homework passes, teacher's assistant, permission to work in library, extra recess time, and so forth. There are countless options to what can be on offer in a token economy. See Table 14–1 for an overview of how to implement a token economy and Figure 14–2 for a sample token economy.

Now, let's consider the following elements in order to create the most successful token economy.

Considerations for Token Economies

Token economies have some clear advantages engrained within the system. Tokens are physical symbols used to acknowledge a target behavior and provide immediate feedback to the student. This is handy when it is simply not feasible to deliver a reinforcer immediately. Delivering tokens immediately following a behavior establishes a link between the behavior and the reward. Token systems are also inherently flexible and can be used with many different types of behaviors, as long as they are clearly defined. For instance, a class attends a school-wide assembly. The teacher would like to recognize and reward the students' quiet

Table 14–1. Steps to Implement a Token Economy

Steps to Implement a Token Economy	Notes and Considerations
1. Select and define target behaviors	• Write clear, objective, measurable definitions and target no more than two to three behaviors • Consider incorporating more wide-ranging behaviors (e.g., following instructions, routines, etc.), particularly for whole classrooms or larger groups
2. Choose what will serve as tokens	• Should be plentiful, portable, durable, inexpensive, hard to replicate, and reusable
3. Choose backup reinforcers and create a "menu" to show what is on offer	• This can be a constantly evolving undertaking; replenish and restock material rewards and tap into creative opportunities and privileges
4. Determine how often to deliver tokens	• At the outset of implementation, tokens should be given each time the student displays the target behavior. Once there is some momentum with the system, begin to fade the frequency of token delivery to offset dependence
5. Determine the "cost" for backup reinforcers	• What is the number of tokens required for a specific backup reinforcer? • Larger rewards or higher-level privileges (e.g., lunch with teacher) should cost more than smaller rewards (e.g., packet of stickers) • Monitor student acquisition of tokens to ensure the items are not cost prohibitive and are within reason
6. Set up a time and place for token exchange	• Only allow for tokens to be exchanged at predetermined times/location • Be creative and create a "Token Marketplace" and establish trading hours

Source: Adapted from Miltenberger, 2008.

Figure 14–2. Example of token economy.

Matthew's Earnings

	Follow Instructions	Raise Hand
Morning Block (9:00-11:30)		
Trade in or Save		
Afternoon Block (12:00-3:00)		

I earn points when:

- I follow a teacher instruction within 10 seconds
- I raise my hand and wait to be called on

When I earn enough points, I can trade my points for really awesome things or save my points to trade later

Reward Menu

Reward	Amount
Library pass with friend	5 points
Computer time (10 mins)	8 points
2 bonus homework points	10 points
Lunch with teacher	12 points

hallway behavior and quiet sitting throughout the assembly. The token system allows the teacher to provide a token to the whole class (a hole punch on a card in this case), which immediately links student behavior to reinforcement. In this way, the tokens serve as a bridge in the delay between the students' behavior and the reward. Token systems are also flexible in that tokens can be delivered by multiple individuals/teachers and across many different environments, helping to promote generalization.

Do token economies sound familiar? These systems are also used in schools using the Positive Behavioral Intervention and Supports (PBIS) framework. Go back to Chapter 4 to review how this works in schools.

As with any intervention, there are some disadvantages associated with token economies. Firstly, token economies require quite a bit of preparation and time. Because it is a physical tracking system, considerations for what types of tokens, number of tokens, and how tokens will be monitored is important. Further, these systems require a certain degree of organization and structure, especially with regard to upkeep of reinforcers/rewards. Ensuring plenty of options and choices can create a demand on resources and be quite costly; however, it is important to keep a variety of backup reinforcers on hand to appeal to different preferences. Planning and organization are also integral once the system is up and running as consistency of implementation can prove challenging with many moving parts, all of which require close supervision. The goal of a token economy is to teach and reward positive behavior that will be generalized to other settings. In order for this to occur, token economies should be faded so they do not foster dependence on behalf of students. Fading is simply done by changing the frequency with which tokens are being delivered. For instance, at the outset of a token economy, providing one token for the target behavior of hand raising is appropriate and sufficient. Begin fading by offering tokens on an intermittent or random schedule while increasing the cost of the backup reinforcers. Additionally, replacing material backup reinforcers with more naturally occurring rewards also supports successful token economy fading.

Potential Problems

Some common issues you may encounter when implementing a token system may be traced back to weak or faulty reinforcers. If you notice students are not motivated to earn tokens, reevaluate the rewards on offer and seek student input. If the rewards do not hold value to the students, they will inevitably not generate desire and motivation to earn. If students start out motivated but quickly lose interest, simplify the token system. Ensure that rewards are clearly linked to a few (no more than three) well-defined behaviors. Mix up the reinforcers on offer and always seek student input for new reward ideas. You could also incorporate a strategically timed reinforcer "sale'" and mark down the cost of some specific items (and can even tie in some math concepts!). If students are motivated, but misbehave or become upset when they do not earn tokens, keep the focus of the token economy positive and reevaluate the frequency with which students are getting tokens. These types of behaviors may also be the result of a procedure called response cost, which is often used in conjunction with a token economy.

Response cost is a negative punishment procedure (i.e., removing a reinforcer with the intention of decreasing future likelihood of behavior) and involves the removal of reinforcement contingent upon an undesirable behavior. While there are situations in which this procedure may be required, it is desirable to keep the token economy as positive as possible. Taking away tokens may seem like a logical consequence for challenging behavior; yet, this goes against positive behavior interventions and intent of the system and against the ethos of an economic system. The student has already earned the token for engaging in a specified positive behavior. This fact remains unchanged regardless of what that student does afterward. Removing tokens can lead to power struggles and de-motivate students. Losing tokens may also make it seem too difficult or nearly impossible for students to regain their previous status. Response cost is often used to illustrate the implications of a token economy; however, let's relate this to a real-life example. As a college student, you complete assignments, take exams, and earn a grade. As an adult, you go to work and earn a paycheck. It would be quite unfair for your professor or your employer to take that grade away or ask for your salary back based off of behavior that occurs *after* you've earned it.

 High-Leverage Practice Alert!

Social behaviors are covered in HLP9 and include explicit instruction of social skills, opportunities to practice skills, and reinforcement considerations.

Social Skills

Often overlooked, but of enormous importance, is the explicit teaching of social skills throughout a student's academic tenure. As adults, we often take for granted the acquisition of social skills and presume the process is acquired via osmosis or mere observation. Yet for many individuals, there are significant struggles associated with poor or underdeveloped social skills that can endure throughout life. Because the spectrum of topics that could be covered under the social skills umbrella is infinite, we will take a broad approach to teaching the foundational elements required for strong social skills. Additionally, we will introduce strategies to effectively engage social skill development as well as touch upon character education within a social-emotional curriculum.

Social skills are the ways in which individuals navigate through interactions with others. By nature, humans are social creatures, and as such, have developed a sophisticated array of skills to vocally and nonvocally communicate thoughts, feelings, and intentions to others. Nuances such as vocal tone, prosody, volume, facial expressions, subtle gestures, and eye contact can all affect the meaning of a message and can cause issues if misinterpreted. Hence, social skills are critical to an individual's social-emotional development and overall adjustment. Further, poor social skills are associated with poorer academic performance, lower social status, and an increased risk for emotional-behavioral problems (Bloom, Karagiannakis, Toste, Heath, & Konstantinopolous, 2007). Proactive social skills instruction can foster acceptance and teach students how to cope effectively within the larger social context.

Social Skills Instruction

While academic performance is often seen as the primary outcome of education, social skills are essential for students to manage themselves across environments. In this way, direct social skills instruction provides a promising avenue for teaching and promoting positive social interactions. Broadly, social skills instruction is an intervention used to address deficits in social skills. Here, the domain of "social skills" may be refined into two distinct concepts: social skills and social competence. Social skills refers to one or more isolated skills an individual must perform within a specific setting or context. For example, some of the social skills required to enter into a conversation include approach individuals talking to one another; wait for a natural pause in their conversation; use a conversation starter; maintain expected physical distance; use appropriate volume, pitch, and pace of voice; and so forth. By contrast, social competence refers to how others judge the outcomes of specific social skills of an individual across settings and situations (Gresham, Elliott, Cook, Vance, & Kettler, 2010). So, for the previous example, an observing teacher may make a judgement on how well a student entered into a conversation. Was the student accepted into the conversation by others? Did the student stay on topic and solicit engagement from others? Did the nonvocal behaviors of others in the group indicate they enjoyed chatting with the student? Essentially, social competence describes how effectively an individual manages within a social context.

Individuals with good social competence consistently obtain successful outcomes from interactions with others, whether be it working in a group, accepting opinions and perspectives of others, or self-monitoring one's own behavior (Spence, 2003). To expand upon the previous example, the teacher may evaluate how socially successful the student is beyond entering into conversation. Can the student successfully establish and maintain quality relationships with others? Are they perceived positively? These are the broader ranging questions to keep at the basis of social skill instruction. So, how does one approach such a vague and sweeping topic? The following is an outline of features found within effective social skills instruction.

Assessment of Need

Just as with any academic content area, teachers must first look toward assessment of need before anything else in order to accurately design instruction. Assessment may be formal or informal but should be conducted across multiple settings and across multiple individuals in order to garner the most complete understanding of where the needs lie. Additionally, and as mentioned in Chapter 10, ensure that the assessment is pinpointed at specific, measurable behaviors that hold social validity. Always, always, always ask yourself the following:

● "Why do I want to target this behavior?"

● "How will (behavior) help this student in (setting/activity/etc.)?"

● "How are other similarly aged students doing (behavior) and how does this differ from what I am seeing?"

Further, being mindful of targeting a focused set of skills is not only more realistic but will also lead to increased success. Consider the difference between targeting skills required for sharing a common work space versus teaching a student to be "socially appropriate" or "get along well with others."

Formal assessment spans many methods, with observation-based data collection, checklists, rating scales, and interviews with caregivers, parents, and/or teachers being the most common. Informal data collection usually consists of observations without data collection; anecdotal reports from teachers, parents, or others; and student self-report. As you may suspect, a direct observation of the student within a specific social context is generally the most useful assessment of need for teachers as it removes subjectivity that may seep into rating scales, checklists, and other types of secondhand reports. However, in order to glean the most reliable source of information, multiple observations of the student across settings along with supplemental input from parents and teachers is ideal.

Accurate assessment begets quality instruction; therefore, the assessment phase should guide educators toward what kind of student need they are facing, as the type of instruction it warrants will vary. Students may demonstrate needs in acquisition, performance, or fluency. Briefly, acquisition needs refer to skills the student does not possess or demonstrate in any capacity but needs to learn, while performance needs refer to skills that are within a student's repertoire but fail to consistently demonstrate it in the appropriate circumstance. Performance-based deficits may stem from an inability or difficulty assessing social situations warranting specific skills or a lack of motivation to perform such skills. These deficits may be particularly frustrating for educators to address as the student may be able to identify and articulate the skill(s) during instruction but flounder when observed in a social transaction. Lastly, a fluency need refers to an individual who has a specific skill, utilizes it under correct situations, and yet may be awkward or unrefined in execution. Considerations and guidelines for identifying instructional need are presented in Figure 14–3.

Create a Plan

After completing assessment and determining the nature of the need, teachers may choose a skill or set of skills to target for instruction. To help guide this decision, consider if the student already has an Instructional Education Plan (IEP) as this should be prioritized; however, if the behaviors compromise the health or safety of the student or others, these should be targeted first.

For acquisition-based needs, teachers must plan for instruction of multiple topographies (i.e., descriptions) of a specific skill. Remember, these are students who do not know how to perform the skill. Take for instance, greeting a peer. Programming multiple ways in which the student can greet others (e.g., saying "hey," waving, pairing eye contact with a smile, etc.) is important to promote generalization and build a hearty skill repertoire. Teaching across settings and individuals is required when planning for performance-based needs. These students are not consistently using skills, despite knowing how to perform them. These deficits require lots of reinforcement to motivate students to continue to perform the skill. Similarly, reinforcement and predetermined mastery criteria should be laid out in advance of teaching a skill; for example, Susanna varies greetings to at least two different peers daily for five consecutive days in order to determine if progress is being made.

Figure 14–3. Considerations for skill instructional need.

Considerations for Skill Instructional Needs

| 1. Can the student accurately tell/model all steps of the skill? (Acquisition) |

- ❖ Yes→ Go to #2
- ❖ No→ Direct instruction of social skill. Explain, model, and practice what each step of skill looks and sounds like. Provide rationale for skill use and describe situations in which skill is used. Provide information in a visual format, reinforce student for practice, and give generalization opportunities.

| 2. Is the student motivated to perform the skill? (Performance) |

- ❖ Yes→ Go to #3
- ❖ No→ Conduct a reinforcer preference assessment and revise reinforcement schedule, with intent to fade over time. Schedule opportunities for practice and reinforcement.

| 3. Does the student understand the context in which to perform the skill? (Performance) |

- ❖ Yes→ Go to #4
- ❖ No→ Direct instruction on when and where skill should be used via examples and non-examples. Recruit student input on examples to increase relevance and provide varied opportunities to practice the skill in different settings, contexts, and with different individuals. Explain how a skill can be used in many ways, across multiple settings, and for different situations.

| 4. Is the student awkward or unpolished performing skill? (Fluency) |

- ❖ Yes→ Provide extensive practice opportunities in both role-play and generalized settings until student can perform each skill step fluently, without support. Deliver immediate and specific positive feedback and reinforcement. Pair constructive feedback with additional models of target skill and more practice.
- ❖ No→ If the student knows the skill, is motivated to perform it, understands its context, and is polished in its performance, then the skill is in the student's repertoire.

Provide Direct Instruction

Now that assessment is complete and there is a plan to move forward, instruction may begin. Just like any other academic skill in the curriculum, social skills instruction starts with a clear lesson plan—complete with objectives, guided practice, independent practice, evaluation, and feedback. Since we know the nature of the skill deficit varies by student, it is imperative to plan for generalization at the outset of instruction. This means having structured practice provided by multiple individuals (e.g., teacher, counselor, etc.) in a variety of settings and among varied individuals to make it the most organic experience possible. Ensuring instruction in this way sets the student up for reinforcement as he or she would in the real-life scenario. If it is not viable or feasible to do this, arrange the location in which you plan to provide instruction to reflect the natural environment as closely as possible.

As with any lesson, there are many ways in which one may approach instruction; however, teaching social skills can be challenging as it requires explicit practice and consistency. A suggested approach to teaching a social skills lesson is outlined in Figure 14–4.

Figure 14–4. Flowchart illustrating phases of teaching social skills.

1. Identify Skill

- Label target skill and identify steps required for performance
- Collaboratively identify rationale for why the skill is important (i.e., social validity)

2. Demonstrate

- Demonstrate and model scenarios requiring target skill
- Use relevant examples, both in and out of school, with adults and peers, etc.

4. Feedback

- During role-play, provide students specific, positive feedback
- Provide constructive suggestions or model skill again to help with skill acquisition

3. Practice & Role-Play

- Use scenarios identified above and practice steps to perform target skill
- Allow students to practice until fluency is reached

5. Generalization

- Provide structured and natural opportunities for students to practice target skill in a variety of settings, situations, and with multiple individuals

First, label the target skill for the student(s), define it measurably and objectively, and provide a rationale. Rationale is so very important because without identifying reasons for why one *should* learn a skill, he or she may either resist or lose interest. Next, the individual leading the lesson demonstrates the skill fluently, providing a visual and auditory representation for the learners. Breaking the skill down into steps is helpful as it provides a sense of structure. Again, here is where having multiple people provide instruction is key as it exposes the students to individual differences and nuances embedded across our social language. Engage the students here; have them provide some scenarios to link the skill to relevant aspects of their lives. This step should be repeated across social skill lessons as multiple opportunities increase the likelihood for successful instruction.

Practice

Next, it is time for students to practice. Use the previously demonstrated scenarios as a starting point and have students engage in repeated practice sessions. Without a doubt, role-play tends to feel forced and artificial initially, but with the proper attitude and approach, it can be one of the most powerful tools to facilitate learning. The other critical element is that role-play is an avenue that allows for feedback. Individualized and specific feedback reinforces what was done well and what steps should be focused on for next time. The immediacy with which feedback is given in this context ensures that mistakes are not practiced; rather, they are corrected. Positive feedback should always be provided first, followed by constructive feedback focusing on what can be done *differently* rather than focusing on what was "wrong." Further, pairing feedback with additional modeling will help to cement exactly what is being targeted.

Generalization

Finally, in order to facilitate student success across time, individuals, and settings, generalization opportunities must be programmed into instruction. Simply, generalization refers to an individual engaging in a particular skill *outside* of the context in which it was learned. For example, a student who learns to take turns playing a card game is then able to transfer this skill to a different group of peers playing a board game. There are many things you can do to promote generalization that should be embedded within your lesson: vary the ways in which you deliver instructions (e.g., "your turn"; "you go now"; "who is next?"; etc.), use a variety of materials (e.g., cards, board games, relay races, etc.), incorporate many individuals (e.g., receiving prompts from classroom teacher, P.E. teacher, librarian, etc.), and change the environment (e.g., large group classroom, after-school groups, lunchtime peers, etc.). Despite being mentioned last, generalization of skills should be considered and planned for from the very beginning of instruction. Specifically, students who have identified needs in fluency are likely to need extra support in generalization of skills. In order for generalization to take hold, instruction must be meaningfully connected to the natural environment.

Character Education and Social-Emotional Curriculum

The word *character* drums up many meanings across individuals, families, cultures, and nations. It has served as the focus of philosophers and scholars for centuries, as many hold it to be at the cornerstone of society. At its core, character is the intentional commitment to live in a way that fosters self-growth, positive moral identities, and healthy communities. Character education can be seen as a way to educate the next generation on ethical values, such as respect, responsibility for self and others, justice, and citizenship.

Character education emphasizes moral, ethical, intellectual, and social-emotional development of students with the goal of creating caring, discerning, and responsible members of society. As a whole, character education is a joint effort, shared by parents, schools, and members of the community. Since youth spend much of their day within a classroom, the call for this branch of education is even more apparent. For the context of this book, we will discuss the role of schools and teachers as facilitators in nurturing students' character.

As discussed within the context of social skills and academics, students must be taught and guided in their development of character. Our charge as educators is to model and shepherd students to act responsibly, engage in decision making, and teach highly regarded features of character held by the culture at large. The U.S. Department of Education has identified key areas that highlight strong character, which include the following:

- Showing compassion
- Having a strong sense of responsibility
- Showing self-discipline
- Making good judgements
- Showing care for their community
- Maintaining self-respect
- Showing respect to others
- Having courage to stand up for beliefs
- Acting with honesty and fairness

So, why is this important? Research consistently tells us that individuals with strong character—specifically those with a sound understanding of emotions and grit or persistence through adversity—are those who are less likely to experience depression and anxiety and are more likely to have happier relationships and higher levels of satisfaction with life (Soutter & Seider, 2013). Emotional intelligence (EQ) is the capacity to be aware of and able to successfully manage one's own emotions while being able to recognize emotions in others in order to foster positive relationships. Thus, in order to have strong character, knowing oneself is of utmost importance.

Take a moment to reflect; do you know individuals, former students, colleagues, or family members who are clearly very intelligent, yet make rather poor decisions? This could be chalked up to the concept of EQ. Different from Intelligence Quotient (IQ), or one's ability to process information about the world around them, EQ is one's ability to process emotional information to make healthy decisions. So, how can we as educators help our students to become responsible, emotionally intelligent humans? There is no one set way to approach character education and social-emotional learning. Much of this depends on the existing school community and its needs. Since character education is largely based on society's socially constructed definitions and norms, culture should be carefully considered. While there are hundreds of character education prepackaged programs available for purchase, be cautious and selective with these curricula. The following section delves into some simple strategies that may be translated into your classroom to promote character development of students.

Modeling

Understanding emotions of others requires careful observation and accurate interpretation of body language, facial expression, tone of voice, and words communicated. Modeling active listening while asking how others are feeling is a great way to demonstrate this to students. However, perhaps the most powerful message we can send to our students is the way in which we respond to the daily stressors that accompany any classroom. No doubt, teaching is one of the most emotionally taxing professions, and tensions can run high following an unexpected disruption to routine. Therefore, the ways in which we as educators cope with our emotions will directly affect what we model to students. Moreover, this extends to the behavior we tolerate and the expectations we convey.

 High-Leverage Practice Alert!

Feedback—particularly positive, timely, and genuine feedback—is covered in HLP20. Remember that ongoing feedback helps students to adjust behaviors and meet goals.

Democratic Classrooms

Contrary to the long-standing model of teacher-centered classrooms, a democratic student community can foster honesty, fairness, and problem solving. Holding regular class meetings builds a collaborative approach to dealing with issues and establishing norms and expectations. Encourage students to take an active role in their learning; recognize and praise positive interactions of kindness and respect. Additionally, build upon the classroom community by encouraging collaboration and cooperation over competition. Provide regular opportunities to work in small groups and prompt students to reflect on how they work together.

Service Learning

Perhaps one of the most transformative methods in character education is through service learning. Service learning is an approach that combines learning objectives with community service. It relies upon both action and reflection with the ultimate goal of identifying and undertaking real-world issues in the student's own communities. Service learning goes beyond spending a day cleaning up a park or volunteering at a local soup kitchen for the afternoon. It is preceded by goal setting, preplanning, and research. Teachers guide students toward identifying pressing community issues and encourage collaboration amongst students to find ways in which to address these. There are projects for all ages and grade levels and can focus on a variety of issues, such as students partnering with other local schools in a cross-tutoring partnership, working with local conservation groups to improve water quality, and launching a campaign to reduce single-use plastics. Both during and after the service learning project, teachers should prompt students to reflect and discuss what is being learned from the process. How were their original goal-setting items connected to the actual work performed? What did they learn about themselves? Keep in mind it is only truly a service learning project if the students are involved from the preplanning phase all the way through to reflection.

Self-Monitoring

Self-monitoring is the intentional use of behavior change strategies to monitor or change one's behavior. It is derived from behavioral principles and sits in the premise that through monitoring and measuring one's own behavior, long-lasting behavior change is possible. This could look like increasing a skill, decreasing challenging behavior, or simply adjusting the environment to create a source of motivation and engagement. This intervention is different in that it relies upon the student to be the agent of change, rather than the teacher or other adult. In an effort to teach students to become more self-aware, self-monitoring requires a student to monitor his or her behavior, make an assessment of the situation, and then engage in desired behaviors or skills.

A self-monitoring intervention is grounded in two key components: self-observation and self-recording. Therefore, prior to implementation, some basic prerequisites must be satisfied. To successfully self-monitor, the student must be able to understand the target behavior, be able to discriminate when to engage or not engage in the target behavior, and be able to accurately report on his or her behavior (Figure 14–5).

Step 1. Define the Target Behavior

While self-monitoring is an excellent intervention to help with motivation for academic performance, reduce challenging behaviors, increase prosocial behaviors, and foster healthy interactions among peers, it is not suitable for teaching an actual skill or behavior. Consider the previous discussion on performance-based deficits with social skills; when deciding to use self-monitoring as an intervention, the initial assessment should verify that the student has the target behavior in

Figure 14–5. Phases of self-monitoring intervention.

| Define target behavior | Choose self-monitoring system | Set self-monitoring schedule | Choose self-monitoring prompt | Teach, practice, reinforce |

his or her repertoire (e.g., raising hand) but is not consistently utilizing it (i.e., performance deficit). Additionally, ensure that the behavior or skill in question is one that will promote positive changes in the student's life. The behavior chosen should be mutually agreed upon by teacher and student and clearly defined. If the focus is to increase a particular behavior, be sure to provide an objective and measurable definition to allow for accurate self-monitoring. For example, rather than stating, "student will complete her work," state, "Clare will read X number of pages and complete Y number of math problems per hour-long independent work block." Alternatively, for reductive behavior targets, be specific and focus on the replacement behavior as an increasing behavior. For example, increasing hand raising to reduce instances of calling out. Recruit student input here as the definition must be clear to him or her and active participation in developing the intervention will increase buy-in and likelihood of adherence.

Step 2. Choose a Monitoring System

Once a behavior has been identified, agreed upon, and defined, it is time to sort out a method to record self-monitoring data. This is a form or method generated to prompt the student to monitor behavior and keep a record of data to share with teachers and parents. A large body of research focuses on three main formats to use for self-monitoring: checklists, frequency counts, and rating scales.

Checklists

Checklists may be used for behaviors that have multiple components or tasks needing to be completed in a certain order. In the previous example of Clare completing work one could generate a self-monitoring checklist that lists out all tasks to be done prior to handing in assignments (e.g., [1] Read X number of pages, [2] Complete Y number of math problems, [3] Hand in folder to teacher before independent work has ended). Similarly, checklists can be used more broadly to help organize students and their workspaces. Perhaps you know a student who could benefit from a checklist of all the items needing to go home in a backpack each afternoon? Checklists can be flexible and easily incorporated into a student's day.

Frequency Counts

A frequency count is a simple tally of the target behavior per specified amount of time. For example, how many times Ben requested teacher help during language arts or how many times Mic initiated interaction with a peer at lunch. Of note, this can become clouded if the target behavior is not well defined. We want to record actual occurrences of behavior, but often this becomes distorted into recording *nonoccurrences of behavior*. For example, record the number of times Ben raised his hand and/or how many times he called out, not how many times he "stopped himself from calling out," as this is impossible to observe.

Frequency counts should be collected in predetermined periods of time in order to garner accurate data. For instance, Nate has identified his target behavior of asking for permission to leave the classroom and will record each instance per 90-min period. Indicating how long the data were collected provides context to behavior and allows it to be compared across time. Consider if the time frame were omitted; Nate's frequency at the beginning of the self-monitoring intervention was three requests versus his current frequency of two requests. On the surface, this looks like a decrease in behavior, which is contrary to the intent of the intervention. However, let's say the first frequency count was three requests over the course of four 90-min periods versus the current frequency count of two requests per one 90-min period. Now, we have context and can see the intervention is producing a desired change in behavior.

Behavior Rating Scales

Behavior rating scales are commonly used tools for self-monitoring and provide a grade or rating about the target behavior. Behavior rating scales are best suited for use with behaviors for which a qualitative score is desired, and as such, tell the student *how well* they demonstrated the target behavior. These measurement tools typically employ a Likert scale, which is a graduated selection of usually 3, 5, or 7 responses that includes a neutral midpoint. Likert scales allow an individual to provide a rating along a continuum, in this case, of how well an individual engaged in the target behavior (e.g., How well did I keep a quiet voice during the lesson? 1. Poor 2. Fair 3. Good).

Step 3. Set a Self-Monitoring Schedule

Self-monitoring requires the student to be aware of how and when to use the system. Setting up a schedule ahead of time preemptively sets the student up to be successful in monitoring and recording his or her data. Consider the target behavior with respect to locations, specific activities, time of day, and individuals. Together with the student, come up with a schedule or outline of when and how often he or she will self-monitor. For instance, a target behavior requiring a checklist of materials to pack for homework may warrant the student self-monitoring during the last interval of the day, whereas a student targeting participation in lessons might self-monitor during her math and language arts block. If the target behavior is not activity specific and occurs throughout the day, such as compliance with instructions, the student may choose to self-monitor during preselected blocks of time throughout the school day (e.g., first 10 min of each hour).

Step 4. Choose a Self-Monitoring Prompt

In order for self-monitoring to work, the student is required to attend to his or her behavior and record it accurately. For many, the act of self-monitoring alone, such as giving oneself a check or crossing things off a list, can be motivating. For others, a prompt to cue the student to self-monitor is required at the outset of the intervention. The prompt may be delivered by the teacher or can be student administered; however, remain considerate and choose a prompt that will be useful to the student but not draw any undue attention. Further, for self-monitoring that occurs at regular intervals (e.g., every 20 min), it may be preferable to have the student manage this. Timers can be set on phones, watches, or discreet kitchen timers at preset intervals. Once it rings, the student engages in self-monitoring and the timer is reset for the next interval. For behaviors that are activity specific, teacher-delivered prompts may be suitable. For instance, a teacher simply delivers a prompt or instruction at the end of the lesson for the student to self-monitor. However, if this is the case, a plan to fade teacher-delivered prompts must be laid out initially as, ultimately, the goal is to shift responsibility to the student.

Step 5. Teach, Practice, and Reinforce

Of course, it should go without saying that any new intervention must be taught and practiced. This is further promoted when the student is an active participant throughout planning stages as he or she then has intimate details of what the target behavior looks and sounds like along with when and how to use the monitoring tool. Purposeful practice of the self-monitoring system allows for opportunities to provide feedback about what is going well along with identifying areas of need. A great way to assess the practice sessions is to have both teacher and student record data and then compare. Then, teachers can strengthen the intervention by including opportunities for reinforcement and embed these within the self-monitoring system. Be sure to clearly define the criteria required to access the reinforcement, such as how much of the target behavior demonstrated will earn reinforcement, how often may the student earn reinforcement, and for how long does student access reinforcement?

Refer to Chapter 3 on how to ensure reinforcers are reinforcing and how to choose suitable motivators for the purpose of behavior change.

Considerations

Some considerations when choosing and developing self-monitoring tools is to first ensure it is as unobtrusive and inconspicuous as possible. Conveniently, the use of technology can be an advantage here, so long as a student's access to devices is consistent with the policies of the classroom and school. Also consider utilizing materials already available to the student, such as a school planner or notebook. In addition to being covert, ensure materials and tools are age-appropriate. Affixing a checklist to the inside of a high-school student's planner or creating a checklist on a smartphone app ensures the intervention does not draw any unnecessary attention. Younger students or those with limited reading abilities could benefit from the use of pictures, but be careful here, just because a seventh grader is not a fluent reader does not warrant the use of cartoon picture symbols. Checklists can be color coded (green for "yes" or "complete" and red for "no" or "incomplete") or have a simple check or X symbol. It is also advisable to periodically check a student's self-monitoring accuracy. Just as teacher and student data were compared in practice sessions, the teacher should check in, record data, and determine if the student is self-monitoring correctly. Doing this periodically improves the integrity of the system overall and ensures that the student is not "practicing a mistake" by reporting inaccurate data.

Self-monitoring holds several advantages, particularly in a classroom setting. It is economical, simple, and recruits student participation, promoting independence and responsibility. Recording one's own behavior results in more immediate feedback than would ever be possible if the teacher were collecting behavioral data and reporting it back to the student. Self-monitoring also incorporates other skills necessary for classroom success such as planning, organizing, counting, and self-awareness/inhibiting. By improving one's awareness of their own behavior, positive results are far more likely.

Conclusion

When implemented with fidelity, positive behavior management strategies are shown to be highly effective methods to manage both individual and class-wide behavior. As described previously, both behavior contracts and token economies are both well suited for classroom use as they are flexible, reinforce prosocial behavior, and teach delayed gratification of reinforcement. While these systems rely upon external reinforcement and teacher-led implementation, self-monitoring systems capitalize on the self as the primary agent of change. Just like behavior contracts and token economies, these systems can target a wide range of behaviors but are particularly ideal for covert behaviors that may be inadvertently overlooked by other behavior change strategies. Having such strategies available allows educators to connect other related interventions, such as social skills instruction, which rely on reinforcement of skills in order to become part of students' repertoires.

Chapter Summary

- Behavior contracts are interventions used to establish a contingency between behavior and reinforcement and include three elements: definition of task/ behavior (i.e., the who, what, when, and how well elements of behavior contract), definition of reward (i.e., who is responsible for or capable of delivering, what are the specific reinforcers, how much of the reinforcer may be accessed, when the reinforcers can be accessed), and task record (i.e., a running record to capture completion of behavior contract components and reward delivery).

- Behavior contracts are not designed to teach new skills or behaviors, rather they are intended to provide guidelines and expectations around behaviors. Consider targeting behaviors that result in a permanent product or requires another individual present. Contracts are most successful when the student is involved in planning the intervention along with effective reinforcement.

- Token economies are interventions rooted in positive reinforcement and operate similarly to a consumer economy. Token economies involve earning tokens contingent on target behaviors and then exchanging tokens for backup reinforcers. The tokens are placeholders and act as currency to purchase activities, privileges, tangibles, or other agreed-upon rewards.

- Token economies create connections between behaviors and rewards and can be done on both the class-wide level or individually.

- Response cost is a negative punishment procedure that may be used in conjunction with a token economy. It involves removal of reinforcement contingent upon undesired behavior, or, in this case, removal of tokens following challenging behavior. This is to be used only as a last resort as removal of tokens goes against the grain of positive behavior support.

- Social skills are the ways in which individuals interact with others vocally and nonvocally. Social skills, just like academic skills, can and should be taught as they enhance student social-emotional development and overall adjustment.

- Social competence refers to how others (e.g., teacher) judge the outcomes of an individual's (e.g., student) social skills in different environments and with different people.

- Social skills instruction involves assessment, creating a plan, providing direct instruction, practice, and generalization.

● Character education seeks to educate students on ethical values such as respect, responsibility for self and others, and citizenship. It emphasizes moral and ethical dimensions of social-emotional development.

● Self-monitoring is an intervention grounded in self-observation and self-recording. It is a powerful way to change one's behavior and relies upon the student, rather than the teacher, to be the agent of change.

● Steps to self-monitoring intervention include the following:

1. Define target behavior objectively so the student knows exactly what the behavior looks and sounds like.

2. Choose a monitoring system to prompt the student to monitor; commonly used are checklists, frequency counts, or behavior rating scales.

3. Set a self-monitoring schedule that defines how and when to record data on the target behavior.

4. Choose a covert prompt to self-monitor to cue the student to self-assess and record.

5. Teach, practice, and reinforce the system prior to actual implementation to ensure accuracy and honesty in self-reporting. Do intermittent checks throughout implementation to ensure integrity is being upheld.

PART IV

CONCLUSION

Chapter 15. **Reflective Practices**

REFLECTIVE PRACTICES

Learning Objectives

- Describe the process of self-reflection and understand its link to teaching
- Identify a variety of ways a teacher may gather information to reflect upon
- Describe the guidelines in the Universal Design for Learning framework
- Understand how the guidelines in the Universal Design for Learning framework can be implemented

Key Terms

Action and Expression
Engagement
Reactivity

Representation
Self-Reflection
Universal Design for Learning

So, what goes on in a classroom? Most people will invariably answer along the lines of "the teacher teaches and the students learn." Yet, the presumption that students are the only ones engaged in learning is simply false. As a highly challenging profession, teaching can often leave educators drained and dejected when lessons don't quite eventuate or if students perform poorly on assessments. So how can we identify and analyze our practices to enhance the collective classroom experience? It's important to acknowledge that no matter how perfect the lesson plan, our teaching practices *can always evolve and improve.* We as educators are in an endless cycle of bettering ourselves and our practice for the benefit of our students. One of the means by which we can become a better version of ourselves is through self-reflection. Self-reflection is a form of personal analysis whereby one aims to connect his or her thoughts and actions to deeply held values.

 High-Leverage Practice Alert!

HLP6 covers the need to evaluate instructional practices and adjust accordingly. Self-reflection is a great way to address the need to self-evaluate.

Teacher Self-Reflection

Teaching is hard. All the moments leading up to your first day of teaching all the way through your very last lesson hold little micro opportunities to become a reflective educator. The essence of being a reflective educator lies in examining what you are doing in your classroom and then think about *why* you are doing it. All too often in work, life, and relationships we abide by certain rules and ascribe to specific routines without giving them much thought. Over time we build up a collection of unconscious responses that can become rather rigid. As Grace Hopper wisely noted, "the most dangerous phrase in our/the language is *we've always done it this way"* (Broome Williams, 2004). Herein lies the very root of why being a reflective educator is so valuable. Once we strip away the "autopilot" from our teaching practices, we allow ourselves to really see what is working well for our students and for us. Once you can identify how your practice is linked to your values and your experiences, you open up opportunities to enhance your teaching.

The value of self-reflection is enormous, and we'll get to that; yet, it may be effort and intention of "doing one more thing" that holds educators back from reaping the full benefit. The practice of becoming a reflective educator does not require sit-down, hardcore, study-mode time, it only requires commitment. More so, some of the best self-reflection comes when you're driving home from work or having a shower. The process of self-reflection can begin any time and starts with jumping into the classroom and teaching. Just like with any other skill, self-reflection takes time and practice. The following are some tips to guide you through the process. Bear in mind this is merely a guide to help you get started, as self-reflection is in no way a linear process.

Identify

Because this process can seem so daunting, it's best to start with identifying an aspect of your teaching to reflect upon. Perhaps it's something academic, like the math block, or nonacademic, like the morning routine. It also does not need to be where you feel your teaching is not going well; in fact, reflecting on something that is going well can help to redirect focus and identify and expand upon strengths. It may also be where you are struggling to find traction with your students. Figure out what to reflect upon. Is it a specific teaching method? How to deal with challenging behavior? Is it the way in which your routine is organized (or not . . .)?

Gather Data

You knew there would be data collection, right? But of course! The only way in which to proceed through the self-reflective process is to actually see, as objectively as possible, what is going on in the classroom. Depending on what you've chosen as your focus, there are many ways in which you can go about gathering information. Also note that you are not bound to one method; combining different sources of information can make for a more robust self-reflective experience.

Reflective Journaling

Grab a notebook, keep it accessible, and use it to jot down observations and notes regarding what happened throughout a block of time, what went well, and/or what fell to pieces. This can be done right after a lesson or even throughout, if feasible. Describe your reactions, responses, and feelings. Also note observations about the students, describing their behaviors. Journaling doesn't need to be neat and tidy, so bullet points and scribbles suit just fine. It's about the conscious process of connecting your behavior to what's happening in the room. Journals can also be divided into two columns, one for what went well and you want to repeat and the other for things you want to change in the future. This will help you recognize what is and what isn't working.

Peer Observation

Sometimes it takes another set of eyes to really see what is going on. Inviting a trusted colleague to observe you teach a lesson can provide some really honest input; however, it is important to recognize that this is in no way intended to be a judgement of your skill as a teacher. Swapping roles and observing one another can create a more comfortable atmosphere and facilitate positive, impartial rapport. Of course, it is perfectly natural to feel self-conscious whilst being observed. Reactivity can occur, which refers to a change in your own behavior that occurs simply because you are aware of being observed. In order to offset this, it is helpful to schedule a series of regularly occurring observations early on. Over time, increased exposure decreases sensitivity to being observed, which allows for a more relaxed and authentic illustration of you as a teacher. Another helpful tool to guide the observer is to use a structured checklist or questionnaire, which can be created cooperatively between you and a trusted colleague.

Video Recording

Videos tell no lies and provide an unbiased permanent product of a lesson. Video recording is used across many disciplines to improve and shape behavior and has been shown to be a powerful learning tool to teach skills such as perspective taking (Hart Barnett, 2018) even improving athletic performance (Boyer, Miltenberger, Batsche, & Fogel, 2009). Just as with having a live observer in your classroom, it may be best to have a camera setup in place and get into the regular practice of recording yourself teaching. Videos have the capabilities of showing us what we don't notice in the moment (e.g., "Do I always give instructions with that tone?"; "I can't believe I'm standing with my back to the class for over a minute!?"; "That student is distracting his neighbors throughout the whole lesson . . . ") and allow us the freedom to pause, rewind, and rewatch. Perhaps the hardest bit is taking the time to sit down and watch the videos back while maintaining a neutral and objective perspective (your hair is *fine* and those pants look great on you; focus on what's important—your teaching!).

Solicit Student Input

If video recording is regarded as the most honest snapshot of your teaching, then receiving student feedback is the next most honest. Students are usually more than eager to provide feedback and giving them the chance to share their perspectives can be empowering. You may also use this as an opportunity to promote their critical thinking and writing skills. As with the observer in the classroom, having a structured checklist or questionnaire to frame the observation may be helpful. Exit tickets are also a great tool for reflection. Beyond capturing how well the students understood the content, this activity can be extended toward gaining information about your teaching: What did the students enjoy? What was confusing? What could be done differently? And what to keep the same?

Questions

Now that you've identified some areas on which to reflect and employed some tools to gather information, the next step is to use the information as a springboard to answer some reflective questions. While there is no exhaustive list of possible questions, there are major areas in which you may direct your focus. Refer to Table 15–1 for some guiding questions related to your teaching, behavior management, activities, materials, student performance, and academic objectives.

Analyze Data

Data are only useful if they are used. Gather what has been collected and start with organizing it in a way that is meaningful and helpful to you. Next, look for trends or common themes that appear. Are there any consistent words or phrases your students use in their feedback? How much time are you spending redirecting students? Is there a sticky or difficult area of classroom management you have recorded in your journaling time and time again? Watch your video feedback. Then watch it again. Think. Brainstorm. If you are comfortable, invite a trusted colleague to view along with you as they may glean different bits of information or notice things you may have missed. This naturally leads to revealing (and hopefully enlightening) discussions about your teaching. Talk about what you've noticed, what you think should change, and brainstorm ideas on how to develop some action items or goals. You may even uncover some commonalities shared between you and colleagues. Perhaps they had a similar issue with their class or have dealt with a particular behavior or classroom management issue you are

Table 15–1. Key Questions to Prompt Self-Reflection

Topic	Question
Activity and Materials	• What materials were used to deliver content? • Did students maintain engagement with the materials or lesson? • Were there any issues with materials (e.g., items inadvertently misused, poor quality, etc.)? • What materials would you use again?
Behavior Management	• Were my behavioral expectations clearly stated prior to the lesson? • Did students actively participate in the lesson? • Did I do anything to ensure equal opportunities for all students to participate? • What did I do to acknowledge and maintain positive behavior (e.g., praise, reinforcement, etc.)? • Did any students engage in challenging behavior? If so, for how long? What was my response?
Lesson/Content	• Were my instructions clearly stated? • Did students follow instructions or seek additional clarification? • Was my pacing appropriate for the content and student ability? • Did the length of the lesson suit the ability and attention levels of the students?
My Students	• Was the lesson too difficult or too easy for students? • Would my students benefit from additional or differentiated supports to access the curriculum and participate? • How did students demonstrate their understanding of the content? • Do I know my students outside of the classroom? • What kind of relationships do I have with students? Is the relationship helpful or hindering?
My Teaching	• Am I talking too much? Too little? • What would I do again? • What would I stop doing? • How did my tone of voice sound when delivering content, managing behavior, or answering student questions? • Does my nonvocal behavior make me seem approachable?

currently facing. Sometimes you will discover that what you thought would be highlighted as a concern, might not be as massive as you had expected; conversely, the data may shed some light on issues you were wholly unaware of.

Next, turn to research and resources for what you can't resolve through reflective discussions and brainstorming. As mentioned in Chapter 1, sources like the What Works Clearinghouse and the IRIS Center are fantastic tools to help with ideas for how to change your practice or incorporate new strategies. If your preferences lean toward the hive mind, utilizing online teaching forums or other platforms can lead you to new perspectives, new ideas, and new directions. Be prudently critical of crowdsourced advice; cross-check strategies and techniques with evidence-based best practice as the internet may be notoriously consultative, but it is certainly not infallible.

> *Don't forget about the resources provided in Chapter 1 as you begin looking for evidence-based and high-leverage practices.*

Implement Change

Finally, it's time to *action* something! Take what you have learned about yourself and your students and systematically implement the changes you have identified. Be purposeful in your approach, especially if you have targeted more than one adjustment to your practice. Begin with implementing one strategy at a time and allow sufficient time for this strategy to take hold. This means *weeks, not days* of implementation! This is the point at which the whole system is reset and the process of self-reflection begins again. Once changes are in play, reflection and evaluation are required to determine next steps. Questions can help continue the flow of self-reflection: Is the strategy working in the way I intended? Are there any barriers preventing success for my students or me? How are the students responding?

Self-reflection is a necessary element to enhance and further learning. Ultimately, the goal of becoming a reflective educator is to intentionally think about your method, your classroom presence, and your overall effectiveness as a teacher. Huge benefits are waiting to be gained, with professional growth being one of the most obvious. Reflective practice allows us to figure out both where our teaching strengths lie and where there are gaps, setting us up to seek out more focused professional development. A natural byproduct of accessing professional development is remaining current, innovative practitioners. Perhaps most importantly, the process of self-reflection helps us to appreciate how we learn, how others learn, and opens us up to recognizing diverse needs. Through this, we are providing strong models to our students and developing them into reflective learners.

High-Leverage Practice Alert!

So many HLPs are covered with the Universal Design for Learning framework. Check out HLP13, HLP14, HLP15, HLP16, and HLP18 for information on adaptations and modifications, cognitive strategies, scaffolding, explicit instruction, and student engagement.

Using a UDL Framework

If you find yourself reflecting on your instruction and classroom management and you're looking to make some broad changes to your instructional practices, look no further than the Universal Design for Learning (UDL) framework! Imagine you're walking down the street and see a mother pushing a stroller on the sidewalk, down a curb cutout, across a side street, and back up another curb cutout to the next sidewalk. Then, on the next corner, you watch an elderly gentleman using a cane shuffle across the street using those same curb cutouts so that he doesn't have to make a step up onto the curb. Finally, you see a young girl in a wheelchair come out of a bookstore and head down the sidewalk, go down the curb cutout, and head toward the back of her father's van. Although that curb cutout was installed to accommodate individuals with disabilities, look at all the other people it helped as well! The curb was altered and designed in such a way that multiple individuals benefited from its design, not just one single individual who absolutely needed it. This is called universal design and the benefits are widespread.

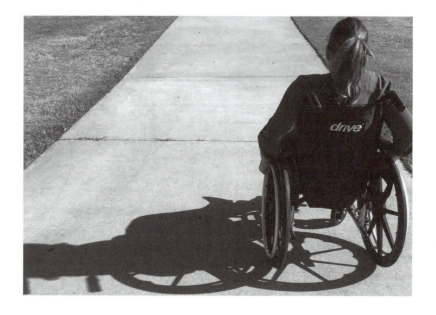

While this book has outlined classroom management strategies for schools, classrooms, and individuals, it is important to recognize that quality instruction is the foundation of any classroom management system. While the UDL framework is designed for instruction, it supports classroom management by creating opportunities for all learners to access the curriculum. Much like a curb cutout, UDL can meet the needs of many individuals. UDL isn't a framework to only support your most challenging students, it's for the range of learners you will inevitably have in your classroom. You might be wondering how UDL relates to behavior and classroom management. Behavior often relates back to meaningful instruction. If students aren't invested or engaged in instruction or do not understand what they are being taught, they are more likely to disengage and find alternative ways to occupy their time in the classroom. While some students may opt to read or draw quietly at their seat, other students may begin to act out through more disruptive behavioral choices. Further, if students aren't challenged or provided with materials and skills to persevere, students may demonstrate behaviors that are rooted in frustration, inadequacy, or boredom. Therefore, it is important that teachers spend some time reflecting on instruction and how their planning, lesson delivery, and assessments impact student learning and success. Rather than focusing on individualized differentiation techniques that only address one student and one situation at a time in isolation, a more universal instructional framework can be used year after year with a range of learners. Consider the idea that architecture is universally designed. The aforementioned curb cutout helped a range of individuals, including ones that probably weren't the intended recipients. That's what UDL can do! It can help you design lessons that meet the needs of learners who may or may not have even entered your classroom yet or aren't on your radar as a student who is struggling to engage or achieve academic success.

The UDL framework uses three guidelines to improve teaching and learning: representation, engagement, and action and expression. In the UDL framework, the first guideline is representation, which focuses on the "what" of learning. This includes all the ways that information is presented to students. To address representation, teachers should consider presenting content in different modalities, including visually and auditorily. This presentation of information should not be limited to one method or example but a range of options. Further, content should be clarified to the greatest extent possible. This might mean clarifying inferential text, teaching vocabulary, pointing out patterns, structures, and relationships, or identifying those big ideas in text. In math, this might also include directly teaching symbols and notations in conjunction with computation skills. Strategies for representation include providing a range of visual, tactile, and auditory representations of material; utilizing read alouds; and scaffolding new material into manageable chunks. Representation can be further developed through thoughtful classroom organization (Chapter 6), building relationships with students (Chapter 9), and self-monitoring (Chapter 14). Remember, the goal with representation is to make information accessible to a range of learners!

The second guideline is engagement. When providing students with multiple means of engagement, the goal is to help students understand the "why" of learning. This includes hooking students early in the lesson, appropriately challenging students on their academic levels, helping students persist through difficult work, and encouraging students to self-reflect and assess. Other ideas to encourage engagement in the classroom include inviting students to participate in their learning goals, encouraging critical thinking and imagination, encouraging and providing opportunities for students to collaborate, and adding variety to instruction. When thinking back to the topics we've discussed in this book, engagement is supported by classroom organization, including "zones" (Chapter 6), procedures and routines (Chapter 7), and teaching new skills (Chapter 14). Each of these supports allows students the opportunity to manage their own behaviors and navigate the learning environment with success.

The final guideline in the UDL framework is action and expression. Action and expression addresses the "how" of learning. Within this guideline, instruction should be focused on options for student responses as well as strategy instruction and progress monitoring. This guideline dives deep into the metacognition of learning and providing students with the tools necessary to know how they learn. In turn, this requires teachers to understand this process to effectively meet the needs of a range of learners. Ideas to support action and expression include using assistive technology, modeling various and different ways to solve a problem, scaffolding skills within lessons, and using graphic organizers, sentence starters, prompts, writing webs, and manipulatives. These short lists are far from comprehensive, but they are a great place to start thinking about designing instruction and lesson planning. To make connections with the ideas listed here, revisit Chapter 8 on engagement, instruction, and motivation as well as Chapter 14 on teaching new skills.

 Make a Connection

Take a moment and consider how the information presented in this text works with and supports the UDL framework. In what other ways are instruction and classroom management connected and how can any disconnects be addressed through UDL?

While the UDL framework uses guidelines for instruction, it is critical for teachers to reach all learners through academic engagement. The implementation of the UDL framework opens doors for more students to engage in instruction, reducing the amount of time they might be off task or discouraged from participating. While implementing the UDL guidelines may feel like a daunting task, teachers should aim to make small changes, one step at a time. It is through this incremental change that teachers will reap the benefits of access for all students. Imagine *not* recreating lessons year after year for individual students but instead adding to your instructional repertoire so that more students are reached each year, therefore needing less individualized differentiation? There are a number of helpful organizations and websites outlining the UDL framework and some of those are listed in Table 15–2.

Planning for the First Year of Teaching

Prior to starting your first year as a teacher, take some time to consider your classroom management philosophy and teaching style. There are a number of classroom management style inventories floating around on the internet, and while not research-based, they may help you identify some of your strengths and weaknesses as a classroom teacher. These inventories typically identify several types of teachers, including authoritarian, authoritative, laissez-faire, indulgent, indifferent, or democratic. Each of these management styles comes with pros and cons, and knowing where you fall, as well as how you might want to grow, is part of both planning and self-reflection. When thinking about your own classroom management philosophy, attempt to create a brief, positive statement under which

Table 15–2. Universal Design for Learning Resources

Name	Website
Centre for Applied Special Technology (CAST)	http://www.cast.org and http://udlguidelines.cast.org/
UDL Center	http://www.udlcenter.org
Accessible Instruction	https://ssbp.mycampus.ca/www_ains_dc/index.html
Access Project	http://accessproject.colostate.edu/
UDL-Universe: A Comprehensive Faculty Development Guide	http://enact.sonoma.edu/udl
The Center for Universal Design in Education	https://www.washington.edu/doit/programs/center-universal-design-education/overview

all of your other classroom management decisions would fit together. Do you believe students are the primary decision makers in your classroom? Where does respect, trustworthiness, fairness, and/or kindness fit into your philosophy? What role will you take in creating an environment that is welcoming and inclusive? Your philosophy should be something you could share with parents or students that conveys what you believe about classroom management and what observers could expect to see with your management plan.

Once you've developed a philosophy statement, imagine how you might get this accomplished. What procedures would you need in your classroom? As we discussed in Chapter 7 this list could be extensive. While you may not know all of the procedures you'll need, there are many that can be established prior to the start of the school year. Even if you don't have these nailed down, generate a list of those procedures that are important to you and your management philosophy. After procedures, consider what expectations you have for your students. Generate a list that not only covers your expectations for your classroom, but also how you can best convey these expectations to students. While rules and consequences may be dependent on your assigned grade level or school policies, you can still prepare for the school year by developing a rough list of ideas for both categories. It will be important to have conversations with your administration and grade- or subject-level team as early as possible to understand how you can plan accordingly in these areas. Finally, use the checklist in Figure 15–1 to get more information to prepare for your first day of school. Having this information will help you establish the kind of environment that will support a well-developed and thoughtful classroom management plan.

Remember, despite all of this planning, nothing is set in stone. While consistency is always best, especially since it creates a predictable and safe environment, the reality in the teaching profession is that we never know what needs our students may bring into our classroom until they arrive. If you find yourself with a plan that just isn't working, self-reflect, take some data, analyze it, and readjust. Stay true to your management philosophy. But what if a procedure isn't working the way you anticipated? Make a new one! Your students aren't responding to reinforcers the way they have in previous years? Find out why and introduce novel ones! If you're worried about what students and parents might say or think about altering your system after the school year has started, remember that recognizing that something isn't working is a sign of reflection and growth. Be honest with students, let them know something isn't working and you'd like their feedback on why. Use the opportunity to problem solve together. You never know, they may propose a solution that is even better than the one we could have imagined. In the end, use the strategies presented throughout this book, but know that no school year is ever the same and every teacher, even the most seasoned, needs to make adjustments now and then.

Figure 15–1. First day of school questions checklist.

First Day of School Questions Checklist

✓ How many students will be in my class or in each section of my courses?

✓ What kind of furniture (desks/ tables) will I have in my classroom?

✓ What materials will be provided?

✓ Is there a master schedule for the school? What are the scheduling expectations for my classroom?

✓ Where do I go if there is a fire drill? Lockdown? Emergency weather event?

✓ Is there a student code of conduct?

✓ What do I need to know about school discipline policies (including PBIS or other frameworks or programs)?

✓ What day-to-day procedures does the county or school have in place that I will need to implement in my classroom?

✓ Is there anything I need to know about lockers, restrooms, water fountains, hallways, the playground, or other areas of the school?

✓ What are the policies or procedures for addressing bullying?

✓ What should I know about arrival and dismissal?

✓ How do I access parent or guardian contact information?

✓ Where can I get a copy of any IEPs, 504s, or documentation about individual students?

✓ Are any support staff available to help me with behavioral challenges in my classroom?

✓ Who can I go to with questions about classroom management or school-wide policies?

Finally, if you are a teacher looking for your first job in education, there are a number of questions you can ask your future principal or administrator about classroom management support. A teacher certainly need not ask every single question, but if your management philosophy strongly hinges on diversity, then a question about cultural awareness might be at the top of your list. If working in a school that implements school-wide supports is appealing to you, be sure to ask about Positive Behavioral Intervention and Supports (PBIS). The interview question list in Figure 15–2 is extensive but not comprehensive. However, it can be used as a guide to learn more about how you might be supported or encouraged in your classroom and behavior management endeavors.

Planning for the 20th Year of Teaching

If you're planning for the 10th, 20th, or the years somewhere in between, this section is for you! Undoubtedly, you've had your fair share of experiences in the classroom and you know what works and doesn't work for you and your students. If you read something in this book that was new or surprising to you, we challenge you to dig in and learn more. Given that there are so many practices that float around our educational system with no, little, or mixed results on effectiveness (e.g., learning styles, growth mindset interventions, corporal punishment, etc.), it's imperative that practitioners are diligent about debunking practices that simply do not work! As mentors and school leaders, our seasoned teachers have the esteemed responsibility to share effective practices—those grounded in research and evidence in settings similar to those where you work. Sharing these practices in practical and positive ways will support the next generation of educators as they build their classroom management strategy repertoire.

Figure 15–2. Job search questions.

Questions to Ask During a Job Search

1. Does this school use multitiered support systems (PBIS, RtI, etc.)?
   a. What role could/would I play in those systems?
   b. How are the procedures outlined in those systems shared with teachers and parents?
2. How are teachers supported with classroom management challenges?
3. What do you expect of your teachers in terms of classroom management?
4. What steps do you believe teachers should take to address challenging behaviors or disciplinary issues before involving the administration?
5. Will I be assigned a mentor who can help me with classroom management planning?

Teacher Stress and Burnout

No matter whether you decide to spend your entire career in the classroom or following an entirely different professional path, you will undoubtably encounter references to, or direct experience with, burnout. Well beyond simple exhaustion or job frustration, burnout is a real and recognized hazard that spans across multiple professions. Burnout is a psychological syndrome resulting from a state of chronic workplace stress. Three main features that characterize burnout are overwhelming physical and emotional exhaustion, cynicism and/or detachment from the job, and an overall sense of ineffectiveness (Maslach & Leiter, 2016). Unfortunately, teachers are exceptionally vulnerable to burnout—not only because of the long hours spent outside of the classroom carefully cultivating lessons, writing sub plans, grading assignments, emailing parents, collaborating with paraprofessionals, maintaining classroom websites, attending collaborative team meetings, IEP meetings, staff meetings, hosting student organizations and clubs, and, and, and, and. . . (you get the point), but also because they tend to be extremely driven, high-achieving individuals, committed to bettering their practice. Taken together, these aspects may also contribute to higher levels of burnout. While much of the appeal of teaching revolves around the selfless nature of the craft, it is so important for teachers to be aware of the potential for burnout, know the warning signs, and have proactive measures in place to offset the demands of the field. Some key indicators of burnout may include sleep issues (e.g., insomnia, difficulty waking, restless sleep, overall fatigue, etc.), difficulty concentrating, absentmindedness, weight or appetite changes, and mood changes (e.g., short fuse, new anxieties, etc.).

The following are some simple suggestions that may be incorporated to counter the effects of burnout and keep you passionate about teaching. First, consciously set boundaries for when you will and will not work, as time spent with family and loved ones as well as on one's own is critical for all-around well-being. Some individuals do well with prescribed work times, such as, "I'll answer emails between 7:00 a.m. and 8:00 a.m. and then again between 4:00 p.m. and 5:00 p.m.," while others operate more broadly, "I'm only answering emails until it's time to eat dinner with my partner." Some schools have even incorporated some of these boundary setting practices by disabling access to email after a certain time every day and on the weekends. It's also helpful to communicate these boundaries to others, including family and friends, so they can help you stay accountable. Next, identify activities, hobbies, and ways to relax and recharge during your downtime. Everyone is different; for some, "active relaxing" on the weekends looks like hitting the gym, spending some time out in the garden, and then going out to a nice meal, while others prefer to get cozy on the couch, watch some reality television, and settle in for the afternoon. Either way, find things you love to do and commit to them. Maybe you'd like to make a point of going out to the movies or a live band once a month—write it on the calendar, invite friends, tell colleagues about your plans—hold yourself accountable. While your students may think you eat, shower, and sleep in your classroom, you actually don't! Remember, you *earn* time off; use it! On the same token, if you are consistently overwhelmed at work and not getting enough time throughout your day to have lunch or use the restroom, speak up! You are your best advocate; you know your limits; and in this way, you teach others how to treat you. Making your needs a priority guarantees a happier, more productive, efficient, and passionate educator.

Conclusion

Throughout this book, we have covered theory and frameworks, school and classroom considerations, and ways to work with individual students on behavioral challenges. While much of the information is deeply rooted in research and evidence, the application of these tenets will range greatly depending on your own philosophy, your setting, the types of students you work with, and a unique combination of factors we cannot begin to categorize. Despite these differences, a successful classroom leader will understand their students and provide a safe and welcoming environment that includes quality instruction and consistency. There is not *one* right answer to classroom management planning, but through self-reflection and continued learning, especially about research and evidence-based practices, both new and seasoned teachers and their students will experience academic and behavioral success.

Chapter Summary

- Self-reflection is an active process through which teachers can examine their practice and make improvements to suit the needs of their learners. Self-reflection begins with a commitment to the practice followed by identifying an aspect of teaching to reflect upon, gathering data, creating and answering questions, analyzing data, and implementing changes.

- Self-reflection allows teachers to further their learning by identifying areas of strength and need and encourages intentional thought about one's method, classroom presence, and overall effectiveness as an educator.

- The Universal Design for Learning (UDL) is a framework that uses checkpoints to support all learners, and while designed for instruction, it also supports classroom behavior management.

- UDL uses the guidelines of representation, engagement, and action and expression to improve teaching and learning.

- Representation involves teachers presenting content through a variety of modalities (e.g., visual, auditory, tactile, scaffolding, read-aloud, etc.) and clarifying as much as possible.

- Engagement refers to the "why" of learning and involves hooking students early in the lesson, providing appropriate challenges, assisting students in persevering through difficult work, and promoting self-reflection.

- Action and expression addresses the "how" of learning. From this guideline, educators bring their focus to various options for student responding and progress monitoring. The goal of this guideline is for students to understand what tools are helpful in their learning and how they learn best.

- Burnout results from a state of chronic workplace stress that is characterized by overwhelming physical and emotional exhaustion, cynicism, and an overall sense of ineffectiveness (Maslach & Leiter, 2016).

- To counter burnout, set boundaries around work and nonwork times and identify activities or hobbies that bring joy and allow you to relax and recharge. Be sure to communicate work/nonwork boundaries to friends and family to help stay accountable to your well-being.

GLOSSARY

A-B-C chart   A form of direct assessment that involves observation and recording of the antecedents and consequences around the target behavior.

Accurate   When the observed value of an event matches its true value.

Action and expression   Addresses the "how" of learning. From this guideline, educators bring their focus to various options for student responding and progress monitoring. The goal of this guideline is for students to understand what tools are helpful in their learning and how they learn best.

Active listening   A technique that encourages the listener to listen for meaning, restating what the speaker is saying, and reserving judgment or advice. Active listening may include asking the speaker questions for clarification and more information.

Antecedent   Stimuli immediately preceding a behavior.

Antecedent strategies   Strategies aimed at adjusting the environment to neutralize or eliminate triggers as well as adjusting behavior teaching strategies to teach a replacement to challenging behavior.

Applied behavior analysis   The scientific discipline based upon learning theory that looks at how to apply empirical techniques to affect socially significant behavior change.

Assertive management style   A style of teaching that clearly and calmly establishes rules, expectations, and consequences in the classroom. Standards of behavior are expected to be followed and both positive and negative consequences are employed based on the adherence to those expectations.

Attention deficit/hyperactivity disorder (ADHD)   A neurological condition causing symptoms of inattention, poor impulse control, distractibility, and/or forgetfulness. ADHD qualifies as a disability under the "Other Health Impairment" (OHI) category of IDEA.

Autism spectrum disorders (ASD)   A developmental disability in which an individual displays persistent deficits in social communication and demonstrates restrictive, repetitive patterns of behavior.

Backup reinforcer   A reinforcer provided in return for tokens earned by engaging in a target behavior.

Baseline   Preintervention condition in which there is no independent variable at play; the period in which a target behavior is being monitored and data are being collected in the *absence* of the intervention.

Behavior   Sometimes referred to as a response, behavior is any activity in which a human engages. Behaviors are actions that are observable and measurable.

Behavior contract   An intervention that establishes a specific contingency, or relationship, between a behavior and a reward and includes three elements: (1) definition of the task; (2) description of the reward/reinforcement; and (3) task record.

Behavior skills training (BST)   A four-step method to teach a new skill, or in the case of a BIP, the replacement behavior. It is comprised of (1) Instruction, (2) Modeling, (3) Practice, and (4) Feedback. In order to use BST, the target behavior should be a skill made up of a chain of behaviors capable of being modeled and role-played.

Behavior-specific praise   A means to reinforce desired behavior that is specific to the student(s), includes a description of the behavior and has a positive praise statement.

Behavioral intervention plan (BIP)   Sometimes referred to as a Behavior Support Plan; a plan designed from data garnered via a functional behavioral assessment to teach prosocial behaviors to replace challenging behavior.

Behavioral momentum   Involves using a series of high-probability requests or tasks to increase compliance with lower-probability requests or tasks.

Character education   Seeks to educate students on ethical values such as respect, responsibility for self and others, and citizenship; it emphasizes moral and ethical dimensions of social-emotional development.

Check-in check-out (CICO)   A Tier 2 intervention whereby students check in with a teacher or mentor prior to a block of instruction to identify observable and measurable goals. Students obtain points for behavior throughout the day. The check-out procedure includes reviewing the daily goals and future goal setting.

Choice theory   Developed by William Glasser, Choice Theory states all behaviors are conscious choices. This theory references internal control, or the belief that we are responsible for our choices, and disregards outside influences as capable of making an individual do or feel anything.

Classical conditioning   A learning process that focuses on respondent, or reflexive, behaviors being elicited by antecedents, or stimuli that immediately precede them.

Classroom management   The ways in which educators implement focused strategies, skills, and techniques to ensure an organized, attentive, and academically productive classroom, free of disruptions resulting from challenging behavior.

Clusters A classroom arrangement, sometimes referred to as a group, which includes four to six student desks pushed together in a square or rectangle shape. Ideal for arranging a small room as less floor space is typically used.

Collaboration Involves voluntarily coming together to engage in joint decision making toward goals.

Competing behavior pathway A strategy for organizing one's approach to functional assessment and provides a series of connections between the steps of the FBA all the way through formulation of the BIP.

Conditioned response A learned reflexive response that is a result of pairing a neutral stimulus with an unconditioned stimulus over time.

Conflict cycle A pattern that may arise from a power struggle between two individuals that leads to a negative and unproductive place and sometimes into a crisis situation. Each individual's behavior can become cyclical, escalating the situation over time.

Consequence strategies Specific strategies designed to strengthen the use of replacement behaviors, giving them more power over challenging behavior.

Consequences Events that occur immediately following a target behavior and influence the future likelihood of that behavior occurring again.

Contingency Refers to the relationship between behaviors and consequences.

Continuous reinforcement The provision of reinforcement for every single response.

Coteaching Involves two teachers working as equals to plan, teach, and evaluate a group of shared students.

Cultural competence The ability to interact, understand, communicate, and interact with people across a range of cultures.

Dependent group contingency A group contingency wherein the reward for the entire group is dependent upon the behavior of either one individual or a small portion of the group.

Dependent variable The variable that is being measured; usually referring to as *target behaviors* and what is being influenced by the independent variable.

Developmental characteristics The typical developmental milestones at specific ages that include cognitive, physical, emotional, and social areas.

Differential reinforcement of low rates (DRL) A procedure used to reduce (but not eliminate) behaviors that are occurring too frequently by delivering reinforcement when behavior levels fall below a predetermined criteria.

Direct assessment Involves direct observation of the student in the environments in which challenging behavior is most likely to occur as well as those environments in which the target behavior does not occur, or is less likely to occur.

Discipline hierarchy A procedure of escalating severity usually starting with small disciplinary actions for first time offences (e.g., verbal warnings). If rule breaking continues, disciplinary actions escalate.

Duration recording   Refers to recording the length of time the behavior occurs; particularly helpful for nondiscrete, or continuous, behaviors.

Emotional and behavioral disorders (EBD)   EBD is a condition in which one or more of the following characteristics are evident over a long period of time, which adversely affects educational performance: (a) an inability to learn, which cannot be explained by intellectual, sensory, or other health factors; (b) an inability to build or maintain satisfactory relationships with peers and teachers; (c) inappropriate types of behavior or feelings under normal circumstances; (d) a general pervasive mood of unhappiness or depression; or (e) a tendency to develop physical symptoms or fears associated with personal and school problems.

Engagement   Refers to the "why" of learning and involves hooking students early in the lesson, providing appropriate challenges, assisting students in persevering through difficult work, and promoting self-reflection.

Environmental factors   Factors such as poverty, homelessness, and a lack of basic needs that students may face that may affect their performance in the classroom.

Errorless prompting   Provides a prompt that directly tells the student how to respond, skipping the hierarchy, but ensuring a correct response.

Event recording   Examines the number of times a behavior occurs across time; suitable for discrete behaviors.

Executive functions   The set of cognitive abilities that allows us to control impulses, problem-solve scenarios, and achieve goals through planning and organization.

Expectations   Communicates to students what behaviors are acceptable and expected and should be written in positive language that outlines what the student *should* be doing, avoiding words like "no" or "don't."

Experimental control   A predictable change in behavior after systematic manipulation of variables.

Extinction   The purposeful withdrawal of the reinforcing variable maintaining challenging behavior.

Extinction burst   A phenomenon in which there is a temporary increase in the frequency, duration, or magnitude of the target response when reinforcement for the behavior is removed (i.e., extinction).

Family values   A family system's beliefs or ideas about what is valued, meaningful, or important.

Fixed interval   A schedule of reinforcement that provides reinforcement for the first target behavior emitted after a fixed time period.

Fixed ratio   A schedule in which a behavior is reinforced after a specified number of required responses.

Force   Also referred to as magnitude; the degree of intensity a behavior emits.

Frequency counts   Also referred to as event recording, this form of data collection examines the number of times a behavior occurs across time—suitable for discrete behaviors.

Functional analysis   An active process whereby a teacher/practitioner manipulates antecedents and consequences of a target behavior in order to "test" what is causing the behavior to occur.

Functional behavioral assessment (FBA)   A systematic process by which the variables that maintain problem behavior are identified; this information is then translated into a behavioral intervention plan (BIP).

Functional communication training (FCT)   A form of differential reinforcement that hinges on using communication to replace disruptive, inappropriate, or otherwise challenging behavior.

Gesture prompt   A visual prompt that uses gestures or actions to show a student what to do.

Good Behavior Game   A form of an interdependent group contingency that uses a point system to reduce challenging or disruptive behavior

Good Student Game   A form of interdependent group contingency that relies upon self-monitoring strategies and points are given for rule-following.

Group contingencies   A behavior management intervention that provides a reinforcer (and sometimes an aversive consequence) to an entire group of people based on either the behavior of one individual within the group, the behavior of a portion of people within the group, or the behavior of the entire group.

Hierarchy of prompts   Refers to the graduated levels of support required to help a student achieve a correct response. Generally sequenced from least to most assistance that includes a visual or gesture prompt, verbal prompts, and physical prompts.

Horseshoe arrangement   A classroom arrangement that places student desks in a horseshoe or u-shaped formation around the perimeter of the room.

Hostile management style   Includes using aversive approaches to manage the classroom that may consist of sarcasm, threats, put-downs, and shouting or yelling.

I-messages   Coined by Thomas Gordon, I-messages may be used to express feelings in a way that allows the listener to understand how the speaker is feeling without making the listener defensive. I-messages include a brief, factual description of the problem and the way the problem makes a person feel as well as a concrete example of the effect of the problem.

Inadvertent reinforcement   A potential disadvantage to group contingencies where there is a risk that students may intentionally or unintentionally alter behaviors and reinforce behaviors other than the ones being targeted.

Inclusive classrooms   A classroom that actively and purposefully involves all students in learning, regardless of background, culture, race, gender, socioeconomic status, or disability.

Independent group contingency   A group contingency wherein all individuals within a group who meet the specified criterion earn the reward.

Independent variable   The variable or intervention that is introduced with the intention to create change; the independent variable is what is expected to produce a change in performance.

Indirect assessment   A means of gathering information through means other than directly observing the target behavior, including rating scales, record reviews, interviews, and checklists.

Individualized education program (IEP)   Both a process and a written document developed by a team for an eligible student with a disability that outlines special education and related services required by a student to receive an appropriate education.

Individuals with Disabilities Education Act (IDEA)   A United States federal law that requires every state to have in effect policies and procedures to ensure a free appropriate public education (FAPE) for all students with disabilities. This federal regulation specifies all students with a disability have specific rights and protections.

Intellectual disability   A combination of deficits in both cognition and adaptive functioning.

Interdependent group contingency   The most commonly used group contingency that requires all members of the group to meet the set criterion, *both individually and as a group,* before earning the reward.

Intermittent reinforcement   Characterized by some responses receiving reinforcement and others not. These schedules operate based on either the number of responses (*ratio*) or the time between reinforcement (*interval*).

Interviews   An indirect measure wherein key people such as parents, caregivers, and teachers, are asked questions aimed gain perspective on a student's concerns.

Latency   Refers to how much time elapses between a prompt, or opportunity to engage in a target behavior, and initiation of the behavior.

Learning zones   A purposeful classroom arrangement that divides the room into specific learning areas; helps to promote organization of materials for specific tasks and instruction.

Level   Refers to value or placement of data on the vertical axis, or *y*-axis.

Locus   Describes where a behavior occurs, typically naming the environment or a specific location.

Magnitude   Also referred to as force; the degree of intensity a behavior emits.

Manifestation determination review (MDR)   The process of determining the relationship between a student's disability and the behavior causing exclusion from school.

Momentary time sampling   A method of data collection that involves observing the target behavior only at the very end of the interval. The behavior is only counted if it is occurring at the precise moment the interval ends.

Motivation   An individual's drive to action.

Multiple baseline design   A single-subject research design characterized by a staggered introduction of the independent variable for at least three different points in time and takes one of three basic forms: across individuals, settings, or behaviors.

Multitiered systems of supports (MTSS)   A framework used to support students academically and behaviorally with early intervention and preventative measures.

Negative reinforcement   Involves the *removal* of a (usually aversive) stimulus after a target response that increases the future likelihood of the behavior.

Neutral stimulus   A stimulus that is neutral to the learner that does not intrinsically produce a response.

No-lose conflict resolution   A tenet of Thomas Gordon, a no-lose conflict resolution involves defining the needs of both the child and the adult, brainstorming solutions, evaluating possible solutions, choosing a solution, implementing a solution, and checking the results.

Nonassertive management style   A management style wherein teachers employ ineffective behavior management strategies and do not follow through on expectations.

Operant behaviors   A learned behavior that is influenced by the consequences that follow it.

Operant conditioning   A method of learning that occurs through rewards and punishments for behavior. The consequences of behaviors either strengthen or weaken future behavior.

Operational definition   Specific means to identifying a target behavior; the operational definition must be measurable, observable, and objective. Measurable behaviors are those that can be counted (e.g., frequency, duration, etc.), observed (e.g., physical movement, sound, or effect on the environment, etc.), and objective (e.g., free from feelings or assumptions).

Pairs   A classroom arrangement whereby all students are typically sat facing forward with desks either parallel to the front of the room or angled to create more space in the center of the room. Pairs requires more floor space than rows or clusters.

Partial interval recording   A data collection recording method suited for behaviors that occur quickly, are short in duration, or occur at high rates. An observation period is divided into equal parts; a positive interval indicates the target behavior occurred, while a negative interval is the complete absence of the target behavior within the interval.

Partnerships   Involve two or more people working together toward a common purpose or goal.

Permanent product   A concrete artifact or an observable outcome of a behavior.

Physical prompt   The least independent form of prompting that provides physical hand-over-hand support to a student.

Planned activity check (PLACHECK)   A way to measure group behavior quickly and easily; best suited for high frequency or continuous behaviors. Using a momentary time sample interval system, the teacher scans the room at the end of each interval and marks/tallies students engaged in target behavior.

Positive behavioral intervention and supports (PBIS)   PBIS is a systems approach for managing student behavior, developing individualized supports, and creating a positive school culture. The foundation of PBIS consists of rules, routines, and physical arrangements that are designed to prevent the occurrence of challenging behaviors.

Positive reinforcement   Positive reinforcement refers to the *addition* of something to the environment after a behavior occurs, increasing the future likelihood of the behavior.

Power struggles   A confrontation between two individuals (e.g., student and teacher) wherein one individual refuses to comply or demonstrates an opposition to requests, followed by the other individual's insistence on follow thorough. Only ends with someone "winning" and can break down relationships in the classroom.

Prediction   The expected outcome of future measurements.

Premack principle   Sometimes referred to as "Grandma's Rule," describes how one can use a high probability behavior to reinforce a lower probability behavior.

Procedures or routines   The behaviors that are expected of all students in a school, on the bus, on the playground, during an athletic event, or in any location where school is in session.

Punishment   When a behavior is immediately followed by a stimulus that decreases the future likelihood of that behavior.

Rate   The frequency, or count, of behaviors across the unit of time measured.

Rating scales   An indirect measure that estimates the extent to which the target behavior occurs across different conditions using a Likert-type scale (e.g., never, sometimes, often, always).

Reactivity   Refers to a change in one's own behavior that occurs simply because one is aware of being observed.

Reinforcement   The provision of a consequence following a behavior that increases the future likelihood of that behavior occurring again in the future.

Reinforcers   A consequence to a behavior that results in an increase in that particular behavior.

Reinforcers (PBIS specific)   Within the PBIS framework, a reinforcer is a reward that may be in the form of verbal praise, tangible items, or activities tied into a ticket or raffle system. These rewards can be delivered to individual students, entire classes, or school wide.

Relatedness   Refers to having safe and satisfying relationships with others.

Reliable   Refers to measurement of data; reliable data produce the same value over repeated measurements.

Replacement behavior   Positive, prosocial behaviors that are functionally equivalent to the target behavior. It is best to select behaviors that are already in a student's repertoire, are efficient, and require the same or less effort than the challenging behavior.

Replication   Repetition of conditions to enforce reliability of results.

Representation   Focuses on the "what" of learning and involves teachers presenting content through a variety of modalities (e.g., visual, auditory, tactile, scaffolding, read-aloud, etc.) and clarifying as much as possible.

Respondent behavior   An involuntary response or reflex.

Response cost   A negative punishment procedure usually used in conjunction with a token economy and involves the removal of reinforcement (e.g., token) contingent upon an undesirable behavior.

Response to intervention (RtI)   A framework that uses universal screening assessments to identify students' academic needs and to provide research-based interventions in a preventive and intensive manner to academically struggling students.

Reversal design   An extension of an A-B design that uses additional conditions. A-B-A returns the participant back to baseline (replication), but it may not be ideal to withdraw intervention. Thus, an A-B-A-B design allows for the participant to go back to intervention and this design satisfies the requirements of replication and verification.

Rows   A classroom arrangement that positions student desks side by side, touching one another to form a straight line. They can be placed facing straight at the front of the room or at an angle.

Rules   Should be framed positively and intended for students to self-monitor, serve as reminders for expected behaviors, and should have corresponding repercussions if broken.

Satiation   Occurs when teachers remain on a lesson or concept too long and is characterized by students showing disinterest in mastered content.

"Saving face"   A situation wherein an individual feels as though they must take measures to avoid feeling embarrassed, humiliated, or disrespected in front of their peers.

Scatterplot   Visual displays of data that help to reveal relationships between two or more variables; they show changes in the value of one variable on one axis with respect to the other axis.

Schedules of reinforcement   The "rule" stating which instances of a target (correct) behavior receive reinforcement. Schedules of reinforcement may either be continuous or intermittent.

Self-monitoring   The intentional use of behavior change strategies to monitor or change one's behavior.

Self-reflection   An active process through which teachers can examine their practice and make improvements to suit the needs of their learners.

Setting event strategies   Involve finding ways to neutralize or minimize the likelihood of a setting event, which may include things like ensuring a comfortable classroom temperature, providing snacks and a drink before a lesson, or providing an area for some quiet down time.

Single-subject design   A type of experimental design (also referred to as single-case designs) that employs a small number of participants and each participant serves as his or her own control.

SMART goals   Goals that are specific, measurable, attainable, realistic, and time-bound.

Social competence   Refers to how others judge the outcomes of specific social skills of an individual across settings and situations.

Social skills   Refers to one or more isolated skills an individual must perform within a specific setting or context.

Social skills instruction   An intervention used to address deficits in social skills and includes assessment, creation of a plan, providing direct instruction, practice, and generalization.

Specific learning disability   A neurological condition in which an individual's ability to understand language, either spoken or written, affects one's ability to listen, think, speak, read, write, spell, or do mathematical calculations.

Stereotyped behaviors   Repetitive or ritualized behaviors described as nonfunctional and repetitive in nature.

Stimulus bound   Coined by Jacob Kounin, wherein teachers become distracted by something or someone in the classroom and lose instructional focus, consequently pulling students off task.

Stoplight system   A classroom management strategy that relies upon a teacher-provided rating system to publicly categorizes student behavior.

Target behavior   The behavior selected for change.

Termination criteria   Provides clear parameters for when one behavior terminates, or is "complete," and another one begins.

Three-term contingency   Describes the relationship between the environment and behavior; also known as the A-B-C contingency.

Tier 1   Part of the RtI framework, Tier 1 interventions are the core interventions, including high-quality classroom instruction for all students.

Tier 2   Part of the RtI framework wherein students receive more intensive interventions, typically in a small group.

Tier 3   The final tier of the RtI framework wherein instruction is individualized and provided with increased frequency and intensity.

Time sampling   A method of data collection that indicates whether or not a behavior occurred during a particular period of time. Three main variations of time sampling: whole interval recording, partial interval recording, and momentary time sampling.

Token economy   An intervention that mirrors a consumer economy whereby desired behaviors are reinforced with tokens that may be exchanged for backup reinforcers.

Tootling   The opposite of tattling; rather than reporting negative behaviors, tootling promotes reports of positive behaviors.

Topography   Refers to the physical form of the behavior, or what the behavior looks and sounds like.

Trend   Describes the direction of the data and labeled as either increasing, decreasing, or zero-trend.

Unconditioned stimulus   A stimulus that *unconditionally,* or automatically, triggers a response or reflex.

Universal design for learning   A framework that uses checkpoints to support all learners, and while designed for instruction, it also supports classroom behavior management.

Valid/validity   A measurement is valid when the data collection is measuring what it is intended to measure.

Variability   The degree to which the data are spread out across time.

Variable interval   A schedule of reinforcement wherein the first correct response following the passage of a *variable* amount of time is reinforced.

Variable ratio   A schedule of reinforcement wherein reinforcement is provided after an *unpredictable* number of responses, which results in high steady rate of responding.

Verbal prompt   Can be direct and indirect. A direct verbal prompt provides explicit instruction to the learner about what to do. An indirect prompt provides the learner with a hint or can be an instruction directed toward the whole group rather than the individual student.

Verification   Showing the dependent variable changed as a result of the independent variable and nothing else.

Visual analysis   The visual interpretation of data that looks at variability, trend, and level.

Whole interval recording   A data recording method suited for continuous behaviors. An observation period is divided into equal parts based off of baseline measures of behavior. A positive interval is noted when the target behavior occurs throughout the entire interval. A negative interval is noted if the behavior does not last throughout the interval or if the behavior stops and restarts within an interval.

Withitness   Defined by Jacob Kounin as the teacher's ability to know what is happening in the classroom at all times.

REFERENCES

Achenbach, T. M., & Edelbrock, C. S. (1991). *Manual for the child behavior checklist*. Burlington, VT: University of Vermont, Department of Psychiatry.

Adkins-Coleman, T. A. (2010). "I'm not afraid to come into your world": Case studies of teachers facilitating engagement in urban high school English classrooms. *Journal of Negro Education, 79*, 41–53. doi:10.2307/25676108

Alberto, P., & Troutman, A. C. (2013). *Applied behavior analysis for teachers*. Boston, MA: Pearson.

Allday, R. A., Hinkson-Lee, K., Hudson, T., Neilson-Gatti, S., Kleinke, A., & Russel, C. S. (2012). Training general educators to increase behavior specific praise: Effects on students with EBD. *Behavioral Disorders, 37*, 87–98. doi:10.1177/019874291203700203

American Psychiatric Association. (2013). *Diagnostic and statistical manual of mental disorders* (5th ed.). Arlington, VA: Author.

Ayres, K., & Ledford, J. R. (2014). Dependent measures and measurement systems. In D. L. Gast & J. R. Ledford (Eds.), *Single case research methodology: Applications in special education and behavioral sciences* (pp. 124–153). New York, NY: Routledge

Babyak, A. E., Luze, G. J., & Kamps, D. M. (2000). The good student game: Behavior management for diverse classroom. *Intervention in School and Clinic, 35*, 216–223. doi:10.1177/105345120003500403

Barrish, H. H., Saunders, M., & Wolf, M. M. (1969). Good behavior game: Effects of individual contingencies for group consequences on disruptive behavior in a classroom. *Journal of Applied Behavior Analysis, 2*, 119–124. doi:10.1901/jaba.1969.2-119

Berlin, L. J., Ispa, J. M., Fine, M. A., Malone, P. S., Brooks-Gunn, J., Brady-Smith, C., & Bai, Y. (2009). Correlates and consequences of spanking and verbal punishment for low-income White, African American, and Mexican American toddlers. *Child Development, 80*, 1403–1420. doi:10.1111/j.1467-8624.2009.01341.x

Biggs, E. E., Gilson, C. B., & Carter, E. W. (2016). Accomplishing more together: Influences to the quality of professional relationships between special educators and paraprofessionals. *Research and Practice for Persons with Severe Disabilities, 41*(4), 256–272. doi:10.1177/1540796916665604

Blair, C., & Raver, C. (2016). Poverty, stress, and brain development: New directions for prevention and intervention. *Academic Pediatrics, 16*, 530–536. doi:10.1016/j.acap.2016.01.010

Bloom, E. L., Karagiannakis, A., Toste, J. R., Heath, N. L., & Konstantinopolous, E. (2007). Severity of academic achievement and social skills deficits. *Canadian Journal of Education, 30*, 911–930. doi:10.2307/20466668

Blum, R. (2005). *School connectedness: Improving the lives of students.* Baltimore, MD: Johns Hopkins Bloomberg School of Public Health.

Boyer, E., Miltenberger, R. G., Batsche, C., & Fogel, V. (2009). Video modeling by experts with video feedback to enhance gymnastics skills. *Journal of Applied Behavior Analysis, 42,* 855–860. doi:10.1901/jaba.2009.42-855

Bradshaw, C., Mitchell, M. M., & Leaf, P. J. (2010). Examining the effects of schoolwide positive behavior interventions and supports on student outcomes: Results from a randomized controlled effectiveness trial in an elementary school. *Journal of Positive Behavior Interventions, 12,* 133–148. doi:10.1177/1098300709334798

Broome Williams, K. (2004). *Grace Hopper: Admiral of the cyber sea.* Annapolis, MD: Naval Institute Press.

Brophy, J. (2006). History of research on classroom management. In C. M. Evertson & C. S. Weinstein (Eds.), *Handbook of classroom management: Research, practice, and contemporary issues* (pp. 17–43). Mahwah, NJ: Erlbaum.

Cardellino, P., Araneda, C., & Alvarado, R. G. (2017). Classroom environments: An experiential analysis of the pupil-teacher visual interaction in Uruguay. *Learning Environments Research, 20,* 417–431. doi:10.1007/s10984-017-9236-y

Carr, E., & Durand, M. (1985). Reducing behavior problems through functional communication training. *Journal of Applied Behavior Analysis, 18,* 111–126. doi:10.1901/jaba.1985.18–111

Children's Defense Fund. (2017). *Child poverty in America 2017: National analysis.* Retrieved from https://www.childrensdefense.org/wp-content/uploads/2018/09/Child-Poverty-in-America-2017-National-Fact-Sheet.pdf

Coffey, J. H., & Horner, R. H. (2012). The sustainability of schoolwide positive behavior interventions and supports. *Exceptional Children, 78,* 407–422. doi.org/10.1177/001440291207800402

Cooper, J. O., Heron, T. E., & Heward, W. L. (2007). *Applied behavior analysis* (2nd ed.). Upper Saddle River, NJ: Pearson Education.

Cooper, J. O., Heron, T. E., & Heward, W. L. (2019). *Applied behavior analysis* (3rd ed.). Upper Saddle River, NJ: Pearson Education.

Cowan, N. (2001). The magical number 4 in short-term memory: A reconsideration of mental storage capacity. *Behavioral and Brain Sciences, 24,* 87–114. doi:10.1017/S0140525X01003922

Crone, D. A., Hawken, L. S., & Horner, R. H. (2015). *Building positive behavior support systems in schools: Functional behavioral assessment.* New York, NY: The Guilford Press.

Dajani, D. R., & Uddin, L. C. (2015). Demystifying cognitive flexibility: Implications for clinical and developmental neuroscience. *Trends in Neurosciences, 38,* 571–578. doi:10.1016/j.tins.2015.07.003

Davis, J. R. (2017). From discipline to dynamic pedagogy: A re-conceptualization of classroom management. *Berkeley Review of Education, 6,* 129–153. Retrieved from http://www.berkeleyreviewofeducation.com

Doran, G. T. (1981). There's a S.M.A.R.T. way to write management's goals and objectives. *Management Review, 70,* 35–36. Retrieved from https://community.mis.temple.edu/mis0855002fall2015/files/2015/10/S.M.A.R.T-Way-Management-Review.pdf

Douglas, S. N., Chapin, S. E., & Nolan, J. F. (2016). Special education teachers' experiences supporting and supervising paraeducators: Implications for special and general education settings. *Teacher Education and Special Education, 39*(1), 60–74. doi.org/10.1177/0888406415616443

Dreikurs, R. (1968). *Psychology in the classroom: A manual for teachers* (2nd ed.). New York, NY: Harper & Row.

Dunn, K. E., Airola, D. T., Lo, W., & Garrison, M. (2013). Becoming data driven: The influence of teachers' sense of efficacy on concerns related to data-driven decision making. *The Journal of Experimental Education, 81*, 222–241. doi:10.1080/00220973.2012.699899

DuPaul, G. J., Gormley, M. J., & Laracy, S. D. (2013). Comorbidity of LD and ADHD: Implications of DSM-5 for assessment and treatment. *Journal of Learning Disabilities, 46*, 43–41. doi:10.1177/0022219412464351

Durand, V. M., & Crimmins, D. B. (1992). *The Motivation Assessment scale* [Measurement instrument]. Topeka, KS: Monaco & Associates.

Dweck, C. (2014). *Carol Dweck: The power of believing that you can improve.* [Video file]. Retrieved from https://www.ted.com/talks/carol_dweck_the_power_of_believing_that_you_can_improve

Ennis, R. P., Royer, D. J., Lane, K. L., Menzies, H. M., Oakes, W. P., & Schellman, L. E. (2018). Behavior-specific praise: An effective, efficient, low-intensity strategy to support student success. *Beyond Behavior, 27*, 134–139. doi:10.1177/1074295618798587

Evan, G. W., & Cassells, R. C. (2014). Childhood poverty, cumulative risk exposure, and mental health in emerging adults. *Clinical Psychological Science, 2*, 287–296. doi:10.1177/2167702613501496

Farmer, T. W., Lines, M. M., & Hamm, J. V. (2011). Revealing the invisible hand: The role of teachers in children's peer experiences. *Journal of Applied Developmental Psychology, 32*, 247–256. doi:10.1016/j.appdev.2011.04.006

Fluke, S. M., & Peterson, R. L. (2013, October). *Positive behavior interventions & supports* [Strategy brief]. Lincoln, NE: Student Engagement Project, University of Nebraska-Lincoln and the Nebraska Department of Education. Retrieved from http://k12engagement.unl.edu

Friend, M., & Cook, L. (1990). Collaboration as a predictor for success in school reform. *Journal of Educational and Psychological Consultation, 1*, 69–86. doi.org/10.1207/s1532768xjepc0101_4

Friend, M., & Cook, L. (2010). Interactions: Collaboration skills for school professionals (6th ed.). Upper Saddle River, NJ: Pearson/Merrill.

Gable, R. A., Hester, P. H., Rock, M. L., & Huges, K. G. (2009). Back to basics: Rules, praise, ignoring, and reprimands revisited. *Intervention in School and Clinic, 44*, 195–205. doi:10.1177/1053451208328831

Gage, N. A., & McDaniel, S. (2012). Creating smarter classrooms: Data-based decision making for effective classroom management. *Beyond Behavior, 22*, 48–55. doi:10.1177/10742956120220108

Garby, L. (2013). Direct bullying: Criminal act or mimicking what has been learned? *Education, 133*, 448–450. Retrieved from http://www.projectinnovation.biz/education.

Gershoff, E. T., & Font, S. A. (2016). *Corporal punishment in U.S. public schools: Prevalence, disparities in use, and status in state and federal policy.* Bethesda, MD: U.S. National Library of Medicine, National Institute of Health. Retrieved from https://www.ncbi.nlm.nih.gov/pmc/articles/PMC5766273/

Gershoff, E. T., Purtell, K. M., & Holas I. (2015). *Corporal punishment in U.S. public schools: Legal precedents, current practices, and future policy.* Springer Briefs in Psychology Series, Advances in Child and Family Policy and Practice Subseries. doi:10.1007/978-3-319-14818-2

Gioia, G. A., Isquith, P. K., Guy, S. C., & Kenworthy, L. (2015). Behavior rating inventory of executive function (2nd ed.) [Measurement instrument]. Lutz, FL: PARInc.

Gordon, T. (2003). *Teacher effectiveness training: The program proven to help teachers bring out the best in students of all ages.* New York, NY: Three Rivers Press.

Gremmen, M. C., van den Berg, Y. H. M., Segers, E., & Cillessen, A. H. N. (2016). Considerations for classroom seating arrangements and the role of teacher characteristics and beliefs. *Social Psychology of Education, 19,* 749–774. doi:10.1007/s11218-016-9353-y

Gresham, F. M., Elliott, S. N., Cook, C. R., Vance M. J., & Kettler, R. (2010). Cross-informant agreement for ratings for social skill and problem ratings: An investigation of the Social Skills Improvement System–rating scales. *Psychological Assessment, 22,* 157–166. doi:10.1037/a0018124

Gresham, F. M., Gansle, K. A., & Noell, G. H. (1993). Treatment integrity in applied behavior analysis with children. *Journal of Applied Behavior Analysis, 26,* 257–263. doi:10.1901/jaba.1993.26-257

Hamilton-Jones, B. M., & Vail, C. O. (2014). Preparing special educators for collaboration in the classroom: Pre-service teachers' beliefs and perspectives. *International Journal of Special Education, 29,* 76–86. Retrieved from http://www.internationaljournalofspecialeducation.com

Hangry. (n.d.). In *OxfordDictionaries.com.* Retrieved from http://www.https://www.lexico.com/en/definition/hangry

Hart Barnett, J. (2018). Three evidence-based strategies that support social skills and play among young children with autism spectrum disorders. *Early Childhood Education Journal, 46,* 665–672. doi:10.1007/s10643-018-0911-0

Hester, P. P., Hendrickson, J. M., & Gable, R. A. (2009). Forty years later—The value of praise, ignoring, and rules for preschoolers at risk for behavior disorders. *Education and Treatment of Children, 32,* 513–535. doi:10.1353/etc.0.0067

Hollingshead, A., Kroeger, S. D., Altus, J., & Trytten, J. B. (2016). A case study of positive behavior supports-based interventions in a seventh-grade urban classroom. *Preventing School Failure: Alternative Education for Children and Youth, 60,* 278–285. doi:10.1080/1045988X.2015.1124832

Horner, R. H., & Sugai, G. (2000). School-wide behavior support: An emerging initiative. *Journal of Positive Behavior Interventions, 2,* 231–232. doi:10.1177/109830070000200407

Horner, R. H., & Sugai, G. (2015). School-wide PBIS: An example of applied behavior analysis implemented at a scale of social importance. *Behavior Analysis in Practice, 8*(1), 80–85. doi:10.1007/s40617-015-0045-4

Horner, R. H., Sugai, G., & Anderson, C. M. (2010). Examining the evidence base for schoolwide positive behavior support. *Focus on Exceptional Children, 42*(8), 1–15. doi:10.17161/foec.v42i8.6906

Horner, R. H., Sugai, G., Todd, A. W., & Lewis-Palmer, T. (2000). Elements of behavioral support plans: A technical brief. *Exceptionality, 8,* 205–216. doi:10.1207/S15327035EX0803_6

Hoy, A. W., & Weinstein, C. S. (2006). Student and teacher perspectives on classroom management. In C. M. Evertson & C. S. Weinstein (Eds.), *Handbook of classroom management: Research, practice, and contemporary issues* (pp. 181–219). Mahwah, NJ: Erlbaum.

Hughes, J. E. A., Ward, J., Gruffydd, E., Baron-Cohen, S., Smith, P., Allison, C., & Simner, J. (2018). Savant syndrome has a distinct psychological profile in autism. *Molecular Autism, 9,* 1–53. doi:10.1186/s13229-018-0237-1

Hughes, K., & Coplan, R. (2017). Why classroom climate matters for children high in anxious solitude: A study of differential susceptibility. *School Psychology Quarterly*, *33*(1), 94–102. doi:10.1037/spq00 00201

Individuals with Disabilities Education Act Amendments of 1997, 20 U.S.C. §§ 1400 et seq. (2003).

Individuals with Disabilities Education Improvement Act of 2004, 20 U.S.C. §§ 1400 et seq. (2018).

Ingraham v. Wright, 430 U.S. 651 (1977).

Iwata, B. A., & DeLeon, I. (1996). *The Functional Analysis Screening Tool* [Measurement instrument]. Gainesville: The Florida Center on Self-Injury, The University of Florida.

Kang, S. (2016). Inequality and crime revisited: Effects of local inequality and economic segregation on crime. *Journal of Population Economics*, *29*(2), 593–626. doi:10.1007/s00148-015-0579-3

Kauffman, J., Mostert, M., Trent, S., & Pullen, P. (2006). *Managing classroom behavior: A reflective case-based approach*. Upper Saddle River, NJ: Pearson.

Keeping All Students Safe Act, H. R. 7124, 115th Cong. (2018).

Kelshaw-Levering, K., Sterling-Turner, H. E., Henry, J. R., & Skinner, C. H. (2000). Random-ized interdependent group contingencies: Group reinforcement with a twist. *Psychology in the Schools*, *37*, 523–533. doi:10.1002/1520-6807(200011)37:63.0.CO

Ketterlin-Geller, L. R., Baumer, P., & Lichon, K. (2015). Administrators as advocates for teacher collaboration. *Intervention in School and Clinic*, *51*(1), 51–57. doi.org/10.1177/1053451214542044

Knackendoffel, A., Dettmer, P., & Thurston, L. P. (2018). *Collaborating, consulting, and working in teams for students with special needs* (8th ed.). New York, NY: Pearson.

Kounin, J. S. (1970). *Discipline and group management in classrooms* (2nd ed.). New York, NY: Holt, Rinehart, and Winston.

Lambert, A. M., Tingstrom, D. H., Sterling, H. E., Dufrene, B. A., & Lynne, S. (2015). Effects of tootling on classwide disruptive and appropriate behavior of upper-elementary students. *Behavior Modification*, *39*, 413–430. doi:10.1177/0145445514566506

Landrum, T., Tankersley, M., & Kauffman, J. (2003). What is special about special education for students with emotional or behavioral disorders? *The Journal of Special Education*, *37*, 148–156. doi:10.1177/00224669030370030401

Lane, K. L., Wehby, J., & Menzies, H. M. (2003). Social skills instruction for students at risk for antisocial behavior: The effects of small-group instruction. *Behavioral Disorders*, *28*, 229–248. doi:10.1177/019874290302800308

LeBlanc, L. A., Raetz, P. B., Sellers, T. P., & Carr, J. E. (2016). A proposed model for selecting measurement procedures for the assessment and treatment of problem behavior. *Behavior Analysis in Practice*, *9*, 77–83. doi:10.1007/s40617-015-0063-2

Lerman, D. C., Hovanetz, A., Strobel, M., & Tetreault, A. (2009). Accuracy of teacher-collected descriptive analysis data: A comparison of narrative and structured recording formats. *Journal of Behavioral Education*, *18*, 157–172. doi:10.1007/s10864-009-9084-7

Lewis, T. J., Scott, T. M., & Sugai, G. (1994). The problem behavior questionnaire: A teacher-based instrument to develop functional hypotheses of problem behavior in general educa-tion classrooms. *Diagnostique*, *19*, 103–115. doi:10.1177/073724779401900207

Lindsley, O. R. (1985). *Quantified trends in the results of behavior analysts*. Presidential address at the Eleventh Annual Convention of the Association for Behavior Analysis, Columbus, OH.

Lindsley, O. R. (1991). From technical jargon to plain English for application. *Journal of Applied Behavior Analysis, 24,* 449–458. doi:10.1902/jaba.1991.24-449

Lum, J. D. K., Tingstrom, D. H., Dufrene, B. A., Radley, K. C., & Lynne, S. (2017). Effects on tootling on classwide disruptive and academically engaged behavior of general-education high school students. *Psychology in the Schools, 54,* 370–384. doi:10.1002/pits.22002

Maldonado-Carreno, C., & Votruba-Drzal, E. (2011). Teacher-child relationships and the development of academic and behavioral skills during elementary school: A within- and between-child analysis. *Child Development, 82,* 601–616. doi:10.1111/j.1467-8624.2010.01533.x

Mandinach, E. B., & Gummer, E. S. (2013). A systemic view of implementing data literacy in educator preparation. *Educational Researcher, 42,* 30–37. doi:10.3102/0013189X12459803

Maslach, C., & Leiter, M. P. (2016). Understanding the burnout experience: Recent research and its implications for psychiatry. *World Psychiatry, 15,* 103–111. doi:10.1002/wps.20311

McHugh, M. B., Tingstrom, D. H., Radley, K. C., Barry, C. T., & Walker, K. M. (2016). Effects of tootling on classwide and individual disruptive and academically engaged behavior of lower-elementary students. *Behavioral Interventions, 31,* 332–354. doi:10.1002/bin.1447.

McIntosh, K., Borgmeier, C., Anderson, C., Horner, R., Rodriquez, B., & Tobin, T. (2008). Technical adequacy of functional assessment checklist: Teachers and staff (FACTS) FBA interview measure. *Journal of Positive Behavior Interventions, 10*(1), 33–45. doi:10.1177/1098300707311619

McKeown, S., Stringer, M., & Cairns, E. (2015). Classroom segregation: Where do students sit and how is this related to group relations? *British Educational Research Journal, 42*(1), 40–55. doi:10.1002/berj.3200

McLeskey, J., Barringer, M-D., Billingsley, B., Brownell, M., Jackson, D., Kennedy, M., . . . Ziegler, D. (2017). *High-leverage practices in special education.* Arlington, VA: Council for Exceptional Children & CEEDAR Center.

McLoyd, V. C., Kaplan, R., Hardaway, C. R., & Wood, D. (2007). Does endorsement of physical discipline matter? Assessing moderating influences on the maternal and child psychological correlates of physical discipline in African American families. *Journal of Family Psychology, 21,* 165–175. doi:10.1037/0893-3200.21.2.165

Mendler, A., & Curwin, R. (1983). *Taking charge in the classroom.* Reston, VA: Reston Publishing.

Miller, L. K. (2006). *Principles of everyday behavior analysis.* Belmont, CA: Wadsworth.

Milner, H., & Tenore, F. B. (2010). Classroom management in diverse classrooms. *Urban Education, 45,* 560–603. doi:10.1177/0042085910377290

Miltenberger, R. (2004). *Behavior modification: Principles and procedure* (3rd ed.). Belmont, CA: Wadsworth.

Miltenberger, R. (2008). *Behavior modification.* Belmont, CA: Wadsworth.

Murawski, W. W. (2012). 10 tips for using co-planning time more efficiently. *Teaching Exceptional Children, 44*(4), 8–15. doi.org/10.1177/004005991204400401

Murphy, E. L., & McKenzie, V. L. (2016). The impact of family functioning and school connectedness on preadolescent sense of mastery. *Journal of Psychologists and Counsellors in Schools, 26,* 35–51. doi:10.1017/jgc.2015.17

Myers, D. M., Simonsen, B., & Sugai, G. (2011). Increasing teachers' use of praise with a response-to-intervention approach. *Education and Treatment of Children, 34*, 35–39. doi:/10.1353/etc.2011.0004

Nasir, N.i.S., Jones, A., & McLaughlin, M. (2011). School connectedness for students in low-income urban high schools. *Teachers College Record, 113*, 1755–1793. Retrieved from http://www.tcrecord.org

National Center for Children in Poverty. (2019). *Child poverty*. Retrieved from http://www.nccp.org/topics/childpoverty.html

National Center on Safe Supportive Learning Environments. (2014). *Office of Special Education Programs Technical Assistance Center on Positive Behavior Interventions*. Retrieved from http://www.pbis.org

Newton, J. S., Horner, R. H., Algozzine, B., Todd, A. W., & Algozzine, K. (2012). A randomized wait-list controlled analysis of the implementation of integrity of team-initiated problem solving processes. *Journal of School Psychology, 50*, 421–441. doi:10.1016/j.jsp.2012.04.002

O'Donnell, A. M., Reeve, J., & Smith, J. K. (2009). *Educational psychology: Reflection for action*. Hoboken, NJ: John Wiley & Sons.

O'Neill, R. E., Horner, R. H., Albin, R. W., Sprague, J. R., Storey, K., & Newton, J. S. (1997). *Functional assessment and program development for problem behavior: A practical handbook* (2nd ed.). Pacific Grove, CA: Brooks/Cole.

Paclawskyj, T., Matson, J., Rush, K., Smalls, Y., & Vollmer, T. (2000). Questions about behavior function (QABF): Behavioral checklist for functional assessment of aberrant behavior. *Research in Developmental Disabilities, 21*, 223–229. doi:10.1016/S0891-4222(00)00036-6

Pinkelman, S. E., McIntosh, K., Rasplica, C. K., Berg, T., & Strickland-Cohen, M. K. (2015). Perceived enablers and barriers related to sustainability of school-wide positive behavioral interventions and supports. *Behavioral Disorders, 40*(3), 171–183. doi:10.17988/0198-7429-40.3.171

Rasmussen, M., Damsgaard, M. T., Holstein, B. E., Poulsen, L. H., & Due, P. (2005). School connectedness and daily smoking among boys and girls: The influence of parental smoking norms. *European Journal of Public Health, 15*, 607–612. doi:10.1093/eurpub/cki039

Rathel, J. M., Drasgow, E., Brown, W. H., & Marshall, K. J. (2014). Increasing induction-level teachers' positive to negative communication ratio and use of behavior-specific praise through e-mailed performance and its effect on students' task engagement. *Journal of Positive Behavior Interventions, 16*, 219–233. doi:10.1177/109800713492856

Ray, K. P., Skinner, C. H., & Watson, T. S. (1999). Transferring stimulus control via momentum to increase compliance in a student with autism: A demonstration of collaborative consultation. *School Psychology Review, 28*(4), 622–628. Retrieved from https://naspjournals.org/loi/spsr

Reinke, W. M., Herman, K. C., & Stormont, M. (2013). Classroom-level positive behavior supports in schools implementing SW-PBIS: Identifying areas for enhancement. *Journal of Positive Behavior Interventions, 15*, 39–50. doi:10.1177/1098300712459079

Royer, D. J., Lane, K. L., Dunlap, K. D., & Ennis, R. P. (2019). A systematic review of teacher-delivered behavior-specific praise on K–12 student performance. *Remedial and Special Education, 40*, 112–128. doi:10.1177/0741932517751054

Rubie-Davies, C. (2014). *Becoming a high expectation teacher: Raising the bar*. London, UK: Routledge.

Sandall, S. R., Schwartz, I. S., & Lacroix, B. (2004). Interventionists' perspectives about data collection in integrated early childhood classrooms. *Journal of Early Intervention, 26,* 161–174. doi:10.1177/105381510402600301

Santos, C. E., & Collins, M. A. (2016). Ethnic identity, school connectedness, and achievement in standardized tests among Mexican-origin youth. *Cultural Diversity and Ethnic Minority Psychology, 22,* 447–452. doi:10.1037/cdp0000065

Simonsen, B., Fairbanks, S., Briesch, A., Myers, D., & Sugai, G. (2008). Evidence based practices in classroom management: Considerations for research to practice. *Education and Treatment of Children, 31,* 351–380. doi:10.1353/etc.0.0007

Skiba, R. J., Horner, R. H., Chung, C. G., Rausch, M. K., May, S. L., & Tobin, T. (2011). Race is not neutral: A national investigation of African American and Latino disproportionality in school discipline. *School Psychology Review, 40,* 85–107. Retrieved from http://www.nasponline.org/publications/spr/sprmain.aspx

Skinner, C. H., Cashwell, C. S., & Dunn, M. S. (2008). Independent and interdependent group contingencies: Smoothing the rough waters. *Special Services in the Schools, 12,* 61–78. doi:10.1300/J008v12n01_04

Skinner, C. H., Cashwell, T. H., & Skinner, A. L. (2000). Increasing tootling: The effects of a peer-monitored group contingency program on students' reports of peers' prosocial behaviors. *Psychology in the Schools, 37,* 263–270. doi:10.1002/(SICI)1520-6807(2000005)37:3<263::AID-PITS6>3.0.CO;2-C

Soutter, M., & Seider, S. (2013). College access, student success, and the new character education. *Journal of College and Character, 14,* 351–356. doi:10.1515/jcc-2013-0044

Spence, S. H. (2003). Social skills training with children and young people: Theory, evidence and practice. *Child and Adolescent Mental Health, 8,* 84–96. doi:10.1111/1475-3588.00051

Steedly, K., Schwartz, A., Levin, M., & Luke, S. (2011). Social skills and academic achievement. *Evidence for Education, 3,* 1–15. Retrieved from http://www.nichcy.org

Straus, M. A. (2001). *Beating the devil out of them: Corporal punishment in American families and its effects on children.* Edison, NJ: Transaction Publishers.

Strom, I. F., Thoresen, S., Wentzel-Larsen, T., & Dyb, G. (2013). Violence, bullying and academic achievement: A study of 15-year-old adolescents and their school environment. *Child Abuse & Neglect, 37,* 243–251. doi:10.1016/j.chiabu.2012.10.010

Sugai, G., Horner, R. H., Dunlap, G., Hieneman, M., Lewis, T. J., Nelson, C. M., . . . Ruef, M. (2000). Applying positive behavioral support and functional behavioral assessment in schools. *Journal of Positive Behavioral Interventions, 2,* 131–143. doi:10.1177/109830070000200302

Sulzer-Azaroof, B., & Mayer, G. R. (1991). *Behavior analysis for lasting change.* New York, NY: Sloan Education.

Sutherland, K. S., Wehby, J. H., & Copeland, S. R. (2000). Effect of varying rates of behavior-specific praise on the on-task behavior of students with EBD. *Journal of Emotional and Behavioral Disorders, 1,* 2–9. doi:10.1177/106342660000800101

Tanol, G., Johnson, L., McComas, J., & Cote, E. (2010). Responding to rule violations or rule following: A comparison of two versions of the good behavior game with kindergarten students. *Journal of School Psychology, 48,* 337–355. doi:10.1016/j.jsp.2010.06.001

Tiger, J. H., Hanley, G. P., & Bruzek, J. (2008). Functional communication training: A review and practical guide. *Behavior Analysis in Practice, 1,* 16–23. doi:10.1007/BF03391716

U.S. Census Bureau. (2019). *Poverty thresholds*. Retrieved from https://www.census.gov/data/tables/time-series/demo/income-poverty/historical-poverty-thresholds.html

U.S. Department of Education. (2007). *NCLB: More local freedom. The facts about school safety*. Retrieved from https://www2.ed.gov/nclb/freedom/safety/keepingkids.html

U.S. Department of Education, Office of Special Education and Rehabilitative Services, Office of Special Education Programs. (2008) *40th Annual Report to Congress on the Implementation of the Individuals with Disabilities Education Act*. Washington, DC.

U.S. Government Accountability Office. (2009). Selected cases of death and abuse at public and private schools and treatment centers. In Kutz, G. D. (Ed.), *Seclusions and Restraints, (GAO-09-719T)* (pp. 3–58). Washington, DC.

van den Berg, Y. H. M., Segers, E., & Cillessen, A. H. N. (2012). Changing peer perceptions and victimization through classroom arrangements: A field experiment. *Journal of Abnormal Child Psychology, 40,* 403–412. doi:10.1007/s10802-011-9567-6

van den Berg, Y. H. M., & Stotlz, S. (2018). Enhancing social inclusion of children with externalizing problems through classroom seating arrangements: A randomized controlled trial. *Journal of Emotional and Behavioral Disorders, 26*(1), 31–41. doi:10.1177/1063426617740561

Walker, J. D., & Barry, C. (2018). Assessing and supporting social-skill needs for students with high-incidence disabilities. *Teaching Exceptional Children, 51,* 18–30. doi:10.1177/0040059918790219

Walker, J. D., & Brigham, F. J. (2017). Manifestation determination decisions and students with emotional/ behavioral disorders. *Journal of Emotional and Behavioral Disorders, 25,* 107–118. doi:10.1177/1063426616628819

Wang, M., & Degol, J. (2016). School climate: A review of the construct, measurement, and impact on student outcomes. *Educational Psychology Review, 28,* 315–352. doi:10.1007/s10648-015-9319-1.

Will, M. N., Currans, K., Smith, J., Weber, S., Duncan, A., Burton, J., . . . Anixt, J. (2018). Evidence-based interventions for children with autism spectrum disorder. *Current Problems in Pediatric and Adolescent Health Care, 48,* 234–249. doi:10.1016/j.cppeds.2018.08.014

Yell, M. (2019). *The law and special education* (5th ed.). New York, NY: Pearson.

Yell, M. L., Katsiyannis, A., Ennis, R. P., Losinski, M., & Christle, C. A. (2016). Avoiding substantive errors in individualized education program development. *Teaching Exceptional Children, 49,* 31–40. doi:10.1177/0040059916662204

INDEX

Note: Page numbers in **bold** indicate non-text material.

A

A-B-A-B design, 230, **230**, 245
A-B-A design, 228–230, **229**, 245
A-B-C charts, 258–261, **261**, 262, 345
A-B-C contingency, 58, 74
A-B-C data collection, **201**, 260, **261**
A-B design, 227–228, **228**, 245
Academic supports, 349
Access behaviors, 267, **279**
Accessible Instruction website, **337**
Access Project, **337**
Accuracy, 213–214, 218
  definition of, 345
  factors that pose threats to, 215
Action and expression, 335–336, 343
  change implementation, 333
  definition, 345
Active listening
  for behavior management, 7
  for classroom management, 115
  for conflict resolution, 185
  definition, 345
Active relaxing, 341–342
Activity-based reinforcers, 91
ADHD. *See* Attention deficit/hyperactivity
  disorder
Administration, 115–117, 119
African American students, 16
All About Me posters, **189**
Alternative behaviors, 73–74
American Indian students, 32

Analysis
  applied behavior analysis (ABA), 5–6, 58,
    222–223
    definition, 345
    summary, 244
  functional, 262–265
    conditions and examples, 262–263, **263**,
      264
    definition, 349
    summary, 270
  visual, 240–243, 245, 356
Anecdotal notes, 258
Anecdotal observation, 258
Antecedent-Behavior-Consequence recording,
  258–262
  A-B-C charts, 258–261, **261**, 262, 345
  A-B-C data collection, **201**, 260, **261**
Antecedent event strategies, 282–284, 293–294,
  345
Antecedents, 6, 58–59, 210–211, 218, 258–259,
  269
  contributing factors, 259
  definition, 258, 345
  summary, 74
Anti-Drug Abuse Act, 16
Antiseptic bounce, 291
Anxiety, 132
Applied behavior analysis (ABA), 5–6, 58,
  222–223
  definition, 345
  summary, 244
ASD. *See* Autism spectrum disorder

Assertive management style, 10, 21, 345
Assessment
    direct, 257, 269, 347
    direct strategies, 256–252
    functional, 268–269. *See also* Functional
        behavior assessments (FBAs)
    indirect, 269
        definition of, 350
        examples, 251–252
        tools for, 256, **257**
    indirect strategies, 251–256
    of need, 309–310
Attainable goals, 160
Attention, 266
    contingent, 262–263, **263**, **264**
    example replacement behaviors for getting,
        279
Attention deficit/hyperactivity disorder
        (ADHD), 39–42, 55
    classroom considerations, 132
    classroom examples, **40**, **41**, **42**
    combined presentation, 41–42
    definition of, 39, 345
    predominantly hyperactive/impulsive
        presentation, 41
    predominantly inattentive presentation, 40
Autism spectrum disorder (ASD), 48–52, 55
    classroom examples, **49**, **50–51**
    definition of, 48, 345
    myths about, 48–49
    umbrella diagnosis of, 50
Automatic behavior, 268, **279**
Avoidance, 266–267
    contingent, 262–263, **263**, **264**
    example replacement behaviors, **279**

B

Backup reinforcers, 303, **304**, 345
Bar graphs, 236, **236**, 245
Baseline conditions, 225
    decreasing, 226, **227**
    definition, 346

multiple baseline design, 230–232, **231**
    definition, 351
    summary, 245
Behavior(s)
    ABCs of, 58
    alternative, 73–74
    antecedents or triggers that precede, 210–211,
        218
    automatic, 268, **279**
    basics of, 57–76
    communicating with parents about, 107–110,
        118
    definition of, 59, 346
    functional assessment of, 248–262, 349
    functions of, 265–268, 270
    intensity scales, 208, **209**
    legal considerations, 15–18
    measurable, objective, and observable (MOO),
        198, 216, 259–260
    operant, 6, 351
    reflexive, 6
    replacement, 274–275. *See also* Target
        behavior(s)
        considerations for selecting, 278–280
        definition of, 353
        examples, **279**
    respondent, 6, 353
    self-stimulatory, 51–52
    stereotyped, 51–52, 354
    teaching alternative behaviors, 73–74
Behavioral data collection, 195–218
    methods, 200–210, **201**
    summary, 216–218
Behavioral disorders. *See* Emotional and
        behavioral disorders (EBDs)
Behavioral intervention plans (BIPs), 14, 19,
        248–249, 273–294, 349
    for classroom management, 110, 116
    construction, 275–280
    critical components, 196
    definition, 346
    summary, 293–294
    team approach to, 292–294

Behavioral interventions. *See also* Positive behavioral intervention and supports (PBIS)
    antecedent event strategies, 282–284
    consequence strategies, 288–289
    setting event strategies, 280–282, 354
    teaching strategies, 284–288
Behavioral momentum, 283, 346
Behavioral skills training (BST), 285–286
    prerequisites, 285
    steps, **285**
Behavioral support plans (BSPs), 248
Behavioral teaching strategies, 284–288
Behavior analysis. *See* Applied behavior analysis (ABA)
Behavior contracts, 298–300, 349
    definition, 346
    example, **300**
    guidelines and considerations, 300–302
    summary, 322
Behavior management, 3–22
    class-wide, 162
    key questions to prompt teacher self-reflection, **332**
    prominent theorists, 5–13
Behavior modification, 222–223
Behavior rating scales, 319
Behavior skills training (BST), 294, 346
Behavior-specific praise (BSP), 181–182, 192, 346
Behavior Support Plan. *See* Behavioral intervention plan
Believability, 225–226
Best practices for positive relationships, 176–181, 192
BINGO activity, **191**
Black students, 32
Board-Certified Behavior Analysts (BCBAs), 73–74, 262
Bounce, antiseptic, 291
Boys, 16
Brown Bag/Warm Fuzzies activity, **189**
BST. *See* Behavior skills training
Burnout, 341–343

C

Canter, Lee and Marlene, 9–10, 21
Center for Universal Design in Education, **337**
Centre for Applied Special Technology (CAST), **337**
Change implementation, 333
Character education, 314–317
    definition of, 308, 346
    key areas for, 308–309
    summary, 323
Chartdog 2.0, **214**
Check-in check-out (CICO), 96, 346
Checklists, 256, 318, 321
Child Behavior Checklist (CBCL), 256, **257**
Choice Theory, 6–7, 21, 346
Classical conditioning, 6, 346
Classroom(s)
    cluster or group arrangements, 124–125, **125**, 347
    considerations for, 128–129, 131–132
    culturally responsive, 35–36, **36**
    democratic, 316
    design planning tools for, 128, **128**
    horseshoe arrangement, 122–123, **123**, 349
    inclusive, 37, 55, 350
    individual considerations, 128–129
    learning zones, 129–131
    movement considerations, 129
    pairs arrangement, 125–126, **126**, 351
    physical layout, 122–129, 135
    questions to ask about arrangement, **133**
    rows arrangement, 123–124, **124**
    safety considerations, 129
    setting up, 137–153
Classroom Architect website, **128**
Classroom climate, 132–134, 182
Classroom Floor Planner tool, **128**
Classroom management
    assertive style, 10, 21, 345
    collaboration for, 103–119
    communication for, 103–119
    definition of, 4, 346

Classroom management *(continued)*
  foundations, 3–76
  general, 284
  hostile style, 9–10, 21, 349
  inclusive classrooms, 37, 55, 350
  nonassertive style, 9, 21, 351
  planning template, **4**
  school-wide systems, 81–102
  stoplight system, 354
Classroom management communities, 79–170
Classroom procedures
  establishing, **139**
  samples, **140**, **141**
  summary, 152–153
  think sheet for identifying and teaching, 142, **143**
Classroom rules, 147, 152–153, 353
  establishing, **139**, 147–150
  key points, 148
  key tenets, 152
  measurable, objective, and observable (MOO), 148
  rights and responsibilities grids, 149, **149**
  ways to teach, 149, **149**
Class-wide behavior management, 162
Climate, classroom, 132–134
Clusters or groups, 124–125, **125**, 347
Cognitive rigidity, 51
Collaboration, 118
  classroom management, 103–119
  coteaching, 113–115, **114**, 347
  definition of, 347
  with other professionals, 111
  questions and prompts for, **114**
  team approach, 292–293
Collaboration for Effective Educator Development, Accountability, and Reform (CEEDAR), 14
Communication
  with administrators, 119
  about behavior, 107–110, 118
  classroom management, 103–119
  functional communication training (FCT), 286–288, 349

  with parents, 107–110, 118
  welcome packets, **106**, 106–107
Community service, 316–317
Competence
  cultural, 34, 347
  social, 308–309, 322, 354
Competing behavior pathways, 275, 293, 347
Competing behavior pathways charts, 275–278, **276**, **277**
Condition change line, 234–235
Conditioned responses, 6, 21, 347
Conditioning
  classical, 6, 346
  operant, 5–6, 58–61
    for classroom management, 93
    definition of, 351
  respondent, 6
Condition labels, 234–235
Conflict cycle, 181, 347
Conflict resolution, 184–185, 192
  no-lose, 8, 351
  problem-solving prompts, 185, **186**
  summary, 192
  ways to facilitate, 185
Confounding, 228
Consequences, 6, 60, 260, 270
  definition, 60, 93, 260, 347
  intervention strategies, 288–289, 294, 347
  legal considerations, 15–18
  logical, 10
  maintaining, 275
  PBIS-specific, 93
Contingency, 63–64
  A-B-C, 58, 74
  definition of, 347
  group. *See* Group contingencies
  three-term, 58, 355
Contingent attention, 262–263, **263**, **264**
Contingent escape/avoid, 262–263, **263**, **264**
Continuous reinforcement, 64–65, 347
Contracts. *See* Behavior contracts
Control conditions, 226, 262–263, **263**, **264**
Control Theory. *See* Choice Theory
Corporal punishment, 16

Coteaching, 113–115, 118
   definition of, 113, 347
   questions and prompts for, **114**
Council for Exceptional Children (CEC), 14
Cultural competence, 34, 347
Cultural differences, 186–188, 192
Cultural factors, 30, 34–36
Culturally responsive classrooms, 35–36, **36**
The Curriculum Corner, **214**
Curwin and Mendler, 12–13, 22

D

Daily schedules, 140–141
   samples, **141**, **142**
Data analysis, 331–333
Data collection
   A-B-C, **201**, 260, **261**
   A-B-C charts, 258–261, **261**, 262, 345
   alternative methods, 134
   behavioral, 195–218
   considerations for, 213–216
   discreet, 134
   interval, **201**. *See also* Partial interval
      recording; Whole interval recording
   methods for, 212, **213**
   momentary time sampling, 206–207, 217,
      351
   partial interval recording, 205–206
     definition, 351–352
     example, 205, **206**
     formula for, 205, 217
     summary, 217
   school-wide, 94–95
   for self-reflection, 329
   staggered, 211, **212**
   timelines for, 210–212, **213**
   tools for, 213, **214**
   websites for, **214**
   whole interval recording, 204, 217, 356
Data displays, 232–233
Data levels, 242, **243**, 245, 350
Data path, 235
Data points, 235

Dead Man Test, 59
Dead Person Test, 59
Democratic classrooms, 316
Demonstration, **312**
Dependent group contingencies, 163, **163**
   definition, 163, 347
   summary, 169
Dependent variables, 223, 225, 347
Design planning tools, 128, **128**
Developmental characteristics, 26–30, **27–29**
   cultural, social, and environmental factors,
      30–37
   definition, 26, 347
Differential reinforcement of low rates (DRL) of
      behavior, 166, 170, 347
Dignity, 12–13
Direct assessment, 269
   definition of, 257, 347
   strategies for, 256–252
Direct instruction, 311–313
Disabilities. *See* Students with disabilities
Disability categories, 37, **38**
Discipline hierarchy, 9, 347
Disrespect, 180–181, 198
Diversity, 186–188, 192
Documentation
   A-B-C sheets, 260, **261**
   records review, 252, **253–255**
Dreikurs, Rudolf, 5, 10, 21
Drug-Free Schools and Communities Act, 16
Duration recording, **201**, 202–203
   definition, 348
   summary, 217

E

Education
   character, 314–317, 346
   social skills instruction, 308–314
Educators. *See* Professionals
Elementary settings
   relationships between students, 184
   sample classroom procedures, **140**, **141**
   sample daily schedule, **141**

Emotional and behavioral disorders (EBDs),
     45–46, 55, 348
Emotional control, 42, **43**
Emotional intelligence (EQ), 309
Engagement, 155–170
   definition, 348
   UDL guidelines for, 334–337, 343
Environmental factors, 30, 32–33, 348
Environmental setting events, 280
EQ (emotional intelligence), 309
Errorless prompting, 151, 348
Escape/avoid, 266–267
     contingent, 262–263, **263**, **264**
     example replacement behaviors for, **279**
Event recording, 202, 348
Evidence-based practices (EBPs), 13–14
   resources, **14**
   summary, 22
Executive function deficits, 42–45, 132
Executive functions (EFs), 42, 55
   classroom considerations for students with
        challenges, 132
   definition, 348
   domains, 42, **43–44**
Expectations
   definition of, 145, 348
   establishing, **139**, 145–147
   explanation of, **106**, 106–107
   measurable, objective, and observable (MOO),
        89–90, 198
   school-wide, 87–88, **88**, **89**
   summary, 152–153
Experimental control, 223, 244, 348
Experiments, 225
   A-B-A-B design, 230, **230**, 245
   A-B-A design, 228–230, **229**, 245
   A-B design, 227–228, **228**, 245
   baseline conditions, 225
   control conditions, 226
   multiple baseline design, 230–232, **231**
     definition, 351
     summary, 245
   reversal design, 228–230, 245
   single-subject design, 223–232, 244, 354

study design, 244
Extinction, 70, 75, 289
   definition, 348
   summary, 294
Extinction burst, 70, 75, 348
Extrinsic motivation, 156–158

F

Family values, 31–32, 348
Feedback, **286**, **312**
First Day of School Questions Checklist, **339**
Five Items activity, **190**
Five Things in Common activity, **190**
Fixed interval (FI) reinforcement, 66–67, 348
Fixed ratio (FR) reinforcement, 66, 348
Force, 208, 349. *See also* Magnitude
Free and appropriate education (FAPE), 18, 110
Frequency counts, **201**, 202, 318–319
   data charts, 202, **203**
   definition, 349
   summary, 217
Functional analysis, 262–265
   conditions and examples, 262–263, **263**, **264**
   definition, 349
   summary, 270
Functional Analysis Screening Tool (FAST), 256
Functional assessment, 268–269. *See also*
        Functional behavior assessments (FBAs)
Functional Assessment Checklist for Teachers
        and Staff (FACTS), 256, **257**
Functional Assessment Interview (FAI), 256, **257**
Functional Assessment Screening Tool (FAST),
        257
Functional behavior assessments (FBAs), 14, 19,
        248–262
   best practice for, 110
   components, 196, 250–251, **251**, 269
   definition, 248, 349
   development of, 292
   indirect strategies, 251–256
   intervention, 96
   methods, 248, 250, **251**, 269
   summary, 269–270, 293

team approach, 292–294

working with administration, 116

Functional communication training (FCT),
    286–288, 349

G

Generalization, **312**, 314

Gesture prompts, 150–151, 349

Glasser, William, 5–7, 21

Goals

mistaken, 10

SMART, 159–161, 169

definition of, 354

guidelines for, **160**

Good Behavior Game, 165–166, 169, 349

Good Student Game, 166–167, 170, 349

Gordon, Thomas, 7–8, 21, 349

Grandma's Rule, 70, 75, 352

Graphs and graphing, 222, 233–240, 244–245

Group arrangements, 124–125, **125**, 347

Group contingencies, 161–162, **163**

considerations for, 167, 170

definition of, 161, 349

dependent, 163, **163**, 169, 347

helpful tips, 167–168

independent, **163**, 164, 169, 350

interdependent, **163**, 165, 169, 350

prerequisite skills, 167–168

risks, 168–170

summary, 169

Gun-Free Schools Act, 16–17

H

High-leverage practices (HLPs), 13–14

alerts, **334**

resources, **15**

High-Leverage Practices: Social/Emotional/
    Behavioral Practices website, **15**

High-Leverage Practices in Special Education
    website, **15**

Hispanic students, 32

Histograms, 236, **236**

Hopper, Grace, 328

Horseshoe arrangement, 122–123, **123**, 349

Hostile management style, 9–10, 21, 349

Humiliation. *See* Saving face

I

IDEA. *See* Individuals with Disabilities
    Education Act

IEP. *See* Individualized education program

I-messages

for behavior management, 7

for classroom management, 108

for conflict resolution, 185

definition, 349

Immediacy, 63–64

Inadvertent reinforcement, 168, 349

Inclusive classrooms, 37, 55, 350

Independent group contingencies, **163**, 164

definition, 164, 350

summary, 169

Independent variables, 223, 225, 350

Indirect assessment, 269

definition of, 350

examples, 251–252

strategies for, 251–256

tools for, 256, **257**

Individualized Education Program (IEP), 18–19,
    110–112, 116

definition of, 350

monitoring goals on, 196

Individualized Education Program (IEP)
    meetings, 249

Individualized Education Program (IEP) teams,
    292

Individualized supports. *See* Tier 3 interventions

Individuals with Disabilities Education Act
    (IDEA), 18–19, 21, 37–38, 110, 248–249

definition, 350

disability categories, 37, **38**

Individuals with Disabilities Education
    Improvement Act (IDEIA), 18, 21, 39,
    45–46, 82

Ingraham v. Wright, 16

Inhibition, 42, **43**

Initiation, 42, **43**

Instruction, 155–170

    direct, 311–313

    identifying instructional needs, 310, **311**

    key questions to prompt teacher self-reflection, **332**

    social skills, 308–314, 322

        considerations for, **311**

        definition of, 354

        suggested approach to, **312**

    UDL guidelines for, 335–336, 343

Intellectual disability (ID), 53–55, 350

Intelligence quotient (IQ), 309

Intensity of behavior scales, 208, **209**

Intensive, individualized supports. *See* Tier 3 interventions

Interdependent group contingencies, **163**, 165

    definition, 165, 350

    summary, 169

Intermittent reinforcement, 64–65, 75, 350

Internal control, 7

Interval data collection, **201**. *See also* Partial interval recording; Whole interval recording

Interview questions, 340, **340**

Interviews, 256, 350

Intrinsic motivation, 156–158

IQ (intelligence quotient), 309

IRIS Center, **14**, **15**, 333

I Trust activity, **191**

J

Job search questions, 340, **340**

Journaling, reflective, 330

Juvenile Justice and Delinquency Prevention Act (JJDPA), 15–16

K

Keeping All Students Safe Act, 18

Kounin, Jacob, 5, 11–12, 22, 354, 356

L

Landmark legislation, policies, and processes, 18

Language, person-first, 38–39

Latency, **201**, 207–208

    definition, 350

    summary, 217

Learning

    service, 316–317

    Universal Design for Learning (UDL), 334–337

        definition of, 342, 355

        guidelines for instruction, 335–336, 343

        resources, **337**

Learning disability. *See* specific learning disability (SLD)

Learning environments

    classroom layouts, 122–129, 135

    environmental factors, 30, 32–33, 348

    environmental setting events, 280

    least restrictive environment (LRE), 18

    physical, 121–135

Learning zones, 129–131, 135, 350

Least restrictive environment (LRE), 18

Legal considerations, 15–18

Legislation, landmark, 18

Level (data), 242, **243**, 245, 350

Line graphs, 233–235, 245

    examples, **234**, **235**, **241**, **242**

Listening, active

    for behavior management, 7

    for classroom management, 115

    for conflict resolution, 185

    definition of, 345

Locus, 260–261, 350

Logical consequences, 10

M

Magnitude (force), 208

    definition, 208, 350

    scales for measuring, 208, **209**

    summary, 218

Manifestation determination review (MDR), 18–21, 351

Materials, **332**

Measurable, objective, and observable (MOO) behaviors, 198, 216, 259–260

Measurable, objective, and observable (MOO) expectations, 89–90, 198

Measurable, objective, and observable (MOO) rules, 148

Measurable goals, 159

Mentoring, 349

Mistaken goals, 10

Modeling, 309–310

Momentary time sampling, 206–207, 217, 351

Money activity, **190**

Monitoring
self-monitoring, 317–321, 354
team approach, 292–293

Monitoring systems, 318–319

Motivation, 62, 156–161, 169
definition of, 156, 351
intrinsic vs extrinsic, 156–158, 169
strategies to motivate students, 158
summary, 169

Motivation Assessment Scale (MAS), 256, **257**

Movement: classroom considerations, 129

Multiple baseline design, 230–232, **231**
definition, 351
summary, 245

Multitiered systems of supports (MTSS), 82, 99, 351

N

Names, 176–177

National Center on Intensive Intervention, **14**

Needs assessment, 309–310

Negative punishment, 73, 76

Negative reinforcement, 67–70, **72**, 75, 351

Negative stimuli, 351

Neutral stimuli, 6, 21

No Child Left Behind Act (NCLB), 17, 21

No-lose conflict resolution, 8, 351

Nonassertive management style, 9, 21, 351

Noncontingent reinforcement, 290

O

Observation
anecdotal, 258
peer, 330

Operant behaviors, 6, 351

Operant conditioning, 5–6, 58–61
for classroom management, 93
definition of, 351

Operational definitions, 197, 216, 351

Organization, 42, **44**

Other Health Impairments (OHIs), 39

Overlapping, 11

P

Pairs arrangement, 125–126, **126**, 351

Paraprofessionals, 113

Parents
communicating about behavior with, 107–110, 118
working with, 104–107, 118

Partial interval recording, 205–206
definition, 351–352
example, 205, **206**
formula for, 205, 217
summary, 217

Partnerships, 104–105, 352

Pavlov, Ivan, 6, 21

PBIS World website, **214**

Peer groups, 184

Peer observation, 330

Peer pressure, 162

Permanent products, **201**, 209–210, 352

Person-first language, 38–39

Philosophy statements, 338

Physical learning environments
classroom layouts, 122–129, 135
setting up, 121–135

Physical prompts, 151, 352

Physiological setting events, 281
Planned Activity Check (PLACHECK), 206–207,
        217, 352
Planning
    1st-year of teaching, 337–340
    20th-year of teaching, 340–341
    behavioral intervention. *See* Behavioral
        intervention plans (BIPs)
    classroom design tools, 128, **128**
    executive function, 42, **44**
    safety plans, 98–100, 291
    for social skills instruction, 310
    whole child, 82
Policy, landmark, 18
Positive Behavioral Intervention and Supports
        (PBIS)
    administrative support for, 115, 117
    for behavior management, 15
    for classroom management, 83–95, 99, 134, 138
    communication of, 107
    consequences, 93
    definition of, 352
    group contingencies, 162
    PBIS-specific reinforcers, 91, 353
    principles of, 85
    school-wide (SWPBIS), 84
    school-wide expectations, 87–88, **88**, **89**
    school-wide procedures or routines, 89–91
    school-wide reinforcement, 91
    summary, 100
    tiers of intervention, **86**, 95–98, 100
Positive punishment, 73
Positive reinforcement, 67–68, **72**, 75
    alternative methods, 134
    definition, 352
Positive relationships: best practices for,
        176–181, 192
Positive statements, 182
    tootling, 185–186, 192
Postreinforcement pause, 66
Poverty, 32
Power struggles, 178–180
    definition, 352
    examples, **179–180**

Practice
    self-monitoring, 320
    social skills, **312**, 313
Praise
    behavior-specific, 181–182, 192, 346
    general, 182
Prediction, 225–226, 244, 352
Premack principle, 70, 75, 352
Problem Behavior Questionnaire, 256, **257**
Problem-solving prompts, 185, **186**
Procedures or routines
    definition of, 89, 138, 352
    establishing, 138–145, **139**
    samples, **140**, **141**, **142**
    school-wide, 89–91
Processes, landmark, 18
Professionals: working with, 111–115, 118
Progress monitoring, 292–293
Promising Practices Network, **14**
Prompts and prompting, 286, 320
    errorless prompting, 151, 348
    gesture prompts, 150–151, 349
    hierarchy of, 137–153, 349
    key questions to prompt self-reflection, **332**
    physical prompts, 151, 352
    problem-solving prompts, 185, **186**
    verbal prompts, 151, 355
Punishers, 61, 76
Punishment, 60–61, 71–76
    corporal, 16
    definition of, 61, 71–72, 352
    negative, 73, 76
    positive, 73
    unintended effects, 74, 76

Q

Questions about Behavior Function (QABF),
        256, **257**

R

Rate, **201**, 202, 352
Rating scales, 256, 352

Reactivity, 330, 352

Realistic goals, 160

Recording

duration, **201**, 202–203

definition, 348

summary, 217

event, 202, 348

partial interval, 205–206

definition, 351–352

example, 205, **206**

formula for, 205, 217

summary, 217

video, 330–331

whole interval, 204, 217, 356

Records review, 252, **253–255**

Redirection, 291

Reflection

for culturally responsive classrooms, 35–36, **36**

self-reflection, 328–334, 354

Reflective journaling, 330

Reflective practices, 327–343

Reflective questions, 331

Reflexive behaviors, 6. *See also* Respondent behaviors

Reinforcement, 60–61, 289–290

alternative methods, 134

behavior-specific praise, 181–182

continuous, 64–65, 347

definition of, 60–61, 75, 353

differential, 166

differential reinforcement of low rates (DRL) of behavior, 166, 170, 347

fixed interval (FI), 66–67, 348

fixed ratio (FR), 66, 348

inadvertent, 168, 349

intermittent, 64–65, 75, 350

negative, 67–70, **72**, 75, 351

noncontingent, 290

positive, 67–68, **72**, 75

alternative methods, 134

definition of, 352

schedules of, **64**, 64–65, **65**, 75, 354

school-wide, 91–94, **92**

self-monitoring, 320

summary, 75, 294

tangible systems, 91–93, **92**

variable interval (VI), 67, 355

variable ratio (VR), 67, 355

Reinforcers, 61–64, 76

activity-based, 91

backup, 303, **304**, 345

contingent, 63–64

definition of, 61, 353

examples, **63**

immediate, 63–64

PBIS-specific, 91, 353

relevant, 167

selecting, 62–63

tangible, 91–93, **92**

Relatedness, 176, 353

Relationship-building activities, 188, **189–191**, 192

Relationships

best practices for positive relationships, 176–181, 192

between students, 183–186

with students, 31, 175–192

Relaxation, active, 341–342

Reliability, 213–216, 218

definition of, 353

factors that pose threats to, 215, 218

Replacement behavior(s), 274–275

considerations for selecting, 278–280

definition, 353

examples, **279**

Replication

definition of, 229, 353

in single-subject designs, 225–226, 229–230, 245

Representation, 335–336, 343, 353

Research. *See* Experiments

Respondent behaviors, 6, 353

Respondent conditioning, 6

Response cost, 306–307, 322, 353

Responses, 59. *See also* Behavior(s)

Response to intervention (RtI), 82

definition, 353

summary, 99–100

Responsibility grids, 149, **149**

Restraint, 18

Reversal design, 228–230, 245, 353

Rewards, 167–168, 299

Rights and responsibilities grids, 149, **149**

Ripple effects, 11

Role-play, **312**

Routines

   definition, 89, 352

   school-wide, 89–91

Rows of desks, 123–124, **124**, 353

Rules. *See* Classroom rules

S

Safety, 17

   classroom considerations for, 129

   questions to ask, 98–99

   school safety plans, 98–100

Safety plans, 291

Sampling. *See* Time sampling

Sarcasm, 178

Satiation, 11–12, 353

Satiety, 62

Satisfaction surveys, 215

Saving face, 180–181, 354

Scatterplots, **201**, 236–239, 245

   definition of, 354

   examples, 239, **240**, **244**

   with negative correlation, 237, **238**

   with no correlation, 237–238, **239**

   with positive correlation, 237, **237**

   with trendline, **244**

Schedules

   daily, 140–141, **141**, **142**

   of reinforcement, **64**, 64–65, **65**

     continuous, 64–65, 347

     definition of, 64–65, 354

     fixed interval (FI), 66–67, 348

     fixed ratio (FR), 66, 348

     intermittent, 64–65, 75, 350

     summary, 75

     variable interval (VI), 67, 355

     variable ratio (VR), 66, 355

   self-monitoring, 319–320

Scholastic Tools website, **128**

School safety plans, 98–100

School-wide data collection, 94–95

School-wide expectations, 87–88, **88**, **89**

School-wide positive behavioral intervention

   and supports (SWPBIS), 84

School-wide procedures or routines, 89–91

School-wide reinforcement, 91–94, **92**

School-wide supports. *See* Tier 1 interventions

School-wide systems, 81–100

Seclusion, 18

Secondary settings, 113

   example classroom procedures, **140**, **142**,

     144

   example schedule, **142**

Secondary supports. *See* Tier 2 interventions

Self-monitoring, 42, **43**, 317–321

   advantages of, 321

   considerations for, 321

   definition of, 323, 354

   monitoring systems, 318–319

   phases of, 317, **317**

   practice, 320

   prompts for, 320

   reinforcement, 320

   schedule for, 319–320

   steps, 323

   teaching, 320

Self-reflection, 328–334

   definition, 328, 354

   key questions to prompt, **332**

   summary, 342

Self-reports, 215

Self-stimulatory behaviors, 51–52

Service learning, 316–317

Setting, 260–261

Setting events, 259, 269, 281–282

   environmental, 280

   examples, 280–281

   intervention strategies, 293

   physiological, 281

social, 280

Setting event strategies, 280–282, 354

Shift, 42, **43**, 50

Single-case design. *See* Single-subject design

Single-mother families, 32

Single-subject design, 223–232, 244

   A-B, 227–228, **228**

   definition of, 223, 354

Skills training. *See* Behavior skills training

Skinner, B. F., 5–6, 21, 58

Small group supports. *See* Tier 2 interventions

SmartDraw tools, **128**

SMART goals, 159–161

  definition of, 354

  guidelines for, **160**

  summary, 169

Social competence, 308–309, 322, 354

Social-emotional curriculum, 308–314

Social factors, 30, 33–34

Social networks, 184

Social setting events, 280

Social skills, 308, 322, 354

Social skills groups, 349

Social skills instruction, 308–314, 322

  considerations for, **311**

  definition of, 354

  planning, 310

  suggested approach to, **312**

Specific goals, 159

Specific learning disability (SLD), 47–48, 55, 354

Stay-put provisions, 18

Stereotyped behaviors, 51–52, 354

Stereotypies, 51–52

Stimuli

  negative, 351

  neutral, 6, 21

  unconditioned, 6, 21, 355

Stimulus-bound teachers, 11–12, 354

Stoplight system, 354

Stress and burnout, 341–342

Student conflict, 192. *See also* Conflict resolution

Student desks

  clusters/group arrangements, 124–125, **125**, 347

  horseshoe arrangement, 122–123, **123**

  individual, 126–127

  pairs arrangement, 125–126, **126**, 351

  rows of, 123–124, **124**

Student of the Week activity, **189–190**

Students

  establishing relationships with, 31, 175–192

  input from, 331

  key questions to prompt teacher self-reflection, **332**

  meeting individual needs of, 175–323

  needs of, 25–55

  relationships between, 183–186

  roles for, 31

  strategies to motivate, 158

Students with disabilities, 16, 37–39

Support

  intensive, individualized. *See* Tier 3 interventions

  multitiered systems of supports (MTSS), 82, 99, 351

  positive behavioral intervention and supports (PBIS), 83–95, 99

    definition of, 352

    tiers of intervention, **86**, 95–98

  school-wide supports. *See* Tier 1 interventions

  secondary or small group supports. *See* Tier 2 interventions

T

Tables, 127–128

Tangible reinforcement systems, 91–93, **92**

Tangible reinforcers, 91–93, **92**

Target behavior(s), 59, 302

  antecedents or triggers that precede, 210–211

  considerations for, 210, **304**

  definition of, 197, 317–318, 354

  examples, **60**

  identifying and defining, 197–200

measurable, objective, and observable (MOO), 198, 216, 259–260

prerequisite skills, 167–168

Task definition, 298–299

Task-monitoring, 42, **44**

Task record, 299–300

T-charts, 197

Teacher-led prompts, 185

Teachers

response styles, 21

stimulus-bound, 11–12

stress and burnout, 341–342

withitness, 11, 127, 356

Teacher self-reflection, 328–334

key questions to prompt, **332**

student input for, 331

Teacher/student relationships, 31, 175–192

Teaching

1st-year planning, 337–340

20th-year planning, 340–341

alternative behavior, 73–74

behavioral, 284–288

coteaching, 113–115

definition of, 113, 347

questions and prompts to consider, **114**

First Day of School Questions Checklist, **339**

job search questions, 340, **340**

key questions to prompt teacher self-reflection, **332**

new skills, 297–323

self-monitoring, 320

social skills instruction, 322

Team approach, 292–294

Termination criteria, 203, 355

Think sheets, 142, **143**

This or That activity, **190–191**

Three-term contingency, 58, 355

Tier 1 interventions

in classroom management, 82, **86**, 95–96, 100

definition, 355

Tier 2 interventions

in classroom management, 82, **86**, 96, 100

definition, 355

Tier 3 interventions

in classroom management, 82, **86**, 97–98, 100

definition, 355

Time-bound goals, 160–161

Timelines for data collection, 210–212, **213**

staggered times, 211, **212**

Timeliness, 182

Time sampling, **201**, 203–205, 217

definition of, 204, 355

momentary, 206–207, 217, 351

Token economies, 302–307

common issues, 306–307

considerations for, 303–307, **304**

definition of, 302, 355

disadvantages, 306

example, **305**

potential problems, 306–307

steps to implement, **304**

summary, 322

Tokens, 91, **92**, 303, **304**

Tootling, 185–186, 192, 355

Topography, 208–209, 218, 355

Training

behavioral skills training (BST), **285**, 285–286

functional communication training (FCT), 286–288, 349

Trendlines, 242–243, **244**

Trends, 242, 245, 355

Trust activity, **191**

Two Truths and a Lie activity, **191**

U

UDL Center, **337**

UDL-Universe: A Comprehensive Faculty Development Guide, **337**

Unconditioned stimuli, 6, 21, 355

United States Department of Education (USDOE), 17–18

Universal Design for Learning (UDL), 334–337

definition of, 342, 355

guidelines for instruction, 335–336, 343

resources, **337**

University of Nebraska–Lincoln Student
Engagement Project, **214**

V

Validity, 213–214, 218
  definition of, 355
  factors that pose threats to, 215, 218
Value(s), 62
  differences in, 32
  family values, 31–32, 348
Variability, 241, 245, 355
Variable interval (VI) reinforcement, 67, 355
Variable ratio (VR) reinforcement, 66, 355
Variables
  dependent, 223, 225, 347
  independent, 223, 225, 350
Verbal prompts, 151, 355
Verification, 225–226, 228, 245, 356
Video recording, 330–331
Video resources, **15**
Virtual Room Designer tools, **128**
Visual analysis, 240–243, 245
  definition of, 356
  examples, **241**, **242**

Visual displays, 232–233, 245
  graphs, 222, 233–240, 244–245

W

Warm Fuzzies activity, **189**
Welcome packets, **106**, 106–107
What Works Clearinghouse, **14**, 333
Whole child planning, 82
Whole interval recording, 204, 217, 356
Withitness, 11, 127, 356
Working memory, 42, **43**

X

x-axis, 233

Y

y-axis, 233

Z

Zero-tolerance policies, 17